THE NEW CALIFORNIA COOK

THE NEW CALIFORNIA COOK

More Than 200 Timeless Recipes

from the Author of *Seriously Simple* and *The Cuisine of California*

by Diane Rossen Worthington
Wine Notes by Anthony Dias Blue
Illustrations by Michael Schwab

CHRONICLE BOOKS
SAN FRANCISCO

First Chronicle Books LLC edition published in 2006.

Text copyright © 1994 and 2006
    by Diane Rossen Worthington.

Illustrations copyright © 2006 by Michael Schwab.

Library of Congress Cataloging-in-Publication Data

Worthington, Diane Rossen.
The new California cook : more than 200 timeless recipes
from Diane Rossen Worthington, author of seriously simple
and the cuisine of California / by Diane Rossen Worthington;
wine notes by Anthony Dias Blue.
p. cm.
Includes index.
ISBN-10: 0-8118-4901-5
ISBN-13: 978-0-8118-4901-2
1. Cookery, American–California style.
I. Dias Blue, Anthony. II. Title.
TX715.2.C34W6726 2006
641.59794—dc22
2005031857

Manufactured in Canada
DESIGNED BY Jacob T. Gardner
ILLUSTRATIONS BY Michael Schwab
TYPESETTING BY Blue Friday
TYPESET IN Adobe Caslon AND ITC Franklin Gothic

Distributed in Canada by Raincoast Books
9050 Shaughnessy Street
Vancouver, British Columbia V6P 6E5
10 9 8 7 6 5 4 3 2 1

Chronicle Books LLC
85 Second Street
San Francisco, California 94105
www.chroniclebooks.com

For my daughter, Laura, with all my love

ACKNOWLEDGMENTS

There are always those people behind the scenes who
help the author and the book reach their goals. Many
thanks to: Ethan Ellenberg, my agent, for his thoughtful
insights. Fran McCullough, editor of the original edition
of this book, who always had another way to look at a
problem and solve it. Bill LeBlond, my editor, who gives
me great encouragement and support. Amy Treadwell,
for her helpful editorial suggestions. Denny Luria, for
her unwavering friendship, sense of humor, and editing
skills. Anthony Dias Blue, for his exceptional knowledge
of pairing California food with California wine. My
colleagues Laurie Burrows Grad, Janice Wald Henderson,
Jan Weimer, and Ciji Ware for their gracious assistance.
My friends and tasters Mary Rose, Kathy Blue, George
and Cathi Rimalower, Connie Engel, Judy Miller, Lucy
Suzar, and Virginia Paca. The Huntington Library, for
the generous use of the library's rare Helen Evans Brown
Collection. All the California chefs and cooks who
continue to inspire me daily. And, finally, my husband,
Michael, and daughter, Laura, for all their love and support.

INTRODUCTION   8

A NOTE ON WINES   13

APPETIZERS AND FIRST COURSES   14

SOUPS   42

SALADS   72

PASTA, PIZZA, POLENTA, RISOTTO, AND EGGS   110

SEAFOOD   148

POULTRY   174

MEAT   204

SIDE DISHES   242

BREADS   272

DESSERTS   296

BASICS   340

MENUS   366

INDEX   370

INTRODUCTION

When my publisher suggested bringing out a new edition of *The California Cook*, I was delighted. I took this well-worn book off my shelf and reread it from cover to cover. Over the years, I had tucked several handwritten notes into the pages with recipes I had created since the book was first published, recipes that seemed like natural additions to this collection. Now I finally have the opportunity to update this book and include them.

For years I have often turned to this cookbook to prepare meals myself, so it came as no surprise to me that most of these recipes are as familiar as if I had written them yesterday. In this edition, you'll find some of my newer favorites as well, calling for California produce and products that I've discovered in my more recent travels across the state.

You don't have to live in California to be a California cook—what you do need is a California spirit. That means having a sense of adventure about food, an appreciation of the freshest seasonal ingredients, and a desire to reinterpret familiar dishes with unexpected twists. It's serving gravlax "Asian-style" with a ginger-mustard sauce; it's firing up lettuce and vegetables on the grill and tossing them with sweet smoky shrimp, or roasting sea bass with a blend of Mexican salsa and Dijon mustard. Present these dishes in a relaxed, homey setting and your table will resemble that of a creative California cook. Simple, lively, and bright tastes are the heart of California cooking—and it's all put together with casual elegance. It can be enjoyed anywhere, as long as you have access to fresh produce and enjoy bold flavors.

As a native Californian, I have been fascinated with flavor ever since I can remember. Even in grade school I would add parsley to dress up deviled eggs or embellish a can of Campbell's tomato soup with a dash of curry, refinements not appreciated by my siblings or parents. As a teenager, I kept a volume of the Escoffier cookbook on my nightstand and would read myself to sleep with thoughts of Roti de Bouef and its variations. Clearly, I was captivated with the magic of cooking.

Years later, I pursued this love of food at the Cordon Bleu School of Cookery in London and then as a curious cook in Paris. I would walk through the open-air markets and happily fill my basket with brightly colored fresh produce, pungent cheeses, and freshly baked breads to prepare exquisitely simple meals. I learned firsthand the exhilarating impact that fresh farmers' market–quality ingredients can have on cooking.

I had that same sense of excitement when I returned to Los Angeles in the early 1970s and found a new cuisine emerging. California Cuisine was a movement towards freshness, simplicity, and originality, defined by the use of the freshest local produce, herbs, fish, and dairy products. Grilling, marinades, and California wines were key elements in this evolving style, which originated in the restaurant kitchens of Chez Panisse and Zuni Café in the San Francisco Bay Area and Spago and Michael's in Los

Angeles. All of these kitchens continue to serve the best in contemporary California cooking, along with a growing roster of fine restaurants from San Diego's Region to Lake Tahoe's Wolfdale's. Many California chefs experiment with fusing influences from different regions such as the Mediterranean, Japan, Italy, and Mexico, to create their individual styles. The common bond among these chefs is their insistence on the use of the freshest ingredients.

When I was writing *The Cuisine of California* in 1982, I had to rely on my friends who were chefs and produce managers to provide me with specialty ingredients like radicchio, arugula, or shiitake mushrooms—ingredients I was sure would soon become widely available in supermarkets. And indeed they have. Today when I walk through the supermarket or one of the many bustling local farmers' markets dotting the state, I see an explosion of colorful produce: orange chanterelle mushrooms; multi-colored heirloom tomatoes; orange, red, and yellow sweet bell peppers; yellow Yukon gold and purple potatoes; green and yellow figs; orange persimmons. What were once "specialty ingredients" are now commonly available as a result of popular demand. As is often the case, the changes in California's culinary landscape influenced the rest of the country, and these foods are steadily appearing more and more in markets from coast to coast.

Other ingredients that I like to sample and use in my cooking include locally produced California artisan foods. Award-winning cheese makers cropping up primarily in Northern California can be found in Sonoma, Point Reyes, and Humboldt County. Small businesses manufacture top-quality olive oils in little towns like Los Olivos, Boonville, and Oroville. San Francisco Bay Area chocolatiers like Scharffen Berger and E. Guittard are also making their mark by developing signature blends for the home cook. Gourmet bottled condiments and flavor enhancers like tapenades, pestos, rubs, salts, and dipping sauces are becoming handy ingredients to use in creating California-inspired dishes.

Other ingredients that have a special role in my cooking are those with their roots in the history of California. When I first wrote this book, it was very important for me to understand the origins of some of the foods and cooking methods that have become integral to California cooking. For example, in the late 1700s, the Spanish missionary fathers establishing themselves in towns from San Diego to Sonoma brought with them corn tortillas, chiles, beans, dried fruits, and Mexican chocolate. They also brought grape seeds and olives from their native lands that later produced the region's first wines and olive oils.

In the early California rancho kitchens, olive oil was used instead of lard for cooking, and meats were usually marinated and then grilled over wood coals. In the early 1800s, a simple tomato-onion mixture called *sarsa* began to appear as an accompaniment to these meats. Tortillas, chiles, beans, olive oil, marinated meats, and salsas have all become ingredients essential to me as a California cook.

Recipes in *The New California Cook* reflect a wide range of my personal cooking style. Some of the recipes draw heavily upon the foods that commonly appeared on the early rancho tables. For example, you'll find traditional flour tortillas used in my recipe for Griddled Quesadillas with Caramelized Onions, Chicken, and Jack Cheese. You can see how I use variations of salsa with fish in recipes such as Grilled Salmon Fillet with Avocado, Cucumber, and Dill Salsa or Grilled Tuna with Vegetable and White Bean Salsa. Dried beans move away from the rancho tradition as a side dish in my White Bean and Artichoke Soup.

Many of the original recipes also include ethnic ingredients that are now considered staples in California cooking. For instance, Japanese ingredients sake and ginger surprisingly accent the recipe I offer for Asian Guacamole. Yogurt and mint, commonly used in Indian dishes, richly flavor the meat in Lamb Brochettes with Raita. Italian pancetta and Mexican ancho chile paste add dimension to Pasta with Ancho Chile and Tomato Cream. My menus may combine a mix of ethnic influences as well. I might begin with a Southwestern-style first course (Black Bean Soup with Lime Cream), followed by an Asian-style entrée (Grilled Swordfish on a Bed of Cucumber "Pasta" with Asian Salsa), and round out the meal with an Italian-influenced dessert (Orange, Almond, and Olive Oil Cake).

This book features some of my own personal favorites, those that friends repeatedly ask me to make. My Pear, Pistachio, and Chicken Liver Mousse appetizer is a surefire hit. Everyone requests it at my holiday parties. Warm Grilled Vegetable and Shrimp Salad, accompanied by a basket of California breads and my dipping sauces, make a success of any luncheon. Don't miss my Crispy Roast Chicken to guarantee that your friends or family have a homey, satisfying meal (it is my family's Friday night tradition). And be careful when you finish off your meal with either my Glazed Lemon–Sour Cream Cake or Chocolate Truffle Brownies; know that your guests will be clamoring for another dinner invitation to your house.

In this edition, I've adapted some of the old recipes and added new ones. I've turned my original recipe for chilled artichokes into one in which the vegetable is freshly grilled, resulting in a smoky, slightly charred flavor that is simply delicious. Subtly flavored caviars cultivated near Sacramento elevate the Smoked Salmon and Caviar Torta into a uniquely California dish. As for my new recipes, a pair of olive oil dipping sauces can be used as flavor enhancers in a number of ways: as a condiment along with a basket of warm homemade bread, as a finishing touch to spoon over freshly grilled chicken or fish, or as a quick but elegant sauce for pasta. As a tasty addition to the soups chapter, you'll find my Asian Chicken Noodle Soup with Tofu and Pea Pods, a hearty but light one-dish meal. Mac and cheese never tasted so good as it does in my contemporary version laced with caramelized leeks, prosciutto, zippy Sonoma pepper jack cheese, and a crispy panko crumb topping. If you want a homey dessert, look no further than the Walnut Cake with Roasted Blueberry Compote. The warm, fruity sauce nicely complements the nutty flavor of the cake. I've loved experimenting with California chocolate, and my family couldn't be happier with my recipe for Warm Mocha Pudding Cakes.

Working on this book has been like revisiting an old friend. There's great comfort in knowing that I can come back to these recipes and keep enjoying them over the years. They are tried and true and can be counted on not to let me down. Many of them are associated with long-cherished traditions. There's my daughter Laura's annual birthday request of Glazed Lemon–Sour Cream Cake, summer lunches with my dear friend Denny celebrating her birthday with Corn and Tomato Soup and Warm Grilled Vegetable and Shrimp Salad, Thanksgiving dinners where my brother Richard gets to feast on his favorite Marinated Roast Turkey, and my mother happily enjoying Roasted Garlic Mashed Potatoes with Leeks. I've returned to these recipes over and over again with warmth and fondness, and they have inspired me to develop new ones. What more can you ask of your friends? I sincerely hope my recipes bring you pleasure as well.

—*Diane Rossen Worthington*

A Note on Wines

The wines selected for a meal should flow from one to the next. It is just as important for the second wine to relate to the first as it is for the first to relate to the dish with which it's served. Just like the meal itself, the wines should offer a beginning, a middle, and an end.

Appetizers would be very easy to match with wine if they weren't followed by a main dish. If they were on their own, you'd simply select a wine to balance the flavors of the dish and leave it at that. But when the appetizer is part of a full meal—which it is by definition—other important considerations are involved in choosing the first wine.

The accepted way to provide a deftly orchestrated range of wines is to move from light to heavy, from white to red, from dry to sweet. Thus an appetizer that calls for a spicy red may have to be matched with a less assertive white in order to preserve the sequence of the meal.

—Anthony Dias Blue

16   Pear, Pistachio, and Chicken Liver Mousse

18   Smoked Salmon and Caviar Torta

20   Asian Gravlax with Ginger-Mustard Sauce

22   Smoked Fish Mousse

23   Shrimp Salsa

24   Assorted Grilled Vegetables

26   Roasted Peppers with Mint Vinaigrette and Goat Cheese Croutons

28   Grilled Artichoke Halves with Red Pepper Aioli

29   Olive Oil Dipping Sauces

31   Green Olive Tapenade

32   Sun-Dried Tomato Tapenade

33   Green Pea Guacamole

34   Asian Guacamole

36   Baked Brie with Sun-Dried Tomato Pesto

37   Griddled Quesadillas with Caramelized Onions, Chicken, and Jack Cheese

39   California Caponata

40   Ricotta Corn Cakes with Smoky Salsa Topping

41   Tuna Tartare

APPETIZERS AND FIRST COURSES

PEAR, PISTACHIO, AND CHICKEN LIVER MOUSSE

SERVES 8 TO 12

Californians love fruit in just about everything, including pâté. In this fluffy pâté-like mousse, juicy Bosc pear and softened black currants add an intriguing essence, while pistachios bring a buttery flavor and crisp texture to the mild chicken liver base. Look for a domestic pear brandy; they're less expensive and will still provide the right flavor. Serve this mousse with mild crackers or sliced French bread.

For a large party, double the recipe and pour the mousse into an 8- or 9-inch springform pan. As a more elaborate alternative to the simple pistachio and parsley garnish, decorate the top with cherry tomato quarters arranged as flower petals and lengths of fresh chives for the flower stems, and trim the border with dill. When ready to serve, unmold the mousse and cover the sides with finely chopped fresh parsley. This mousse makes a wonderful gift for the holidays.

2 tablespoons dried black currants

¼ cup pear brandy

3 tablespoons unsalted butter

2 tablespoons olive oil

1 medium onion, finely chopped

1 medium Bosc pear, peeled, cored, and finely chopped

2 garlic cloves, minced

1 teaspoon salt

¼ teaspoon dried thyme

⅛ teaspoon ground allspice

⅛ teaspoon freshly ground white pepper

1 pound cream cheese, at room temperature, cut into 2-inch pieces

1 pound chicken livers, trimmed of excess fat, rinsed, and patted dry

2 tablespoons coarsely chopped unsalted roasted pistachio nuts

GARNISH

Whole unsalted roasted pistachios

Fresh parsley sprigs

Simple crackers and/or thinly sliced French bread for serving

Recommended Wine

My first instinct here would be to suggest a late-harvest wine to balance the sweetness of the fruit and the richness of the chicken liver. Keeping in mind the next course, however, it may be better to opt for a crisp, off-dry (1 to 2 percent residual sugar) Riesling or Gewürztraminer.

Advance Preparation

Can be prepared up to 3 days ahead, covered well, and refrigerated. Freeze for up to 2 months; let thaw in the refrigerator a day ahead.

1   Soften the currants by pouring the pear brandy over them and letting them steep for at least 4 hours and up to 24 hours.

2   In a large skillet over medium heat, melt 2 tablespoons of the butter and 1 tablespoon of the oil. Add the onion and sauté for 3 to 5 minutes, or until softened. Add the pear and continue cooking until softened. Add the garlic and cook for another minute.

3   Transfer the mixture to a food processor fitted with the metal blade and purée. Add the salt, thyme, allspice, pepper, and cream cheese and process to a smooth purée.

4   Heat the remaining 1 tablespoon oil and 1 tablespoon butter in the same skillet. Add the chicken livers and sauté over medium-high heat until cooked through and just slightly pink, 5 to 7 minutes. Strain the pear brandy from the currants, set aside the currants, and add the brandy to the skillet. Ignite the brandy with a long match, averting your face and making sure any overhead fan is off.

5   When the flame has gone out, add the liver mixture to the onion-pear mixture in the food processor and process for about 30 seconds, or until the mousse is smooth. Add the softened currants and the chopped pistachios and process just until combined, making sure the currants and pistachios retain their texture. Taste for seasoning.

6   Pour into a 4-cup crock or mold and decorate with the whole pistachios and sprigs of parsley. Refrigerate for at least 4 hours or until well set. Serve with the crackers or bread.

SMOKED SALMON AND CAVIAR TORTA

SERVES 6 TO 8

Recommended Wine

A crisp, dry sparkling wine does well here. The shimmering bubbles underscore the festive quality of the torta. A fresh Sauvignon Blanc will also do the trick, with the smokiness of the wine complementing the smokiness of the salmon.

Advance Preparation

Can be prepared through step 4 up to 1 day ahead and refrigerated.

This pretty starter is particularly festive for a cocktail party or as an appetizer at a more formal dinner party. Layers of crunchy cucumber and velvety smoked salmon star here. Combining ricotta cheese with the cream cheese base lightens the mixture.

Sparkling beads of colorful red and yellow American "caviars" make a dazzling design on the top of the torta. Purists insist that only the processed roe of the sturgeon can be called caviar, but you can find jars of various other processed fish eggs called caviar in most specialty stores. Here salmon and whitefish caviar are used.

Tsar Nicoulai, a California caviar producer, is creating some very interesting variations. Whitefish roe can be found in flavors like ginger, black truffle, beet and saffron, or wasabi. You can substitute the salmon and golden whitefish roes with these colorful and flavorful new options; you could also use other smoked fish, like the sturgeon now being produced in California, in place of the salmon.

Ask for the less expensive lox or smoked salmon end pieces since you will be chopping them anyway. Accompany with simple crackers or toasts so that the full flavor of the torta is highlighted. Follow with Rack of Lamb with Mint Crust (page 218) and Confetti Rice Pilaf (page 269).

½ pound ricotta cheese

½ pound cream cheese, at room temperature, cut into 2-inch pieces

1 tablespoon finely chopped fresh dill

1 tablespoon finely chopped fresh chives

1 tablespoon fresh lemon juice

¼ teaspoon salt

Pinch of freshly ground white pepper

½ cup peeled, seeded, and diced cucumber

7 ounces smoked salmon, finely chopped

GARNISH

2 ounces salmon roe

2 ounces golden whitefish caviar

Fresh dill sprigs

Thinly sliced French bread, lightly toasted, and/or simple crackers for serving

1 Oil a 3½-by-6-by-2½-inch loaf pan. Place plastic wrap inside so that it is tucked into all the corners, leaving enough overhang to cover the top after you've made the torta.

2 Combine the ricotta, cream cheese, chopped dill, chives, lemon juice, salt, and pepper in a food processor fitted with the metal blade and process until completely blended. Using a rubber spatula, spread one-third of the cheese mixture on the bottom of the pan. Make sure the layer is even.

3 Carefully spoon half of the chopped cucumber on top of the cheese mixture, patting it in an even layer. Top with half of the chopped salmon, patting it in an even layer.

4 With the rubber spatula, spread another one-third of the cheese mixture on top. Again, make sure to spread it evenly. Repeat with the remaining cucumber and salmon. Spread the remaining cheese mixture on top, making sure that the salmon and cucumber do not show through. Cover the torta completely with the plastic wrap and refrigerate for at least 4 hours, or until well set. (If you have any cheese mixture left over, refrigerate it and enjoy it later spread on toast or French bread.)

5 To unmold, fold back the top layer of plastic wrap, lift the whole torta from the pan, and invert it on a rectangular platter. Remove the plastic wrap and garnish the top with alternating stripes of the golden whitefish caviar and salmon roe. Garnish the sides with the dill sprigs. Serve with the freshly toasted bread or crackers.

ASIAN GRAVLAX WITH GINGER-MUSTARD SAUCE

SERVES 8 TO 12

A crisp and lively Sauvignon Blanc is ideal with the gravlax.

Recommended Wine

A crisp and lively Sauvignon Blanc is ideal with the gravlax.

Advance Preparation

Can be prepared up to 3 weeks ahead, covered, and refrigerated.

Gravlax—cured fresh salmon—is traditionally marinated with dill. This California variation uses the stronger, more aromatic cilantro along with fresh peeled ginger and spicy Sichuan peppercorns. Sometimes called anise pepper or Chinese pepper, Sichuan peppercorns can be found in Chinese markets. If they aren't available, use white peppercorns.

The fish is actually cooked, or cured, by the marinade, but the curing takes time, so begin 4 days before you plan to serve. Follow with Braised Stuffed Shoulder of Veal (page 234) and Roasted Winter Vegetables (page 247).

2 to 2½ pounds fresh salmon fillet (1 large piece)

3 tablespoons sugar

2 tablespoons kosher or coarse salt

2 teaspoons Sichuan peppercorns or white peppercorns

1 teaspoon coriander seeds

1 tablespoon peeled and finely chopped fresh ginger

4 large bunches fresh cilantro

GARNISH

Lemon wedges

Fresh cilantro leaves

Ginger-Mustard Sauce (recipe follows)

Thinly sliced French or sourdough bread for serving

1   Lay the salmon on a sheet of wax paper. Combine the sugar, salt, peppercorns, coriander seeds, and ginger in a small bowl. Rub the top of the salmon with half of the peppercorn mixture. Turn the fillet and rub the second side with the remaining mixture. Press down firmly on the salmon to help the seasonings adhere, and be sure to coat the fish evenly.

2   Arrange 2 bunches of the cilantro on the bottom of a large, shallow, non-aluminum pan. Place the salmon on top, then arrange the remaining 2 bunches of cilantro over the salmon, covering it as completely as possible.

3   Cover the salmon well with aluminum foil or plastic wrap, place a weight on top—a heavy pot lid, brick, or large can—and refrigerate. Turn the salmon twice a day for 4 days. Make sure the cilantro and peppercorn mixture remains evenly distributed.

4   To serve, remove all the cilantro and peppercorn mixture. Lightly pat the salmon dry with paper towels, making sure all the salt and sugar is removed. Slice crosswise very thinly on the diagonal and garnish with the lemon wedges and cilantro leaves. Serve with the Ginger-Mustard Sauce and the bread.

Ginger-Mustard Sauce
Makes 1 cup

This sweet mustard and herb sauce has a texture similar to mayonnaise. It's great with poached salmon or gravlax.

¼ cup Dijon or whole-grain mustard
3 tablespoons dark brown sugar
2 tablespoons cider vinegar
1 teaspoon dry mustard
⅓ cup vegetable oil
1 tablespoon peeled and finely chopped fresh ginger
2 tablespoons finely chopped fresh cilantro
1 tablespoon finely chopped fresh parsley

1   In a blender or food processor fitted with the metal blade, combine the prepared mustard, brown sugar, vinegar, and dry mustard and process for a few seconds. With the machine running, slowly add the oil in a steady stream and process until the sauce is thick and smooth. Add the ginger, cilantro, and parsley and process for another minute, or until blended.

2   Pour the sauce into a small bowl. Refrigerate for 2 to 3 hours, or until ready to use.

SMOKED FISH MOUSSE

MAKES 1 CUP; SERVES 4 TO 6

This quick appetizer always wins raves from my guests. Ask to taste the smoked fish before buying it to make sure it's evenly balanced, not too oily and not too smoky. Add the lemon juice sparingly, since it tends to bring out the saltiness of smoked fish. Remember to make this ahead, even up to a few days, so that the flavors can blend and the saltiness mellow.

1 small shallot
½ pound lean smoked trout, whitefish, or bluefish, all skin and bones removed
3 tablespoons mayonnaise
2 tablespoons cream cheese
1 to 2 tablespoons fresh lemon juice
Pinch of freshly ground white pepper
Pinch of cayenne pepper
1 tablespoon finely chopped fresh parsley

GARNISH

Fresh parsley sprigs

Simple crackers or thinly sliced egg bread, lightly toasted, for serving

Recommended Wine

Try a crisp and slightly smoky Sauvignon Blanc (Fumé Blanc), which offers nice balance to this smoky mousse.

Advance Preparation

Can be prepared up to 3 days ahead, covered well, and refrigerated.

1   Mince the shallot in a food processor fitted with the metal blade. Add the remaining ingredients and process to a smooth purée. Taste for seasoning. If the mousse tastes overly salty, don't worry; it will balance out as it sits. Spoon into a 1½-cup crock and garnish with the parsley sprigs. Serve with the crackers or freshly toasted bread.

This variation on one of my favorite recipes, Guacamole Salsa, from my book *The Taste of Summer,* blends sweet cooked shrimp with crunchy colorful vegetables. The spices here are Mexican, but you can use fresh basil or dill instead of the cilantro. Warm Crisp Tortilla Chips (page 282) are my first choice for dipping. For a lighter appetizer, try Belgian endive leaves, celery sticks, or even jicama sticks.

SHRIMP SALSA

MAKES 6 CUPS; SERVES 6

2 large tomatoes (about 1 pound), peeled, seeded, and diced

½ medium red bell pepper, seeded and diced (about ½ cup)

½ medium yellow bell pepper, seeded and diced (about ½ cup)

1 cup peeled and diced jicama

½ English (hothouse) cucumber, diced

½ cup fresh corn kernels (from about 1 medium ear), preferably white

2 tablespoons finely chopped fresh cilantro

2 tablespoons finely chopped fresh parsley

1 jalapeño chile, seeded and finely chopped (see note)

2 tablespoons fresh lime juice

1 teaspoon salt

¼ teaspoon freshly ground black pepper

1 ripe medium avocado, pitted, peeled, and cut into ½-inch pieces

½ pound cooked and peeled medium shrimp, diced

GARNISH

Fresh cilantro leaves

Crisp Tortilla Chips, good-quality store-bought tortilla chips, or crudités (see recipe introduction) for serving

1   Combine all the ingredients except the avocado and shrimp in a medium mixing bowl. Cover and refrigerate for at least 1 hour.

2   Spoon the salsa into a serving bowl. Right before serving, add the avocado and shrimp and taste for seasoning. Garnish with the cilantro leaves and serve with the chips or crudités.

Recommended Wine
A slightly off-dry Gewürztraminer would be a spicy complement to this spicy appetizer. The salsa also works well with a wood-aged Sauvignon Blanc.

Note
When working with chiles, always wear rubber gloves. Wash the cutting surface and knife immediately.

Advance Preparation
Can be prepared up to 6 hours ahead, covered, and refrigerated.

ASSORTED GRILLED VEGETABLES

SERVES 6

Picture a large platter of colorful vegetables, each with its own grill marks, decoratively arranged. Pretty barbecued vegetables are one of the signature clean flavors of California cooking. This dish is an elegant beginning to lunch or dinner as well as an excellent side accompaniment.

Don't restrict yourself to the vegetable choices listed here. Whatever is fresh and at its seasonal best is appropriate for the grill and your table. Roma tomatoes, asparagus, Belgian or California endive, and small rounds of fresh corn on the cob are other good choices.

A drizzle of olive oil, a squirt of lemon juice, and a sprinkling of fresh herbs heighten the pure flavors of grilled vegetables. Or make a more elaborate presentation by arranging bowls of Smoky Salsa (page 360), Red Pepper Aioli (page 352), or any of the tapenades (pages 31 and 32) and dipping sauces (page 29) alongside the vegetables.

2 red bell peppers
2 yellow bell peppers
4 medium Japanese eggplants
4 medium zucchini
1 small butternut squash
1 medium fennel bulb
½ cup olive oil

GARNISH

Olive oil
Fresh lemon or lime juice
Assorted finely chopped fresh herbs

Recommended Wine

Try a crisp, fruity Sauvignon Blanc with this dish. The herbal qualities of the wine will blend nicely with the vegetables.

Advance Preparation

Can be prepared up to 2 days ahead, covered well, and refrigerated. Remove from the refrigerator ½ hour before serving.

1. Prepare a grill for medium-high-heat grilling. Grill the peppers about 4 inches from the heat until the skin is blistered and slightly charred on all sides, using long tongs to turn the peppers. Do not pierce the peppers or the juices will escape. Put the peppers in a brown paper bag and close it tightly. Let the peppers rest for 10 minutes. Remove the peppers from the bag and drain them. Peel off the skins with your fingers. Make a slit in each pepper and open it up. Core and cut off the stem. Scrape the seeds and ribs from the peppers. Cut the peppers into ½-inch-wide slices.

2. Trim the stems off the eggplants and zucchini and cut them lengthwise into slices ¼ inch thick. Cut the squash in half lengthwise and remove the seeds and stringy pulp with a spoon. Carefully slice the peel off and then cut the flesh into ¼-inch-thick slices. Trim the fennel bulb and cut it into quarters.

3. Brush the eggplant and zucchini slices with oil and grill for about 3 minutes on each side, or until the vegetables have grill marks and are beginning to soften. Repeat with the squash, which may take 4 to 5 minutes per side. Repeat with the fennel, 3 to 4 minutes per side.

4. Arrange the vegetables on a large platter in an attractive design. Drizzle them with the olive oil and lemon juice, and sprinkle with the fresh herbs.

ROASTED PEPPERS WITH MINT VINAIGRETTE AND GOAT CHEESE CROUTONS

SERVES 6

Recommended Wine

A steely, crisp Sauvignon Blanc is an excellent match for the peppers.

Advance Preparation

The marinated peppers can be prepared up to 3 days ahead, covered, and refrigerated. Remove from the refrigerator 2 hours before serving. Add the goat cheese croutons just before serving.

When I wrote *The Cuisine of California* in the early 1980s, California French-style goat cheese had just arrived on the scene. Laura Chenel was a pioneer in the California goat cheese industry, and it was with much excitement that I visited her small Sonoma factory at the inception of this cottage industry.

Cheese making is still a labor of love for Laura, but it's also become a viable business that continues to expand. Many different varieties of California goat's milk cheese, from fresh to aged, are now available from the cheese makers. The fresh cheese has a mild flavor and a soft, spreadable texture. Aged cheeses like crottin or Taupinière boast a complex, sophisticated flavor, perfect on their own or accompanying a simple green salad. This recipe uses fresh goat cheese in a simple, colorful, and easy appetizer.

Here, colorful sweet bell peppers, available much of the year, make a lovely first course. Fresh mint is a surprise with the sweet peppers, and goat cheese croutons add a creamy dimension. You could also serve the goat cheese croutons topped with the minted pepper mixture on a serving platter.

DRESSING

2 teaspoons fresh lemon juice

3 tablespoons red wine vinegar

1 garlic clove, minced

2 tablespoons minced fresh mint

6 tablespoons olive oil

¼ teaspoon salt

Pinch of freshly ground white pepper

6 red or yellow bell peppers or a combination, roasted, peeled (facing page), seeded, and cut into ½-inch slices

GOAT CHEESE CROUTONS

¾ cup fresh goat cheese, at room temperature

Eighteen ¼-inch-thick slices French or sourdough baguette, lightly toasted

GARNISH

Fresh mint sprigs

1 To make the dressing, in a bowl, combine the lemon juice, vinegar, garlic, and mint and mix well. Slowly add the oil in a steady stream, whisking until it is incorporated and emulsified. Add the salt and pepper, whisk to combine, and taste for seasoning.

2 Place the peppers in a bowl and pour the dressing over them. Marinate for at least 2 hours or up to 3 days.

3 When ready to serve, make the croutons: Spread the cheese on the bread slices. Drain the peppers and place them on a serving platter. Arrange the croutons around the outside of the platter. Garnish the peppers with the mint sprigs and serve.

HOW TO PEEL A BELL PEPPER

Select firm-fleshed, thick-skinned peppers so they'll retain their texture when grilled or broiled. Preheat the broiler or prepare a grill for medium-high-heat grilling. Place the whole peppers on a broiler pan or on a barbecue grill rack and broil or grill about 4 inches from the heat until the skin is blistered and slightly charred on all sides, using long tongs to turn the peppers. Never pierce the peppers or the juices will escape. Put the peppers in a brown paper bag and close it tightly. Let the peppers rest for 10 minutes. Remove the peppers from the bag and drain them. Peel off the charred skins with your fingers. Make a slit in each pepper and open it up. Core and cut off the stem. Scrape the seeds and ribs from the peppers. Cut the peppers with a sharp knife or a pizza cutter as desired.

GRILLED ARTICHOKE HALVES WITH RED PEPPER AIOLI

SERVES 6

America's entire commercial artichoke crop is grown on just over 9,000 acres concentrated in only five California counties—a meager harvest compared to Italy's 150,000 acres of artichokes. In recent years even fewer farmers have been growing artichokes because the demand has declined. Sadly, some artichoke enthusiasts think the decline is linked to Italian families not passing on their culinary traditions and instead opting for quicker cooking solutions. But Californians love artichokes, consuming nearly 40 percent of the domestic crop.

People always seem surprised that artichokes can be barbecued. In fact, grilled artichokes, with their smoky flavor, taste decidedly different from steamed artichokes. I love to serve these at a casual dinner along with small bowls on the table for guests to discard the remaining leaves.

3 large artichokes

3 slices of lemon

¼ cup olive oil

GARNISH

¾ cup Red Pepper Aioli (page 352)

2 tablespoons finely chopped fresh parsley

Recommended Wine

Although artichokes are thought to be unfriendly to wine, a dry Chenin Blanc or spicy Sauvignon Blanc goes nicely with this dish.

Advance Preparation

Can be prepared through step 3 up to 1 day ahead, covered, and refrigerated. Bring to room temperature before grilling.

1   Cut the sharp points off the artichoke leaves with kitchen shears. Remove the small dry outer leaves from around the base of the artichoke. Cut off the stem of each artichoke. Soak the artichokes in cold water for at least 15 minutes to clean them.

2   Place the artichokes upright in a saucepan with about 4 inches of water and add the lemon slices. Bring to a boil, reduce the heat to medium, and cook for 30 to 40 minutes, partially covered, or until the leaves pull off fairly easily. (You want to make sure the artichokes will hold together when grilling.) Drain thoroughly.

3   Let the artichokes cool to room temperature and then cut them in half lengthwise. Scoop out the fuzzy choke with a teaspoon and discard.

4   While the artichokes are cooling, prepare a grill for medium-high-heat grilling. Using half of the oil, brush the leaf side of each artichoke half. Arrange on the grill, leaf side down, and grill for 3 to 4 minutes, or until the artichokes have grill marks. Brush the cut sides of the artichoke halves with the remaining oil and turn over. Grill the cut sides until they have grill marks, 3 to 4 more minutes.

5   Transfer the artichokes to a platter. Dollop 2 to 3 tablespoons Red Pepper Aioli in the center of each half. Sprinkle with the parsley just before serving.

Interesting olive oil combinations have taken the place of butter as an accompaniment for bread. Here are two renditions to add to your repertoire. I like to serve these sauces in small glass bowls with a spoon for people to help themselves. Make sure to have a basket of assorted breads, like walnut, sourdough, and foccacia, along with bread plates. These sauces also make a wonderful glaze on grilled chicken, fish, or vegetables, or can be used as a simple sauce for pasta or a quick dressing to drizzle on your favorite greens.

There are over three hundred California olive oil producers today, compared to twenty only a decade ago. Willow Creek Olive Oil in Paso Robles makes a glorious Meyer lemon olive oil that inspired the first dipping sauce here. The small town of Paso Robles, in central California, is emerging as a center for food artisans: There are bread bakers, cheese makers, and wineries in addition to producers of fine olive oil. I love the warmth and enthusiasm of these local businesses.

Meyer Lemon, Olive, and Dried Cherry Dipping Sauce

½ cup Meyer or other lemon olive oil

2 tablespoons good-quality balsamic vinegar

2 garlic cloves, ends removed and sliced into very thin slivers

2 or 3 sprigs fresh thyme, stems removed

2 tablespoons chopped Kalamata olives

2 tablespoons chopped dried cherries

Freshly ground black pepper to taste

Anchovy, Sun-Dried Tomato, and Tapenade Dipping Sauce

½ cup extra-virgin olive oil

2 tablespoons good-quality balsamic vinegar

2 tablespoons chopped drained anchovies, preferably white anchovies (see note)

2 tablespoons green olive tapenade, homemade (page 31) or store-bought

2 tablespoons chopped drained oil-packed sun-dried tomatoes

¼ to ½ teaspoon hot sauce or spicy chile paste, or to taste

1   For either recipe, combine all of the ingredients in a glass mixing bowl and mix to combine. Taste for seasoning. Cover and let rest for at least 4 hours to allow the flavors to blend. Pour into small glass bowls or plates for serving with bread.

OLIVE OIL DIPPING SAUCES

EACH RECIPE SERVES 4 TO 6

Note
You can find white anchovies at gourmet specialty-food stores in the refrigerated section. They have a sweeter, milder flavor than regular canned anchovies.

Advance Preparation
Can be prepared up to 1 week ahead, covered tightly, and refrigerated. Return to room temperature before serving.

Special Super Colossal: California's Olive Industry

Sometime around 1785, a few olive pits were planted in California's missions, and from that humble beginning the Golden State now produces 99 percent of the nation's table olives. The bland Mission olive, as it came to be known, was the only olive on the scene for many years, because Americans' taste for olives and the oil produced from them was slow to develop.

It was not until the 1920s that olive production in the state began on a serious scale, and size designations had to be made for the fledgling industry. These, of course, were based on the Mission olive: small, medium, large, and extra large. Then came the arrival of the "Queen of Olives," the Sevillano, which quickly became popular for its lack of oiliness and much larger size. This new olive necessitated a new system of size definition, giving rise to the somewhat confusing labels *giant, jumbo, colossal* and *super colossal.*

Since the birth of the industry in this country, and even to a large extent today, demand has been largely for the "black ripe" olive. This is simply a green olive that has been allowed to ripen on the tree before harvesting, then cured in a very mild brine. To lovers of the myriad black, green, or purple, spicy, sour, and vinegary Mediterranean olives, this product seems bland, overly rich, and much too large. The olive industry has clearly sensed this demand trend and has recently responded by producing several different green and even black olives in a more Mediterranean style. Though these olives tend to be packed in a very strong brine, they offer a vastly improved flavor over the standard "black ripe."

With orchards of European olive trees flourishing throughout Napa and Sonoma counties, observers are comparing today's California olive oil industry to the Napa Valley wine industry of the 1950s. This recipe for tapenade uses California's plentiful green olives as a less pungent alternative to the traditional black Niçoise olives. Pitted French green olives also work well. Either way, be sure to rinse the olives well, since they're often packed in strong brine.

This intensely flavored olive paste is excellent as a spread for crackers and interesting-flavored breads and as a dipping sauce for raw vegetables. It also has many uses as a flavor enhancer; stir it into mayonnaise or salad dressing, or spread it on chicken before roasting or grilling.

GREEN OLIVE TAPENADE

MAKES ABOUT 1 CUP

2 garlic cloves

20 large or 30 medium pitted green olives, drained and rinsed

2 tablespoons capers, rinsed and well drained

2 anchovy fillets, drained

2 teaspoons Dijon mustard

2 tablespoons fresh lemon juice

2 tablespoons finely chopped fresh basil

¼ cup finely chopped fresh parsley

⅛ teaspoon cayenne pepper

⅓ cup olive oil

Recommended Wine
This tapenade goes nicely with crisp, dry sparkling wine, such as dry Chenin Blanc or Sauvignon Blanc.

Advance Preparation
Can be prepared up to 1 week ahead, covered, and refrigerated.

1   Mince the garlic in a food processor fitted with the metal blade. Add the remaining ingredients except the oil and process until puréed, using a rubber spatula to scrape down the sides of the bowl and push down the ingredients that do not get puréed, as needed.

2   With the machine running, slowly add the oil in a steady stream and process until it is incorporated and emulsified. Taste for seasoning. Transfer to an airtight container and refrigerate until needed.

SUN-DRIED
TOMATO
TAPENADE

MAKES ABOUT 1 CUP

Chef Gary Danko of Gary Danko's in San Francisco is known for his innovative blending of classic French cooking style with California ingredients. This rich, thick paste, a variation on Gary's recipe, is perfect to serve as a dip or as a spread on Parmesan Toasts (page 274) or simple crackers. I like to serve the Green Olive Tapenade (page 31) alongside this one for a marvelous contrast of colors and flavors. It's fun to watch your guests decide which they prefer. You can be sure that opinions will change more than once.

2 garlic cloves
One 8-ounce jar oil-packed sun-dried tomatoes, undrained
¼ cup capers, rinsed and well drained
3 anchovy fillets, drained
1 tablespoon finely chopped fresh parsley
1 tablespoon finely chopped fresh basil
2 teaspoons Dijon mustard
2 teaspoons balsamic vinegar
2 tablespoons olive oil or hot water
Pinch of freshly ground black pepper

Recommended Wine

Dry sparkling wine, dry Chenin Blanc, or Sauvignon Blanc is ideal.

Advance Preparation

Can be prepared up to 1 week ahead, covered, and refrigerated.

1   Mince the garlic in a food processor fitted with the metal blade. Add the remaining ingredients except the oil and pepper and process until puréed, using a rubber spatula to scrape down the sides of the bowl and push down the ingredients that do not get puréed, as needed.

2   With the machine running, add the oil and pepper and process until combined. Taste for seasoning. Transfer to an airtight container and refrigerate until needed.

The late Michael Roberts was an inventive Southern California chef who always came up with unusual variations on classic dishes. When I first tasted his green pea guacamole, I was puzzled by the unusual yet pleasing quality of the green peas he used instead of avocado. I have combined the two in this adaptation to create a refreshing, clean flavor. If you like a creamier consistency, add a bit more sour cream. You can also serve this with Crisp Tortilla Chips (page 282), Griddled Quesadillas (page 37), or Grilled Flank Steak with Smoky Salsa (page 211).

8 ounces thawed frozen baby peas

½ medium or 1 small very ripe avocado, pitted, peeled, and cubed

2 tablespoons fresh lemon juice

2 tablespoons Tomatillo Salsa (page 358)

2 tablespoons sour cream

2 tablespoons finely chopped fresh cilantro

1 small jalapeño chile, seeded and finely chopped (see note)

¼ teaspoon ground cumin

¼ teaspoon salt

GARNISH

Fresh cilantro leaves

Crudités or yellow or blue tortilla chips for serving

1 In a food processor fitted with the metal blade, combine all the ingredients and process until the peas are puréed. Taste for seasoning. Spoon into a small serving bowl and garnish with the cilantro leaves. Serve with the crudités or tortilla chips.

GREEN PEA GUACAMOLE

SERVES 4 TO 6

Recommended Wine
A fresh, youthful Chardonnay or a dry Chenin Blanc complements the creaminess of this guacamole.

Note
When working with chiles, always were rubber gloves. Wash the cutting surface and knife immediately.

Advance Preparation
Can be prepared up to 4 hours ahead, covered, and refrigerated.

ASIAN GUACAMOLE

SERVES 4 TO 6

Famed Hawaiian chef Alan Wong is renowned for his intriguing twists on traditional recipes. He serves this simple but uniquely flavored guacamole with taro chips. If you can't find them, substitute shrimp chips or blue or yellow tortilla chips for a great beginning to an informal Asian-inspired dinner. If available, use Hass avocados, which have a fuller flavor than other types.

2 medium very ripe avocados, pitted, peeled, and coarsely chopped
1 small tomato, peeled, seeded, and finely chopped
2 tablespoons finely chopped red onion
1 serrano chile, seeded and finely chopped (see note)
Juice of 1 lime
1 tablespoon sake
1 tablespoon finely chopped fresh cilantro
1 tablespoon finely chopped scallion, white and light green parts only
1 tablespoon peeled and finely chopped fresh ginger
½ teaspoon salt

Taro chips, shrimp chips, tortilla chips, carrot and celery sticks, and/or endive leaves for serving

1 Combine all the ingredients in a medium mixing bowl and stir. Taste for seasoning.

2 Transfer the guacamole to a serving bowl and serve with the chips and/or vegetables.

Recommended Wine
A crisp, dry Gewürztraminer will balance nicely with the spiciness of this dish.

Note
When working with chiles, always wear rubber gloves. Wash the cutting surface and knife immediately.

Sun-Dried Tomatoes

Southern Italians were the first to come up with the idea of drying tomatoes in the sun. In the dry and sunny Mediterranean summer the plump, meaty plum tomatoes are reduced to a leathery state, covered with olive oil, and bottled for winter use. Today California, and the rest of the world, seems to have gone sun-dried-tomato crazy, but the first casualty in the industrialization of the product was ironically, the sun. On a recent visit to Sonoma County's largest dried-tomato producer, I expected to see racks of deep red tomatoes drying picturesquely in the sun. I was told, "That's the romance; dehydrators are the reality."

Drying tomatoes greatly intensifies their flavor and gives them a chewy texture, though the quality can vary widely between producers. The characteristic sunny, earthy flavor marries well with other Mediterranean ingredients such as polenta, grilled vegetables, and pasta. Dried tomatoes, along with goat cheese, have become a quintessential ingredient for California pizza and are often paired with fresh tomatoes for a deep, complex flavor.

Recipes that call for sun-dried tomatoes must be read carefully: are they dry-packed or oil-packed, halved or chopped? Dry-packed tomatoes should always be reconstituted before using: Pour boiling water over them in a bowl and let them steep for at least 10 minutes. Drain well and cover with a good-quality olive oil. Keep them in the refrigerator and use the oil for dressings or as a condiment.

- Make a Sun-Dried Tomato Pesto (page 350) and use it on baked potatoes, in salad dressings, in pasta sauces, and in dips.

- Add chopped sun-dried tomatoes to a cheese torta or mix with ricotta for stuffing pastas.

- Garnish an omelet with sour cream and chopped sun-dried tomatoes, or mince the tomatoes very finely and add them to a soufflé mixture.

- To make sun-dried tomato butter mix 2 tablespoons of chopped dried tomatoes with softened butter. Form the tomato butter into a log in wax paper and freeze. Slice off the tomato butter as needed to garnish grilled steaks, poultry, or vegetables.

BAKED BRIE WITH SUN-DRIED TOMATO PESTO

SERVES 8 TO 10

Sun-dried tomato pesto contributes an earthy-sweet contrast to soft-ripened, creamy Brie. Dry-packed sun-dried tomatoes can either be softened in hot water or marinated in olive oil, which will also soften them. For a richer flavor, you may need to add a bit more oil to the pesto if you choose water-softened tomatoes.

This baked cheese is perfect for a cocktail party, beautiful as well as utterly delicious. California produces soft-ripened Brie and Camembert, but for this dish I prefer a French Brie. Wheels of Brie come in a variety of sizes; just adjust the pesto quantity if you want to use a larger cheese than called for here. Accompany the Brie with thinly sliced toasted French bread.

You can also serve this appetizer at room temperature with a few minor variations. Working with the Brie cold, remove the rind from the edges and top of the cheese carefully with a very sharp knife. Press the toasted pine nuts all around the edges. Spread the top thickly with the pesto. Place on a serving platter, bring to room temperature, and decorate with the basil. This is particularly enjoyable on warmer evenings.

½ cup Sun-Dried Tomato Pesto (page 350)

One 1-pound round of Brie

GARNISH

¼ cup pine nuts

Fresh basil leaves

Crisp crackers or thinly sliced French baguette or bread, lightly toasted, for serving

1   If the pesto is very thick, you may need to add a bit of olive oil. Place the Brie in an ovenproof dish. Make about 8 wheel-spoke cuts down into the cheese, leaving a little circle in the center uncut to hold the wheel together during baking. With a spoon, carefully push a few tablespoons of pesto down into each slit so it's flush with the top. Tie a piece of cooking string around the circumference of the Brie to hold its shape.

2   Preheat the oven to 350°F. Spread the pine nuts on a baking sheet and toast for 5 minutes, or until lightly browned. Watch carefully, as they burn quickly. Transfer immediately to a plate and set aside.

3   Place the cheese in the oven and bake for 10 to 15 minutes, or until it just begins to melt. Remove from the oven, untie the string, sprinkle the pine nuts on top, and decorate with a garland of fresh basil leaves around the base of the cheese. Serve immediately.

Recommended Wine

Brie is best with a red wine—serve Syrah, Merlot, Pinot Noir, or Zinfandel. Another possibility is a chilled dry Vin Gris—a blush wine usually made from Pinot Noir.

Advance Preparation

Can be prepared through step 2 up to 2 days ahead, covered, and refrigerated. Keep the pine nuts covered at room temperature. Bring the cheese to room temperature before baking.

Quesadillas, those puffy "little whims," as the Mexicans call appetizers, can be found in most Mexican restaurants in many variations. Sometimes called *empanadas,* these turnovers have evolved through the years. Traditionally, masa dough is flattened and folded over to enclose a variety of fillings.

In California we make quesadillas with either corn or flour tortillas. They can be simple, with a melted cheese center, or more complicated creations, like this one. Olive oil spray on the pan or griddle keeps the outside crispy without being overly greasy. If you don't have the spray, add a tablespoon of vegetable or light-flavored olive oil to the pan and make sure it is very hot before cooking the tortillas. These small triangles are wonderful served as a first course before a Mexican-style main course like Grilled Skirt Steak with Avocado-Tomato Salsa (page 206) or as a main course for brunch or lunch.

GRIDDLED QUESADILLAS WITH CARAMELIZED ONIONS, CHICKEN, AND JACK CHEESE

SERVES 6

3 cups Chicken Stock (page 342) or water, or a combination

1 boneless medium chicken breast or 1½ cups shredded cooked chicken breast

1 tablespoon vegetable oil

2 large red onions, thinly sliced

½ cup beer, a medium-bodied lager

2 tablespoons balsamic vinegar

1 teaspoon sugar

1 medium jalapeño chile, seeded and finely chopped (see note)

1 teaspoon finely chopped fresh oregano or ½ teaspoon dried

¼ teaspoon salt

⅛ teaspoon freshly ground black pepper

Olive oil cooking spray

Three 12-inch flour tortillas

1½ cups shredded jack cheese

GARNISH

½ cup Green Pea Guacamole (page 33)

½ cup salsa of your choice

½ cup sour cream

Recommended Wine
A spicy, rich, central coast Chardonnay is perfect with this flavorful appetizer.

continued on next page

1   In a deep medium skillet or a large saucepan, bring the chicken stock (or enough of a combination of chicken stock and water to cover the chicken) to a simmer. If you're using water only, add ½ teaspoon salt. Add the chicken breast and simmer for 10 to 12 minutes, or until just tender and opaque throughout. Let the chicken cool in the stock. Drain the chicken, remove the skin, and shred it into bite-sized pieces. Set aside. (Skip this step if using precooked chicken.)

2   Heat the oil in large, nonaluminum skillet over medium-high heat. Add the onions and sauté, stirring frequently, for 10 to 15 minutes, or until well softened.

3   Add the beer, vinegar, sugar, and jalapeño to the onions and simmer over low heat until almost all of the liquid has evaporated. The onions should be very tender and slightly caramelized. Add the oregano, salt, and pepper. Taste for seasoning and let cool.

4   Lightly coat a 12-inch nonstick skillet or griddle with cooking spray and place over medium-high heat. Place a tortilla in the skillet and spoon ½ cup of the onion mixture evenly over one half. Sprinkle with ½ cup of the chicken and top evenly with ½ cup of the cheese; fold the tortilla in half, pressing down with a spatula. Cook the quesadilla until the bottom is lightly browned, then turn and cook the second side until lightly browned. Place on a cutting board, slice into bite-sized wedges, and keep warm under aluminum foil.

5   Repeat to cook the remaining quesadillas. Arrange on a large serving platter and serve immediately, accompanied by the Green Pea Guacamole, salsa, and sour cream.

Caponata, the popular Sicilian appetizer, is often served at room temperature on toasted croutons. Traditionally it includes tomatoes, eggplant, onions, and capers to produce a pronounced sweet-and-sour taste. In this California version there's no tomato; roasted eggplant is paired with sweet onion and California blue cheese or pungent Italian Gorgonzola to become a fragrant, warm spread for crisp toasts or warm French bread.

CALIFORNIA CAPONATA

SERVES 4 TO 6

1 medium eggplant

1 tablespoon olive oil

1 large red onion, finely chopped

2 tablespoons balsamic vinegar

¼ cup water

2 tablespoons finely chopped fresh parsley

Salt and freshly ground black pepper

⅓ pound Point Reyes Original Blue, Gorgonzola dolcelatte, or other creamy blue cheese, cut into small pieces

Thinly sliced French or sourdough bread, warmed or toasted, for serving

1   Preheat the oven to 400°F. Place the eggplant on a baking sheet and prick in several spots. Bake for 50 minutes, or until very tender. Remove from the oven. Let cool, then peel and cut into ½-inch cubes.

2   While the eggplant is baking, heat the olive oil in a large skillet over medium heat. Add the onion and sauté until nicely browned, 7 to 10 minutes. Add 1 tablespoon of the vinegar and continue cooking until the onions are nicely glazed, about 5 minutes longer. Continue cooking the onions, adding the water a tablespoonful at a time as the liquid evaporates to keep them moist and prevent burning, until very soft, about 30 minutes longer.

3   Add the eggplant and the remaining 1 tablespoon vinegar to the onions. Add the parsley and salt and pepper to taste. Gently cook over medium heat until heated through, 3 to 5 minutes. Add the cheese to the eggplant mixture and cook briefly, just until the cheese is melted and distributed. Spoon the mixture into a 2-cup crock and serve immediately, with the bread.

Recommended Wine
Use a rich, oaky Chardonnay to balance the richness of this dish.

Advance Preparation
Can be prepared up to 8 hours ahead and refrigerated. Bring to room temperature and then reheat gently before serving.

RICOTTA CORN CAKES WITH SMOKY SALSA TOPPING

SERVES 8

When I first made light and fluffy Ricotta Pancakes with Sautéed Spiced Pears (page 116), I wondered how a similar mixture would go with corn. These Ricotta Corn Cakes are the result. The sweet flavors of fresh corn and ricotta cheese are a perfect contrast to the Smoky Salsa. For an equally delicious variation, combine the salsa and sour cream and spoon it over the corn cakes. For your main course, consider Roasted Cornish Hens with Honey-Tangerine Marinade (page 191) and Tricolor Vegetable Sauté (page 245).

4 tablespoons unsalted butter
4 scallions, white and light green parts only, thinly sliced
4 large eggs
1 cup low-fat ricotta cheese
⅓ cup all-purpose flour
⅓ cup yellow cornmeal
1 teaspoon salt
¼ teaspoon freshly ground white pepper
1 cup fresh corn kernels (from about 2 medium ears)

GARNISH

½ cup Smoky Salsa (page 360)
½ cup sour cream

Recommended Wine

Use a crisp, spicy Sauvignon Blanc to balance the smokiness of this dish.

Advance Preparation

The batter can be made up to 1 day in advance, covered well, and refrigerated. The corn cakes can be made up to 1 hour ahead and kept warm in a 250°F oven.

1   In a medium skillet over medium heat, melt 3 tablespoons of the butter. Add the scallions and sauté until softened and slightly caramelized, about 7 minutes. Transfer to a food processor fitted with the metal blade.

2   Add the eggs, ricotta, flour, cornmeal, salt, and pepper and process until you have a smooth batter. Add the corn kernels and pulse a few times, being sure not to break up the corn too much.

3   Melt the remaining 1 tablespoon butter in a large, nonstick skillet or griddle over medium heat. Using a small ladle or measuring cup with a pouring spout, pour about 1 tablespoon of batter into the skillet for each cake (the pancakes should be about the size of silver dollars). Cook for about 2 minutes, or until the cakes bubble and are just set. Flip the cakes and cook for another minute.

4   To serve, place the cakes on large serving platter and garnish each with a dollop of the salsa and the sour cream. Serve immediately.

Los Angeles's Chaya Brasserie Restaurant is known for its innovative cross-cultural blending of French, Italian, and Japanese cuisine with a California point of view. The appetizers are among the best in Los Angeles. In the Chaya version of tuna tartare (which might be called a double tuna sashimi), thick slices of raw tuna and a refreshing tuna tartare sit on top of a crispy wonton square. It is important to use only the freshest top-quality (sushi-grade) tuna since it is not cooked.

TUNA TARTARE

SERVES 6

DRESSING

2 tablespoons Champagne vinegar

1 teaspoon fresh lemon juice

1 teaspoon whole-grain mustard

¼ cup light olive oil

Salt and freshly ground black pepper

1 pound sushi-grade fresh tuna, cut into ½-inch pieces

1 teaspoon whole-grain mustard

2 tablespoons finely chopped scallion, both white and green parts

2 tablespoons finely chopped cornichons

½ cup finely chopped English (hothouse) cucumber

1 to 2 teaspoons finely chopped fresh tarragon

1 to 2 teaspoons green peppercorns, rinsed, drained, and crushed

½ medium ripe avocado, pitted, peeled, and cut into ½-inch pieces

GARNISH

1 tablespoon finely chopped scallion, both white and green parts

Simple crackers or thinly sliced French bread, lightly toasted, for serving

Recommended Wine

A big, rich, oaky Chardonnay should do the trick here. It will balance nicely with the tangy cornichons and the herbs. If you want to be a bit daring, try champagne.

Advance Preparation

Can be prepared up to 2 hours ahead, covered, and refrigerated.

1   To make the dressing, whisk together the vinegar, lemon juice, and mustard in a small mixing bowl. Slowly add the olive oil in a steady stream, whisking until it is incorporated and emulsified. Add salt and pepper to taste.

2   In a medium mixing bowl, combine the tuna, mustard, scallion, cornichons, cucumber, tarragon, green peppercorns to taste, and avocado.

3   Pour the dressing over the tuna mixture, stir to blend thoroughly, and spoon it into a small serving bowl. Serve with the crackers or freshly toasted bread, garnished with the scallion.

44 Roasted Garlic and Butternut Squash Soup with Ancho Chile Cream

46 Roasted Vegetable Soup

48 Sweet Potato–Jalapeño Soup with Tomatillo Cream

50 Spinach, Pasta, and Fagioli Soup

52 White Bean and Artichoke Soup

54 Yellow Split Pea Soup with Mushrooms and Smoked Turkey

57 Lentil Soup with Thyme and Balsamic Vinegar

59 Pinto Bean Soup with Gremolata

60 Black Bean Soup with Lime Cream

62 Broccoli-Leek Soup with Parmesan Cream

63 Asian Chicken Noodle Soup with Tofu and Pea Pods

64 Chicken Minestrone with Mixed-Herb Pesto

66 Grilled Seafood Bisque with Red Pepper Aioli

68 Corn and Tomato Soup

70 Cucumber-Avocado Gazpacho

71 Squash Vichyssoise

S O U P S

ROASTED GARLIC AND BUTTERNUT SQUASH SOUP WITH ANCHO CHILE CREAM

SERVES 4 TO 6

I like to serve this soup in mugs on Thanksgiving or during the holidays, when there's lots of excitement in the kitchen and a fire in the fireplace. Butternut squash is sweetest during these months and is well complemented by the spicy ancho chile cream. Roasting the garlic with the squash allows the sweet nutty flavors to develop fully. Slowly sautéed onions turn caramel brown and add another layer of flavor. For a large crowd, this recipe can easily be doubled.

1 large butternut squash (about 4 pounds)

1 medium head of garlic, cloves separated and peeled, ends cut off (about 20 cloves)

¼ cup olive oil

¼ cup water

2 medium onions, finely chopped

5 cups Chicken Stock (page 342) or vegetable stock

½ teaspoon salt

½ teaspoon freshly ground white pepper

ANCHO CHILE CREAM

1 tablespoon Ancho Chile Paste (page 351)

½ cup sour cream or store-bought crème fraîche

GARNISH

2 tablespoons finely chopped fresh chives

Advance Preparation

The soup and Ancho Chile Cream can be prepared through step 6 up to 3 days ahead, covered, and refrigerated. Reheat the soup gently and taste for seasoning.

1   Preheat the oven to 350°F. Slice the squash in half lengthwise and remove the seeds and stringy pulp with a serrated spoon. Carefully slice the peel off and then cut the flesh into 1-inch-thick slices.

2   In a medium roasting pan, combine the squash and garlic. Drizzle 2 tablespoons of the olive oil over the squash and mix with a spoon until all of the ingredients are well coated. Add the water. Roast in the middle of the oven, stirring occasionally, until the squash and garlic cloves are soft and caramelized, about 50 to 60 minutes. Add a bit more water if the squash begins to burn. Let cool slightly.

3   While the squash is roasting, heat the remaining 2 tablespoons of olive oil in a heavy medium skillet over medium heat. Add the onions and sauté slowly for about 20 minutes or until the onions are golden and caramelized. Set aside.

4 Working in batches, spoon the roasted squash and garlic cloves into a blender with 1 cup of the stock. Add the caramelized onions and purée the mixture in the blender for about 1 minute or until very smooth.

5 Pour the squash into a large saucepan. Add the remaining stock and the salt and pepper to the saucepan and bring to a simmer. Taste for seasoning.

6 To make the chile cream, in a small bowl, combine the ancho chile paste with the sour cream. Blend completely. Taste for seasoning.

7 When you're ready to serve, ladle the soup into soup bowls or mugs and place a dollop of the Ancho Chile Cream on top. Sprinkle with the chives and serve immediately.

GREAT GADGETS: THE IMMERSION BLENDER

Sometimes called a hand blender, this innovative kitchen tool can be used for making soup, sauces, salad dressings, and drinks. The long and narrow-handheld blender with a rotary blade at one end goes right into the pot to purée or emulsify and eliminates the extra step of transferring the mixture to a blender or food processor.

The trick here is to keep the blade at the bottom of the vessel. Occasionally lift it gently, but *never* above the surface of the liquid, so the mixture stays in the pot and doesn't splatter all over. You can use this blender in a saucepan, a pitcher, or a deep bowl—just be sure there is enough mixture to cover the blades. You'll love this gadget.

ROASTED VEGETABLE SOUP

SERVES 6 TO 8

Roasting the vegetables adds an extra taste dimension to this soup, bringing out each vegetable's unique flavor. Use your favorite vegetables in this hearty, rustic, low-fat soup. Plain nonfat yogurt contributes a creamy consistency while adding only a few extra calories. This is a great main-course lunch soup with toasted Country Sourdough Bread (page 286) and Farmers' Market Chopped Salad (page 78).

2 leeks, white parts only, cleaned and finely chopped

½ pound mushrooms, brushed clean and coarsely chopped

3 medium carrots, peeled and cut into 2-inch pieces

2 medium zucchini, cut into 2-inch pieces

2 large tomatoes, quartered

2 medium white potatoes, peeled and cut into 2-inch pieces

½ medium head of green cabbage, shredded

2 tablespoons olive oil

½ cup Chicken Stock (page 342)

Pinch of freshly ground black pepper

TO FINISH

6 to 7 cups Chicken Stock (page 342)

2 tablespoons finely chopped mixed fresh herbs such as parsley, basil, chives, and thyme

2 tablespoons fresh lemon juice

Salt and freshly ground black pepper

GARNISH

½ cup plain nonfat or low-fat yogurt

2 tablespoons finely chopped mixed fresh herbs such as parsley, basil, chives, and thyme

Advance Preparation

Can be prepared through step 2 up to 3 days ahead, covered, and refrigerated. Reheat gently and taste for seasoning.

1   Preheat the oven to 425°F. Place all the vegetables in a large, heavy roasting pan. Add the oil, the ½ cup stock, and a pinch of pepper and mix until all the vegetables are well coated. Roast the vegetables for 40 minutes, or until soft, turning once to make sure they do not burn.

2   Working in batches, place the vegetables in a food processor fitted with the metal blade or a blender and process to a smooth purée. Transfer the purée to a large saucepan. Add 6 cups of the stock, the herbs, and the lemon juice and stir to mix well. Add more stock if needed to reach the desired consistency and cook over low heat for 10 minutes to allow the flavors to blend. Season with salt and pepper to taste.

3   To serve, ladle the soup into soup bowls. Swirl a tablespoon of the yogurt into each and garnish with the fresh herbs. Serve immediately.

SWEET POTATO–JALAPEÑO SOUP WITH TOMATILLO CREAM

SERVES 6 TO 8

Most California markets sell only two sweet potato varieties: moist and dry. The moist sweet potato variety is often erroneously labeled *yam*. For this soup you want the reddish brown moist sweet potato, not the drier one, which has a light brown-yellow skin and a pale flesh—they are decidedly less sweet.

If you find that this soup lacks a sweet flavor, add a pinch of brown sugar for balance. Served by itself, this soup does not reach the spectacular flavor it attains when served with the Tomatillo Cream and the garnishes; the crunch of whole sweet corn kernels and a final squirt of lime juice brings all the flavors together harmoniously. If you're not serving sweet potatoes for Thanksgiving, begin the dinner with this soup. It is also great as a main dish on a cool autumn afternoon served with a salad and a glass of Beaujolais Nouveau.

1 tablespoon olive oil

2 medium leeks, white parts only, cleaned and finely chopped

1 garlic clove, minced

¼ teaspoon ground cumin

3 pounds moist (reddish brown–skinned) sweet potatoes (about 6 medium), peeled and cut into 2-inch pieces

6 to 7 cups Chicken Stock (page 342)

1 small jalapeño chile, seeded and finely chopped (see note)

½ teaspoon salt

¼ teaspoon freshly ground white pepper

2 tablespoons fresh lime juice

1 teaspoon dark brown sugar (optional)

1 cup cooked fresh corn kernels (from about 2 medium ears) or thawed frozen kernels

TOMATILLO CREAM AND GARNISH

½ cup sour cream or plain low-fat yogurt

2 tablespoons Tomatillo Salsa (page 358)

3 tablespoons finely chopped fresh cilantro

¼ teaspoon salt

Pinch of freshly ground white pepper

½ cup cooked fresh corn kernels (from about 1 medium ear) or thawed frozen kernels

6 to 8 teaspoons fresh lime juice

Note

When working with chiles, always wear rubber gloves. Wash the cutting surface and knife immediately.

Advance Preparation

Can be prepared through step 2 up to 3 days ahead, covered, and refrigerated. Reheat gently and taste for seasoning.

1 In a 6-quart soup pot or Dutch oven over medium-high heat, heat the oil. Add the leeks and sauté for 5 minutes, or until softened. Add the garlic and cumin, reduce the heat to medium, and cook for another minute. Add the sweet potatoes, 6 cups of the stock, the jalapeño, salt, and pepper and bring to a simmer. Cook, covered, for 20 to 25 minutes, or until the sweet potatoes are very tender. Remove from the heat.

2 Purée the soup in the pot using an immersion blender or in batches in a food processor fitted with the metal blade. Add the remaining 1 cup stock if the soup is too thick. Return the soup to the pot if necessary and bring it to a simmer. Add the 2 tablespoons lime juice, the brown sugar if desired, and the 1 cup corn kernels and cook the soup 3 more minutes to allow the flavors to blend. Taste for seasoning.

3 To make the Tomatillo Cream, in a small bowl, combine the sour cream, salsa, 1 tablespoon of the chopped cilantro, and the salt and pepper and mix together. Taste for seasoning.

4 To serve, ladle the soup into soup bowls and garnish each with a tablespoon of the Tomatillo Cream, a tablespoon of the corn kernels, a sprinkling of the remaining chopped cilantro, and a squeeze of fresh lime juice. Serve immediately.

SPINACH, PASTA, AND FAGIOLI SOUP

SERVES 6

Adding spinach to this classic bean and pasta soup enriches its taste and color. Great Northern, cannellini, or any other white bean all work nicely here.

1 cup (½ pound) dried white beans, picked over and rinsed

2 tablespoons olive oil

2 medium onions, coarsely chopped

2 carrots, peeled and coarsely chopped

1 small bunch spinach, tough stems removed, cut into julienne

6 cups Chicken Stock (page 342)

2 garlic cloves, minced

2 medium tomatoes, peeled, seeded, and coarsely chopped, or 1 cup chopped well-drained canned tomatoes

2 tablespoons finely chopped fresh basil or 2 teaspoons dried

¾ cup fine egg noodles or broken capellini

1 teaspoon salt

½ teaspoon freshly ground white pepper

2 tablespoons finely chopped fresh parsley

GARNISH

2 tablespoons finely chopped fresh parsley

6 tablespoons freshly grated Parmesan cheese

Advance Preparation

Can be prepared through step 5 up to 3 days ahead, covered, and refrigerated. Reheat gently. This soup also freezes well. Be sure to adjust the seasonings and add fresh herbs when you reheat the frozen soup.

1   Soak the beans overnight in enough cold water to cover generously. (Alternatively, do a quick soak: Bring the beans to a boil in just enough water to cover, boil for 2 minutes, then cover and let stand for 1 hour.) Drain the beans and set aside.

2   In a 6-quart soup pot over medium heat, heat the oil. Add the onions and sauté for about 5 minutes, or until softened. Add the carrots and sauté until slightly softened, about 3 minutes longer. Add half of the spinach and sauté until it wilts, about 2 to 3 minutes. Add the stock, beans, garlic, tomatoes, and basil and simmer for about 1 hour, partially covered, or until the beans are tender. Remove from the heat.

3   Meanwhile, cook the noodles in a medium saucepan of boiling water until al dente, 5 to 7 minutes, depending on their thickness. Drain in a colander and set aside.

4   Purée the soup in the pot with an immersion blender or in batches in a food processor fitted with the metal blade, making sure the vegetables still have some texture.

5   Return the soup to the pot if necessary, place over medium-high heat, and add the noodles and remaining spinach. Cook for about 5 minutes, then add the salt, pepper, and parsley and taste for seasoning.

6   To serve, ladle the soup into soup bowls and garnish with the parsley and Parmesan.

WHITE BEAN AND ARTICHOKE SOUP

SERVES 6

White beans and artichoke hearts are a surprisingly winning combination. The artichoke hearts add just a hint of pleasant bitterness to this soup; using frozen artichoke hearts cuts down the preparation time without sacrificing any flavor. Straining the soup creates a silken texture. Follow with Sautéed Pork Medallions with Mustard-Herb Sauce (page 237) and Roasted Broccoli with Toasted Bread Crumb Gremolata (page 248).

1 cup (½ pound) dried white beans, picked over and rinsed

2 tablespoons olive oil

2 medium onions, coarsely chopped

2 carrots, peeled and coarsely chopped

¾ pound thawed frozen artichoke hearts

7 cups Chicken Stock (page 342), plus more if needed

3 garlic cloves, minced

3 medium tomatoes, peeled, seeded, and coarsely chopped,

or one 14½-ounce can diced tomatoes

Salt and freshly ground white pepper

2 tablespoons finely chopped fresh parsley

GARNISH

½ cup of your favorite croutons (optional)

6 tablespoons freshly grated Parmesan cheese

2 tablespoons finely chopped fresh parsley

Advance Preparation

Can be prepared through step 3 up to 3 days ahead, covered, and refrigerated. Reheat gently. This soup also freezes well. Be sure to adjust the seasonings and add fresh herbs when you reheat the frozen soup.

1 Soak the beans overnight in enough cold water to cover generously. (Alternatively, do a quick soak: Bring the beans to a boil in just enough water to cover, boil for 2 minutes, then cover and let stand for 1 hour.) Drain the beans and set aside.

2 In a 6-quart soup pot over medium heat, heat the oil. Add the onions and sauté for about 5 minutes, or until softened. Add the carrots and sauté for 3 minutes, or until slightly softened. Add the artichoke hearts and sauté for 2 to 3 minutes longer, or until slightly softened. Raise the heat to high and add the stock, beans, garlic, and tomatoes. Bring to a boil, then reduce the heat to low, cover partially, and simmer for 1 to 1¼ hours, or until the beans are tender. Remove from the heat.

3 Purée the soup in the pot using an immersion blender or in batches in a food processor fitted with the metal blade. Strain the soup through a fine-mesh strainer into a large saucepan. Add a bit more stock if it's too thick. Gently reheat the soup over medium heat. Add the salt, pepper, and parsley and taste for seasoning.

4 To serve, ladle the soup into soup bowls and garnish with the croutons (if using), Parmesan, and parsley.

YELLOW SPLIT PEA SOUP WITH MUSHROOMS AND SMOKED TURKEY

SERVES 4 TO 6

This simple soup has a couple of surprises: smoked turkey instead of the usual ham and a garnish of shredded sugar snap or snow peas for a garden-sweet crunch. Most of the turkey goes in right before serving so the texture is preserved. Serve with Sourdough Rye Rolls (page 288) or Focaccia (page 294).

2 tablespoons olive oil

1 medium onion, finely chopped

1 celery rib, sliced

2 carrots, peeled and sliced

¾ pound mushrooms, brushed, cleaned, and sliced

1 medium yellow bell pepper, seeded and coarsely chopped

1 cup (½ pound) dried yellow split peas, picked over and rinsed

½ pound smoked turkey breast, coarsely chopped

6 cups Chicken Stock (page 342)

¼ cup finely chopped fresh flat-leaf parsley

½ teaspoon finely chopped fresh sage or ¼ teaspoon dried

½ teaspoon finely chopped fresh thyme or ¼ teaspoon dried

¼ teaspoon salt

¼ teaspoon freshly ground black pepper

¼ pound sugar snap or snow peas, trimmed and thinly sliced

GARNISH

¼ cup finely chopped fresh parsley

Fresh thyme leaves

Advance Preparation

Can be prepared through step 3 up to 3 days ahead, covered, and refrigerated. Reheat gently. This soup also freezes well. Be sure to adjust the seasonings and add fresh herbs when you reheat the frozen soup.

1 In a 6-quart soup pot over medium heat, heat the oil. Add the onion and sauté for 5 minutes, or until softened. Add the celery, carrots, mushrooms, and bell pepper and sauté for 2 minutes longer, or until slightly softened.

2 Add the split peas, ¼ cup of the smoked turkey, the stock, and the herbs and bring to a simmer over medium-low heat. Partially cover and cook for about 50 to 60 minutes, or until the peas are tender. Remove from the heat.

3 Coarsely purée the soup in the pot using an immersion blender or in batches in a food processor fitted with the metal blade. Return the soup to the pot if necessary. Add the remaining turkey, the salt, and the pepper. Bring to a simmer and cook for 5 minutes longer. Taste for seasoning.

4 Just before serving, add the sliced fresh peas and heat through. Ladle into soup bowls and serve immediately, garnished with the parsley and thyme.

Balsamic Vinegar

Think of balsamic vinegar as a cook's best friend—a flavor enhancer that brings out underlying complex flavors and sparks up simpler flavors. From pasta sauce to salad dressings, from complex meat reductions to soup enhancers, balsamic vinegar is an essential ingredient in California cooking. It has, in fact, become so popular in the United States that imitations are being sold right along with the real thing. A true balsamic comes from only one region of Italy, around the town of Modena in Emilia-Romagna.

There are three categories of balsamic vinegar: artisan and commercially produced balsamic vinegar, both made in the provinces of Modena and Reggio, and imitations made outside the provinces of Modena and Reggio. Balsamic vinegar is made by combining a high-quality wine vinegar, reduced grape must (the partially fermented juice and pulp of the grapes), some young balsamic vinegar as a starter, and sometimes caramel. Aging takes place in a succession of wooden casks and can require from a few years up to 120 years.

Prices for a bottle range from a few dollars to over $100. The really expensive artisan-produced vinegars are much too good for cooking. In Italy they are used by the drop or sometimes sipped as liqueurs.

For cooking, a commercial (*industriale*) vinegar from Modena or nearby Reggio will be fine. Look on the label for either API MO (referring to Modena) or API RE (referring to Reggio) to be sure you aren't buying an imitation from another area.

When selecting a good *industriale* balsamic, look for a refined, sweet-tart balance. It shouldn't taste too acidic or too sweet—the balance is important. If you find the vinegar is too strong and tart, reduce it by half over high heat to tame the acid and give it a syrupy glaze consistency with a richer, subtler flavor. You can keep this on hand in the refrigerator and use it as needed. Another way to help balance it is to add a pinch of dark brown sugar to each tablespoon.

As an ingredient in a marinade or as part of the acid content of a vinaigrette, balance its strength with other acids like lemon juice or other wine vinegars so that it doesn't overwhelm the dish.

Here are a few ideas for how to use balsamic vinegar:

- Add it to a vinaigrette with lemon, red wine, or rice wine vinegar.
- Add it to cooked beans or bean soups just before serving.
- Add it to roasted and caramelized onions or garlic.
- Add a teaspoon to salsas or your favorite pesto.
- Use it as a salt substitute.
- Add a teaspoon to fruit jams, roasted or grilled tomatoes, or fruit compotes.
- Drizzle it over simple grilled fish, meat, or poultry.
- Add it to sautéed vegetables.
- Drizzle it over ripe sliced tomatoes with a fresh basil garnish.
- Drizzle it over mixed grilled vegetables along with some lemon juice, extra-virgin olive oil, and chopped fresh herbs.
- Drizzle it over baked potatoes, or combine a bit of olive oil and balsamic and roast new potatoes in this blend.
- Add a tablespoon when you deglaze the pan before you make a sauce for poultry dishes.
- Drizzle it over sliced melon.
- Drizzle it over strawberries and sprinkle with freshly ground black pepper.

This classic Middle Eastern soup has a sweet American accent: honey-cured ham. Use brown lentils, sometimes called *masoor dal,* since they cook quickly and purée well. If fresh tomatoes are not at their best, use diced well-drained canned tomatoes.

LENTIL SOUP WITH THYME AND BALSAMIC VINEGAR

SERVES 6 TO 8

2 tablespoons olive oil

1 large onion, finely chopped

3 carrots, peeled and coarsely chopped

2 celery ribs, finely chopped

2 cups (1 pound) dried brown lentils, picked over and rinsed

½ pound coarsely chopped honey-cured or other sweet-flavored ham

2 quarts Chicken Stock (page 342)

2 cups peeled, seeded, and finely chopped fresh tomatoes (about 2 large) or diced well-drained canned tomatoes

4 tablespoons finely chopped fresh parsley

1 teaspoon finely chopped fresh thyme or ⅓ teaspoon dried

2 teaspoons balsamic vinegar

1 teaspoon salt

¼ teaspoon freshly ground black pepper

GARNISH

1 large tomato, peeled, seeded, and finely chopped

¼ cup finely chopped fresh parsley

continued on next page

Advance Preparation

Can be prepared through step 4 up to 3 days ahead, covered, and refrigerated. Reheat gently. This soup also freezes well. Be sure to adjust the seasonings and add fresh herbs when you reheat the frozen soup.

1   In a 6-quart soup pot over medium heat, heat the oil. Add the onion and sauté
    for about 3 minutes. Add the carrot and celery and continue sautéing until
    softened, about 5 minutes longer.

2   Add the lentils, ½ cup of the ham, the stock, tomatoes, and 2 tablespoons
    of the parsley. Bring to a boil, then reduce the heat to medium-low, cover
    partially, and simmer, stirring occasionally for about 30 minutes, or until the
    lentils are tender. Remove from the heat.

3   Process the soup in the pot using an immersion blender or in batches in a food
    processor fitted with the metal blade, pulsing until the soup is partially puréed
    but still has plenty of texture.

4   Return the soup to the pot if necessary. Add the remaining ham, the remaining
    2 tablespoons parsley, the thyme, vinegar, salt, and pepper. Bring to a simmer
    and cook for 5 minutes longer. Taste for seasoning.

5   To serve, ladle the soup into soup bowls and garnish with the tomato
    and parsley.

Gremolata, an Italian flavoring blend of lemon zest, garlic, and parsley, is traditionally used as a finishing touch for osso buco. This savory herb blend is even better
as a garnish for less complicated flavors, as in this puréed soup. Try using turkey
bacon—it's much lower in fat but still gives the desired smoky flavor. For a satisfying
lunch, follow with Grilled Steak and Potato Salad (page 96).

2 cups (1 pound) dried pinto beans, picked over and rinsed

2 tablespoons olive oil

1 medium onion, finely chopped

1 carrot, peeled and finely chopped

2 garlic cloves, minced

7 cups Chicken Stock (page 342)

4 strips bacon

Salt and freshly ground black pepper

GREMOLATA

2 garlic cloves, minced

¼ cup chopped fresh parsley

Zest of 1 lemon, finely chopped

1   Soak the beans overnight in enough cold water to cover generously. (Alterna-
    tively, do a quick soak: Bring the beans to a boil in just enough water to cover, boil
    for 2 minutes, then cover and let stand for 1 hour.) Drain the beans and set aside.

2   In a 6-quart soup pot over medium heat, heat the oil. Add the onion and sauté
    for about 5 minutes, or until softened. Add the carrot and sauté until slightly
    softened, about 3 minutes longer. Add the garlic and sauté for another minute.

3   Add the beans, stock, and bacon. Bring to a boil, then reduce the heat to low,
    cover partially, and simmer for 50 to 60 minutes, or until the beans are tender.
    Remove from the heat.

4   Purée the soup in the pot using an immersion blender or in batches in a food
    processor fitted with the metal blade. Return the soup to the pot if necessary
    and reheat gently. Add the salt and pepper to taste.

5   To make the gremolata, stir together the garlic, parsley, and lemon zest in a
    small bowl.

6   To serve, ladle the soup into soup bowls and garnish with the gremolata.

Advance Preparation
Can be prepared through step 4 up to
3 days ahead, covered, and refrigerated. Reheat gently. This soup also
freezes well. Be sure to adjust the
seasonings and add fresh herbs when
you reheat the frozen soup.

BLACK BEAN SOUP WITH LIME CREAM

SERVES 6 TO 8

Black beans have become a welcome staple in many California kitchens, where they're blended into soups, stews, pancakes, salsas, and relishes. The lime cream adds a sophisticated touch to ordinary black beans. Most black bean soups are coarse textured, but I like to purée this soup and put it through a fine-mesh strainer to achieve a velvety texture. I prefer a mild smoky flavor, so I don't add the meat from the ham bone.

Salsa makes a wonderful accompaniment—try Tomatillo (page 358), Spicy Tomato (page 357), or your favorite store-bought salsa. Serve warm tortillas or tortilla chips on the side.

2 cups (1 pound) dried black beans, picked over and rinsed

2 tablespoons olive oil

2 medium onions, finely chopped

1 to 2 medium jalapeño chiles, seeded and finely chopped (see note)

3 garlic cloves, minced

1 small red bell pepper, seeded and finely chopped

1 teaspoon ground cumin

1 teaspoon ground coriander

2 teaspoons finely chopped fresh oregano or 1 teaspoon dried

2 quarts water

½ small ham hock or ham bone

2 tablespoons fresh lime juice

2 tablespoons finely chopped fresh cilantro

Salt and freshly ground black pepper

LIME CREAM

½ cup sour cream

1 to 2 tablespoons fresh lime juice

¼ teaspoon salt

Pinch of freshly ground white pepper

GARNISH

Fresh cilantro sprigs

½ cup salsa of your choice (optional)

Advance Preparation

Can be prepared through step 4 up to 2 days ahead, covered, and refrigerated. Reheat gently. This soup also freezes well. Be sure to adjust the seasonings and add fresh herbs when you reheat the frozen soup.

Note

When working with chiles, always wear rubber gloves. Wash the cutting surface and knife immediately.

1   Soak the beans overnight in enough cold water to cover generously. (Alternatively, do a quick soak: Bring the beans to a boil in just enough water to cover, boil for 2 minutes, then cover and let stand for 1 hour.) Drain the beans and set aside.

2   In a large soup pot over medium heat, heat the oil. Add the onions and sauté for about 3 minutes, or until softened. Add the jalapeño to taste, the garlic, bell pepper, cumin, coriander, and oregano and sauté for another 10 minutes, stirring frequently.

3   Add the drained beans, water, and ham hock. Bring to a boil, then reduce the heat to medium-low, cover partially, and simmer for 1½ to 2 hours, or until the beans are tender. Remove from the heat and discard the ham hock.

4   Purée half of the bean mixture in a food processor fitted with the metal blade or in a blender and return it to the soup pot, or purée the soup in the pot using an immersion blender, leaving a bit of texture. Reheat gently. Add the lime juice, chopped cilantro, and salt and black pepper to taste. If the soup is too thick, thin it with water. (If you prefer a velvety texture, purée all of the soup well and then pour it through a fine-mesh strainer into a saucepan.)

5   To make the Lime Cream, combine the sour cream, lime juice to taste, salt, and white pepper in a small bowl. Taste for seasoning.

6   To serve, ladle the soup into soup bowls and garnish with lime cream, a sprig of cilantro, and a dollop of salsa, if desired.

BROCCOLI-LEEK SOUP WITH PARMESAN CREAM

SERVES 4

This quick soup works in many roles, from an informal family dinner to an elegant starter for a dinner party. Parmesan cream is a lovely counterpoint to the distinctive, bright green broccoli-leek purée. Using a handheld immersion blender saves on preparation time and cleaning.

2 tablespoons olive oil
2 medium leeks, white and light green parts only, cleaned and finely chopped
1 pound red potatoes (about 2 medium), peeled and finely chopped
1½ pounds broccoli, florets and stalks trimmed and cut into 1-inch pieces
5 cups Chicken Stock (page 342)
½ teaspoon salt
¼ freshly ground white pepper

PARMESAN CREAM

½ cup sour cream or plain nonfat yogurt
¼ cup finely grated Parmesan cheese
Pinch of freshly ground white pepper

GARNISH

2 tablespoons finely chopped fresh chives

Advance Preparation

The soup and Parmesan Cream can be prepared through step 3 up to 1 day ahead, covered, and refrigerated. Gently reheat the soup and taste for seasoning. Whisk the Parmesan Cream before serving.

1   In a large soup pot over medium heat, heat the oil. Add the leeks and sauté for about 3 to 5 minutes, or until softened. Add the potatoes and broccoli and sauté for 2 minutes, stirring frequently. Add the stock and bring it to a simmer. Partially cover and simmer for about 15 to 20 minutes, or until the vegetables are tender when pierced with the tip of a sharp knife. Remove from the heat.

2   Purée the soup in the pot using an immersion blender or in batches in a food processor fitted with the metal blade. Return the soup to the pot if necessary and reheat gently. Add the salt and pepper and taste for seasoning.

3   To make the Parmesan Cream, combine the sour cream, cheese, and pepper in a small bowl and whisk until combined.

4   To serve, ladle the soup into soup plates or bowls, spoon a dollop of the Parmesan Cream on top, and garnish with the chives. Serve immediately.

Noodle shops have sprung up all over California. Mishima in Los Angeles makes many variations on a classic Asian noodle soup; this recipe is based on a soup I enjoy there from time to time. I like to use soba noodles, which are made from buckwheat flour and are enormously popular in Japanese noodle shops. You'll find miso paste and dried soba noodles in the Asian section of your supermarket.

If you put the noodles right into the broth, they will soak up much of the liquid; it's best to divide up the noodles among the soup bowls and pour over the broth for a good balance of noodles to broth. This is a meal-in-one.

ASIAN CHICKEN NOODLE SOUP WITH TOFU AND PEA PODS

SERVES 6

10 ounces dried soba noodles

6 cups Chicken Stock (page 342)

2 cups water

⅓ cup light yellow miso paste (shiromiso)

2 teaspoons peeled and grated fresh ginger

1 pound boneless, skinless chicken breast, cut into thin strips

½ pound firm tofu, cut into 1-inch cubes

¼ pound Chinese pea pods or sugar snap peas, trimmed and julienned

2 carrots, peeled and julienned

2 cups packed baby spinach leaves

2 scallions, white and light green parts only, thinly sliced

2 tablespoons fresh cilantro leaves

1   Bring a large saucepan three-fourths full of water to a boil over high heat. Add the noodles and cook for about 4 minutes, or until they are just tender. Drain and set aside.

2   Combine the stock, water, miso paste, and ginger in a large saucepan over medium-high heat. Whisk together and bring to a simmer, whisking until the miso is completely dissolved.

3   Reduce the heat to medium and add the chicken strips. Cook for another 3 to 4 minutes, or until the chicken is just tender and opaque throughout. Add the tofu, pea pods, and carrots and cook for 2 more minutes, or until the vegetables are crisp-tender. Add the spinach and cook for about another minute, just until the leaves have softened but the spinach is still bright green. Add the scallions and cilantro leaves and cook for another minute. Taste for seasoning.

4   To serve, using tongs, divide the noodles among soup bowls. Ladle the soup over and serve immediately.

CHICKEN MINESTRONE WITH MIXED-HERB PESTO

SERVES 8 AS A MAIN COURSE

This informal one-dish meal is a family favorite. Italian Arborio rice and an assertive mixed-herb pesto balance the soup in a most pleasing way. Shiitake mushrooms introduce a slightly chewy texture. Cutting all the vegetables is labor-intensive, so I make the soup in large quantities to enjoy on more than one occasion. Serve with warm Jalapeño Cheese Bread (page 292) or Country Sourdough Bread (page 286) for a satisfying lunch or dinner.

Advance Preparation

The soup and pesto can be prepared through step 4 up to 3 days ahead and refrigerated. Bring both to room temperature, then gently reheat the soup and serve. This soup also freezes well. Be sure to adjust the seasonings and add fresh herbs when you reheat the frozen soup.

3 quarts Chicken Stock (page 342) or water, or a combination

2 medium boneless, skinless whole chicken breasts

2 tablespoons olive oil

2 medium onions, finely chopped

4 carrots, peeled and cut into 1-inch pieces

2 large zucchini, cut into 1-inch pieces

½ pound green beans, trimmed and cut into 1-inch pieces

1 Japanese eggplant, unpeeled, cut into 1-inch pieces

½ small head of green cabbage, shredded

¼ pound mushrooms, preferably shiitake, brushed clean and sliced

2 garlic cloves, minced

1 cup diced well-drained canned tomatoes or 2 medium tomatoes, peeled, seeded, and finely chopped

2 tablespoons finely chopped fresh basil or 1 tablespoon dried

¼ cup Arborio rice

2 cups cooked white beans such as cannellini, or one 15-ounce can white beans, drained and rinsed well

½ teaspoon salt

½ teaspoon freshly ground black pepper

GARNISH

½ cup Mixed-Herb Pesto (page 348)

1   In a deep medium skillet or a large saucepan, bring the stock (enough to cover the chicken) to a simmer. If using water only, add ½ teaspoon salt. Add the chicken breasts and simmer for 8 to 10 minutes, or until just tender and opaque throughout. Remove from the heat and let the chicken cool in the stock. Drain the chicken, reserving the stock, and cut into 1-inch pieces. Set aside.

2   In a 6-quart soup pot over medium heat, heat the oil. Add the onions and sauté for about 5 minutes, or until softened, stirring occasionally. Add the carrots, zucchini, green beans, and eggplant and sauté for about 3 minutes, stirring frequently. Add the cabbage and sauté just until softened. Add the mushrooms and sauté for 2 minutes. Add the garlic and sauté for 1 minute longer.

3   Add the tomatoes, the reserved stock plus enough water to make 3 quarts, and the basil and bring to a boil. Reduce the heat to medium-low and simmer until all the vegetables are tender, about 15 minutes. The soup will be slightly thickened.

4   Add the rice and beans and cook for about 15 minutes, or until the rice is al dente. Add the reserved chicken and cook until heated through. Add the salt and pepper and taste for seasoning.

5   To serve, ladle the soup into soup bowls and swirl a tablespoon of pesto into each bowl.

GRILLED SEAFOOD BISQUE WITH RED PEPPER AIOLI

SERVES 4 TO 6

A rich orange saffron broth with chunks of tomato is paired with grilled scallops and shrimp for an unusual twist on cioppino, the seafood soup that San Franciscans made famous. Cooking seafood in broth tends to make the fish a bit rubbery, so here the fish is grilled instead, with outstanding results.

The leek-flecked tomato broth is poured into soup bowls, and grilled seafood is arranged decoratively on top. With the simple Red Pepper Aioli spooned over the seafood, the soup becomes a satisfying main course. You can also garnish the soup with plain toasted French bread topped with a dollop of the aioli. Begin with California Caponata (page 39) and serve the bisque with plenty of warm Country Sourdough Bread (page 286). For dessert, try Banana Split Ice Cream Torte (page 334).

Recommended Wine

Try a crispy, lively Sauvignon Blanc with this smoky soup.

Advance Preparation

Can be prepared through step 1 up to 1 day ahead, covered, and refrigerated. Reheat gently and taste for seasoning.

2 tablespoons olive oil

2 medium leeks, white and light green parts only, cleaned and thinly sliced

1 carrot, peeled and finely chopped

3 garlic cloves, minced

1 cup fish stock or bottled clam juice

2 cups dry white wine such as Sauvignon Blanc

One 28-ounce can diced tomatoes, with juice

Large pinch of saffron threads

One 2-inch-long strip of orange zest

Salt and freshly ground black pepper

12 large shrimp, peeled and deveined, tails left on

12 medium sea scallops

GARNISH

½ cup Red Pepper Aioli (page 352)

2 tablespoons finely chopped fresh chives

1   Heat the oil in a 4-quart nonaluminum Dutch oven or pot over medium heat. Add the leeks and carrot and sauté, stirring occasionally, for about 5 minutes, or until softened. Add the garlic and sauté for another minute. Add the stock, wine, tomatoes, saffron, and orange zest, bring to a simmer over medium-low heat, and cook for 20 minutes. Add the salt and pepper to taste. Remove from the heat and discard the orange zest. Using an immersion blender or in batches in a food processor fitted with the metal blade, purée the soup, leaving some texture. Return the soup to the pot if necessary.

2   Thread the shrimp and scallops on metal skewers. Lightly sprinkle them with salt and pepper. When you're ready to serve, prepare a grill for medium-high-heat grilling. Place the skewers on the grill 3 to 4 inches from the heat, flat side down, and grill until the shrimp and scallops are just opaque throughout, 3 to 4 minutes on each side. Remove the seafood from the skewers with a fork, and place on a plate. Cover and keep warm.

3   To serve, reheat the soup gently and ladle the bisque into soup plates. Arrange 2 or 3 shrimp and 2 or 3 scallops on top of each in a decorative circular pattern. Dollop the aioli in the center and garnish with the chives. Serve immediately.

CORN AND TOMATO SOUP

SERVES 8

This soup has won rave reviews from students and guests alike. What makes it so special is the layering of flavors. First a simple corn and tomato soup is simmered with hints of sun-dried tomato and basil and chilled. Next a rosy, mahogany cream bursting with sun-dried tomato essence is spooned on top of crispy sun-dried tomato toasts. Finally a corn-and-tomato relish is garnished on the toasts. While this may sound like too much tomato, I urge you to try it. It gets my vote for best summer soup.

If you love corn and cook with it frequently, you might want to invest in a gadget that removes the corn kernels from the cob in a single swoop. If you prefer the old-fashioned method, take a very sharp chef's knife, stand the husked ear of corn in a bowl, and slice down on an angle, separating the corn from the cob and letting it fall into the bowl. Sweet white corn is particularly delicious in this soup.

Advance Preparation

The soup, relish, and tomato cream can be prepared through step 4 up to 1 day ahead and refrigerated. This soup can also be served warm, if desired. Gently reheat and taste for seasoning before serving.

2 tablespoons olive oil

4 medium leeks, white and light green parts only, cleaned and finely chopped

1 carrot, peeled and finely chopped

1 celery rib, finely chopped

6 large tomatoes, coarsely chopped

3 tablespoons all-purpose flour

3½ cups fresh corn kernels (from about 7 medium ears)

2 garlic cloves, minced

6 dry-packed sun-dried tomatoes

8 fresh basil leaves

2 tablespoons tomato paste

6 cups Chicken Stock (page 342)

1 teaspoon salt

¼ teaspoon freshly ground black pepper

CORN-TOMATO RELISH

½ cup reserved chopped tomato (from above)

½ cup reserved fresh corn kernels (from above)

1 tablespoon finely chopped fresh basil

⅛ teaspoon salt

Pinch of freshly ground black pepper

SUN-DRIED TOMATO CREAM

½ cup dry-packed sun-dried tomatoes

½ cup sour cream

¼ teaspoon salt

Pinch of freshly ground white pepper

Sun-Dried Tomato Toasts (page 275) for serving

1   In a large soup pot over medium heat, heat the oil. Add the leeks, carrot, and celery and sauté for about 5 minutes, or until softened. Set aside ½ cup of the tomatoes for the relish; add the remaining tomatoes, and cook for about 3 minutes, or until slightly softened. Add the flour and stir with a wooden spoon, making sure that the flour is dissolved. Continue cooking for 2 minutes.

2   Reserve ½ cup of the corn kernels for the relish and add the remaining corn kernels, the garlic, sun-dried tomatoes, basil, tomato paste, and stock. Bring to a simmer and cook, partially covered, for about 25 minutes, or until the corn and sun-dried tomatoes are tender. Purée the soup in the pot using an immersion blender or in batches in a food processor fitted with the metal blade. Pour the soup through a fine-mesh strainer into a large container. Add the salt and black pepper and taste for seasoning. Let cool to room temperature and then refrigerate until well chilled, at least 2 hours.

3   To make the relish, finely dice the reserved chopped tomato and place in a small mixing bowl. Add the reserved corn kernels, the basil, salt, and black pepper. Taste for seasoning, and cover and refrigerate until serving.

4   To make the tomato cream, in a bowl, pour boiling water over the sun-dried tomatoes and soften for about 20 minutes. Drain the tomatoes and combine them with the sour cream, salt, and white pepper in a food processor fitted with the metal blade. Purée and taste for seasoning. Cover and refrigerate until serving.

5   To serve, ladle the soup into soup bowls and place 2 or 3 toasts on top. Place a spoonful of the tomato cream on top of the toasts and then garnish each toast with a spoonful of the relish.

CUCUMBER-AVOCADO GAZPACHO

SERVES 4

Here, a refreshing uncooked purée of cucumber and avocado is accented by crunchy chopped cucumber and creamy diced avocado. If you don't have time to make your own salsa, use the jalapeño salsa that comes in a jar or the fresh store-bought variety, but be careful—it can be very spicy. Serve the gazpacho icy cold, followed by Grilled Chicken Niçoise (page 176) with Assorted Grilled Vegetables (page 24).

BASE

1 large ripe avocado, pitted, peeled, and cut into 2-inch chunks

1 large English (hothouse) cucumber, cut into 2-inch chunks

1½ cups Chicken Stock (page 342)

2 tablespoons finely chopped fresh chives

2 tablespoons finely chopped red onion

3 tablespoons fresh lemon juice

½ cup sour cream

2 tablespoons Tomatillo Salsa (page 358), or to taste

Salt and freshly ground white pepper

VEGETABLES

2 cups finely chopped English (hothouse) cucumber

1 medium avocado, pitted, peeled, and cut into ½-inch dice

GARNISH

¼ cup sour cream

4 teaspoons Tomatillo Salsa (page 358)

¼ cup finely chopped fresh chives

Advance Preparation
Can be prepared through step 2 up to 4 hours ahead excluding the lemon juice, covered, and refrigerated. Add the lemon juice about 2 hours before serving.

1   In a food processor fitted with the metal blade, combine the chunks of avocado and cucumber and process until smooth. Add the stock, chives, red onion, lemon juice, sour cream, and salsa and process until combined. Season to taste with the salt and white pepper.

2   Pour the soup into a medium bowl and add the chopped cucumber and diced avocado, stirring to distribute. Taste for seasoning and refrigerate until well chilled, at least 2 hours.

3   To serve, ladle the soup into glass soup bowls and garnish with the sour cream, salsa, and chives.

This cool and refreshing potato soup includes green zucchini and yellow squash for color and subtle flavor. Onions are used in place of the usual leek, and lots of fresh basil adds a fragrant garden freshness. Remember not to chop the fresh basil until just before using it or it will turn black. If you prefer a lighter soup, use plain nonfat yogurt as an alternative to sour cream. Serve as a prelude to Grilled Lamb Chops with Cranberry-Rosemary Marinade (page 217) and Roasted Onions and Baby Potatoes (page 263).

2 tablespoons olive oil

1 medium onion, finely chopped

3 medium yellow crookneck squash, thinly sliced

3 medium zucchini, thinly sliced

3 medium White Rose potatoes (about 1 pound), peeled and thinly sliced

7 cups Chicken Stock (page 342)

2 tablespoons finely chopped fresh basil or 1 tablespoon dried

1½ teaspoons salt

¼ teaspoon freshly ground white pepper

1 tablespoon fresh lemon juice

½ cup sour cream or plain nonfat yogurt

GARNISH

¼ cup sour cream or plain nonfat yogurt

2 tablespoons finely chopped fresh basil

Advance Preparation
Can be prepared through step 3 up to 1 day ahead, covered, and refrigerated. Add the lemon juice and sour cream just before serving.

1   In a medium saucepan over medium heat, heat the oil. Add the onion and sauté for about 3 minutes, or until softened. Add the squashes and potatoes and sauté for about 3 minutes longer.

2   Add the stock and basil. Bring to a simmer and cook, partially covered, for about 15 minutes, or until the vegetables are tender. Add the salt and white pepper.

3   Purée the soup in the pan using an immersion blender or in batches in a food processor fitted with the metal blade. Transfer to a large container. Let cool to room temperature and then refrigerate until well chilled, at least 2 hours.

4   Whisk the lemon juice and sour cream into the soup until well combined. Taste for seasoning. To serve, ladle the soup into soup bowls and garnish with the sour cream and basil.

74 Caesar Salad with Mixed Baby Lettuces and Parmesan Toasts

76 Arugula and Jerusalem Artichoke Salad with Shaved Pecorino and Orange Vinaigrette

77 La Scala Chopped Salad

78 Farmers' Market Chopped Salad

80 Peppery Greens with Gorgonzola and Pine Nuts

82 California Salad

84 Mixed Greens with Beets and Peppers

86 Spinach and Mushroom Salad with Warm Tomato-Bacon Vinaigrette

88 Blood Orange, Mushroom, and Avocado Salad

90 Wheat Berry Vegetable Salad

92 Long-Grain and Wild Rice Salad with Corn and Salmon

94 Pasta Salad with Parmesan Dressing

96 Grilled Steak and Potato Salad

98 Grilled Chicken, Black Bean, and Corn Salad with Salsa Dressing

100 Warm Grilled Chicken Salad with Pesto

102 Chicken Salad with Chinese Noodles

104 Wine Country Chicken Salad

106 Warm Grilled Vegetable and Shrimp Salad

108 Springtime Salmon Salad

SALADS

CAESAR SALAD WITH MIXED BABY LETTUCES AND PARMESAN TOASTS

SERVES 4 TO 6

Advance Preparation

The toasts can be prepared up to 1 week ahead and stored in an airtight container. The dressing can be prepared up to 1 day ahead and refrigerated.

Caesar salad is a favorite of mine, but the undercooked egg in the traditional version—actually it's a coddled egg—is out of the question in the age of salmonella scares. Giving up Caesar salad seems equally out of the question.

But there's an alternative. Cook the egg completely and then blend it into the dressing. The result is a particularly creamy dressing. In this version, thin, crispy oven-baked Parmesan toasts replace the overused fried crouton. The usual romaine lettuce is mixed with radicchio and butter lettuce. And though it's far from traditional, I like to garnish this salad with ripe, juicy chopped tomatoes.

DRESSING

1 large egg

3 garlic cloves

¼ cup fresh lemon juice

1 to 2 teaspoons anchovy paste to taste

¼ teaspoon freshly ground black pepper

½ cup olive oil

¼ cup freshly grated Parmesan cheese

SALAD

1 medium head of radicchio, torn into bite-sized pieces

1 medium head of butter lettuce, torn into bite-sized pieces

1 medium head of romaine lettuce, heart only, torn into bite-sized pieces

¼ cup freshly grated Parmesan cheese

12 Parmesan Toasts (page 274) or store-bought toasts

GARNISH

1 large tomato (½ pound), peeled, seeded, and finely chopped

12 Parmesan Toasts (page 274) or store-bought toasts

1   To make the dressing, submerge the egg in a small saucepan of boiling water. Remove the pan from the heat and cover it for 10 minutes. Remove the egg from the water and let cool for 10 minutes.

2   With the machine running, mince the garlic in a food processor fitted with the metal blade; add the lemon juice, anchovy paste to taste, and pepper and process to combine. Crack the egg and spoon it out of the shell into the food processor. Pulse the egg with the other ingredients until combined. With the machine running, slowly add the oil in a steady stream and process until it is emulsified. Whisk in the Parmesan. Taste for seasoning.

3   In a large salad bowl, combine the radicchio and lettuces and toss with the dressing and Parmesan. Add the 12 toasts, breaking them into smaller bite-sized pieces, and toss again. Divide the salad among serving plates and garnish the center of each with the chopped tomatoes and the whole toasts.

HAIL CAESAR

There are many stories about how Caesar salad came into being. One legend has it that on July 4, 1924, Tijuana restaurateur Caesar Cardini found himself in a bit of a pickle. He was running low on food during this particular holiday weekend, but he was stocked up with the staple ingredients for this salad—garlic, bread, romaine lettuce, and Parmesan cheese. From these humble ingredients sprang the first Caesar salad, prepared and served tableside. As the tale goes, the salad was a lifesaver for Mr. Cardini on that Fourth of July weekend; he later moved to California, and since 1948 his family has bottled Cardini's Caesar Salad Dressing.

ARUGULA AND JERUSALEM ARTICHOKE SALAD WITH SHAVED PECORINO AND ORANGE VINAIGRETTE

SERVES 4 TO 6

Advance Preparation

The dressing can be prepared up to 1 day ahead and refrigerated. Whisk well before using.

The Jerusalem artichoke, or sunchoke, is a small tuber grown from the sunflower plant. It has a delightful, sweet, nutty flavor and is a little crunchy when you bite into it. Remember that sunchokes grow underground, so use a good vegetable scrub brush to remove any excess dirt. Scrub them thoroughly, but avoid removing the skin since most of the nutrients are found just below the surface.

This salad is wonderful before or after dinner. You can also add the segments from 2 oranges for an extra dose of citrus. If in season, try slightly tart, crimson-colored blood oranges for a delicious treat.

VINAIGRETTE

2 tablespoons fresh orange juice

1 tablespoon plus 1 teaspoon red wine vinegar

1 teaspoon Dijon mustard

5 tablespoons olive oil

Salt and freshly ground black pepper

10 ounces arugula leaves

½ pound Jerusalem artichokes, scrubbed well and ends trimmed, thinly sliced

2 ounces Pecorino Toscano or Pecorino Romano cheese, shaved

1   To make the vinaigrette, in a small bowl, whisk together the orange juice, vinegar, and mustard. Slowly whisk in the olive oil in a steady stream until completely incorporated and emulsified. Season with salt and pepper to taste.

2   In large salad bowl, combine the arugula leaves with the Jerusalem artichokes. Sprinkle on the shaved Pecorino. When ready to serve, toss the salad with the vinaigrette and serve on individual salad plates.

La Scala Restaurant, opened in 1957 in Beverly Hills, catered to Hollywood celebrities and politicians. Today there are boutique La Scala branches all over Los Angeles, where this salad of enduring popularity is still the number-one seller.

There is much disagreement about the value of iceberg lettuce in terms of both nutrition and flavor. While it's true that iceberg doesn't have the panache of the so-called designer greens, there are times when I prefer its simple flavor and crunchy character. The creators of this salad were obviously aware of these characteristics when La Scala first introduced its chopped salad over thirty years ago.

To separate the core from the lettuce easily, hit the core against a hard surface. Use a stainless-steel or ceramic knife to cut the lettuce to slow the browning of the cut edges. Vary the salad, adding olives, mushrooms, or other embellishments as you like. Begin with Roasted Vegetable Soup (page 46) and serve with warm, crusty Country Sourdough Bread (page 286).

1 medium head of iceberg lettuce, cleaned, cored, and finely chopped
½ pound Italian fontina or Jarlsberg cheese, finely chopped
½ pound salami or fresh cooked turkey breast, finely chopped
1 cup well-drained cooked garbanzo beans (chickpeas)
1 red bell pepper, peeled (page 27), seeded, and finely chopped
1 large tomato, peeled, seeded, and finely chopped
⅓ cup Basic Vinaigrette (page 355)
2 tablespoons finely chopped fresh parsley
¼ teaspoon freshly ground black pepper

Recommended Wine
Serve a ripe, oaky Chardonnay or an oak-aged Sauvignon Blanc with this full-flavored salad.

1   In a medium salad bowl, combine the lettuce, cheese, salami, beans, red pepper, and tomato. Add the vinaigrette, parsley, and black pepper and toss. Taste for seasoning. Serve immediately. (This is best made just before serving to retain the individual texture of the ingredients.)

FARMERS' MARKET CHOPPED SALAD

SERVES 2 TO 3

AS A MAIN COURSE

OR 4 TO 6 AS A FIRST COURSE

Recommended Wine

This fresh garden salad requires a crisp, dry white wine to balance its creamy dressing. Try a bone-dry Sauvignon Blanc or Riesling.

Advance Preparation

The dressing can be prepared up to 1 day ahead and refrigerated. Whisk well before using. The salad can be assembled up to 2 hours ahead and refrigerated. (Since the salad is chopped with a metal knife, the lettuce may begin to brown after 2 hours.)

Growing up in Los Angeles, I had the opportunity to enjoy just about every version of the famous Brown Derby Cobb salad that was offered. You can still find the original Cobb salad, named after Bob Cobb, the owner of the Brown Derby, at any number of California restaurants. Chopped iceberg lettuce is the basic ingredient, with blue cheese, cooked chicken, crisp crumbled bacon, diced avocado, and tomato garnishes.

I've reinterpreted this salad by adding a mix of more flavorful greens, including arugula and watercress, and blending in fresh corn kernels and shreds of imported Parmesan. I often forgo the chicken and serve this as a first course. While the old standards of blue cheese, avocado, and bacon are delicious, this lighter version is a welcome change.

DRESSING

1 medium shallot, finely chopped

1½ tablespoons balsamic vinegar

2 teaspoons fresh lemon juice

1 teaspoon Dijon mustard

3 tablespoons olive oil

2 tablespoons plain nonfat yogurt

¼ teaspoon salt

Pinch of freshly ground black pepper

SALAD

1 medium head of romaine lettuce, light green and white leaves only, finely chopped

1 bunch of arugula, tough stems removed, coarsely chopped

1 bunch of watercress, leaves only, coarsely chopped

1 boneless, skinless medium whole chicken breast, cooked and diced into ¼-inch pieces

½ medium red bell pepper, seeded and diced into ¼-inch pieces

¼ English (hothouse) cucumber, diced into ¼-inch pieces

½ cup fresh white or sweet yellow corn kernels (from about 1 ear)

¼ cup coarsely shredded Parmesan cheese (use a shredder or vegetable peeler)

1 To make the dressing, in a small bowl, combine the shallot, vinegar, lemon juice, and mustard and whisk to combine. Slowly add the oil in a steady stream, whisking until incorporated and emulsified. Add the yogurt, salt, and pepper and blend well. Taste for seasoning.

2 Combine all the salad ingredients in a large salad bowl. Add the dressing and toss until all the ingredients are well coated. Sprinkle freshly ground pepper on the salad if desired and serve.

PEPPERY GREENS WITH GORGONZOLA AND PINE NUTS

SERVES 4 TO 6

Advance Preparation

The dressing can be prepared up to 3 days ahead, covered, and refrigerated. The salad can be assembled up to 4 hours ahead and refrigerated.

Tangy, soft Gorgonzola and rich toasted pine nuts are the perfect complement to a bed of peppery greens. There are a number of varieties of Gorgonzola cheese, Italy's oldest blue cheese. Ask to taste the cheese at the market to make sure it's the right strength for you. If you're going for a mild version, specify dolcelatte, also called sweet Gorgonzola, which is younger and much less pungent than regular Gorgonzola.

Use a good-quality sherry vinegar for best results. Since this salad is richer than a simple dinner salad, follow it with a simple grilled or roasted main course like Grilled Lamb Chops with Cranberry-Rosemary Marinade (page 217) or Grilled Orange-Mustard Chicken (page 180).

¼ cup pine nuts

VINAIGRETTE

1 medium shallot, finely chopped

1 teaspoon Dijon mustard

2 tablespoons sherry wine vinegar

¼ cup olive oil

Salt and freshly ground black pepper

SALAD

1 bunch of watercress, leaves only

1 head of butter lettuce, torn into bite-sized pieces

1 small head of radicchio, torn into bite-sized pieces

1 bunch of arugula, tough stems removed, torn into bite-sized pieces

¼ cup crumbled Italian Gorgonzola, preferably dolcelatte

GARNISH

10 red or yellow cherry tomatoes or a combination, halved

1 Preheat the oven to 350°F. Spread the pine nuts in a single layer on a baking sheet and toast for 5 to 7 minutes, or until lightly browned. (Alternatively, place them in a skillet and toast over medium heat for a few minutes, shaking constantly.) Watch carefully, as they burn quickly. Transfer immediately to a plate and set aside.

2 To make the vinaigrette, whisk together the shallot, mustard, and vinegar in a small bowl and then slowly add the oil in a steady stream, whisking until it is incorporated and emulsified. Season with salt and pepper to taste.

3 Place all of the greens in a salad bowl. Toss with the vinaigrette. Add the pine nuts and Gorgonzola and toss again. Arrange on salad plates and garnish with the cherry tomato halves.

OLIVE OIL

Which olive oil is right for cooking? There's no single answer because you really need more than one olive oil. Not unlike wines, olive oils differ dramatically depending on the type of olive used and where and how the olives were grown. Each olive oil has its own distinctive signature based on the olive variety, the climate and soil of the grove, and how the olives are processed.

Extra-virgin olive oils are not heated when processed and are very rich and full-flavored. Pure olive oils, which have been heated and pressed to extract the last bit of oil, are much milder in flavor. A cold-pressed extra-virgin oil is usually fruity, green, and redolent of olives. Used unheated in a salad dressing, drizzled over sliced tomatoes or a crusty piece of bread, or simply as a condiment, it's heavenly.

Sautéing with a heavy, fruity, extra-virgin olive oil, however, can often overwhelm the delicate flavors of a particular dish—it's better to use a lighter-style oil. Ultimately your decision should be based on what you like and what works with what you're cooking. Just remember that the oil should be a flavoring agent and not dominate the taste of a dish. I think that the best way to judge a particular oil is to taste it.

For many years, California olive oils were considered inferior, but the industry has developed into a serious business that is fast becoming competitive with its Mediterranean counterpart. Now California producers of extra-virgin olive oil who are members of the California Olive Oil Council must submit their oil annually for evaluation for the certification program according to standards that ensure an authentic product to consumers. In 1997, the California Olive Oil Council helped pass a state senate bill legislating olive oil labeling that included truth in labeling as to where the oil is produced.

California entrepreneurs have begun importing and planting Mediterranean olive trees, bringing over the latest technology for milling and pressing the olives and then blending the oil in consultation with their fellow producers. California chefs are also experimenting with blending their own private oils.

CALIFORNIA SALAD

SERVES 6

This salad sounds like all the California culinary buzzwords wrapped into one, but it's truly outstanding. Roasted garlic adds a nutty-rich character to the dressing. You can prepare the dressing several days ahead so the salad can be assembled quickly at the last minute. Spokes of red pepper and crumbled fresh goat cheese add a pretty California touch. Serve as a first course with Roast Crispy Fish with Warm Lentils (page 156) or Grilled Chicken Niçoise (page 176).

Advance Preparation

The dressing can be prepared up to 3 days ahead, covered, and refrigerated. The salad can be assembled up to 4 hours ahead and refrigerated.

DRESSING

1 medium head of garlic or 30 garlic cloves

¼ cup fresh lemon juice

1 teaspoon Dijon mustard

2 teaspoons finely chopped fresh parsley

2 teaspoons finely chopped peeled, seeded red bell pepper (page 27)

2 teaspoons finely chopped fresh chives

¼ teaspoon salt

⅛ teaspoon freshly ground black pepper

½ cup olive oil

SALAD

1 medium head of butter lettuce, torn into bite-sized pieces

1 small head of radicchio, torn into bite-sized pieces

4 medium heads of Belgian endive

1 medium yellow bell pepper, peeled (page 27), seeded, and thinly sliced

1 medium red bell pepper, peeled (page 27), seeded, and thinly sliced

¼ pound goat cheese, crumbled

1   To make the dressing, preheat the oven to 425°F. With a sharp knife, cut off the top of the whole head of garlic. Score it gently, cutting through just a few layers of the papery skin, all around the diameter, and pull off the loose skin from the top half; you don't need to remove every shred. (This will make it easier to squeeze out the cooked cloves later.) Wrap the garlic head (or peeled cloves, if using) tightly in a piece of aluminum foil. Place on a baking sheet and bake for 45 to 60 minutes, or until the garlic is soft when pierced with a knife. Remove from the oven and let cool. Using your fingers, squeeze the soft garlic pulp into a bowl. (If using peeled cloves, mash the softened cloves with a spoon until smooth.)

2   Combine the garlic pulp, lemon juice, mustard, parsley, chopped red pepper, chives, salt, and pepper in a food processor fitted with the metal blade and process to a purée. With the machine running, add the oil and process until emulsified. Taste for seasoning.

3   Arrange the butter lettuce and radicchio in a shallow salad bowl. Slice 2 of the endives into ¼-inch slices (use a stainless-steel knife) and scatter them on top of the lettuce. Separate the leaves of the remaining 2 endives and arrange on the outer edge of the salad bowl. Arrange the pepper slices in a spokelike fashion around the salad and sprinkle the crumbled goat cheese on top.

4   When you're ready to serve, pour enough dressing over the top to coat the salad lightly, then toss and serve.

MIXED GREENS WITH BEETS AND PEPPERS

SERVES 6

Advance Preparation

Can be prepared through step 3 up to 8 hours in advance, covered, and refrigerated. Let the dressing come to room temperature before serving.

Lawry's Restaurant in Los Angeles specializes in prime rib and is renowned for the salad carts that servers bring to the tableside. As a child, I loved to watch that salad bowl spin as the servers theatrically poured the sweet sherry dressing over it. This first-course salad is a contemporary version of that childhood favorite of mine, including the traditional beets and chopped egg but updated with roasted peppers and a zingy lemon-balsamic dressing. Follow the salad with Grilled Steaks with Olivada and Port Wine Sauce (page 212) and Potatoes Vaugirard (page 261).

DRESSING

1 medium shallot, finely chopped

1 tablespoon whole-grain mustard

2 tablespoons fresh lemon juice

2 tablespoons balsamic vinegar

¾ cup olive oil

½ teaspoon salt

¼ teaspoon freshly ground black pepper

2 tablespoons finely chopped fresh parsley

SALAD

2 large eggs

2 medium beets, tops removed

2 medium heads of butter lettuce, torn into bite-sized pieces

1 small head of radicchio, torn into bite-sized pieces

1 bunch of arugula or watercress, tough stems removed, torn into bite-sized pieces

2 heads of Belgian endive, thinly sliced

1 medium yellow bell pepper, peeled (page 27), seeded, and thinly sliced

1 medium red bell pepper, peeled (page 27), seeded, and thinly sliced

1   To make the dressing, combine the shallot, mustard, lemon juice, and vinegar in a mixing bowl. Slowly add the oil in a steady stream, whisking until incorporated and emulsified. Add the salt, pepper, and parsley and taste for seasoning.

2   Place the eggs in a saucepan with cold water to cover and bring to a rolling boil. Turn off the heat and cover the pan for 12 minutes. Cool the eggs under cold running water. Peel and finely chop. Set aside.

3   Bring a medium saucepan three-fourths full of water to a boil. Submerge the beets and cook them until tender but slightly resistant, about 25 minutes. Drain, set aside until cool enough to handle, then peel and let cool completely. When the beets are cool, finely chop them and set aside.

4   In a large mixing bowl, combine the lettuce, radicchio, arugula, and endives and toss with half of the dressing. Divide the greens among serving plates, then decorate with beets and pepper slices and finish with the chopped egg. Serve the remaining dressing on the side.

SPINACH AND MUSHROOM SALAD WITH WARM TOMATO-BACON VINAIGRETTE

SERVES 2 AS A MAIN COURSE

OR 4 AS A FIRST COURSE

Recommended Wine

A smoky and crisp Sauvignon Blanc works really well with this salad.

Advance Preparation

The salad can be prepared through step 3 up to 2 hours ahead and kept at room temperature. Make the dressing just before serving.

Warm spinach salads were popular back in the 1960s and '70s. Most versions had one thing in common: Bacon grease was the foundation of the salad dressing. In this contemporary version, a warm vinaigrette, enhanced by finely chopped fresh tomatoes and crisp bacon, is an updated healthful and flavorful adaptation. Golden egg yolks and bright red tomatoes set off the dark green spinach leaves and make a pleasing presentation. To reduce the fat even more, use turkey bacon. This is a nice prelude to Grilled Chicken with Pesto Bean Sauce (page 178) or Roast Crispy Fish with Warm Lentils (page 156). I also like to serve this as a brunch dish since it contains all the components for both breakfast and lunch.

SALAD

2 medium bunches of baby spinach, leaves only, cleaned, well dried, and torn into bite-sized pieces

½ pound mushrooms, brushed clean and thinly sliced

4 large eggs

8 strips of bacon, cut into 1-inch pieces

DRESSING

6 tablespoons olive oil

2 medium shallots, finely chopped

¼ cup sherry vinegar or red wine vinegar

⅛ teaspoon coarsely cracked freshly ground black pepper

1 medium tomato, peeled, seeded, and finely chopped

1 Place the spinach and mushrooms in a large salad bowl. Set aside.

2 Place the eggs in a medium saucepan and cover by 1 inch with cold water. Bring the water to a boil over high heat. Immediately remove the pan from the heat, cover, and let stand for 10 minutes. Cool the eggs under cold running water. Peel and quarter the eggs lengthwise. Set aside.

3 In a medium skillet over medium-high heat, sauté the bacon until crisp. Remove the bacon from the pan and drain on a paper towel. Set aside. Discard the bacon grease.

4 To make the dressing, add the oil to the skillet and reduce the heat to medium. Add the shallots and sauté for about 2 minutes, or until just softened. Add the vinegar and pepper and boil for another minute. Taste for seasoning. Add the tomatoes and all but 2 tablespoons of the bacon to the dressing and heat through for another minute.

5 Pour the hot dressing over the spinach and mushrooms and toss to coat.

6 Divide the salad among serving plates. Arrange the egg quarters on the outside edge of the plates. Garnish with the reserved bacon. Serve immediately.

BLOOD ORANGE, MUSHROOM, AND AVOCADO SALAD

SERVES 4 TO 6

Advance Preparation

The dressing can be prepared up to 2 days ahead, covered, and refrigerated. The salad can be assembled through step 2 up to 4 hours ahead, covered, and refrigerated.

This first course salad is best in the winter and early spring months, when vivid maroon-colored blood oranges, now grown commercially in California, make their appearance. Blood oranges, which have a distinctively rich orange flavor with raspberry overtones, have been featured in the Mediterranean diet for centuries.

This update on the classic grapefruit and avocado combination includes thinly sliced white mushrooms, which offer a pleasant textural contrast. Serve as a prelude to Roast Crispy Fish with Warm Lentils (page 156) and Home Ranch Butternut Squash (page 251).

DRESSING

1 medium shallot

Juice of 1 medium blood orange (about ⅓ cup)

1 tablespoon balsamic vinegar

½ cup olive oil

½ teaspoon salt

¼ teaspoon freshly ground black pepper

SALAD

2 medium heads of butter lettuce, torn into bite-sized pieces

2 blood oranges, peeled and membrane removed, cut into 1-inch pieces

6 medium mushrooms, brushed clean and thinly sliced

1 medium ripe avocado, pitted, peeled, and cut into ¼-inch slices

1 To make the dressing, mince the shallot in a food processor fitted with the metal blade. With the machine running, add the orange juice and vinegar and process to combine. Slowly add the oil in a steady stream and process until it is completely incorporated and emulsified. Add the salt and pepper. Taste for seasoning.

2 Arrange the butter lettuce in a shallow salad bowl. Place the orange pieces and mushrooms on top of the lettuce in an attractive pattern, in order to make a pretty presentation before tossing.

3 When you're ready to serve, arrange the avocado slices around the outside edge of the bowl. Toss the salad with the dressing and serve.

Guacamole is only one way to appreciate avocados; try them in omelets, chilled soups, salads, salsas, or even to replace the mayonnaise in a sandwich. Here are a few avocado facts to help you enjoy them.

Eighty percent of California avocado production is of the Haas variety, with its characteristic knobby skin and pale green, creamy flesh. Available most of the year, the Haas is considered the best avocado, but during the few winter months when it's out of season, look for the smooth-skinned but less full-flavorful Fuerte.

To test for ripeness, squeeze the fruit gently; it should just yield to pressure. Haas avocados change from green to purple-black as they ripen, but the Fuerte remains green even when completely ripe. To speed up ripening, place the avocados in a paper bag at room temperature for a few days. When ripe, avocados can be stored in the refrigerator for up to 5 days.

Ideally, don't peel the avocado until just before serving, then sprinkle all cut surfaces with lemon or lime juice to help prevent discoloration. For mashed or cubed avocado, be sure there is lemon juice in the mixture if the dish is to be held in the refrigerator for any length of time, and cover tightly.

Avocado oil (extracted from the flesh, not the seed of the avocado) is a healthy choice for cooking since it's high in monounsaturated fatty acids. It also has a high smoking point, which makes it a nice option for sautéing. Because it's light in both flavor and aroma, avocado oil is versatile enough to use in any dish.

WHEAT BERRY VEGETABLE SALAD

SERVES 4 TO 6

Advance Preparation
This salad can be prepared up to 4 hours ahead, covered, and refrigerated.

This is a variation on tabouli, the Middle Eastern cracked-wheat salad traditionally made with olive oil, lemon, mint, tomato, and loads of parsley. Wheat berries, which are actually unprocessed whole wheat kernels, must be soaked before cooking and will have a distinctive al dente crunchiness to them. You can find wheat berries in natural-foods stores. In this recipe, the mint and tomatoes are replaced by chopped cucumber, radishes, and fresh goat or feta cheese. Serve with White Bean and Artichoke Soup (page 52) for a satisfying lunch or supper.

1 cup dried wheat berries

½ teaspoon salt

2 tablespoons finely chopped red onion

½ cup finely diced English (hothouse) cucumber

¾ cup finely diced radishes

¾ cup peeled and finely diced carrots

2 tablespoons finely chopped fresh parsley

2 tablespoons finely chopped fresh chives

3 tablespoons finely chopped fresh cilantro

DRESSING

½ cup Basic Vinaigrette (page 355)

2 tablespoons fresh lemon juice

Salt and freshly ground black pepper

½ pound goat or feta cheese, crumbled

GARNISH

Fresh cilantro leaves

1 Soak the wheat berries overnight in cold water to cover generously. (Alternatively, do a quick soak: Bring the wheat berries to a boil in water to cover, boil for 2 minutes, cover, and let stand for 1 hour.) Drain the wheat berries.

2 Put the wheat berries in a saucepan with water to cover by 2 inches, add the salt, and bring to a boil. Cover, reduce the heat to medium-low, and simmer for 40 minutes, or until the wheat berries are tender and most of the liquid is absorbed. Uncover and cook for 10 minutes longer to remove excess liquid. Drain the wheat berries well and transfer to a serving bowl. Let cool to room temperature.

3 Add the red onion, cucumber, radishes, and carrots. Mix with a two-pronged fork, adding the parsley, chives, and cilantro.

4 To make the dressing, combine the vinaigrette, lemon juice, and salt and pepper to taste in a medium bowl and whisk until incorporated. Taste for seasoning.

5 Pour the dressing over the wheat berries and mix with a fork. Add the goat or feta cheese and toss gently. Taste for seasoning, garnish with the cilantro leaves, and serve.

LONG-GRAIN AND WILD RICE SALAD WITH CORN AND SALMON

SERVES 4 TO 6

This colorful salad, tinged with yellow and pink, is beautiful on a buffet table. I like to shuck just-picked corn and put it in the salad immediately for a garden-to-table flavor. If the corn is a bit older, drop it in boiling water for a minute and then let cool before adding to the salad.

For a smart luncheon menu, begin with Broccoli-Leek Soup (page 62) and serve this salad as a light main course. For dessert, try Orange, Almond, and Olive Oil Cake (page 302). Or serve this on a buffet table along with other cold salads. If you're serving on individual plates, line the plates with pretty lettuce leaves, place a mound of the rice salad on top, and garnish with the dill sprigs.

One 6-ounce box long-grain and wild rice mixture

1 pound salmon fillet

DRESSING

3 tablespoons fresh lemon juice

1 teaspoon Dijon mustard

6 tablespoons olive oil

½ teaspoon salt

Pinch of freshly ground white pepper

3 tablespoons finely chopped fresh chives

3 tablespoons finely chopped fresh dill

1 cup fresh corn kernels (from about 2 medium ears)

GARNISH

Fresh dill sprigs

Recommended Wine

A full-bodied Sauvignon Blanc is very effective with this salad. If you are serving it as a main course, Pinot Noir would also perform nicely.

Advance Preparation

This salad gets even better if it sits for a day, so you may prepare it up to 1 day ahead and refrigerate, covered, until serving. Add the salmon and adjust the seasonings just before serving.

1   Cook the rice according to the package directions. Set aside and let cool to room temperature.

2   Prepare a grill for medium-heat grilling. Wrap the salmon tightly in aluminum foil or place it directly on the grill rack 3 inches from the heat. Grill until opaque throughout, 5 or 6 minutes per side, depending on the thickness. (Alternatively, preheat the oven to 425°F and roast the salmon for 12 to 15 minutes in a roasting pan.) Let the salmon cool for 15 minutes. Remove the skin and any brown parts of the flesh and break the rest into 1-inch pieces. Refrigerate until ready to use.

3   To make the dressing, in a small mixing bowl, combine the lemon juice and mustard. Slowly whisk in the oil until incorporated and emulsified. Add the salt and pepper and taste for seasoning.

4   In a deep serving bowl, combine the herbs, rice, and dressing and toss to mix. Taste for seasoning. Just before serving, add the corn and salmon and toss gently, being sure not to break up the salmon pieces. Garnish with the dill sprigs and serve.

PASTA SALAD WITH PARMESAN DRESSING

SERVES 6

Pasta salads have become a standard dish for lunch or even dinner in the last few years. This vegetarian recipe, filled with colorful vegetables and two cheeses, is vastly different from the macaroni salad of my youth. The dressing has enough body and flavor to stand up to the inherent blandness of chilled pasta.

Pick your favorite vegetables and make sure that once they have been cooked they retain some crunch. Include contrasting colors and cut all the vegetables into same-sized pieces. You can add some shredded chicken, turkey, or even seafood.

Advance Preparation

Can be prepared, excluding the basil, up to 8 hours ahead, covered, and refrigerated. Remove from the refrigerator ½ hour before serving. Do not add the basil until immediately before serving.

1 tablespoon olive oil

1 teaspoon salt

1 pound dried pasta wheels, fusilli, or small shells

4 cups vegetables—any combination of carrots, zucchini, broccoli, asparagus, red or seeded yellow bell peppers—cut into 1-inch pieces, or about the same size as the pasta

DRESSING

¼ cup whole-grain mustard

2 garlic cloves, minced

¼ cup fresh lemon juice

2 tablespoons sherry vinegar or red wine vinegar

¼ teaspoon salt

¼ teaspoon freshly ground black pepper

½ cup olive oil

¼ cup freshly grated Parmesan cheese

1 tablespoon sour cream or plain nonfat yogurt

1 pound whole-milk mozzarella cheese, cut into 1-inch pieces

½ cup finely chopped fresh basil

¼ cup freshly grated Parmesan cheese

1   Have ready a bowl of ice water mixed with the 1 tablespoon oil. Add the salt
    to a large pot of boiling water. Add the pasta and cook over high heat for
    10 minutes, or until al dente. Drain and transfer to the bowl of ice water to
    cool. Drain thoroughly.

2   Bring another large pot of water to a boil. Add the vegetables and cook until
    barely tender. Drain and pour cold water over the vegetables to stop the cooking.
    Drain again thoroughly and set aside.

3   To make the dressing, in a small bowl, combine the mustard, garlic, lemon
    juice, vinegar, salt, and pepper. Slowly add the oil in a steady stream, whisk-
    ing until incorporated and emulsified. Add the Parmesan and sour cream and
    continue whisking until well blended. Taste for seasoning.

4   In a serving bowl, combine the drained pasta, the vegetables, and the dressing
    and toss to coat. Add the mozzarella, basil, and Parmesan and toss again. Taste
    for seasoning. Refrigerate for 1 hour before serving.

GRILLED STEAK AND POTATO SALAD

SERVES 4 AS A MAIN COURSE

OR 6 TO 8 ON A BUFFET

The favorite American combination of steak and potatoes is reinterpreted here as a hearty salad. I like to leave the peel on the red skinned potatoes for extra texture and color. If you have any dressing left over, save it and use it for other marinades or on a simple green salad. Begin with Corn and Tomato Soup (page 68) and serve warm Country Sourdough Bread (page 286) or French bread with the salad. For dessert, try Glazed Lemon–Sour Cream Cake (page 304).

MARINADE AND DRESSING

2 garlic cloves, minced

2 teaspoons Dijon mustard

2 tablespoons finely chopped fresh chervil or basil

⅔ cup fresh lemon juice

1 cup extra-virgin olive oil

½ teaspoon salt

¼ teaspoon freshly ground black pepper

SALAD

1¼ pounds triangle tip (bottom sirloin) roast

1 pound red-skinned potatoes (about 3 medium)

½ pound green beans, trimmed and cut into 1½-inch pieces

3 celery ribs, thinly sliced on the diagonal

1 small red onion, thinly sliced and cut into 1½-inch pieces

2 tablespoons capers, well drained and rinsed

2 tablespoons finely chopped fresh chervil or basil

¼ teaspoon freshly ground black pepper

GARNISH

3 hard-cooked eggs, quartered

1 pint yellow or red cherry tomatoes, halved

Fresh chervil sprigs, or basil leaves or flowers

Recommended Wine

Serve a hearty red wine with this main-course salad. The best choices are Pinot Noir, Zinfandel, or Syrah, although Cabernet Sauvignon would work, too.

Advance Preparation

Can be prepared through step 6 up to 1 day ahead. Refrigerate the salad, covered well, making sure the potatoes are on the bottom of the bowl. The dressing can be left at room temperature. The salad can be made completely, including garnish, up to 2 hours ahead. Cover well and refrigerate.

1   To make the marinade and dressing, combine the garlic, mustard, chervil, and lemon juice in a small bowl. Slowly add the oil in a steady stream, whisking until it is incorporated and emulsified. Add the salt and pepper and taste for seasoning.

2   Place the meat in a shallow, nonaluminum dish and spoon over ½ cup of the marinade, reserving the rest for the salad dressing. Rub the marinade all over the meat and marinate for 2 to 4 hours, covered and refrigerated.

3   In a large pot of boiling water, cook the potatoes for 20 to 30 minutes, or until tender but slightly resistant when pierced with a fork. Drain and let cool. When cool, cut into thick julienne. Place in a large bowl and set aside.

4   Have ready a bowl of ice water. Bring a medium saucepan three-fourths full of water to a boil. Immerse the green beans in the water and cook for 5 to 7 minutes, or until tender but slightly resistant when pierced with a fork. Drain the beans and plunge them into the ice water to stop the cooking. When the beans are cool, drain well and place them in the bowl with the potatoes.

5   Add the celery, onion, capers, chervil, and pepper to the vegetable mixture and stir to combine.

6   When the meat is ready, prepare a grill for medium-heat grilling. Remove the beef from the marinade and place it on the grill rack about 3 inches from the heat. Sear each side for about 3 minutes. Cover and grill for about 10 minutes longer on each side, or until it registers 135°F on an instant-read thermometer. (Alternatively, preheat the oven to 425°F and roast the meat for 30 minutes in a roasting pan.) Remove from the heat and let cool. When the meat has cooled, slice it into thick julienne and add it to the vegetable mixture.

7   To serve, add just enough of the reserved dressing to the salad to moisten it. Toss gently to combine, being sure not to break up the capers. Taste for seasoning.

8   Arrange the steak salad in a large, shallow serving bowl, mounding it high. Alternate the egg wedges and cherry tomato halves around the outside edge. Garnish with the herbs and serve, passing the remaining dressing at the table.

GRILLED CHICKEN, BLACK BEAN, AND CORN SALAD WITH SALSA DRESSING

SERVES 4 TO 6

Black beans and corn often appear together on the California table in salsas, soups, salads, and vegetable dishes. In this salad, grilled marinated chicken is combined with corn and beans for a substantial and satisfying main course.

Black beans have a slightly earthy mushroom flavor that gives a distinctive dimension to this Mexican-style grilled chicken salad. If you're in a hurry, use canned black beans, rinsed and well drained. You can serve this either warm or chilled. Begin with Sweet Potato–Jalapeño Soup with Tomatillo Cream (page 48).

MARINADE AND DRESSING

¼ cup fresh lemon juice

1 tablespoon whole-grain mustard

½ cup olive oil

2 tablespoons Spicy Tomato Salsa (page 357) or mild or spicy store-bought salsa

¼ teaspoon salt

Pinch of freshly ground black pepper

SALAD

2 large boneless, skinless whole chicken breasts, halved

2 medium or 1 large head of romaine lettuce, light green and white parts only, torn into bite-sized pieces

2 medium carrots, peeled and thinly sliced

½ English (hothouse) cucumber, thinly sliced

2 cups well-drained cooked black beans

1 cup blanched fresh corn kernels (from about 2 medium ears) or thawed frozen corn

1 medium ripe avocado, pitted, peeled, and cut into ½-inch pieces

GARNISH

Blue or yellow tortilla chips

Additional tomato salsa

Recommended Wine

A lively red wine is the answer here. Try Cabernet Sauvignon or Merlot to bring out the earthiness of the salad flavors.

Advance Preparation

Can be prepared, excluding the avocados, through step 3 up to 4 hours ahead. Add the avocado just before serving. Cover and refrigerate until you are ready to grill the chicken breasts.

1 To make the marinade and dressing, whisk together the lemon juice and mustard in a small bowl. Slowly add the oil in a steady stream, whisking until it's incorporated and emulsified. Stir in the salsa, salt, and pepper and taste for seasoning.

2 Arrange the chicken breasts in a shallow, nonaluminum dish and spoon over ⅓ cup of the marinade, reserving the rest for the salad dressing. Rub the marinade all over the chicken and marinate for at least ½ hour and no more than 2 hours, covered and refrigerated.

3 Place the lettuce in a large serving bowl. Arrange the carrots, cucumber, beans, corn, and avocado on top of the lettuce.

4 Prepare a grill for medium-low-heat grilling. Remove the chicken breasts from the marinade and grill about 3 inches from the heat until opaque throughout, 7 to 10 minutes per side, depending on the thickness. Transfer to a carving board and cut on the diagonal into ½-inch slices.

5 To serve, arrange the warm strips of chicken on top of the salad. Add just enough of the reserved dressing to the salad to moisten it, and toss gently. Garnish with the tortilla chips. Drizzle salsa decoratively on top. Pass the remaining dressing at the table.

WARM GRILLED CHICKEN SALAD WITH PESTO

SERVES 6 AS A MAIN COURSE

Recommended Wine
Try a Zinfandel, Pinot Noir, Gamay, Beaujolais, or Syrah here.

Advance Preparation
Can be prepared through step 4 up to 4 hours ahead. Cover and refrigerate until you're ready to grill the chicken breasts.

This unusual chicken salad always wins raves from guests and works either for a luncheon or as a main course for a picnic under the stars. Warm grilled chicken salads are a satisfying solution to summer dining when you're not in the mood for a heavy meal. This is very easy to assemble and can be served cold with equally satisfying results. If you're in a hurry, use your favorite store-bought pesto. Begin with Pinto Bean Soup with Gremolata (page 59) and serve the salad with Country Sourdough Bread (page 286). For dessert, try a plate of Chocolate Truffle Brownies (page 339).

¼ cup pine nuts

MARINADE AND DRESSING

⅓ cup fresh lemon juice

⅔ cup olive oil

¼ cup Pesto (page 349) or store-bought pesto

Salt and freshly ground white pepper

SALAD

3 medium boneless, skinless whole chicken breasts, halved

2 heads of romaine lettuce, light green and white parts only, torn into bite-sized pieces

3 medium carrots, peeled and shredded

½ pound jicama, peeled and cut into julienne

¼ pound white mushrooms, brushed clean and thinly sliced

2 medium tomatoes, thinly sliced or cut into eighths

1   Preheat the oven to 350°F. Spread the pine nuts in a single layer on a baking sheet and toast for 5 to 7 minutes, or until lightly browned. Watch carefully, as they burn quickly. Transfer immediately to a plate and set aside.

2   To make the marinade and dressing, in a small bowl, whisk together the lemon juice, olive oil, and pesto until incorporated. Add the salt and pepper to taste.

3   Arrange the chicken breasts in a shallow, nonaluminum dish and pour ¼ cup of the marinade over them, reserving the rest for the salad dressing. Turn to coat and marinate for at least ½ hour or up to 4 hours, covered and refrigerated.

4   Place the lettuce in a large serving bowl. Arrange the carrots, jicama, and mushrooms on top of the lettuce. Arrange the sliced tomatoes in a ring around the outside.

5   Prepare a grill for medium-heat grilling. Remove the chicken breasts from the marinade and grill about 3 inches from the heat until opaque throughout, 6 to 8 minutes per side, depending on the thickness. Transfer to a carving board and cut on the diagonal into ½-inch slices.

6   To serve, arrange the warm strips of chicken on top of the salad. Scatter the pine nuts on top, add just enough of the reserved dressing to moisten the salad, and toss gently. Pass the remaining dressing at the table.

CHICKEN SALAD WITH CHINESE NOODLES

SERVES 6

Be sure to use a thick noodle that can stand up to the concentrated peanut-tahini dressing in this recipe. I like the sturdier wheat or egg noodles that you can find at a Chinese grocery, or you can substitute fettuccine if you can't find the Chinese noodles. The spicy-sweet peanut sauce, crunchy peanuts, and refreshing carrot and cucumber garnish offset the comforting but bland noodles. Serve this as a main-course luncheon dish. To start, consider Squash Vichyssoise (page 71). This salad also goes well with other vegetable salads on a buffet.

3 cups Chicken Stock (page 342) or water, or a combination
2 medium boneless whole chicken breasts
1 pound dried Chinese-style noodles or your favorite thick noodles
2 tablespoons dark sesame oil

DRESSING

1 tablespoon vegetable oil
6 tablespoons peanut butter
¼ cup water
5 tablespoons soy sauce
6 tablespoons tahini (sesame paste)
2 tablespoons dry sherry
¼ cup rice wine vinegar
¼ cup honey
3 garlic cloves, minced
1 tablespoon peeled and minced fresh ginger
1 to 2 teaspoons Hot Pepper Oil (page 356)
½ cup very hot water, or as needed

1 medium carrot, peeled and cut into julienne
½ English (hothouse) cucumber, seeded and cut into julienne
2 scallions, white and light green parts only, thinly sliced

Recommended Wine

A robust and ripe Chardonnay balances nicely with this spicy salad, or, if you're feeling a bit daring, try a crisp, off-dry Gewürztraminer.

Advance Preparation

Can be prepared through step 4 up to 1 day ahead, covered, and refrigerated. Bring the dressing to room temperature before tossing. Extra dressing will keep for up to 1 month in the refrigerator; it's great as a sauce with lamb.

1 carrot, peeled, cut in half lengthwise, and shaved with a vegetable peeler

½ medium English (hothouse) cucumber, cut in half lengthwise, seeded, and shaved with a vegetable peeler

2 scallions, thinly sliced

½ cup roasted peanuts, coarsely chopped

1   In a deep medium skillet or a large saucepan, bring the stock to a simmer. If using water only, add ½ teaspoon salt. Add the chicken breasts and simmer for 10 to 12 minutes, or until just opaque throughout.

2   Let the chicken cool in the liquid, then drain. Remove and discard the skin. Shred the chicken by tearing it into long, thin pieces (or slice it with a knife). Place in a bowl and set aside.

3   Cook the noodles in a large pot of boiling water over medium heat for about 2½ to 3 minutes, or until barely tender and still firm. Drain the noodles immediately and rinse them with cold water until cooled. Drain again well, place in a large serving bowl, and toss with the sesame oil so that they don't stick together. Set aside.

4   To make the dressing, combine all the ingredients except the hot water in a blender or a food processor fitted with a metal blade and blend until smooth. Thin with the hot water to the consistency of heavy cream.

5   Add the chicken, the julienned vegetables, and the scallions to the bowl with the noodles. Add enough of the dressing to coat the noodles generously and toss. Garnish with the shaved carrot and cucumber, the scallions, and the peanuts. Refrigerate for ½ hour before serving.

WINE COUNTRY CHICKEN SALAD

SERVES 4

I enjoyed this main-course salad at the Robert Mondavi Winery in Napa Valley. Sitting outside overlooking the vines and mountains and enjoying the beautiful weather, I thought about how this salad represents the best of California's fresh, lively flavors.

This salad is perfect for a hot summer day or evening since it can be prepared well ahead of time. Begin with California Caponata (page 39) on French bread. Finish with sliced fresh seasonal fruit and White Chocolate and Pistachio Cookies (page 336).

Recommended Wine

An oak-aged Sauvignon Blanc (such as Mondavi's Fumé Blanc) or a crisp, medium-weight Chardonnay is a perfect foil for this lively salad.

Advance Preparation

Can be prepared through step 5 up to 6 hours ahead, covered, and refrigerated. The dressing can be left at room temperature. The salad can be made completely up to 2 hours ahead, covered well, and refrigerated.

3 cups Chicken Stock (page 342), or water, or a combination

2 medium boneless whole chicken breasts

½ pound pencil-thin asparagus, trimmed and cut into 2-inch lengths

½ cup pitted Niçoise olives

10 cherry tomatoes, quartered

2 tablespoons capers, well drained and rinsed

2 tablespoons finely chopped fresh chervil or basil

¼ teaspoon freshly ground black pepper

DRESSING

1 medium shallot, minced

2 teaspoons finely chopped fresh thyme

1 tablespoon finely chopped fresh parsley

¼ cup fresh lemon juice

½ cup extra-virgin olive oil

½ teaspoon salt

¼ teaspoon freshly ground black pepper

GARNISH

Butter lettuce leaves

Fresh chervil sprigs or basil leaves

1   In a deep medium skillet or a large saucepan, bring the stock to a simmer. If you're using only water, add ½ teaspoon salt. Add the chicken breasts and simmer for 10 to 12 minutes, or until just opaque throughout.

2   Let the chicken cool in the liquid, then drain. Remove and discard the skin. Shred the chicken by tearing it into long, thin pieces (or slice it with a knife). Place in a large bowl and set aside.

3   In a medium skillet of boiling water, cook the asparagus pieces for 3 to 4 minutes or until tender but slightly resistant when pierced with a fork. Drain and cool under running water. Add to the bowl with the chicken.

4   Add the olives, tomatoes, capers, chopped chervil, and pepper to the bowl with the chicken and toss to combine.

5   To make the dressing, combine the shallot, thyme, parsley, and lemon juice in a small bowl. Slowly add in the oil in a steady stream, whisking until it's incorporated and emulsified. Add the salt and pepper and taste for seasoning.

6   When you're ready to serve, add just enough dressing to the chicken salad to moisten it. Stir gently to combine, being sure not to break up the capers. Taste for seasoning.

7   On a serving platter, make a bed of the butter lettuce. Arrange the chicken salad on top. Garnish with the chervil sprigs and serve . Pass the remaining dressing at the table.

WARM GRILLED VEGETABLE AND SHRIMP SALAD

SERVES 6 TO 8

Picture the vibrant colors of grilled shrimp, asparagus, scallions, corn, and fresh lettuce. In this quintessential California salad, the shrimp and all accompanying ingredients are grilled and slightly charred, chopped, and combined into a lightly smoked medley.

This salad is fun to prepare for guests because you can chat with them as the vegetables and shrimp are grilling. For a lighter beginning to your meal, serve the salad without the shrimp. For a main course, begin with Baked Brie with Sun-Dried Tomato Pesto (page 36) and sliced Country Sourdough Bread (page 286) or French bread.

1 pound large shrimp, peeled and deveined

¾ cup Basic Vinaigrette (page 355)

1 teaspoon Dijon mustard

3 medium zucchini, cut lengthwise into ¼-inch-thick slices

16 asparagus spears, trimmed

8 scallions, white and light green parts only

2 ears of corn, husked

2 medium heads of Belgian endive

2 medium heads of radicchio

2 medium heads of butter lettuce

1 medium ripe avocado, pitted, peeled, and diced

2 tablespoons finely chopped fresh herbs: any combination of basil, parsley, dill, and chives

Recommended Wine

A crisp, spicy Sauvignon Blanc or a dry Chenin Blanc will offer an attractive contrast to the richness of the shrimp.

Advance Preparation

Can be prepared up to 1 day ahead and served cold. Add the avocado just before serving.

1   Thread the shrimp on metal or bamboo skewers (soak bamboo skewers in cold water for ½ hour before grilling) and lay them flat in a shallow, nonaluminum dish. In a small bowl, combine the vinaigrette and mustard. Pour ¼ cup of the vinaigrette mixture over the shrimp, reserving the rest for the salad dressing. Marinate for ½ hour in the refrigerator, turning once or twice.

2   Prepare a grill for medium-heat grilling. Place the zucchini, asparagus, and scallions on the grill rack 3 inches from the heat and grill for about 4 minutes per side, or until slightly charred. Transfer the vegetables to a cutting board and chop them into 1-inch pieces. Transfer to a large salad bowl.

3   Place the corn on the grill and grill on all sides, turning as it just begins to darken. Remove from the grill and, when cool enough, shuck the corn kernels with a sharp knife into the salad bowl with the other vegetables.

4   Place the endives, radicchio, and lettuce on the grill and grill for about 3 minutes per side, turning to evenly cook. Transfer to the cutting board and chop coarsely. Place them in the salad bowl.

5   Place the skewered shrimp flat on the grill. Baste each side with the vinaigrette mixture and grill until just opaque throughout, 3 to 4 minutes per side. Transfer to the cutting board, withdraw the skewers, and chop the shrimp into 1-inch pieces. Place in the salad bowl. Add the avocado and herbs and then drizzle on the reserved dressing. Toss and serve immediately.

SPRINGTIME SALMON SALAD

SERVES 4

Salmon and asparagus are at their peak in the spring. I love this salad for its piquant herbed dressing, which perfectly accents the vegetables and the salmon. Buttery Yellow Finn or Yukon gold potatoes give the salad a superb flavor. Serve with Sourdough Rye Rolls (page 288).

1 pound salmon fillet

1 pound Yellow Finn or Yukon gold potatoes, peeled

1 pound thin asparagus, trimmed and cut into 1½-inch pieces

2 large eggs

DRESSING

¼ cup fresh lemon juice

1 garlic clove, minced

1 tablespoon drained capers, well drained and rinsed

3 tablespoons finely chopped fresh dill

2 tablespoons finely chopped fresh parsley

1 teaspoon finely chopped lemon zest

¼ teaspoon salt

⅛ teaspoon freshly ground black pepper

½ cup olive oil

GARNISH

1 head of red leaf lettuce, cleaned and torn into 2-inch pieces

Red and yellow teardrop cherry tomatoes

Recommended Wine

A rich, nicely oaked Chardonnay does well with this hearty salad. A chilled Gamay Beaujolais or light Pinot Noir is a more daring choice.

Advance Preparation

Can be prepared through step 5 up to 4 hours ahead, covered, and refrigerated.

1   Bring enough water to cover the salmon to a simmer in a medium sauté pan over medium heat. Add the salmon and poach for about 10 to 12 minutes, depending on the thickness. Remove the salmon from heat and let it cool in the liquid. When the salmon is cool, remove the skin and break it up into 1½-inch pieces.

2   In a medium saucepan of boiling water, cook the potatoes until they are tender but slightly resistant when pierced with a fork, 20 to 30 minutes. Drain and cool, then cut into 1½-inch strips.

3   Bring a large saucepan of salted water to a boil and cook the asparagus for about 3 to 5 minutes, or until just tender. Drain and let cool.

4   Place the eggs in a pan with cold water to cover and bring to a rolling boil. Turn off the heat and cover the pan for 12 minutes. Cool the eggs under cold running water. Peel and cut into quarters. Set aside.

5   To make the dressing, combine all the ingredients in a blender or food processor fitted with a metal blade and blend until creamy. Taste for seasoning.

6   Combine the salmon, potatoes, and asparagus in a medium mixing bowl and add ⅓ cup of the dressing. Toss to combine. Taste for seasoning.

7   To serve, arrange the lettuce leaves on serving plates. Place some salmon salad on top and then garnish with alternating egg quarters and red and yellow cherry tomato halves. Pass the remaining dressing at the table.

112   Golden Frittata with Tomatillo Salsa

113   Puffed Apple-Orange Oven Pancake

114   Scrambled Eggs with Asparagus and Smoked Salmon

115   Herbed Scrambled Eggs with Goat Cheese

116   Ricotta Pancakes with Sautéed Spiced Pears

118   Pasta with Ancho Chile and Tomato Cream

120   Indian Summer Pasta

122   Baked Vegetable Rigatoni with Tomatoes and Provolone Cheese

124   Three-Cheese Macaroni with Caramelized Leeks, Prosciutto, and Peas

126   Wonton Butternut Squash Ravioli with Spinach Pesto

128   Pasta with Tomatoes, Basil, and Balsamic Vinaigrette

129   Holiday Lasagne with Roasted Vegetables and Pesto

132   Risotto with Leeks, Tomatoes, and Niçoise Olives

134   Garden Risotto

136   Two-Mushroom Barley Risotto

138   Soft Polenta with Sun-Dried Tomato Pesto

140   Grilled Polenta with Confit of Red Onions and Prosciutto

142   Grilled Polenta with Yellow Cornmeal

143   Confit of Red Onions and Prosciutto

144   Jewish Breakfast Pizza

146   Grilled Pizza with Leeks, Mozzarella, Tomatoes, and Pancetta

PASTA, PIZZA,
POLENTA,
RISOTTO, AND EGGS

GOLDEN FRITTATA WITH TOMATILLO SALSA

SERVES 4 TO 6

This large, golden, pancake-style omelet looks like an egg pizza. A nonstick skillet makes it easy to invert the frittata onto a serving platter. Begin with a fruit platter and serve with Ciji's Scones with Currants (page 278) or Fresh Pear Bread (page 279). Chicken and Apple Sausage (page 201) makes a nice accompaniment.

2 tablespoons olive oil
2 medium leeks, white and light green parts only, cleaned and finely chopped
1 pound mushrooms, brushed clean and thinly sliced
1 medium yellow bell pepper, seeded and thinly sliced
1 garlic clove, minced
½ teaspoon salt
¼ teaspoon freshly ground black pepper
12 large eggs
1½ cups shredded Swiss Gruyère or sharp Cheddar cheese

GARNISH

½ cup sour cream
½ cup Tomatillo Salsa (page 358)

Recommended Wine

A light, fresh Chardonnay or a dry Chenin Blanc works well with the flavors of this frittata.

Advance Preparation

Can be prepared through step 1 up to 4 hours ahead, covered, and kept at room temperature. Although it will have a heavier texture, the frittata can be made completely 1 day ahead, refrigerated, and served at room temperature.

1 In a 12-inch nonstick skillet with an ovenproof handle or a shallow paella pan over medium-high heat, heat the olive oil. Add the leeks and sauté until softened but not browned, about 3 minutes. Add the mushrooms and sauté for 2 minutes, and then add the yellow pepper. Cook for a few more minutes, until the pepper is slightly softened. Add the garlic and cook for another minute. Season with the salt and pepper.

2 Preheat the oven to 425°F. In a bowl, whisk the eggs until well blended. Stir in 1¼ cups of the shredded cheese. Pour the egg mixture over the vegetables in the skillet and cook over medium-low heat, stirring occasionally, until the bottom of the mixture is lightly browned, about 5 minutes. Sprinkle the remaining cheese on top.

3 Transfer the skillet to the middle rack of the oven and bake until the frittata is puffed and brown, about 10 to 15 minutes. Remove it from the oven and invert onto a plate. Invert again onto a serving platter, so the browned top faces up. Arrange a large dollop of sour cream in the middle, and then spoon on the salsa in an attractive pattern. Serve immediately. (You can also serve the frittata right out of the pan, if you prefer.)

Like a popover, this giant vanilla-scented pancake magically puffs up into a light yet satisfying breakfast or brunch main course. Serve this pancake with grilled assorted sausages and big cups of cappuccino.

¾ cup milk

½ cup all-purpose flour

2 large eggs

2 tablespoons sugar

1 teaspoon vanilla extract

1 teaspoon finely chopped orange zest

1 small pippin, Granny Smith, or Golden Delicious apple, peeled, cored, and finely chopped (about 1 cup)

2 tablespoons unsalted butter

GARNISH

Powdered sugar

Recommended Wine
Serve a crisp, slightly off-dry Johannisburg Riesling with this fruity pancake.

1 Preheat the oven to 450°F. Combine the milk, flour, eggs, sugar, vanilla, and orange zest in a food processor fitted with the metal blade, a blender, or a bowl and process or whisk until smooth. Add the apple pieces and stir to combine.

2 Place the butter in a 10-inch pie pan or ovenproof skillet and put it in the oven to melt. Brush the inside of the pan to coat it evenly with the butter.

3 Pour the batter into the prepared pan and bake for 15 minutes. Reduce the heat to 350°F and bake for 15 minutes longer, or until the pancake is nicely browned, cooked in the center, and well puffed. Remove from the oven and sprinkle the powdered sugar generously on top. Serve immediately.

SCRAMBLED EGGS WITH ASPARAGUS AND SMOKED SALMON

SERVES 4 TO 6

Scrambled eggs are particularly appealing when paired with crisp, green asparagus and delicate pink smoked salmon. Try this recipe with toasted Country Sourdough Bread (page 286) and fresh fruit salad.

1 pound asparagus
⅛ pound sliced smoked salmon
2 tablespoons unsalted butter
12 large eggs
¼ teaspoon salt
Pinch of freshly ground white pepper

1   Peel, trim, and rinse the asparagus. Cut off the asparagus tips and set aside. Slice the asparagus stalks into 1½-inch pieces.

2   Finely dice all but 1 slice of the salmon. Cut the remaining slice into strips and reserve for garnish.

3   Add the asparagus pieces to a saucepan of boiling salted water and boil for 3 minutes, or until barely tender. Drain thoroughly.

4   Melt the butter in a medium saucepan over medium heat. Add the asparagus pieces and sauté, stirring, for 2 minutes.

5   Meanwhile, cook the asparagus tips in another saucepan of boiling salted water for about 3 minutes, or until bright green and barely tender. Drain and cover to keep them warm.

6   In a bowl, whisk the eggs with the salt and pepper. Add the eggs to the sauce-pan containing the asparagus pieces and cook over low heat, stirring constantly, until the egg mixture becomes thick but not dry, about 4 to 5 minutes. Stir in the diced smoked salmon and remove from the heat. Taste for seasoning.

7   Transfer the egg mixture to a serving bowl. Arrange the asparagus tips facing outward around the scrambled eggs and then sprinkle with the reserved smoked salmon strips. Serve immediately.

Recommended Wine

A smoky Sauvignon Blanc is just right with the smokiness of the salmon here.

Advance Preparation

Can be prepared through step 5 up to 2 hours ahead and kept at room temperature.

Goat cheese has become a staple in California cooking and is readily available in local supermarkets. The fresh soft variety is used here to give the eggs a fluffy texture.

California or other American goat cheeses are generally fresher than imported ones, which have to travel a long way to reach you. Fresh goat cheese should have a tangy, lively flavor; as it ages, it unfortunately develops a sharper, bitterer, and sometimes chalky flavor and an ammonia scent, so check the date on the package.

This is a sensational Sunday brunch dish accompanied by sautéed or grilled Chicken and Apple Sausage (page 201) and crispy roasted potatoes. Serve Mixed Exotic Fruit Gazpacho (page 300) with Orange, Almond, and Olive Oil Cake (page 302) for dessert.

12 large eggs

½ teaspoon salt

¼ teaspoon freshly ground black pepper

2 tablespoons unsalted butter

1 cup crumbled fresh goat cheese

3 tablespoons finely chopped mixed fresh herb combination such as parsley, chives, basil, thyme, and burnet

GARNISH

Fresh herb sprigs such as parsley, chives, basil, burnet, or thyme

Recommended Wine
A slightly chilled Gamay Beaujolais or a Pinot Noir underlines the richness and creaminess of the cheese.

1   In a bowl, whisk the eggs with the salt and pepper.

2   Melt the butter in a heavy medium saucepan over low heat. Add the egg mixture and cook, whisking constantly, until the mixture becomes thick but not dry, about 4 to 5 minutes. Remove from the heat. Gently stir in the goat cheese and fresh herbs so that they blend in well. Taste for seasoning.

3   Transfer the egg mixture to a serving bowl. Garnish with the fresh herb sprigs. Serve immediately.

RICOTTA PANCAKES WITH SAUTÉED SPICED PEARS

SERVES 4

On a trip to the Sonoma wine country, I spent the evening at a charming bed-and-breakfast called the George Alexander House in the little town of Healdsburg. I awoke the next morning to find a version of these heavenly, fluffy pancakes awaiting me in the cozy country dining room. Those pancakes were flavored with lemon extract and lemon zest, but I like the addition of orange with the pear topping. Some crisp bacon and fresh fruit juice are all you need to make this a breakfast or brunch you won't soon forget. Serve these on a lazy Sunday morning with caffe latte.

Recommended Wine

Accompany these pancakes with a crisp, fruity Johannisburg Riesling or a spicy Gewürztraminer.

Advance Preparation

The pear topping can be prepared up to 1 day ahead and refrigerated. Reheat gently to serve.

PEAR TOPPING

2 tablespoons unsalted butter

3 large Bosc or Anjou pears, peeled, cored, and cut into 1-inch dice

2 tablespoons sugar

¼ teaspoon ground ginger

¼ teaspoon ground cinnamon

1 tablespoon fresh orange juice

1 teaspoon vanilla extract

PANCAKES

4 large eggs, separated

1 cup low-fat ricotta cheese

2 tablespoons sugar

1 tablespoon finely chopped orange zest

½ cup all-purpose flour

Pinch of salt

4 tablespoons unsalted butter

1. To make the pear topping, melt the butter in a large sauté pan over medium-high heat. Add the pears and sauté for about 5 minutes, or until the pears are softened. Add the sugar and continue cooking until the pears are soft and the sauce is slightly caramelized, about 3 minutes longer. Add the ginger, cinnamon, orange juice, and vanilla and cook for another minute. Cover and set aside, keeping warm.

2. For the pancakes, combine the egg yolks, ricotta, sugar, orange zest, and flour in a medium bowl and whisk until well combined.

3. In a large bowl, using an electric mixer, combine the egg whites and pinch of salt and beat on medium speed until the egg whites are stiff but not dry. Add one-third of the egg whites to the pancake mixture and fold them in gently. Fold in the remaining egg whites, making sure no white streaks are left in the batter.

4. Melt 2 tablespoons of the butter in a large griddle or sauté pan over medium heat. Pour in about ¼ cup batter for each pancake and cook for about 2 to 3 minutes on each side, or until lightly browned. Add more butter as needed.

5. Serve the pancakes immediately with a large dollop of pear topping. You can also serve these with some warm maple syrup, if you like.

PASTA WITH ANCHO CHILE AND TOMATO CREAM

SERVES 4 TO 6

Ancho chile has a smoky, rich flavor that brings a Southwestern touch to this typical Italian dish. The addition of Sun-Dried Tomato Pesto provides a subtle, sweet undertone to the sauce. This twist on pasta with pesto becomes particularly colorful with bright green peas and crisp, mahogany brown pancetta.

I like to make the Ancho Chile Paste and Sun-Dried Tomato Pesto in advance and keep them in my refrigerator for future use. I find these versatile condiments useful in ways I would never have imagined had they not been readily available for experimentation. (If you don't have time to make the chile paste or pesto, you can buy the packaged supermarket versions.)

Adding chicken stock to the sauce gives it both flavor and lightness, so less cream is required. I like to serve this dish for lunch or dinner as a main course. Start with Farmers' Market Chopped Salad (page 78) and finish with Peach Melba Buckle (page 306).

½ pound pancetta or other bacon, thinly sliced

SAUCE

½ cup Ancho Chile Paste (page 351)

½ cup Sun-Dried Tomato Pesto (page 350)

2 cups Chicken Stock (page 342)

½ cup heavy cream (whipping cream)

¼ teaspoon freshly ground black pepper

1 teaspoon salt

1 pound dried fusilli or small pasta shells

1 cup thawed frozen baby peas or fresh baby peas cooked until tender

GARNISH

½ cup freshly grated Parmesan cheese

Recommended Wine
A crisp, medium-weight Chardonnay is a good companion to this rich dish.

Advance Preparation
Can be prepared through step 2 up to 4 hours ahead and refrigerated. Gently reheat the sauce.

Variation
You can substitute julienned cooked chicken, shrimp, or scallops for the pancetta. You can also let cool and stir in ½ cup Basic Vinaigrette (page 355) for a pasta salad.

1 Cook the pancetta in a medium skillet over medium heat, turning it occasionally until crisp and brown, about 4 to 5 minutes. Drain on paper towels and crumble into bite-sized pieces. Set aside.

2 To make the sauce, combine the chile paste, pesto, stock, cream, and pepper in a medium saucepan over medium heat and bring to a simmer. Whisk to blend the ingredients and cook for 5 minutes. Taste for seasoning.

3 Add the salt to a large pot of boiling water. Add the pasta and cook over high heat until al dente, about 7 to 10 minutes. Drain well and place in a large pasta bowl. Pour the sauce over the pasta and then carefully add the peas and pancetta, tossing gently to combine. Taste for seasoning. Serve immediately, garnished with the Parmesan.

INDIAN SUMMER PASTA

SERVES 6 TO 8

Every year I look forward to the time when summer drifts away into the cool, crisp days of autumn. From a cook's point of view, I can recognize the signals: The tomatoes, corn, fresh herbs, and summer fruits are slowly being replaced in the markets by sturdier produce fit for fall weather. Just before this change of season occurs, I have a compelling desire to enjoy all the tastes of summer one last time. That's how this dish came into being.

As I stood at the produce stand eyeing the possibilities, I wondered how to reinterpret the ingredients before me. This light, simple sauce takes into account a broad array of seasonal vegetables and includes your choice of grilled sausages for a substantial main course. If you have any left over, refrigerate it and add some vinaigrette to make it into a pasta salad. Begin with Squash Vichyssoise (page 71) and serve a simple dessert of Baked Pears in Burgundy and Port Glaze (page 298).

Recommended Wine

This dish will be best with a fruity red wine that will balance its strong flavors. Try a Zinfandel, Gamay Beaujolais, or Rhône variety.

Advance Preparation

The sauce can be prepared up to 8 hours ahead, covered, and refrigerated. Remove from the refrigerator ½ hour before reheating. Gently reheat the sauce.

1½ pounds assorted sausages: sweet, hot, or Turkey Sausages with Sun-Dried Tomatoes (page 203)

SAUCE

3 tablespoons olive oil

2 garlic cloves, minced

¾ pound green beans, yellow wax beans, or sugar snap peas, cut into 2-inch pieces and cooked until crisp-tender

2½ pounds peeled, seeded, and coarsely chopped ripe red and, if available, yellow tomatoes

1 cup fresh corn kernels (from about 2 ears)

¼ cup finely chopped fresh basil

1 tablespoon finely chopped fresh parsley

1 teaspoon salt

½ teaspoon freshly ground white pepper

1 teaspoon salt

1 pound dried small pasta shells

GARNISH

1 tablespoon finely chopped fresh basil

1 cup freshly grated Parmesan cheese

1   Prepare a grill for medium-high-heat grilling. Arrange the sausages on the grill rack and grill 3 inches from the heat for about 20 minutes, rotating them on all sides until the fat runs clear. (Alternatively, place them on a microwave-safe plate and cook on high power for 4 minutes, or until the fat runs clear.) Transfer to a platter and let cool. When cool, slice into ¼-inch pieces or crumble, if desired.

2   To make the sauce, in a large, deep skillet over medium heat, heat the oil. Add the garlic and sauté for 1 minute, making sure it does not burn. Add the green beans and sauté for 2 minutes. Add the tomatoes and cook for 5 minutes, stirring occasionally, until some of the liquid has evaporated. Add the corn and cook for 2 minutes. Add the basil, parsley, salt, and pepper and taste for seasoning. Add the sausages to the sauce and taste again for seasoning.

3   Add the salt to a large pot of boiling water. Add the pasta and cook over high heat until al dente, 7 to 10 minutes. Drain well.

4   Place the pasta in large serving bowl. Pour the sauce over the pasta and mix well. Garnish with the basil and a few tablespoons of the Parmesan. Pass the remaining cheese separately. Serve immediately.

BAKED VEGETABLE RIGATONI WITH TOMATOES AND PROVOLONE CHEESE

SERVES 6

I particularly like this great party dish because it won't overwhelm whatever else I might serve with it. Roasting the vegetables before baking them with the pasta brings a rustic, rich flavor to this dish. You can add zucchini, leeks, or other peppers for a more complex flavor. The melted smoky provolone adds a comforting touch.

Try this for a party when you don't want to prepare a sit-down dinner. Choose simple roast chicken breasts with herbs, sliced roast leg of lamb, or tenderloin of beef to complete the menu.

ROASTED VEGETABLES

2 tablespoons olive oil

1 small onion, finely chopped

8 medium Japanese eggplants or 1 large eggplant, cut into 1-inch slices

1¼ pounds medium mushrooms, brushed clean and quartered

2 large red bell peppers, seeded and cut into 1-inch pieces

1 teaspoon salt

½ teaspoon freshly ground black pepper

1 teaspoon salt

1 pound dried rigatoni

4 cups Double-Tomato Herb Sauce (page 347) or your favorite cooked tomato sauce

2 tablespoons finely chopped fresh basil

½ pound provolone cheese, cut into ½-inch pieces

¾ cup freshly grated Parmesan cheese

Recommended Wine

A medium-weight, fruity red wine is an excellent match for this dish. The acidic nature of eggplant and tomatoes pairs nicely with Gamay Beaujolais, Zinfandel, or Pinot Noir.

Advance Preparation

Can be prepared through step 4 up to 1 day ahead, covered, and refrigerated. Remove from the refrigerator ½ hour before baking.

1   To roast the vegetables, preheat the oven to 425°F. In a large roasting pan, combine the oil, onion, eggplants, mushrooms, and bell peppers and mix to coat all the ingredients. Roast the vegetables until softened, about 40 to 45 minutes, turning them occasionally to keep them from sticking. Remove from the oven, let cool, and season with the salt and pepper. Set aside.

2   Add the salt to a large pot of boiling water. Add the rigatoni and cook over high heat until al dente, about 12 minutes. Drain well.

3   Place the pasta in a large mixing bowl. Pour 3½ cups of the tomato sauce over the pasta and mix well. Add the basil, provolone, ¼ cup of the Parmesan, and the roasted vegetables and mix well. Taste for seasoning.

4   Grease a 9-by-13-inch ovenproof baking dish. Spoon the pasta mixture into the dish and dot the top with the remaining ½ cup tomato sauce. Sprinkle the remaining Parmesan cheese on top.

5   When you're ready to serve, preheat the oven to 400°F. Bake the pasta for 20 minutes, or until bubbling hot. Serve immediately.

THREE-CHEESE MACARONI WITH CARAMELIZED LEEKS, PROSCIUTTO, AND PEAS

SERVES 6

Combining Cheddar cheese with spicy peppery Monterey jack cheese and a touch of Parmesan elevates this mac and cheese to a sophisticated dish. Since I often make pasta with pesto, peas, and prosciutto, I added those ingredients as well. I think the caramelized leeks are the secret ingredient that takes the dish to a new level, along with the crispy bread-crumb topping. I have served this at parties to rave reviews. This is a perfect one-dish meal, along with Mixed Greens with Beets and Peppers (page 84). To make this a vegetarian dish, just omit the prosciutto.

Butter for pan

CARAMELIZED LEEKS

3 tablespoons olive oil

6 leeks, white and light green parts only, cleaned and finely chopped

Salt and freshly ground black pepper

1 tablespoon salt

3 cups dried macaroni (about ¾ pound large elbow macaroni)

¼ pound sliced prosciutto, finely chopped

1 cup frozen baby peas

SAUCE

3 tablespoons unsalted butter

3 tablespoons all-purpose or Wondra flour

3 cups warm milk or half-and-half

2 cups shredded Sonoma pepper jack cheese

2 cups shredded sharp Cheddar cheese

¼ cup freshly grated Parmesan cheese

½ teaspoon salt

½ teaspoon freshly ground white pepper

1 tablespoon Dijon mustard

Recommended Wine

Try this with a medium Chardonnay or a spicy Zinfandel.

Advance Preparation

Can be prepared and baked up to 2 days ahead, covered, and refrigerated. Bring to room temperature before reheating in a 350°F degree oven for 20 minutes. You may need to cover it with aluminum foil so the top does not burn.

½ cup bread crumbs, preferably Japanese panko crumbs

¼ cup freshly grated Parmesan cheese

2 tablespoons unsalted butter, cut into tiny pieces

1   Preheat the oven to 375°F. Butter an 8-inch square or 9-by-11-inch baking dish.

2   To make the leeks, heat the olive oil in a large, nonaluminum skillet over medium-high heat. Add the leeks and sauté, stirring frequently, for about 15 minutes, or until well softened and nicely caramelized. Season with salt and black pepper to taste. Transfer to a large mixing bowl. Set aside.

3   Bring a large pot of water to a rapid boil and add the salt. Add the macaroni and stir to separate. Cook over high heat until al dente, 5 to 7 minutes, or according to package directions, stirring occasionally. Drain well. Place the macaroni in the bowl with the leeks and toss. Add the prosciutto and peas and toss again. Set aside.

4   To make the sauce, in a large saucepan over medium-low heat, melt the butter. Sprinkle the flour over the butter and whisk to mix well. Cook, stirring constantly, for about 2 minutes, or until the flour is well absorbed and the mixture is gently bubbling and golden. Add the warm milk gradually, continuing to whisk constantly, and bring the sauce to a simmer over medium heat. Continue to cook until the white sauce is smooth and slightly thickened, about 3 to 4 minutes. Add the three cheeses. Remove from the heat and whisk constantly until the cheese is completely melted. Stir in the salt, white pepper, and mustard. Taste for seasoning. Pour the sauce over the macaroni-leek mixture and mix to evenly combine and coat the ingredients.

5   Place the prepared baking dish on a baking sheet. Transfer the macaroni mixture to the dish. Make the topping: In a small bowl, combine the bread crumbs and Parmesan and mix well. Sprinkle on top of the macaroni in an even layer. Dot with the butter pieces and bake, uncovered, for 35 to 40 minutes, or until the top is bubbling, beginning to form a crust, and golden brown. Be very careful not to let the bread crumbs burn. Let stand for at least 10 minutes before serving.

WONTON BUTTERNUT SQUASH RAVIOLI WITH SPINACH PESTO

MAKES ABOUT 38 RAVIOLI,

SERVES 6 TO 8

If you've never made ravioli with wonton skins instead of pasta, you'll be amazed at how easy and how good they are. These plump pasta bundles signal the arrival of autumn for me. Pumpkin is another well-loved filling for this ravioli, but I find butternut squash has a better texture and flavor.

Spinach pesto heightens the sweetness of the squash, and its emerald green color looks particularly pretty with the bright orange ravioli triangles. You can serve these either in individual bowls with a drizzle of pesto on top or gently tossed with the pesto in a large serving bowl.

These ravioli make a wonderful beginning to an Italian-inspired menu or a main course followed by Essencia Zabaglione with Fresh Fruit Compote (page 299).

FILLING

1 large butternut squash (about 2 pounds)

2 tablespoons olive oil

¼ cup water

2 medium shallots, minced

¼ cup freshly grated Parmesan cheese

¼ teaspoon minced fresh sage

¼ teaspoon salt

⅛ teaspoon freshly ground white pepper

⅛ teaspoon freshly grated nutmeg

⅛ teaspoon ground sage

Thirty-eight 3-by-3½-inch square wonton wrappers

1 large egg white, beaten

SPINACH PESTO

2 garlic cloves, peeled

2 cups well-packed fresh spinach leaves

1 cup well-packed fresh basil leaves

½ cup olive oil

¼ teaspoon freshly ground black pepper

⅔ cup freshly grated Parmesan cheese

Recommended Wine

The flavors of this dish lend themselves to both Chardonnay and Pinot Noir. A Rhône variety would also do the trick.

Advance Preparation

The ravioli can be prepared through step 3 up to 6 hours ahead and refrigerated. The pesto can be prepared 2 days ahead, covered, and refrigerated. Bring to room temperature before serving. Refrigerate any remaining pesto in a tightly covered container.

2 tablespoons freshly grated Parmesan cheese

1   To make the filling, preheat the oven to 350°F. Cut the squash in half length-
    wise and rub 1 tablespoon of the oil evenly over the cut sides. Place the squash
    halves, cut side down, in a roasting pan, add the water, and bake for about 1
    hour, or until tender, adding a little more water if it evaporates during cook-
    ing. (Alternatively, microwave the squash: Place the halves cut side down in
    a microwave-safe dish, cover with plastic wrap, and cook on high power for 6
    minutes. Remove the plastic and cook until tender, about 6 minutes longer.)
    Let the squash cool and remove and discard the seeds. Spoon out the flesh and
    place in a food processor fitted with the metal blade. Process until completely
    puréed. Drain any accumulated juices. Transfer to a medium mixing bowl.
    Clean and dry the work bowl and blade of the food processor.

2   In a small skillet over medium heat, heat the remaining 1 tablespoon oil. Add
    the shallots and sauté for 3 to 5 minutes, or until softened. Add the shallots
    and the remaining filling ingredients to the squash and mix to combine. Taste
    for seasoning. The filling should be firm enough to hold together. Refrigerate
    the filling until it is needed.

3   For each ravioli, place a wrapper on a work surface. Put 1 rounded teaspoon of
    filling in the center. Brush the edges with egg white and then fold over to make
    a triangle, pressing the edges together firmly so that the filling will not leak.
    Place the finished ravioli on a floured baking sheet and cover with a very damp
    kitchen towel.

4   To make the pesto, mince the garlic in the food processor. Add the spinach and
    basil and process until finely chopped. With the machine running, add the oil
    in a fine stream and process until blended. Add the black pepper and Parmesan
    and process until well blended. Taste for seasoning.

5   Bring a large, deep skillet of water to a simmer. Cook half of the ravioli until
    they're hot in the center and float to the top, about 3 minutes. Using a slot-
    ted spoon, transfer to a large serving bowl or individual shallow soup plates.
    Repeat to cook the remaining ravioli.

6   To serve, spoon on just enough pesto to coat the ravioli, mixing very gently so
    they don't break. Drizzle with a little extra pesto and sprinkle with the Parmesan.
    Serve immediately.

PASTA WITH TOMATOES, BASIL, AND BALSAMIC VINAIGRETTE

SERVES 4 TO 6

Balsamic vinegar is the vital ingredient in this no-cook pasta sauce. Light and refreshing, this is a great side dish for any simple grilled entrée. You could also serve it as a main course for lunch.

SAUCE

2 pounds plum (Roma) tomatoes, peeled, seeded, and finely chopped

Leaves of 1 medium bunch basil, finely chopped

4 garlic cloves, minced

¼ cup olive oil

2 tablespoons balsamic vinegar

½ teaspoon salt

¼ teaspoon freshly ground black pepper

¼ cup freshly shaved Parmesan cheese

1 teaspoon salt

1 pound capellini or linguini

GARNISH

Fresh basil leaves

¼ cup freshly shaved Parmesan cheese

1   To make the sauce, in a medium pasta serving bowl, combine all the sauce ingredients and toss gently to mix.

2   Add the salt to a large pot of boiling water. Add the pasta and cook over high heat until al dente, about 5 to 8 minutes. Drain well. Add the pasta to the bowl with the sauce and toss to mix. Garnish with the fresh basil leaves and pass the Parmesan at the table. Serve immediately.

Recommended Wine

Pairing wine with vinegar is always a problem, but the sweetness in the balsamic vinegar takes the edge off its volatile acidity. Pour a rich, complex Chardonnay with this dish.

Advance Preparation

The sauce can be prepared up to 4 hours ahead, covered, and left at room temperature.

This one-dish pasta recipe evolved with the help of my dear friend Laurie Burrows Grad. One of our first cooking days together was spent making Ed Giobbi's delectable lasagne recipe, which took the two of us 10 hours to put together.

This streamlined interpretation will win raves from your guests. I like to serve this for holiday buffet dinners.

ROASTED VEGETABLES

2 tablespoons olive oil

6 medium zucchini (about 1½ pounds), sliced into ½-inch rounds

2 large red bell peppers, seeded and cut into 1-inch pieces

2 large leeks, white and light green parts only, cleaned and thinly sliced

1¼ pounds medium mushrooms, brushed cleaned and quartered

Salt and freshly ground black pepper

½ cup Mixed-Herb Pesto (page 348), Sun-Dried Tomato Pesto (page 350), or store-bought pesto

WHITE SAUCE

3 tablespoons unsalted butter

3 tablespoons all-purpose flour

2 cups warm milk

¼ teaspoon freshly grated nutmeg

Salt and freshly ground white pepper

RICOTTA-CHEESE LAYER

1½ pounds ricotta cheese

3 large eggs

1 cup freshly grated Parmesan cheese

2 tablespoons finely chopped fresh flat-leaf parsley

Salt and freshly ground white pepper

1 teaspoon salt

1 pound fresh or dried green or white lasagne noodles

¾ pound thinly sliced Muenster cheese, diced

⅓ cup freshly grated Parmesan cheese

continued on next page

Recommended Wine

This dish works well with Sauvignon Blanc or a bright and lively Chardonnay. A tangy Gamay Beaujolais or Pinot Noir would also be a good choice.

Advance Preparation

Can be prepared through step 5 up to 2 days ahead, covered tightly with plastic wrap or aluminum foil, and refrigerated. Bring to room temperature before baking. The lasagne also freezes well. Bake the lasagne without thawing for 1 hour at 375°F, or until piping hot in the center.

Layering Order

If you get as confused as I do with all the separate layers in this dish, here's the sequence:

½ white sauce
⅓ lasagne noodles
½ roasted vegetables with pesto
½ ricotta-cheese mixture
½ Muenster
⅓ lasagne noodles
The rest of the white sauce
The rest of the roasted vegetables with pesto
The rest of the lasagne noodles
The rest of the ricotta-cheese mixture
The rest of the Muenster
A sprinkling of Parmesan cheese

1   To roast the vegetables, preheat the oven to 450°F. In a large roasting pan, combine the oil, zucchini, bell peppers, leeks, and mushrooms and toss to coat all the ingredients. Roast the vegetables until softened, about 45 to 50 minutes, turning occasionally to keep them from sticking. (If water accumulates in the pan during cooking, pour off the excess and continue to roast.) Transfer the vegetables to a mixing bowl, let cool, and season with salt and black pepper to taste. Gently toss the vegetables with the pesto, taste for seasoning, and set aside.

2   To make the white sauce, melt the butter in a heavy medium saucepan over medium heat. Remove from the heat and whisk in the flour until blended. Return the pan to the heat and cook the flour for 2 minutes, whisking constantly, until the mixture is bubbling but has not changed color. Remove from the heat and gradually whisk in the warm milk, beating to prevent lumps. Return to the heat and bring to a boil. Reduce the heat to low and whisk until thickened, about 10 minutes. Remove from the heat and season with the nutmeg and salt and white pepper to taste. Let cool slightly, then cover with plastic wrap, pressing it directly on the surface of the sauce to prevent a skin from forming. Set aside.

3   To make the ricotta-cheese layer, combine the ricotta, eggs, Parmesan, parsley, and salt and white pepper to taste in a medium mixing bowl and mix well. Set aside.

4   Add the salt to a large pot of boiling water. Add the lasagna noodles and cook until just al dente (about 10 minutes if dried, 3 to 4 if fresh). Drain and place the noodles in a mixing bowl; cover with lukewarm water. When the noodles are tepid, lay them in a single layer on paper towels to drain. Blot the noodles dry.

5   Preheat the oven to 375°F. To assemble the lasagne, spread half of the white sauce on the bottom of a deep 10-by-13-inch lasagne dish. Top the sauce with one-third of the noodles, then half of the vegetable-pesto mixture, then half of the ricotta-cheese mixture. Scatter half of the Muenster on top of the ricotta-cheese mixture. Continue building the lasagne with another one-third of the noodles, the remaining white sauce, the remaining vegetables, and the last third of the noodles. Spread the remaining ricotta-cheese mixture over the last layer of noodles. Add the remaining Muenster and then sprinkle the Parmesan evenly on top. With a serrated knife, cut the lasagne into even squares, which will help when you serve it.

6   Bake the lasagne for about 45 minutes, or until piping hot and bubbling throughout. Recut the squares and serve immediately.

Parmesan Cheese

True Italian Parmigiano-Reggiano cheese comes from an area of the Emilia-Romagna region, where it is strictly licensed and has been produced in much the same way for almost 700 years. The 80-pound wheels were exported to enthusiasts from England to Constantinople as early as the seventeenth century, and today some of the cheeses are so valuable that they are aged in special "cheese banks."

Once you've tasted an aged block of Parmigiano-Reggiano, it's difficult to settle for anything less. The cheese should be straw yellow in color and have a crumbly but moist texture. Look for the words Parmigiano-Reggiano stamped on the rind of the cheese to be sure it's authentic.

In Sonoma, California, the Vella Cheese Factory produces a dry jack cheese that is aged for 9 months. It has a buttery, nutty quality similar to Parmesan, but less piquant and grainy. It is excellent grated for pasta or shaved for salads or vegetables.

Parmesan Tips

- Store the cheese in plastic wrap in the refrigerator for up to 3 weeks. If it becomes dry, wrap it in moist cheesecloth and leave it in the refrigerator for a few hours, then rewrap it in plastic.

- It's best to grate the Parmesan just when needed for the best flavor, since the cheese begins to lose its punch and texture soon after it's grated.

- Parmesan can also be shaved with a swivel-bladed vegetable peeler into long or short curls for garnishes.

- Remember that pasta dishes containing fish don't require Parmesan.

- Try shaved pieces of Parmesan with sliced apples or pears for dessert.

RISOTTO WITH LEEKS, TOMATOES, AND NIÇOISE OLIVES

SERVES 6

Recommended Wine

When this risotto is served as a first course, a ripe Chardonnay is the wine to serve, since it leads logically to the next wine, a red of some sort. If served as a main course, the Chardonnay will be fine, but so will a Zinfandel or Pinot Noir.

Californians have been making risotto for decades. Both Helen Brown's *West Coast Cook Book* (1952) and Genevieve Callahan's *The California Cook Book* (1946) refer to risotto, but they never mention the crucial ingredient—Italian short grain rice—that is vital to the authentic and slightly al dente consistency.

Now that Arborio rice is widely available in supermarkets and specialty-food stores, the traditional risotto has become commonplace on California-style restaurant menus. While Arborio rice is most commonly available, you can also use Vialone Nano or Carnaroli rice. All of these Italian varieties will create a true risotto—al dente grains bound in a velvety sauce. A key to making this dish taste so good without using excessive fat is a trio of Mediterranean flavoring agents—tomatoes, leeks, and olives—that offsets the blandness of the rice.

But the real secret ingredient in this dish is the olives. You don't need a lot of them—a little goes a long way with the pungent Niçoise variety. I've tried using other types of olives with less success. Pitting olives can be tedious; you can press down on the olive with your thumb or you can use an olive pitter. Either way, try to keep the olive meat in coarse pieces. Pitted Niçoise olives and other special varieties are also becoming more widely available in well-stocked markets. I like to serve this dish before Rack of Lamb with Mint Crust (page 218).

3 tablespoons olive oil
1 large leek, white part only, cleaned and finely chopped
2 medium tomatoes, peeled, seeded, and finely chopped
¼ teaspoon salt
Pinch of freshly ground black pepper
5 cups Chicken Stock (page 342)
1½ cups Arborio rice
¼ cup pitted and coarsely chopped Niçoise olives
2 tablespoons finely chopped fresh parsley
½ cup freshly grated Parmesan cheese

1 In a medium sauté pan over medium heat, heat 1 tablespoon of the olive oil. Add the leek and sauté until softened, about 5 minutes. Add the tomatoes and cook for about 4 minutes, raising the heat if necessary to reduce the excess tomato juice. Season with the salt and pepper and set aside.

2 In a medium saucepan over medium-high heat, bring the stock to a simmer. In a heavy 4-quart saucepan over medium heat, heat the remaining 2 tablespoons olive oil. Add the rice and stir, making sure all the grains are well coated. Ladle in ½ cup of the hot stock and stir, using a wooden spoon, until all of the stock is absorbed. Continue adding the stock ½ cup at a time, making sure the rice has absorbed the previous stock before the next addition and stirring constantly to prevent burning or sticking. The rice will develop a very creamy consistency as you continue to add the stock. (This should take 20 to 25 minutes.)

3 Reserve the last ¼ cup of the stock and add it to the risotto with the leek and tomato mixture. Cook over low heat for another 2 minutes. Remove from the heat, add the olives, parsley, and Parmesan, and stir well to combine evenly with the rice. Serve immediately.

RISOTTO

Look for Arborio *superfino* rice from Italy, a small, oval variety high in amylopectin starch. This starch lends a creaminess to the finished risotto that is accentuated by the slow addition of liquid and constant stirring. Another unique feature of Arborio rice is the firm central core it retains when cooked, giving it a distinctive al dente texture. Other Italian rices good for risotto are Carnaroli and Vialone Nano, but they're a bit more difficult to find.

Risotto Tips

- Never wash the rice; you'll be washing away the starch that gives risotto its creamy character.
- Use a heavy pot with a handle so you can mix the risotto with one hand while holding the pot with the other.
- Use a wooden spoon for stirring.
- Keep the rice at a very low boil so that it cooks evenly and retains a creamy yet firm quality.
- Serve the risotto immediately in warm shallow bowls.

GARDEN RISOTTO

SERVES 6

Recommended Wine

This is a classic match for a rich, creamy Chardonnay. The wine enhances the flavors of the vegetables.

I first tasted a version of this dish at Campanile Restaurant in Los Angeles. Each vegetable had an individual character that was preserved in a fresh clean way. The vegetables were picked that day at Chino Ranch in Rancho Santa Fe, just north of San Diego. Chino Ranch (or, as the retail stand is called, the Vegetable Shop) specializes in unusual produce for Chez Panisse in Berkeley and select Southern California restaurants like Spago and Campanile. The tender sweet peas, carrots, and squash were truly memorable for their straight-from-the-garden flavor.

Don't worry if you can't pick vegetables from your garden; what's important is to select the freshest available. Feel free to alter this basic recipe to include what's in season, for instance, asparagus, fresh exotic mushrooms, peas, and summer squash all make delectable variations. For an informal dinner, begin with Blood Orange, Mushroom, and Avocado Salad (page 88). Try Tiramisu with Toasted Hazelnuts and Chocolate (page 316) for dessert.

3 tablespoons olive oil

1 large leek, white and light green parts only, cleaned and finely chopped

3 ounces cremini mushrooms, brushed clean and cut into ½-inch pieces (about 1 cup)

1 small carrot, peeled and cut into ½-inch pieces

½ cup sugar snap peas, cut into ½-inch pieces

½ medium red bell pepper, peeled (page 27), seeded, and cut into ½-inch pieces

¼ teaspoon salt

Pinch of freshly ground black pepper

5 cups Chicken Stock (page 342)

½ cup dry white wine

1½ cups Arborio rice

2 tablespoons finely chopped fresh parsley

½ cup freshly grated Parmesan cheese, plus extra for serving

1   In a medium sauté pan over medium heat, heat 1 tablespoon of the oil. Add
    the leek and sauté until softened, about 5 minutes. Add the mushrooms and
    cook for about 3 minutes. Add the carrot and peas and sauté for 2 minutes
    longer. Add the red pepper and cook for another minute. Season with the salt
    and pepper and set aside.

2   In a medium saucepan over medium-high heat, bring the stock and wine to
    a simmer. In a heavy 4-quart saucepan over medium heat, heat the remaining
    2 tablespoons oil. Add the rice and stir, making sure all the grains are well
    coated. Ladle in ½ cup of the hot stock and stir, using a wooden spoon, until
    all of the stock is absorbed. Continue adding the stock ½ cup at a time, making
    sure that the rice has absorbed the previous stock before the next addition and
    stirring constantly to prevent burning or sticking. The rice will develop a very
    creamy consistency as you continue to add the stock. (This should take 20 to
    25 minutes.)

3   Reserve the last ¼ cup of the stock and add it to the risotto with the vegetable
    mixture. Cook over low heat for another 2 minutes. Remove from the heat,
    add the parsley and ½ cup Parmesan, and stir well to combine evenly with the
    rice. Serve immediately. Pass additional Parmesan at the table.

TWO-MUSHROOM BARLEY RISOTTO

SERVES 4 TO 6

Most of us think of barley as a hearty ingredient in soup or as a side dish with meat. Here the creamy texture and sophisticated taste of barley are a pleasant surprise.

Use dried shiitake or other earthy-flavored mushrooms and freshly grated good-quality Parmesan cheese. Adding the strained shiitake liquid to the barley intensifies the mushroom flavor. Pearl barley, available in most markets, takes less time to cook and requires a bit less liquid. The barley should not be cooked until soft all the way through but should have a nutty, slightly crunchy center.

This takeoff on risotto is best served as a main course in shallow soup bowls. Begin with Farmers' Market Chopped Salad (page 78) and serve Banana Split Ice Cream Torte (page 334) for dessert.

¾ cup dried shiitake mushrooms

3 cups Chicken Stock (page 342)

2 tablespoons olive oil

1 large onion, finely chopped

1 pound fresh white mushrooms, brushed clean and coarsely chopped

1 garlic clove, minced

1½ cups pearl barley

1 cup dry white wine

2 tablespoons Marsala

1 teaspoon salt

¼ teaspoon freshly ground black pepper

3 tablespoons finely chopped fresh parsley

½ cup freshly grated Parmesan cheese

Recommended Wine

The earthy flavors of this dish blend well with a young Cabernet Sauvignon or Merlot.

Advance Preparation

Can be prepared through step 2 up to 4 hours ahead, covered, and kept at room temperature.

1   Place the dried mushrooms in a medium bowl and cover with 2 cups boiling water. Let soften for at least ½ hour. Drain the mushrooms, reserving the soaking liquid. Cut off and discard the tough stems and coarsely chop. Strain the soaking liquid through cheesecloth and set aside.

2   In a medium saucepan over medium-high heat, bring the stock to a simmer. Stir in the mushroom soaking liquid.

3   In a large saucepan over medium-high heat, heat the oil. And the onion and sauté for 3 to 5 minutes, or until softened. Add the fresh mushrooms and sauté for 3 minutes. Add the garlic and sauté for another minute. Add the barley and stir to coat completely with the onion-mushroom mixture.

4   Reduce the heat to medium and ladle in 1 cup of the hot stock. Cook, stirring frequently, until all the liquid has been absorbed, about 7 to 10 minutes. Stir in another 1 cup stock and continue cooking, stirring frequently, until all the liquid has been absorbed, about 7 to 10 minutes longer. Add the white wine and continue cooking, stirring frequently, until all the liquid has been absorbed, another 7 to 10 minutes.

5   Add the remaining stock and the Marsala and continue to cook until the barley is tender but still slightly firm in the enter. (If you like it al dente, watch carefully.) If there is excess liquid, raise the heat to medium-high and continue cooking the barley until it evaporates. (Total cooking time should be about 35 minutes.) Add the salt, pepper, and parsley and mix to combine. Spoon into shallow pasta or soup bowls, sprinkle with the Parmesan, and serve immediately.

SOFT POLENTA WITH SUN-DRIED TOMATO PESTO

SERVES 6 TO 8

I remember the first time I tasted a warm bowl of this thick cornmeal porridge on a cold summer day in an Italian mountain village. I wondered how this creamy, soul-satisfying dish would taste in a California climate. Little did I know that years later it would become an adopted dish of chefs and home cooks alike, with as many variations as one can imagine.

Traditional polenta takes at least 30 minutes of cooking in a copper pot over low heat with constant stirring. Fortunately, an imported instant (precooked) polenta with a finer texture has become widely available. This fine-grained polenta yields an excellent flavor as well as texture.

Here the polenta is served with a big dollop of Sun-Dried Tomato Pesto on top and sprinkled with freshly grated Parmesan cheese. You can also top it with a soft goat's milk cheese or Gorgonzola dolcelatte. This dish is good as a first course or as an accompaniment to Crispy Roast Chicken (page 188) or Grilled Veal or Lamb Chops (pages 228 or 217).

| Double recipe of Sun-Dried Tomato Pesto (page 350) |
| Olive oil if needed |

POLENTA

| 2 tablespoons olive oil |
| 1 medium onion, very finely chopped |
| 2 garlic cloves, minced |
| 7 cups Chicken Stock (page 342) |
| 2 cups (one 13-ounce box) imported instant polenta |
| ¾ cup freshly grated Parmesan or pecorino romano cheese |

1   If the pesto is very thick, you may need to add a bit of olive oil. Set aside.

2   To make the polenta, in a large saucepan over medium heat, heat the oil. Add the onion and sauté for 5 to 7 minutes, or until softened and just beginning to caramelize. Add the garlic and sauté for 1 minute, making sure not to let it brown. Add the stock and bring to a boil over medium-high heat.

Recommended Wine

This dish is particularly good with young, fruity red wines such as Zinfandel, Sangiovese, and Rhône varieties. If it's a first course, a ripe, full-bodied Chardonnay will be quite pleasant.

Advance Preparation

The pesto can be made up to 1 week ahead, covered, and refrigerated. Bring to room temperature before serving.

3   Very slowly, in a thin stream (I use a liquid measuring cup), add the polenta, stirring constantly with a wooden spoon. Reduce the heat to low and continue cooking for about 5 minutes, stirring almost constantly to prevent sticking, until the polenta is very thick, smooth, and creamy. Add ½ cup of the Parmesan and stir to combine until the cheese has melted into the polenta.

4   Spoon the polenta into shallow soup bowls and spoon on a large dollop of the pesto and a sprinkling of the remaining Parmesan. Serve immediately.

POLENTA—INSTANT VS. TRADITIONAL

Many enthusiastic cooks have stopped making polenta because of the long, labor-intensive cooking. The arrival on the scene of instant polenta (a finer-grained cornmeal) has changed all that, and, unless you are a purist, there is very little difference in the final result except the texture. Traditional polenta is simply coarse yellow cornmeal added to boiling water with salt and stirred, constantly, for 30 to 40 minutes. Instant polenta, which has long been used in Italy, takes only 5 minutes to prepare, after which you can serve it immediately or cool and slice it for grilling. Substituting chicken stock for part or all of the water called for in the package recipe will produce a more flavorful result, but polenta is really a foil, like pasta or pizza, for its topping.

GRILLED POLENTA WITH CONFIT OF RED ONIONS AND PROSCIUTTO

SERVES 8

Advance Preparation

Can be prepared through step 2 up to 6 hours ahead, covered, and kept at room temperature.

Here are two versions of grilled polenta—this one using instant polenta and another using yellow cornmeal (page 142)—and each has its own virtues. If time is a factor, use instant polenta. What you give up in texture is compensated for in preparation speed. Yellow cornmeal takes 15 to 20 minutes longer to cook but offers a superior coarse texture. The addition of garlic, onions, chicken stock, and Parmesan cheese makes for a surprising improvement in flavor over the traditional cornmeal-and-water mixture. Make sure in both versions to cook the polenta until it is very stiff, so it will hold up when grilled.

Two overlapping slices of grilled polenta make a wonderful accompaniment to other grilled dishes like grilled Turkey Sausages with Sun-Dried Tomatoes (page 203), Grilled Veal Chops with Zucchini-Corn Relish (page 228), or Grilled Chicken Niçoise (page 176).

POLENTA

1 tablespoon olive oil

½ small onion, very finely chopped

1 garlic clove, minced

½ teaspoon salt

3½ cups Chicken Stock (page 342)

1 cup imported instant polenta

2 tablespoons freshly grated Parmesan cheese

FOR GRILLING

2 tablespoons olive oil

Freshly ground black pepper

Warm Confit of Red Onions and Prosciutto (page 143) for serving

1   To make the polenta, in a large, deep saucepan over medium heat, heat the oil. Add the onion and sauté for 5 to 7 minutes, or until softened. Add the garlic and sauté for 1 minute, making sure not to let it brown. Add the salt and stock and bring to a boil over medium-high heat. In a thin stream (I use a liquid measuring cup), very slowly add the instant polenta, stirring constantly with a wooden spoon.

2   Reduce the heat to low and continue cooking for about 5 minutes, stirring almost constantly to prevent sticking, until it is very smooth and stiff. Stir in the Parmesan and then quickly pour the polenta into an 8-inch nonstick square baking dish that has been rinsed out with cold water, smoothing the top with a spatula if necessary. Allow the polenta to rest for 2 hours, covered.

3   With a round-bladed knife (a pizza wheel works well), cut the polenta into nine squares. With a sharp chef's knife, carefully cut each of the squares in half horizontally to make eighteen squares.

4   Prepare a grill for medium-heat grilling. Brush the polenta squares with the oil and sprinkle with a little pepper. Grill the squares for 6 to 7 minutes on each side, until browned and crispy but not blackened. Use 2 flat spatulas to turn the squares.

5   Place overlapping slices on individual serving plates or a platter and garnish with the warm confit. Serve immediately.

GRILLED POLENTA WITH YELLOW CORNMEAL

SERVES 8

Advance Preparation

Can be prepared through step 2 up to 6 hours ahead, covered, and kept at room temperature.

POLENTA

1 tablespoon olive oil

½ small onion, very finely chopped

1 garlic clove, minced

½ teaspoon salt

1 quart Chicken Stock (page 342)

1 cup coarse yellow cornmeal

2 tablespoons freshly grated Parmesan cheese

FOR GRILLING

2 tablespoons olive oil

Freshly ground black pepper

Warm Confit of Red Onions and Prosciutto (opposite) for serving

1 To make the polenta, in a large saucepan over medium heat, heat the oil. Add the onion and sauté for 5 to 7 minutes, or until softened. Add the garlic and sauté for 1 minute, making sure not to let it brown. Add the salt and stock and bring to a boil over medium-high heat. In a thin stream (I use a liquid measuring cup), very slowly add the cornmeal, stirring constantly with a wooden spoon.

2 Reduce the heat to low and continue cooking for about 15 to 20 minutes, stirring almost constantly to prevent sticking, until it is very smooth and stiff. Stir in the Parmesan and then quickly pour the polenta into an 8-inch nonstick square baking dish that has been rinsed out with cold water, smoothing the top with a spatula if necessary. Allow the polenta to rest for 2 hours, covered,

3 With a round-bladed knife (a pizza wheel works well), cut the polenta into nine squares. With a sharp chef's knife, carefully cut each of the squares in half horizontally to make eighteen squares.

4 Prepare a grill for medium-heat grilling. Brush the polenta squares with the oil and sprinkle with a little pepper. Grill the squares for 6 to 7 minutes on each side, until browned and crispy but not blackened. Use 2 flat spatulas to turn the squares.

5 Place overlapping slices on individual serving plates or a platter and garnish with the warm confit. Serve immediately.

This topping for grilled polenta is also an excellent flavor enhancer for scrambled eggs, omelet fillings, stir-fries, pasta, or as a topping for pizza or focaccia.

2 tablespoons olive oil

2 large red onions, coarsely chopped

¾ cup dry red wine

¼ cup balsamic vinegar

2 teaspoons sugar

¼ cup finely chopped prosciutto (about 2 ounces)

2 tablespoons finely chopped fresh basil or 1 tablespoon dried

¼ teaspoon salt

¼ teaspoon freshly ground black pepper

¼ cup Chicken Stock (page 342), or as needed

1 In a large skillet over medium-low heat, heat the oil. Add the onions and sauté for about 20 minutes, or until very soft. Add the wine, vinegar, and sugar and continue to cook until almost all of the liquid has evaporated, about 7 to 10 minutes longer. The onions should be very tender and caramelized. Stir in the prosciutto, basil, salt, pepper, and enough of the stock to give the mixture a thick, saucelike consistency. Taste for seasoning.

Advance Preparation
Can be prepared up to 5 days ahead and refrigerated. Reheat gently, adding more chicken stock if necessary to achieve a thick, saucelike consistency.

JEWISH
BREAKFAST
PIZZA

SERVES 2

After a busy morning in downtown San Francisco, I stopped into Wolfgang Puck's Postrio restaurant and enjoyed a version of this combination deli dish/pizza. It's a wonderful main course for an early lunch or a weekend late-morning breakfast.

The objective here is to have a slightly bready center. To accomplish this, let the dough sit after it has baked to collect a bit of moisture. Then turn it over so the bottom is crisp and the top has a nice texture for topping. Be sure to buy mild, not too salty, smoked salmon. If you like extra color, use a mixture of different caviars. Start with a simple mixed green salad and serve Essencia Zabaglione with Fresh Fruit Compote (page 299) for dessert.

½ recipe Pizza Dough (page 283)

CREAM SPREAD

2 tablespoons sour cream

1 teaspoon very finely chopped red onion

1 teaspoon finely chopped fresh chives

Pinch of salt

Pinch of freshly ground white pepper

TOPPING

4 large eggs

⅛ teaspoon freshly ground black pepper

1 tablespoon unsalted butter

1 ounce smoked salmon, coarsely chopped

GARNISH

2 tablespoons sour cream

1 ounce smoked salmon, cut into thin strips

1 teaspoon finely chopped fresh chives

1 ounce golden whitefish caviar

Recommended Wine

A crisp, dry sparkling wine makes this pizza appropriately festive. A lively Sauvignon Blanc is a good alternative.

Advance Preparation

The pizza can be prepared through step 2 up to 2 hours ahead. Refrigerate the sour cream mixture, then bring to room temperature before continuing.

1 Preheat the oven to 475°F. Press the pizza dough into a 9-inch round on a lightly oiled baking sheet and dimple the surface of the dough all over with your fingertips. Bake for 20 minutes, or until puffed and golden. Remove and let cool on the baking sheet for 10 minutes. (This will allow the bottom to become soft enough to use as the top for filling the pizza.) Invert and place on a serving plate.

2 To make the cream spread, combine the sour cream, onion, chives, salt, and white pepper in a small bowl. Set aside.

3 To make the topping, whisk the eggs with the black pepper in a small bowl. Melt the butter in a heavy medium saucepan over low heat. Add the eggs and cook, stirring constantly, until the mixture becomes thick but not dry. Remove from the heat. Carefully stir in the chopped smoked salmon and blend well. Taste for seasoning.

4 Spread the pizza shell evenly with the sour cream mixture and then spoon on the egg mixture, distributing evenly. Dollop the sour cream in the center. Garnish with the smoked salmon strips, chives, and caviar. Serve immediately.

GRILLED PIZZA WITH LEEKS, MOZZARELLA, TOMATOES, AND PANCETTA

MAKES 2 MEDIUM PIZZAS,

SERVES 2 TO 4 AS A MAIN

COURSE OR 6 TO 8 AS AN

APPETIZER

Recommended Wine

Try a fruity red wine, such as a Rhône variety, that will balance this pizza's strong, complex flavors. Or consider a full-bodied beer.

Advance Preparatiom

Can be prepared through step 2 up to 2 hours ahead.

I first made this recipe in my book *The Taste of Summer,* and it's still my favorite pizza, with a delightful smoky taste and crispy grill-marked crust. A grill with a lid works best for melting the cheese. If pancetta (Italian cured bacon) isn't available, substitute thick-sliced bacon. If you're in the mood to experiment, try your hand at one of the other toppings, opposite.

½ pound plum (Roma) tomatoes
7 tablespoons olive oil
3 medium leeks, white and light green parts only, cleaned and thinly sliced
¼ teaspoon salt
⅛ teaspoon freshly ground black pepper
½ pound pancetta, cut into 1-inch pieces
1 recipe Pizza Dough (page 283)
1½ cups shredded mozzarella cheese
¼ cup finely chopped fresh basil

1 Slice the tomatoes crosswise into ¼-inch slices. Put the slices in a colander and let stand for ½ hour to drain excess liquid.

2 In a deep sauté pan over low heat, heat 3 tablespoons of the oil. Add the leeks and mix thoroughly. Cover and cook, stirring often, for about 20 minutes, or until softened and caramelized. If any liquid remains in pan, uncover and continue cooking, stirring often, until it evaporates. Add the salt and pepper and taste for seasoning. Set aside.

3 In medium skillet over medium-low heat, cook the pancetta until crisp and slightly browned, about 4 to 5 minutes. Transfer to paper towels to drain.

4 When you're ready to barbecue, prepare a grill, preferably one with a lid, for medium-high-heat grilling.

5 Oil 2 round baking sheets or pizza pans. Knead the dough again briefly and divide it into 2 equal parts. Place each on a baking sheet. With oiled hands, pat each piece of dough into a 9-inch circle. (Alternatively, use a rolling pin to roll out the dough on a lightly floured work surface and transfer it to baking sheets.)

6 Brush the top of the pizzas with 2 tablespoons of the remaining olive oil. Using a spatula, transfer the pizzas to the center of the grill rack and grill for about 2 minutes, or until the dough begins to puff and there are grill marks on the bottom.

7   Using a large spatula, turn the pizzas over and move them to the coolest part of the grill. Brush the grilled pizza tops with the remaining 2 tablespoons olive oil. Divide the leek mixture between the two pizzas, spreading it evenly, and then sprinkle half of the mozzarella over each pizza. Divide and arrange the pancetta on top of each. Divide and overlap the tomatoes in an attractive pattern. Sprinkle with the basil.

8   Move the pizzas back to the center of the rack, cover the grill, and cook for about 3 minutes longer. Check the pizzas and rotate them if necessary. Recover the grill and cook for another 2 to 3 minutes. Watch carefully so that they do not burn on the bottom. The cheese should be completely melted. (If you want them hotter on top, you can place them under a preheated broiler for a minute or two.) They should be slightly charred. Transfer to a cutting board or platters and cut into wedges with a pizza wheel. Serve immediately.

PIZZA TOPPINGS

Thinking up toppings for pizza is a lot of fun—and the possibilities are almost endless. I tend to prefer simple combinations, but every now and then I want one with "the works" like the Mexican-inspired pizza below. Here are some of my favorites.

- Italian-Style Roma tomato, mozzarella, basil
- Mixed-Herb Pesto (page 348), Italian fontina, and cooked scallops or shrimp
- Green Olive and Sun-Dried Tomato Tapenades (pages 31 and 32) with goat cheese
- Grilled eggplant and zucchini, tomato, Parmesan cheese, and thyme

Mexican Style

- Sautéed onion, roasted chiles, tomatoes, Cheddar cheese, and fresh cilantro. Top with avocado, and sour cream

California Style

- Mascarpone, smoked salmon, and caviar
- Confit of Red Onions and Prosciutto (page 143) with Niçoise olives
- Grilled mixed vegetables with Gorgonzola dolcelatte

150   Tomatillo Grilled Shrimp

152   Roasted Sea Bass with Mustard-Salsa Sauce

153   Grilled Salmon Fillet with Avocado, Cucumber, and Dill Salsa

154   Baked Salmon with Red Onion Sauce

156   Roast Crispy Fish with Warm Lentils

158   Grilled Halibut with Red Pepper–Mint Sauce

160   Glazed Halibut with Orange-Chive Sauce

161   Grilled Swordfish on a Bed of Cucumber "Pasta" with Asian Salsa

164   Broiled Orange Roughy with Salsa Glaze

165   West Coast Crab Cakes with Grapefruit Sauce

168   Grilled Tuna with Vegetable and White Bean Salsa

172   Grilled Scallop Brochettes with Almond-Caper Relish

SEAFOOD

TOMATILLO GRILLED SHRIMP

SERVES 4

A satisfying spicy flavor and quick preparation time are two good reasons to make this dish. Shrimp benefits from the tangy, hot flavors of tomatillo salsa.

Arrange the skewers on a platter with the sauce in the center and let your guests help themselves. This works nicely for a buffet. Accompany the dish with Confetti Rice Pilaf (page 269) and warm corn tortillas.

MARINADE

½ cup Tomatillo Salsa (page 358)

1 tablespoon fresh lime juice

1 tablespoon olive oil

2 tablespoons finely chopped fresh cilantro

1 pound large shrimp (4 to 6 per person), peeled and deveined, tails left on

SAUCE

½ cup sour cream

¼ cup Tomatillo Salsa (page 358)

2 tablespoons finely chopped fresh cilantro

1 teaspoon fresh lime juice

¼ teaspoon salt

Pinch of freshly ground white pepper

1 head red leaf lettuce, cored and leaves separated

Recommended Wine

The shrimp go equally well with a crisp, spicy Sauvignon Blanc or a lively, well-balanced Chardonnay.

Advance Preparation

The marinade and sauce can be made up to 1 day ahead and refrigerated.

1   To make the marinade, combine the ingredients in a small mixing bowl and mix well. Taste for seasoning.

2   Thread the shrimp onto metal or bamboo skewers (soak bamboo skewers in cold water for ½ hour before using), dividing evenly. Lay the skewers flat in a shallow, nonaluminum dish. Pour the marinade over the shrimp and turn to coat evenly. Cover and refrigerate for ½ hour, turning once or twice.

3   To make the sauce, in a small glass serving bowl, combine the ingredients and mix well. Taste for seasoning and set aside.

4   When you're ready to serve, prepare a grill for medium-high-heat grilling. Remove the shrimp from the marinade and place flat on the grill, about 3 inches from the heat. Baste each side with the marinade and cook for about 3 minutes on each side, or until just opaque throughout.

5   Arrange the lettuce leaves on a serving platter. Put the bowl of sauce in the middle, place the skewers of grilled shrimp around the bowl, and let your guests help themselves. (You can also remove the shrimp from the skewers and serve them on a platter with a fork.)

ROASTED SEA BASS WITH MUSTARD-SALSA SAUCE

SERVES 4 TO 6

Oven-roasting fish in individual aluminum foil or parchment packets is quick and keeps the fish moist. The sauce, a low-calorie mix of salsa and Dijon mustard, takes only a minute to assemble. You can use any fresh white sea bass or halibut for this recipe. Serve with Cauliflower Purée with Two Cheeses (page 246) and simple steamed green beans.

SAUCE

⅔ cup Spicy Tomato Salsa (page 357) or fresh store-bought salsa

⅓ cup Dijon mustard

1 tablespoon olive oil

2 tablespoons finely chopped fresh cilantro or parsley

1 tablespoon fresh lemon juice

4 to 6 sea bass fillets, each ⅓ to ½ pound, about 1 inch thick

1   To make the sauce, combine the ingredients in a medium mixing bowl and mix well.

2   Preheat the oven to 425°F. Cut 4 to 6 pieces of parchment paper or aluminum foil into heart or rectangular shapes large enough to overlap over the fish.

3   Arrange each fillet in the center of a piece of parchment or foil. Spoon a good tablespoon or so of the sauce over each. Fold the paper or foil in half over the fish. Overlap the edges, holding down the creased edges with one index finger and using your other index finger and thumb to pinch and fold. Tuck under the excess and place the packets on baking sheets; 2 to 3 packets will fit on 1 baking sheet.

4   Roast for 8 to 10 minutes, depending on the thickness of the fillets. The fish should be very moist. Place the packets on serving dishes, open the packets, and serve immediately. Serve the remaining sauce separately.

Recommended Wine
Accompany with a smoky, well-balanced Sauvignon Blanc.

Advance Preparation
Can be prepared through step 3 up to 4 hours ahead and refrigerated.

This salsa is lighter and more refreshing than the traditional creamy mayonnaise-based sauce for salmon; it tastes more like a crunchy relish. I prefer to use English (hothouse) cucumber because you don't have to peel it and the dark green skin is pretty mixed with the lighter green avocado. Serve this with Confetti Rice Pilaf (page 269) and a simple steamed vegetable like asparagus or green beans.

SERVES 4

SALSA

1 medium English (hothouse) cucumber, cut into ¼-inch pieces

2 tablespoons finely chopped fresh dill

2 tablespoons olive oil

2 tablespoons rice wine vinegar

1 tablespoon fresh lemon juice

½ teaspoon salt

½ teaspoon sugar

1 small ripe avocado, pitted, peeled, and cut into ¼-inch pieces

Two pounds salmon fillet or four ½-pound pieces

1 tablespoon fresh lemon juice

1 tablespoon finely chopped fresh dill

GARNISH

Lemon slices

Fresh dill sprigs

1 Prepare a grill for medium-high-heat grilling.

2 To make the salsa, combine the ingredients in a medium mixing bowl and mix well. Taste for seasoning. Set aside.

3 Place the salmon on wax paper and sprinkle evenly with the lemon juice and chopped dill. Grill the salmon about 3 inches from the heat until opaque throughout, about 7 minutes on each side, depending on the thickness and size.

4 Remove the salmon from the grill, cut it into serving pieces if it's one large piece, and place the pieces on serving plates. Spoon the salsa over the salmon and garnish with the lemon slices and dill sprigs. Serve immediately.

Recommended Wine

A well-balanced Sauvignon Blanc that has spent some aging time in oak is a good match for this dish of textural and flavor contrasts.

Advance Preparation

The salsa can be prepared up to 4 hours ahead, covered, and refrigerated.

BAKED SALMON WITH RED ONION SAUCE

SERVES 6

Fish with a red sauce? They go together perfectly here. An assertive, sweet yet slightly tart sauce brings this salmon dish to new heights. The balsamic vinegar is important for its full-bodied acidic-sweet character. This is an excellent dinner party dish because the sauce can be prepared hours ahead. Begin with White Bean and Artichoke Soup (page 52) or Peppery Greens with Gorgonzola and Pine Nuts (page 80). Sautéed Green and Yellow Beans with Garlic and Basil (page 244) make a colorful accompaniment.

SAUCE

2 tablespoons olive oil

2 large red onions, very finely chopped

1 cup full-bodied red wine

2 tablespoons balsamic vinegar

1½ cups Chicken Stock (page 342)

3 tablespoons heavy whipping cream

¼ teaspoon salt

⅛ teaspoon cayenne pepper

Three pounds salmon fillet or six ½-pound pieces

GARNISH

2 tablespoons finely chopped fresh parsley

Recommended Wine

A crisp and youthful red such as a Gamay Beaujolais, Pinot Noir, or Syrah is very effective with this dish.

Advance Preparation

Can be prepared through step 4 up to 6 hours ahead, covered, and refrigerated. Reheat gently.

1   To make the sauce, in a large skillet over medium heat, heat the oil. Add the onions and sauté until completely softened and beginning to caramelize, 15 to 20 minutes; reduce the heat if they begin to burn. Add the wine and vinegar and raise the heat to medium-high. Cook until the mixture is reduced to a syrupy glaze, about 5 to 7 minutes.

2   Transfer the onion mixture to a food processor fitted with metal blade. Process the onion mixture until you have a fine purée.

3   Return the onion purée to the skillet and add the stock. Bring to a boil. Simmer for about 5 minutes, or until the liquid is reduced by one-third.

4   Pour the sauce into a fine-mesh strainer set over a medium saucepan. With a wooden spoon, push the sauce through the strainer, making sure to get out as much of the pulp as possible. Using a rubber spatula, scrape off the solids on the underside of the strainer into the saucepan.

5   Add the cream and place the pan over high heat. Cook for 3 to 5 minutes, or until reduced to a nice glaze. Add the salt and cayenne and cook for another minute. Taste for seasoning and set aside.

6   Preheat the oven to 450°F. Place the salmon on an oiled baking sheet and bake until opaque throughout, about 12 minutes, depending on the thickness and size.

7   Remove the salmon from the oven and cut it into serving pieces if it's one large piece, and place the pieces on serving plates. Spoon the sauce over the salmon, garnish with the parsley, and serve immediately.

ROAST CRISPY FISH WITH WARM LENTILS

SERVES 4

This unusual combination tastes wonderful. After the lentils are braised, part of the mixture is puréed to become a sauce for the fish. The simple, clear flavors of lemon, parsley, and basil are well suited to the lentil mixture. Spraying the fish rather than brushing it with olive oil gives it a crunchy coating without an oily aftertaste. Begin with California Salad (page 82) as a first course.

LENTILS

1 cup (½ pound) dried brown lentils, picked over and rinsed

3 cups Chicken Stock (page 342)

3 tablespoons olive oil

1 medium red onion, finely chopped

1 medium celery rib, finely diced

1 medium carrot, peeled and finely diced

1 small red bell pepper, seeded and finely diced

3 tablespoons fresh lemon juice

2 tablespoons finely chopped fresh parsley

2 tablespoons finely chopped fresh basil or 1 tablespoon dried

1 teaspoon salt

¼ teaspoon freshly ground black pepper

One 2-pound sea bass or halibut fillet, about ½ inch thick

2 tablespoons fresh lemon juice

3 tablespoons dried bread crumbs

Olive oil cooking spray

GARNISH

Fresh parsley or basil leaves

Recommended Wine

The earthy flavors of this dish are best combined with a Syrah or a Sangiovese among reds; if you want to pour a white, an oaky Chardonnay does very nicely.

Advance Preparation

The lentils can be prepared through step 3 up to 4 hours ahead and kept covered at room temperature. Reheat gently.

1   To make the lentils, in a medium saucepan, combine the lentils and 2 cups of the stock and bring to a boil. Reduce the heat and simmer, partially covered, for about 20 minutes, or until tender but not mushy. Drain and set aside

2   In a large skillet over medium heat, heat 2 tablespoons of the oil. Add the onion and sauté until softened, about 5 to 7 minutes. Add the celery and carrot and sauté for about 5 minutes. Add the bell pepper and cook for 2 more minutes.

3   Add the lentils to the vegetables in the skillet and cook for 2 minutes over medium heat. Add the lemon juice, the remaining 1 tablespoon oil, the chopped parsley, the basil, salt, and pepper and mix well. Transfer 1 cup of the lentil mixture to a food processor fitted with the metal blade. Add ¾ to 1 cup of the remaining stock, or enough to make it a saucelike consistency. Process to a purée, return the purée to the skillet with the whole lentils, mix well, and taste for seasoning. Remove from the heat and cover to keep warm while you cook the fish.

4   Preheat the oven to 450°F. Place the fish in an oiled roasting pan and sprinkle on the lemon juice and then the bread crumbs in an even layer. Spray with a thin, even coating of olive oil spray. Roast the fish for 10 to 15 minutes, or until browned and crispy.

5   To serve, cut the fish into 4 equal pieces. Place a portion of lentils on each serving plate and place a piece of fish on top of the lentils. Garnish with the herb leaves and serve immediately.

LENTILS

California cooks have rediscovered this diminutive legume, which is technically in the family of pulses. Lentils now appear often, not only in soups but also in salads, as a side dish, or as a bed for seafood. Lentils don't require soaking, and they cook quickly.

Most chefs and many home cooks prefer the smaller, plump slate-green French Le Puy lentils, which are more expensive but have a firmer texture and a subtle, peppery flavor. Other lentils, like the brown masoor dal, cook faster and break down more quickly, making them ideal for soups and purées. If you want your lentils to hold their shape for a salad or as a bed for fish or chicken, use the French green lentils; they'll take just a little longer to cook.

Red lentils, whether domestic or imported, have a milder flavor than the brown ones and turn a sort of dull gold after cooking. They break down into a purée quickly and can be mixed with other varieties that take longer to reach a purée, giving a soft, creamy background to the whole lentils.

GRILLED HALIBUT WITH RED PEPPER– MINT SAUCE

SERVES 6

Sweet bell peppers seasoned with fresh mint are the foundation for this sauce. Fortunately, you don't need to roast and peel the peppers. Think about preparing this dish whenever red peppers are plentiful in the market. The sauce is also perfect with grilled chicken or shrimp. Begin with Green Olive Tapenade (page 31) with Parmesan Toasts (page 274) and serve the fish with Home Ranch Butternut Squash (page 251) or Spinach Rice Timbales (page 271).

MARINADE

1 tablespoon finely chopped fresh mint

1 garlic clove, minced

2 tablespoons balsamic vinegar

2 tablespoons olive oil

6 halibut fillets or steaks, ⅓ to ½ pound each

SAUCE

1 tablespoon olive oil

2 garlic cloves, minced

4 red bell peppers, seeded and finely chopped

2 tablespoons finely chopped fresh mint

1 tablespoon balsamic vinegar

1¼ cups dry white wine

3 tablespoons heavy (whipping) cream

½ teaspoon salt

Pinch of freshly ground white pepper

GARNISH

Fresh mint leaves

Roasted red pepper slices (page 27) (optional)

Recommended Wine

This is a very difficult dish to match with wine. The herbal flavors of mint and bell peppers can be contrasted by a spicy, crisp Sauvignon Blanc or augmented by a youthful Cabernet Sauvignon. The Sauvignon Blanc is the safer choice, but the Cabernet will certainly provoke conversation.

Advance Preparation

Can be prepared through step 6 up to 2 hours ahead. Refrigerate the fish and sauce. Gently reheat the sauce.

1   To make the marinade, mix together the ingredients in a small mixing bowl.

2   Arrange the fish pieces in a large, shallow, nonaluminum dish. Pour the marinade over the fish and turn to coat evenly. Cover and refrigerate for at least 30 minutes and up to 2 hours.

3   To make the sauce, heat the oil in a large saucepan over low heat. Add the garlic and sauté for 30 seconds. Raise the heat to medium, add the bell peppers and mint, and sauté for 5 minutes, stirring frequently. Add the vinegar and cook the peppers until they are glazed, 1 to 2 minutes.

4   Reduce the heat to low. Add the wine, cover, and simmer for about 15 minutes, or until the peppers are softened. Purée the mixture in the pan with an immersion blender or in a food processor fitted with the metal blade.

5   Pour the sauce into a fine-mesh strainer set over a medium saucepan. With a wooden spoon, push the sauce through the strainer, making sure to get out as much of the pulp as possible. Using a rubber spatula, scrape off the solids on the underside of the strainer into the saucepan.

6   Add the cream, salt, and white pepper and place over high heat. Cook for 3 to 5 minutes, or until the sauce just coats a spoon. Taste for seasoning. Remove from the heat and cover to keep warm while you cook the fish.

7   Prepare a grill for medium-high-heat grilling. Remove the fish from the marinade and grill about 3 inches from the heat until opaque throughout, 5 to 7 minutes on each side, or until done to taste. Arrange the fish on serving plates and spoon some sauce over each portion. Garnish with the fresh mint leaves and the roasted pepper slices, if desired. Serve immediately.

GLAZED HALIBUT WITH ORANGE-CHIVE SAUCE

SERVES 4

This simple recipe brings out the fine texture and flavor of halibut. The yogurt gives the creamy citrus sauce extra tang. Be sure to sprinkle with more fresh chives just before serving because the chives in the cooked sauce will have darkened. Serve this with Oven-Roasted Potatoes with Parmesan (page 262) and steamed asparagus.

SAUCE

1 tablespoon fresh orange juice

1 teaspoon finely chopped orange zest

2 garlic cloves, minced

1 tablespoon finely chopped fresh chives

½ cup mayonnaise (low-fat if desired)

2 tablespoons plain nonfat yogurt

4 halibut fillets, ⅓ to ½ pound each

GARNISH

2 tablespoons chopped fresh chives

Recommended Wine

The citrus flavors in this dish suggest a dry Riesling or a tangy, bright Chardonnay with lots of lively acidity.

Advance Preparation

Sauce can be prepared up to 1 day ahead and refrigerated.

1   To make the sauce, in a small mixing bowl, whisk together the ingredients. Set aside.

2   Preheat the broiler. Place the fillets on an oiled broiler pan and spread 1 tablespoon of the sauce on top of the each fillet. Broil about 3 inches from the heat for 3 to 5 minutes, or until nicely browned. Remove from the broiler, turn the fillets carefully with a spatula, and spread each with another 1 tablespoon of the sauce. Return to the broiler and broil for another 3 to 5 minutes, or until bubbly and well browned. Be careful not to let the fish burn. Transfer the fillets to serving dishes, garnish with the chives, and serve with the remaining sauce.

Swordfish is a meaty, substantial fish that benefits from an intensely flavored marinade. This light and refreshing entrée brings together the flavors of Italy and Asia with tomatoes, ginger, and sesame oil in the sauce. The cucumber should not be cut more than an hour before serving, or it will become soft and mushy. Begin your dinner with Asian Guacamole (page 34) and serve the fish with Tricolor Vegetable Sauté (page 245).

MARINADE

2 garlic cloves, minced

1 tablespoon peeled and finely chopped fresh ginger

3 tablespoons fresh lime juice

1 tablespoon dark sesame oil

2 tablespoons olive oil

¼ teaspoon salt

⅛ teaspoon freshly ground black pepper

6 swordfish steaks, ⅓ to ½ pound each

SALSA

3 medium tomatoes, peeled, seeded, and finely chopped

2 garlic cloves, minced

2 teaspoons peeled and finely chopped fresh ginger

2 tablespoons finely chopped scallions

2 tablespoons rice wine vinegar

2 teaspoons dark sesame oil

½ teaspoon salt

⅛ teaspoon freshly ground black pepper

CUCUMBER "PASTA"

2 medium English (hothouse) cucumbers, halved lengthwise and seeded

2 tablespoons olive oil

2 tablespoons rice wine vinegar

¼ teaspoon salt

Pinch of freshly ground black pepper

Recommended Wine
Match this dish with a crisp Graves-like Sauvignon Blanc.

Advance Preparation
The salsa can prepared up to 4 hours ahead, covered, and refrigerated. The fish can be marinated 2 hours ahead and refrigerated.

continued on next page

1   To make the marinade, combine the garlic, ginger, and lime juice in a small mixing bowl. Add the sesame and olive oils and whisk to blend completely. Add the salt and pepper and taste for seasoning.

2   Arrange the swordfish steaks in a large, shallow, nonaluminum dish. Pour the marinade over the fish and turn to coat evenly. Cover and refrigerate for at least 30 minutes and up to 2 hours.

3   To make the salsa, combine the ingredients in a medium mixing bowl and mix well. Taste for seasoning.

4   Just before serving, shred the cucumber with a mandoline or in a food processor fitted with a thin julienne blade. *Do not do this more than 1 hour before serving.* Put the cucumber in a paper towel–lined bowl and refrigerate.

5   Prepare a grill for medium-high-heat grilling. Remove the fish from the marinade and grill about 3 inches from the heat until opaque throughout, 5 to 6 minutes on each side, or until done to taste.

6   To serve, remove the paper towel from the bowl of cucumbers (discard all extra moisture) and add the olive oil, vinegar, salt, and pepper. Stir the cucumbers with a fork to coat them evenly. Taste for seasoning. Arrange a few tablespoons of the cucumber "pasta" on each of 6 serving plates, place a swordfish steak on top, and spoon the salsa over. Serve immediately.

Salsa: A California Tradition

It may seem surprising that salsa has been a California tradition since the rancho days of the late 1800s. According to Jacqueline Higuera McMahan in *California Rancho Cooking* (The Olive Press, 1988), it was known as *sarsa* and was made from fresh ingredients grown on the ranchos. Salsa was served at the table to accompany barbecued meats, to spoon over beans, or to spread over big hunks of French bread.

Today the field is wide open to create your own signature salsa with a vast array of fruits and vegetables. Just remember that salsa is a way to heighten simple grilled fish, poultry, meat, and vegetables, so think of complementary flavors. Here are a few ideas to get you thinking.

- Cucumbers or avocados combined with fresh tomato salsa
- Oranges and grapefruit with scallions, fresh chiles, and fresh mint
- Blood oranges and green or black olives with fresh lemon juice
- Papaya, mango, and pineapple with fresh chiles and lemon juice
- Mixed fresh and dried chiles with tomatoes, red onions, vinegar, and cilantro
- Grilled corn, red onion, and tomato salsa
- Pineapple-peach salsa with balsamic vinegar, brown sugar, fresh chiles, and orange zest
- Corn, black bean, garlic, and roasted red bell pepper salsa
- Yellow and red cherry tomato salsa with roasted red and yellow bell peppers, fresh basil, olive oil, and lemon juice

BROILED ORANGE ROUGHY WITH SALSA GLAZE

SERVES 6

Recommended Wine

This spicy dish is charming with an oak-aged Sauvignon Blanc.

Advance Preparation

The glaze can be prepared up to 1 day ahead, covered, and refrigerated.

In the early 1980s orange roughy, a delicate-textured fish, was just a funny name for inexpensive frozen fish. Now it is available fresh nine months of the year, flown in from Australia and New Zealand. One fish salesman told me he thought the reason for the high demand for orange roughy is that home cooks have discovered it is difficult to overcook.

If you can't find fresh orange roughy, consider snapper, sole, or ling cod as substitutes. This last-minute dish relies on a zippy salsa glaze to elevate the simple flavors of the fish into a casually elegant main course. Serve with Orange-Glazed Beets (page 264) and Roasted Onions and Baby Potatoes (page 263).

GLAZE

1 tablespoon fresh lime juice

2 tablespoons Spicy Tomato Salsa (page 357) or store-bought

½ cup mayonnaise (low-fat if desired)

2 tablespoons plain nonfat yogurt

6 fresh orange roughy fillets, ⅓ to ½ pound each

GARNISH

2 tablespoons chopped fresh flat-leaf parsley

1 Preheat the broiler. To make the glaze, in a small mixing bowl, combine the ingredients and mix well. Taste for seasoning.

2 Place the fillets on an oiled broiler pan and spread half of the glaze on top. Broil the fish about 3 inches from the heat for 3 minutes, or until nicely browned. Remove from the broiler, turn the fish over carefully with a large spatula, and spread with the remaining glaze. Return to the broiler and broil about 3 more minutes, until bubbly and well browned. Be careful not to let the fish burn. Using the large spatula, transfer the fish to serving plates, taking care not to break the pieces. Garnish with the parsley and serve immediately.

The sleepy seaside village of Mendocino, California, puts on a crab festival every January. Recently, I was invited to judge the crab cake competition. It felt like a step back in time when we ate at the gigantic Crab Feed, which took place at the local church. Picture enormous stainless-steel bowls spilling over with fresh Dungeness cracked crabs, accompanied by homemade cocktail sauces, salad, bread, and wine, served continuously to the crowd seated at long picnic tables. This was truly an unforgettable feast.

For the competition, we tasted twenty crab cake entries in search of the best, and this recipe is based on what I learned that day. These crab cakes call for Dungeness crab meat because of its naturally sweet, buttery flavor. Chunky crab pieces combine with a bare minimum of bread crumbs, and then are chilled to absorb the extra moisture so that the cakes will hold together well. Juicy grapefruit accents the crab flavor and cuts the richness of the butter sauce. Pink grapefruit sections make a pretty presentation. Serve these crab cakes with a simple mixed green salad lightly dressed with vinaigrette.

WEST COAST CRAB CAKES WITH GRAPEFRUIT SAUCE

MAKES 8 CRAB CAKES;

SERVES 8 AS A FIRST COURSE

OR 4 AS A MAIN COURSE

CRAB CAKES

1 large egg

1 tablespoon heavy (whipping) cream

1 teaspoon Dijon mustard

¼ teaspoon salt

Pinch of cayenne pepper

1 tablespoon finely chopped fresh chives

1 pound fresh Dungeness crabmeat, pulled apart into ½-inch chunks, not completely shredded

½ cup fine fresh bread crumbs

½ cup dried bread crumbs

GRAPEFRUIT SAUCE

½ cup fresh grapefruit juice

2 tablespoons white wine vinegar

2 medium shallots, minced

½ teaspoon salt

¼ teaspoon freshly ground white pepper

¾ cup cold unsalted butter, cut into cubes

continued on next page

Recommended Wine
Pour a crisp, lively Chardonnay with this dish—it will highlight the interesting citrus flavors.

Advance Preparation
Can be prepared through step 2 up to 4 hours ahead and refrigerated.

1   To make the crab cakes, beat the egg in a medium mixing bowl. Add the cream, mustard, salt, cayenne, and chives and mix well. Add the crabmeat and fresh bread crumbs. Mix gently, being careful not to break up the crab too much.

2   Spread the dried bread crumbs on a baking sheet. Divide the crab mixture into 8 crab cakes, shaping them into patties about ¾ inch thick and 3 inches in diameter. Squeeze well to remove any excess liquid. Using a spatula, roll the crab cakes in the dried bread crumbs to coat on all sides and place on a large plate. Cover the crab cakes with plastic wrap and refrigerate for at least 1 hour or up to 4 hours.

3   While the crab cakes are chilling, make the sauce: In a heavy saucepan over high heat combine the grapefruit juice, vinegar, and shallots and bring to a boil. Cook until reduced to about 2 tablespoons of liquid, about 3 to 5 minutes. Add the salt and pepper.

4   Reduce the heat to low and begin adding the cubes of cold butter, 1 or 2 at a time, to the shallot mixture, whisking constantly. Wait until they're absorbed before adding more; the sauce should thicken, but the butter should not turn clear. If the pan begins to get very hot, remove it from the heat and add some of the butter cubes off the heat so the sauce cools slightly. Remove the sauce from the heat as soon as the last butter cube is added.

5   Strain the sauce through a fine-mesh strainer if a smoother consistency is desired. Taste for seasoning. Keep the sauce warm in a double boiler or thermos and serve as soon as possible.

6   Preheat the oven to 300°F. Melt 1 tablespoon of the butter with 1 tablespoon of the oil in a medium nonstick skillet or griddle over medium-high heat. Add 4 crab cakes and cook until golden brown on both sides, 3 to 4 minutes on each side. Be careful when turning them so they stay together. Transfer to a baking sheet and place in the oven to keep warm. Melt the remaining 1 tablespoon

butter with the remaining 1 tablespoon oil and cook the rest of the crab cakes in the same way.

7   To serve, place a small mound of the chopped grapefruit in the center of each serving plate and arrange 1 or 2 crab cakes on top, overlapping slightly if serving more than one. Spoon some sauce on top and around the cakes. Garnish with the whole grapefruit sections, arranging them around the perimeter of each plate, and serve immediately.

GRILLED TUNA WITH VEGETABLE AND WHITE BEAN SALSA

SERVES 6

In the early 1980s Zuni Café opened in San Francisco and was immediately recognized as one of the leaders in contemporary California cooking. Twenty years later Zuni is still going strong. On any given day you can find the best chefs from other San Francisco restaurants dining there. Chef Judy Rogers turns out her own brand of California cooking using Mediterranean products.

This recipe is based on one of Chef Rogers's signatures, grilled fish with unusual light salsas. The fresh flavors are allowed to speak for themselves, calling to mind the old adage that less is more. Here a simple salsa is created using cooked white beans, earthy Niçoise olives, and a hint of mint. The salsa is spooned over a rare grilled ahi tuna steak. Ask for the center cut of the tuna loin, which will be less oily. To determine the freshness of the tuna, look for a deep red color. Begin with Assorted Grilled Vegetables (page 24) and serve this with a simple pasta or rice.

Recommended Wine

The beefiness of the tuna and the richness of the beans combines very nicely with a young Cabernet Sauvignon or Merlot. A Syrah or Rhône blend also does very nicely here.

Advance Preparation

The salsa can be prepared up to 4 hours ahead and refrigerated.

MARINADE

2 medium shallots, minced

6 tablespoons fresh lemon juice

1 teaspoon finely chopped lemon zest

¼ cup olive oil

¼ teaspoon salt

Pinch of freshly ground black pepper

6 tuna steaks cut from the center with no bone, ⅓ to ½ pound each

SALSA

1 large shallot, minced

1 cup cooked white beans such as cannellini

½ cup coarsely chopped English (hothouse) cucumber

4 small red radishes, thinly sliced and slices halved

2 tablespoons finely chopped fresh mint

¼ cup Niçoise olives, pitted and halved

3 tablespoons extra-virgin olive oil

3 tablespoons fresh lemon juice

½ teaspoon salt

¼ teaspoon freshly ground black pepper

1   To make the marinade, whisk together the ingredients in a small mixing bowl. Taste for seasoning.

2   Place the tuna in a large, shallow, nonaluminum dish. Pour the marinade over the tuna and turn to coat evenly. Cover and refrigerate for at least ½ hour but no more than 1 hour. The citrus in the marinade will begin to "cook" the tuna and will change the texture if left longer.

3   To make the salsa, in a small mixing bowl, combine the ingredients and mix well. Taste for seasoning.

4   Prepare a grill for medium-high-heat grilling. Remove the fish from the marinade and grill about 3 inches from the heat for about 3 minutes on each side. The tuna should be rare.

5   Transfer the tuna to serving plates and garnish with a large dollop of salsa. Serve immediately.

Grilling Tips

When Is the Fire Ready?

Knowing just when to put your food on the fire is crucial to successful grilling. A fire that's too hot will char the outside of the food while leaving the center raw. If the fire is too cool, the food just won't cook properly.

Charcoal and wood fires are ready 30 to 45 minutes after the initial lighting. For most foods the fuel should have a layer of gray ash. If there is a high flame, the fire is not quite ready.

Medium-High-Heat Grilling

The fire should have red-hot coals with just a thin layer of gray ash and an occasional flare-up. You can test the heat by holding your hand about 6 inches from the grill rack; you should be able to keep it there for only a few seconds. Medium-high-heat grilling is excellent for boneless chicken breasts or thinly sliced pieces of seafood, poultry, or meat.

Medium-Heat Grilling

The coals should be covered with a thick layer of gray ash, and there should be no flames. This is a good way to cook thicker pieces of meat or poultry. You may want to use the cover on your grill for this lower-temperature cooking.

Grilling in Aluminum Foil

While grilling in aluminum foil may not produce the same smoky-grilled flavor of other grilled foods, this method works well for individual pieces of delicate-textured fish like sea bass, salmon, and halibut that may fall apart on the grill. Season the fish and then enclose it in foil, making sure the edges are sealed. Grill over medium-high heat until the fish reaches the desired doneness, then remove it from the heat and let it rest for a few minutes before opening the foil.

Grilling Times and Temperatures

These basic guidelines will tell you how long and at what temperature to cook the food, but remember that the food will continue to cook off the grill, so remove it a minute or so before it is perfectly done.

Fish

Fish steaks and fillets are best cooked on an open grill over a medium-high heat since they do not require long cooking. Brush the fish liberally with oil before placing on the grill to prevent sticking. A hinged basket is useful for grilling a whole fish because you can turn the fish without breaking it. It's best to cook whole fish over medium heat with a cover. Cooking times will vary according to the type of fish and its thickness. Prod the fish with a fork to see if it's done; it should just begin to flake. Avoid overcooking the fish, because it will change not only the texture but also the flavor.

Poultry

Most poultry is best cooked on a covered grill over medium heat because it requires a longer and slower cooking time. Boneless chicken breasts and turkey slices are the exception; they require medium-high heat and quick grilling. Boneless chicken breasts require 6 to 8 minutes per side, while bone-in pieces require 8 to 14 minutes per side. Use these times as a guideline for other types of poultry.

If you don't have a covered grill, baste the poultry often to retain moisture, and allow a slightly longer cooking time. Make sure that there's a heavy layer of gray ash on the coals before you begin cooking to ensure an even cooking temperature.

Meats

An instant-read thermometer is handy when grilling large pieces of meat. Here are some general guideline temperatures: beef and lamb—130° to 135°F in the thickest part for rare, 135° to 145°F for medium-rare, and 150°F for medium. Pork roasts should have an internal temperature of 160°F—more than that and they tend to be very dry.

Steaks and chops can be cooked according to the thickness of the cut. Sear them on each side for 30 seconds and then cook according to these guidelines, with the lower number indicating the time for rare and the higher number for well done: 1 inch, 3 to 6 minutes per side; 1½ inches, 4 to 9 minutes per side; 2 inches, 6 to 10 minutes per side. Season the meat with salt and freshly ground pepper after it has cooked.

Vegetables

Clean the vegetables and slice them for the grill. Certain vegetables, like pearl onions and summer squash, should be blanched in boiling water for just a minute to eliminate the raw taste that quick grilling might not remove. Brush the vegetables with olive or avocado oil and place them on the grill with whatever else you're grilling. Sear over medium-high heat to seal in the juices, and then move them to the edges of the grill to finish cooking. Thinly sliced vegetables will take 6 to 10 minutes on each side to cook. Vegetables such as tomatoes or onions, which fall apart easily, should be placed in a grilling basket. All vegetables can be threaded on metal or bamboo skewers if desired. Remember to soak the bamboo skewers in cold water for at least 30 minutes before grilling.

GRILLED SCALLOP BROCHETTES WITH ALMOND-CAPER RELISH

SERVES 6

Recommended Wine

A crisp, lively Graves-style Sauvignon Blanc is a bright contrast to the sweetness of the scallops and the richness of the almonds.

Advance Preparation

The relish can be prepared up to 4 hours ahead, covered, and left at room temperature. Add the almonds just before serving.

The larger sea scallops work best for this recipe because they grill evenly and don't dry out as quickly as bay scallops. The light citrus relish includes blanched almonds, which gives it a crunchy, toasty flavor. You'll need about six limes for this dish. Scallop Brochettes go nicely with Confetti Rice Pilaf (page 269) and Sautéed Green and Yellow Beans with Garlic and Basil (page 244).

MARINADE

2 garlic cloves, minced

2 tablespoons fresh lime juice

1 teaspoon minced lime zest

2 tablespoons olive oil

¼ teaspoon salt

⅛ teaspoon freshly ground black pepper

2 pounds large sea scallops

RELISH

⅓ cup slivered blanched almonds

½ cup finely chopped fresh flat-leaf parsley leaves

1 medium shallot, finely chopped

1 garlic clove, minced

2 tablespoons finely chopped seeded red bell pepper

1 tablespoon well-drained capers, finely chopped

¼ cup fresh lime juice

¼ teaspoon salt

⅛ teaspoon freshly ground black pepper

¼ cup olive oil

1   To make the marinade, combine the garlic and lime juice and zest in a small mixing bowl and stir to mix. Add the oil and whisk to blend completely. Add the salt and pepper and taste for seasoning.

2   Thread the scallops onto metal or bamboo skewers (soak bamboo skewers in cold water for ½ hour before grilling) and lay them in a large, shallow, non-aluminum dish. Pour the marinade over the scallops and turn to coat evenly. Cover and refrigerate for ½ hour but not more; the citrus in the marinade will begin to "cook" the scallops if left longer.

3   To make the relish, preheat the oven to 350°F. Spread the almonds in a single layer on a baking sheet and toast for 5 to 7 minutes, or until lightly browned. Immediately transfer to a plate and set aside.

4   In a medium mixing bowl, toss together the parsley, shallot, garlic, bell pepper, capers, lime juice, salt, and pepper. Pour the oil in a steady stream into the mixture and stir until well incorporated. Spoon into a serving dish and gently stir in the toasted almonds. Taste for seasoning.

5   Prepare a grill for medium-high-heat grilling. Remove the scallops from the marinade and grill about 3 inches from the heat until opaque throughout, 3 to 4 minutes on each side, or until done to taste.

6   Arrange the brochettes on a serving platter. Spoon the relish on top or serve on the side. Serve immediately.

176 Grilled Chicken Niçoise

178 Grilled Chicken with Pesto Bean Sauce

180 Grilled Orange-Mustard Chicken

181 Lemon Chicken with Roasted Garlic Sauce

184 Chicken with Garlic and Lime

186 Arroz con Pollo

188 Crispy Roast Chicken

190 Glazed Orange-Hoisin Chicken

191 Roasted Cornish Hens with Honey-Tangerine Marinade

193 Grilled Turkey Breast in Mustard-Bourbon Sauce

194 Marinated Roast Turkey

196 Rich Turkey Gravy

198 Turkey Vegetable Cobbler

201 Chicken and Apple Sausage

203 Turkey Sausages with Sun-Dried Tomatoes

POULTRY

GRILLED CHICKEN NIÇOISE

SERVES 4 TO 6

Sun-dried tomatoes contribute a depth of flavor that fresh or canned tomatoes can't match. California dry-packed sun-dried tomatoes are about a quarter of the price of imported Italian varieties and work well for this recipe. Be sure to soften the tomatoes in boiling water for at least 10 minutes before proceeding.

The thick Mediterranean-influenced marinade here is low in acid, so you can marinate the chicken for up to 8 hours without changing the texture—in fact the flavor will improve. Begin with California Caponata (page 39) with Parmesan Toasts (page 274) and serve the chicken with Garden Risotto (page 134) or Assorted Grilled Vegetables (page 24). For dessert try Tiramisu with Toasted Hazelnuts and Chocolate (page 316) or Orange, Almond, and Olive Oil Cake (page 302).

MARINADE

½ cup dry-packed sun-dried tomatoes

2 to 3 garlic cloves, to taste

2 teaspoons extra-virgin olive oil

15 Niçoise or other black olives, pitted

1 teaspoon capers, well drained and rinsed

2 tablespoons finely chopped fresh basil

2 tablespoons finely chopped fresh parsley

1 tablespoon Dijon mustard

1 tablespoon balsamic vinegar

¼ teaspoon salt

⅛ teaspoon freshly ground black pepper

3 large whole boneless chicken breasts, skin on, halved

SAUCE

2 tablespoons reserved sun-dried tomato marinade (above)

2 teaspoons fresh lemon juice

¼ cup crème fraîche

¼ teaspoon salt

⅛ teaspoon freshly ground black pepper

Recommended Wine

Try a fresh, youthful Pinot Noir with this full-flavored dish.

Advance Preparation

Can be prepared through step 5 up to 8 hours ahead. Refrigerate the chicken and sauce.

1   To make the marinade, in a small bowl, pour boiling water over the sun-dried tomatoes. Let soften for 15 to 30 minutes. Drain the tomatoes well and pat them dry.

2   Mince the garlic in a food processor fitted with the metal blade. Add the sun-dried tomatoes and the rest of the marinade ingredients and process until puréed to the consistency of a thick paste, stopping to scrape down the sides of the bowl as needed. Reserve 2 tablespoons of the marinade for the sauce. Taste for seasoning.

3   Place each chicken breast half between 2 pieces of plastic wrap and, using a mallet or the bottom of a saucepan, pound to an even ½-inch thickness.

4   Place the chicken breasts in a large, shallow, nonaluminum dish. Pour the marinade over the chicken and turn to coat evenly. Make sure you put some marinade *under* the skin. Cover and refrigerate the chicken for at least 2 hours and up to 8 hours, turning several times to make sure the marinade adheres.

5   To make the sauce, combine the reserved marinade, lemon juice, crème fraîche, salt and pepper in a small mixing bowl and whisk until smooth. Taste for seasoning. Set aside.

6   Prepare a grill for medium-high-heat grilling. Remove the chicken from the marinade and grill about 3 inches from the heat for about 7 minutes on each side, or until opaque throughout.

7   To serve, place the sauce in a small saucepan over low heat and gently heat it until just simmering. Place the chicken on serving plates and spoon on some sauce. Serve immediately. Pass the remaining sauce at the table.

GRILLED CHICKEN WITH PESTO BEAN SAUCE

SERVES 4 TO 6

Chicken breasts are probably my favorite poultry because they're a perfect backdrop for sauces or marinades. Here beans are combined with pesto and made into a sauce to spoon over grilled chicken—a marvelous surprise. Serve this with steamed asparagus for a pretty presentation.

MARINADE

¼ cup dry white wine

¼ cup Mixed-Herb Pesto (page 348)

¼ teaspoon salt

¼ teaspoon freshly ground black pepper

3 large whole boneless chicken breasts, halved

SAUCE

2 cups cooked Italian red beans, cannellini, or black beans, with ½ cup bean juice or Chicken Stock (page 342)

¼ cup Mixed-Herb Pesto (page 348)

2 tablespoons sour cream

GARNISH

¼ cup sour cream

2 tablespoons Mixed-Herb Pesto (page 348)

2 tablespoons freshly grated Parmesan cheese

Fresh herb sprigs such as basil, thyme, or parsley

Recommended Wine

The herbal nature of this dish goes very nicely with an oak-aged Sauvignon Blanc. This dish is also complemented by soft-textured Merlots.

Advance Preparation

Can be prepared through step 3 up to 4 hours ahead and refrigerated.

1   To make the marinade, combine the ingredients in a small mixing bowl and mix well. Taste for seasoning.

2   Place each chicken breast half between 2 pieces of plastic wrap and, using a mallet or the bottom of a saucepan, pound to an even ½-inch thickness.

3   Place the chicken breasts in a large, shallow, nonaluminum dish. Pour the marinade over the chicken and turn to coat evenly. Refrigerate, covered, for at least 30 minutes and up to 4 hours.

4   Prepare a grill for medium-heat grilling. Remove the chicken from the marinade and grill about 3 inches from the heat for about 7 minutes on each side, or until opaque throughout.

5   While the chicken is cooking, make the sauce: In a medium saucepan over medium heat, bring the beans, bean juice, and pesto to a simmer. Cook for about 5 minutes. Remove from the heat. Using a potato masher or immersion blender, purée the bean mixture in the pan, leaving some texture. Place over low heat. Add the sour cream and cook only another minute, or the sauce may begin to curdle. If you want a thinner consistency, add a bit more sour cream, chicken stock, or bean liquid.

6   To serve, place the chicken on serving plates and spoon some bean sauce over it. Place a dollop each of the sour cream and pesto on top. Sprinkle with the Parmesan and garnish with the herb sprigs. Serve immediately.

GRILLED ORANGE-MUSTARD CHICKEN

SERVES 4 TO 6

Recommended Wine

A ripe, oaky Chardonnay does well with this dish, as does a crisp, young red such as a Zinfandel or a Rhône blend.

Advance Preparation

Can be prepared through step 2 for up to 4 hours ahead, covered, and refrigerated.

Whole-grain mustard adds texture and a mixture of fresh herbs brings out the flavor in this light and zesty marinade. Sweet orange juice is nicely balanced by the piquant mustard-herb combination. Adding a touch of balsamic vinegar brings the contrasting flavors together. Begin with Grilled Artichoke Halves with Red Pepper Aioli (page 28) and serve the chicken with Ricotta Corn Cakes with Smoky Salsa Topping (page 40) or Sautéed Green and Yellow Beans with Garlic and Basil (page 244).

MARINADE

¼ cup whole-grain mustard

¼ cup Dijon mustard

¼ cup fresh orange juice

1 teaspoon finely chopped orange zest

1 tablespoon balsamic vinegar

1 tablespoon olive oil

¼ to ½ teaspoon Hot Pepper Oil (page 356) or store-bought pepper oil

2 tablespoons finely chopped fresh herbs: any combination of tarragon, mint, chives, thyme, basil, and/or parsley

¼ teaspoon freshly ground black pepper

3 medium whole chicken breasts, halved (boneless and skinless if desired)

GARNISH

Fresh herb leaves

Orange slices

1 To make the marinade, whisk together the ingredients in a small mixing bowl. Taste for seasoning.

2 Arrange the chicken pieces in a large, shallow, nonaluminum dish. Pour the marinade over the chicken and turn to coat evenly. Cover and refrigerate for at least 30 minutes and up to 4 hours.

3 Prepare a grill for medium-high-heat grilling. Remove the chicken from the marinade and grill about 3 inches from the heat for 7 to 10 minutes on each side, or until opaque throughout. Place the chicken on a platter or serving plates and garnish with the herb leaves and orange slices.

This is a variation on my most-requested party dish, which first appeared in *The Cuisine of California.* In this version I've adjusted the flavor of the sauce with puréed roasted garlic and Dijon mustard and roasted the chicken instead of sautéing it. Easy to prepare and incredibly fragrant, these plump browned chicken breasts need only an accompaniment of Roasted Onions and Baby Potatoes (page 263) and Sautéed Green and Yellow Beans (page 244) to make a casually elegant statement. They are also wonderful served cold for lunch.

LEMON CHICKEN WITH ROASTED GARLIC SAUCE

SERVES 6

MARINADE

⅓ cup fresh lemon juice

1 tablespoon finely chopped lemon zest

1 tablespoon olive oil

⅓ cup Chicken Stock (page 342)

¼ cup finely chopped fresh herbs: any combination of rosemary, thyme, parsley, basil, and/or oregano

⅓ cup dry white wine

1 teaspoon honey

½ teaspoon salt

¼ teaspoon freshly ground black pepper

4 large whole boneless chicken breasts, halved

¼ cup heavy (whipping) cream

2 teaspoons Dijon mustard

2 tablespoons Roasted Garlic Purée (page 353)

Salt and freshly ground black pepper

2 tablespoons finely chopped fresh parsley

GARNISH

1 bunch of fresh watercress

1 lemon, sliced

2 tablespoons finely chopped fresh flat-leaf parsley

Recommended Wine

This is one of those dishes (most of them involve chicken) that will be great with almost any wine. Since it uses white wine, a barrel-fermented Sauvignon Blanc or a Chardonnay would be fine, but a medium-weight Cabernet Sauvignon would be good, too.

Advance Preparation

Can be prepared through step 2 up to 2 hours ahead, covered, and refrigerated.

continued on next page

1   To make the marinade, whisk together the ingredients in a small mixing bowl. Taste for seasoning.

2   Place the chicken pieces in a large, shallow, nonaluminum dish. Pour the marinade over the chicken and turn to coat evenly. Cover and refrigerate for at least 30 minutes and up to 2 hours.

3   Preheat the oven to 425°F. Arrange the chicken pieces in a roasting pan, reserving the marinade, and roast for 20 to 25 minutes, or until nicely browned and opaque throughout.

4   While the chicken is roasting, transfer the reserved marinade to a medium saucepan and boil until reduced to about ½ cup, 5 to 7 minutes. Add the cream, mustard, and garlic purée and boil for another few minutes, until the sauce is slightly thickened. When the chicken is done, pour the pan drippings into the sauce and reduce again until slightly thickened, about 3 more minutes. Add the salt and pepper to taste and the parsley.

5   To serve, arrange the chicken breasts on a platter. Spoon some sauce over them, surround with the watercress and lemon slices, and sprinkle with the parsley. Serve immediately. Pass the remaining sauce at the table.

Garlic Tips

I can't imagine what California cooking would be like without this scented pearl. It has a chameleonlike character when taken from its raw state to baked. Its basic integrity is still intact, but the subtle, nutty, magical flavor will surprise you.

- Roast a whole head of garlic and squeeze the mild, creamy cloves directly out of their skin onto a thick wedge of country bread. Place the heads, with most of the papery skin removed, in an earthenware casserole or on a square of heavy aluminum foil, drizzle with olive oil, sprinkle with salt and freshly ground pepper, and roast, covered, at 425°F for about 45 minutes to 1 hour, until the cloves are very soft. Plan on at least 1 whole head per person—these are addictive!

- Subtle garlic flavoring: Put a few peeled garlic cloves in the water you are using to cook vegetables, potatoes, or rice to add a mild garlic flavor to the food. Remove and discard the garlic before serving.

- Sautéing garlic in oil can sometimes produce a burned flavor. To avoid that, use a good-quality olive oil or a combination of unsalted butter and olive oil and sauté over medium heat. Sauté the garlic after cooking the other ingredients, for no more than a minute. This will soften its sharp edge and bring out the garlic's inherent qualities.

- To remove the garlic odor from your hands, rinse them under *cold* water—hot will simply cook the smell onto your skin.

- Chop, press, or process? Hand-chopping garlic will yield the greatest quantity since you won't leave behind all that pulp in the press. (A garlic press may be quick and easy to use, but it often produces a strong, bitter flavor.) Adding any salt that is called for in the recipe to the cutting board while chopping makes it easier to scoop up the garlic afterwards. Chopping garlic by hand will release its aromatic oils, giving it a more assertive bite. The more finely it is chopped, the more intensely flavored it will be. Mincing the garlic in a food processor fitted with the metal blade is a good technique since it brings out the garlic's aromatic oils without the bitterness.

CHICKEN WITH GARLIC AND LIME

SERVES 4 TO 6

Californians love garlic. One method I use with the "stinking rose" is to sauté it lightly and then slowly simmer it in a stock until it's caramelized. In this dish a layered garlic flavor is achieved by simmering a garlic–lime juice sauce with the chicken, and then garnishing it with glazed baby pearl onions and whole garlic cloves. You'll need about 6 limes for the sauce. Make sure your guests love garlic before you serve them this one! Begin with Farmers' Market Chopped Salad (page 78) and serve the chicken with simple roasted baby potatoes. For a refreshing finish, try Mixed Exotic Fruit Gazpacho (page 300).

Recommended Wine

This pungent dish needs a full-flavored wine as an accompaniment. A ripe Zinfandel, Rhône varietal, or big, complex Cabernet Sauvignon will work nicely.

Advance Preparation

Can be prepared through step 5 up to 4 hours ahead, covered, and refrigerated. Reheat gently.

1 tablespoon unsalted butter

1 tablespoon olive oil

4 medium whole skinless, boneless chicken breasts, halved

2 heads of garlic, cloves separated but unpeeled, about 50 cloves

⅓ cup fresh lime juice

2 cups Easy Brown Veal Stock (page 344) or Chicken Stock (page 342)

2 tablespoons heavy (whipping) cream

½ teaspoon salt

⅛ teaspoon freshly ground white pepper

GLAZED ONIONS AND GARLIC

18 pearl onions or small shallots

1 tablespoon unsalted butter

1 tablespoon olive oil

1 cup Easy Brown Veal Stock (page 344) or Chicken Stock (page 342)

¼ teaspoon salt

Pinch of freshly ground white pepper

1 head of garlic, cloves separated and peeled, about 25 cloves

GARNISH

2 tablespoons finely chopped fresh parsley

1   In a medium skillet over medium-high heat, melt the butter with the olive oil. Add the chicken breast halves in batches and brown for about 5 minutes on each side. Transfer the chicken to a platter and cover.

2   Place the unpeeled garlic cloves in the same skillet and brown them quickly. Don't worry about the papery peels; they're removed during straining. Pour off any excess oil and add the lime juice and stock. Scrape up the browned bits from the bottom of the pan. Bring to a boil, then reduce the heat to a simmer. Cover and cook for about 20 minutes, or until the garlic is soft.

3   Place the garlic mixture in a food processor fitted with the metal blade and process to purée. Strain the mixture through a fine-mesh strainer and return it to the skillet, discarding the solids. Add the cream, any juices from the chicken breasts that have collected on the platter, the salt, and the pepper and bring to a simmer. Remove from the heat and cover to keep warm while you cook the onions.

4   To make the Glazed Onions and Garlic, submerge the onions in boiling water in a medium saucepan for 10 seconds, then rinse them in cold water. Trim off the tops and bottoms, then remove the outside skin and first layer with your fingers. Cut a shallow X into the root ends of the onions so they will cook evenly and not burst. Pat the onions dry.

5   In a medium saucepan over medium heat, melt the butter with the olive oil. Add the onions and brown for about 7 to 10 minutes, using a large spoon to roll them or shaking the pan occasionally. Add ½ cup of the stock, the salt, and the pepper and bring to a simmer. Add the peeled garlic cloves and remaining ½ cup stock, reduce the heat to medium-low, and continue cooking until the onions and garlic are tender; they should retain their shape but be tender when pierced with a fork. The liquid should be the consistency of a glaze. Watch carefully to avoid overcooking.

6   Return the chicken to the skillet with the garlic-lime sauce and cook over medium heat for about 5 more minutes, or until just tender and opaque throughout. Taste for seasoning.

7   Arrange the chicken on a large serving platter and pour the sauce over it. Spoon the glazed garlic and onions on top of the chicken and garnish with the chopped parsley. Serve immediately.

ARROZ CON POLLO

SERVES 4

Recommended Wine

A bright, well-oaked Chardonnay is the answer to this earthy dish, or you might try a brisk Gamay Beaujolais.

Advance Preparation

Can be prepared through step 4 up to 2 hours ahead. Reheat gently.

"The poor man's paella" and "a Mexican party dish with a Spanish ancestry" are just two descriptions given to this homey one-dish chicken and rice main course. According to Jacqueline Higuera McMahan, author of *California Rancho Cooking* (The Olive Press, 1988), *arroz con pollo* was served at large parties on the California ranches when it was not possible to barbecue outdoors.

I like to add fresh mint leaves to lightly infuse the rice and punch up the flavor. Traditionally *arroz con pollo* is served "as is," but I prefer it with salsa and a dollop of sour cream. Make your own salsa or purchase a fresh store-bought variety that is as spicy as you like. Begin with Shrimp Salsa (page 23) and serve the Arroz con Pollo with a mixed green salad. Finish with Vanilla Caramel Cream (page 318) or Orange, Almond, and Olive Oil Cake (page 302).

1 large whole skinless, boneless chicken breast
3 cups water
2 tablespoons olive oil
1 small onion, finely chopped
1½ cups long-grain rice
1 medium carrot, peeled and cut into ½-inch dice
2 tablespoons fresh lemon juice
3 large fresh mint sprigs
½ cup finely diced red bell pepper
1 cup thawed frozen baby peas
1 teaspoon salt
¼ teaspoon freshly ground black pepper

GARNISH

Fresh mint sprigs
¼ cup sour cream or plain nonfat yogurt
¼ cup homemade or store-bought tomatillo salsa (page 358) or tomato salsa (pages 357, 359, and 360)

1   Place the chicken breast in a medium saucepan and add the water. Bring to a simmer and cook for 10 minutes. Cover the pan, and remove from the heat, and let stand for 10 minutes. Remove the chicken from the pan and shred it into bite-sized pieces. Set aside the chicken and reserve the stock.

2   In a medium saucepan over medium heat, heat the oil. Add the onion and sauté for 2 to 3 minutes, or until slightly softened. Raise the heat to high and add the rice and carrot. Sauté for about 3 minutes, stirring constantly.

3   Add the reserved stock and the lemon juice to the rice mixture, stir with a fork, and bring to a boil. Reduce the heat to medium-low.

4   Add the reserved chicken, mint sprigs, and bell pepper, cover, and cook for 10 to 12 minutes, or until the rice is nearly tender. Add the peas and continue simmering until all the liquid has been absorbed and the rice is tender, about 3 minutes longer. Add the salt and pepper and taste for seasoning.

5   Remove the mint sprigs and spoon the rice mixture into a serving dish. Garnish with the fresh mint sprigs and serve with the sour cream and salsa on the side.

CRISPY ROAST CHICKEN

SERVES 4

Recommended Wine

This dish calls for an assertive red wine, specifically a Merlot, a Cabernet Sauvignon, or a Rhône varietal such as Syrah.

Advance Preparation

Can be prepared through step 2 up to 8 hours ahead, covered, and refrigerated. The roasted chicken is also excellent served cold.

Like most cooks, I've had many conversations on the proper way to roast a chicken. Some argue that roasting with the breast side down is the very best way to keep the bird moist enough, while others insist that method produces a zebra-striped bird stamped with its roasting lines. And what's the correct roasting temperature?

This controversy isn't new. In *The California Cookbook* (1946), Genevieve Callahan wrote, "I am inclined to feel that the temperature and the length of time of roasting have more bearing on juiciness than has position during roasting." I agree with her, although her recipe suggests a 325°F oven. In an "unorthodox note," Ms. Callahan mentions high–heat roasting and cites "an old Italian short time/high temperature method." This roast chicken is modeled after that old Italian technique.

I find that cooking whole chickens at 425°F keeps them juicy inside and crispy-brown on the outside. The marinade adds color and depth of flavor to the chicken and its juices.

I like to carve the chicken and spoon the vegetables and juices on top. If you want to roast a larger bird, use a 5- to 6-pound roasting chicken and increase the cooking time by 20 to 25 minutes. Watch the chicken carefully and tent with aluminum foil if it seems to be getting too brown.

This chicken is great with Soft Polenta and Sun-Dried Tomato Pesto (page 138). Begin with Peppery Greens with Gorgonzola and Pine Nuts (page 80). For dessert, try Banana Cake with Chocolate Fudge Frosting (page 326).

MARINADE

2 tablespoons whole-grain Dijon mustard

¼ cup balsamic vinegar

2 tablespoons soy sauce

3 garlic cloves, minced

¼ teaspoon freshly ground black pepper

One 3½- to 4½-pound fryer chicken, rinsed and patted dry

1 onion, sliced

2 carrots, peeled and thinly sliced

2 cups Chicken Stock (page 342)

1 To make the marinade, whisk together the ingredients in a small mixing bowl. Taste for seasoning.

2 Place the chicken in a large, nonaluminum mixing bowl. Starting around the main body cavity, carefully slip your hand under the skin, being sure not to tear it. (You may need to use gloves if you have long fingernails.) Pat the marinade under the skin and all over the bird on both sides on top of the skin. Cover the chicken and marinate for at least a few minutes and up to 8 hours in the refrigerator.

3 Preheat the oven to 425°F. Place the chicken, breast side up, on a rack in a roasting pan or on a vertical roaster. Sprinkle the onion and carrots in the bottom of the pan and add 1 cup of the stock. Roast the chicken for about 45 minutes to 1 hour, or until the juices run clear when a thigh is pierced with a knife. Halfway through the cooking, add the remaining 1 cup of chicken stock to keep the bottom of the pan from scorching. Let the chicken rest for 10 minutes before carving. Carve the chicken and arrange on a serving platter. Scrape up the juices and vegetables and pour them over the chicken pieces. Serve immediately.

GLAZED ORANGE-HOISIN CHICKEN

SERVES 4

My friend Barbara Windom is a great cook who typically produces delicious food that's short on preparation time and long on taste and presentation. Her Asian chicken can be served on a moment's notice as long as you have the ingredients in your pantry. Barbara prefers Dundee orange marmalade for this dish because it's not too sweet.

This is superb right from the oven or chilled. If it's warm, accompany with Rice Pilaf with Fresh Corn and Peanuts (page 270). If the chicken is cold, a platter of Assorted Grilled Vegetables (page 24) would be a fine accompaniment.

Recommended Wine

The strong, sweet flavors of this dish blend well with Zinfandel, Syrah, or Pinot Noir.

Advance Preparation

The chicken can be marinated for up to 2 hours, covered and refrigerated. The chicken can be roasted 1 day ahead, refrigerated, and served chilled.

MARINADE

3 tablespoons hoisin sauce

1 teaspoon chile paste with garlic

⅓ cup soy sauce

1 tablespoon honey

1 tablespoon dark sesame oil

2 tablespoons peeled and finely chopped fresh ginger

¼ cup orange marmalade, preferably Dundee

One 3½- to 4½-pound fryer chicken, rinsed, patted dry, and cut into quarters

GARNISH

2 tablespoons finely chopped scallions

Orange slices

1 To make the marinade, whisk together the hoisin sauce, chile paste, soy sauce, honey, sesame oil, and ginger in a large, nonaluminum bowl. Add the marmalade and whisk to mix well. Taste for seasoning.

2 Add the chicken quarters to the marinade and turn to coat evenly. Cover and refrigerate for at least 30 minutes and up to 2 hours, turning once or twice.

3 Preheat the oven to 425°F. Place the chicken quarters skin side up with the marinade in a large, shallow roasting pan and roast for 50 to 55 minutes, or until the chicken is golden brown and the juices run clear when a thigh is pierced with a knife. Baste it with the juices once or twice while it is roasting.

4 To serve, remove the chicken from the pan and degrease the drippings. Arrange the chicken on a large serving platter, spoon the pan juices over it, and garnish with the scallions and orange slices. Serve immediately.

Honey tangerines make their market appearance in the winter months. If you've never treated yourself to a juicy, exotic, honey tangerine, you've missed a flavor sensation. This zesty marinade is a wonderful complement to the slightly gamy flavor of the Rock Cornish hens. You can use oranges if honey tangerines are unavailable. This dish goes well with Confetti Rice Pilaf (page 269).

MARINADE

4 honey tangerines

1 tablespoon peeled and finely chopped fresh ginger

1 medium shallot, finely chopped

1 garlic clove, minced

2 tablespoons olive oil

2 tablespoons soy sauce

2 tablespoons finely chopped fresh mint

½ teaspoon salt

½ teaspoon freshly ground black pepper

6 Rock Cornish hens, rinsed, patted dry, and split in half

1 cup water

SAUCE

1 cup reserved marinade (above)

2 tablespoons heavy (whipping) cream (optional)

3 tablespoons finely chopped fresh mint

GARNISH

Tangerine or orange slices

continued on next page

ROASTED CORNISH HENS WITH HONEY-TANGERINE MARINADE

SERVES 6 TO 8

Recommended Wine

The citrus flavors of this dish are matched nicely by a crisp Chardonnay. Pinot Noir is also quite compatible.

Advance Preparation

The hens can be marinated for up to 4 hours, covered and refrigerated. The hens can be roasted up to 2 days ahead and refrigerated—they are excellent served slightly chilled.

1 To make the marinade, zest the tangerines and mince the zest. Juice 2 of the tangerines to make about 1 cup juice.

2 In a large, nonaluminum mixing bowl, combine the tangerine zest and juice with the rest of the marinade ingredients and whisk until well incorporated. Taste for seasoning. Reserve 1 cup of the marinade for the sauce.

3 Carefully separate the skin from the hens by placing your fingers gently under the skin and loosening it. (You may need to wear gloves if you have long fingernails.) Place the hens in the bowl. Massage the marinade underneath the skin. Rotate the hens until they are completely covered with the marinade. Cover and refrigerate for at least 2 hours and up to 4 hours.

4 Preheat the oven to 425°F. Remove the hens from the marinade and reserve the marinade in the bowl for basting. Arrange the hens close enough together to fit on a large roasting rack set in a large roasting pan. Pour in the water to keep the drippings from burning. Roast the hens for 35 to 45 minutes, or until golden brown, basting a few times. If some of the hens are not golden brown, put them under the broiler for a couple of minutes. Transfer the hens to a large serving platter.

5 Pour the juices from the roasting pan into a fat separator, and then transfer them to a medium saucepan. Add the 1 cup reserved marinade and bring to a boil over medium-high heat. Cook until reduced by one-fourth, about 5 minutes. Add the cream, if desired, and the mint and cook for another 3 to 4 minutes to allow the flavors to blend. Taste for seasoning.

6 Garnish the hens with the tangerine slices and serve immediately, with the sauce on the side.

It wasn't so long ago that veal scaloppine was the quick, last-minute dish that many home cooks relied on in a pinch. Now that veal is so expensive, turkey has become a healthy alternative. This Southern-style marinade is zesty and simple to prepare. If you don't have a grill handy, try a grill pan or sauté the turkey. Serve this with Rice Pilaf with Fresh Corn and Peanuts (page 270) and Fava Beans with Red Onions and Bacon (page 252).

MARINADE

2 tablespoons Dijon mustard

¼ cup fresh orange juice

1 tablespoon bourbon

1 tablespoon molasses

¼ teaspoon salt

¼ teaspoon freshly ground black pepper

1½ pounds turkey breast, cut into ½-inch slices

SAUCE

½ cup Chicken Stock (page 342)

1 tablespoon heavy (whipping) cream

GARNISH

2 tablespoons finely chopped fresh cilantro or parsley

Recommended Wine
This dish goes equally well with ripe, rich Chardonnay or Pinot Noir.

Advance Preparation
The marinade can be prepared up to 1 day ahead and refrigerated.

1 To make the marinade, whisk together the ingredients in a small mixing bowl. Place the turkey slices in a large, shallow, nonaluminum dish. Pour half of the marinade over the turkey and turn to coat evenly. Cover and refrigerate for at least 2 hours and up to 4 hours. Reserve the remaining marinade for the sauce.

2 Prepare a grill for medium-high-heat grilling. Remove the turkey slices from the marinade and grill about 3 inches from the heat for about 3 minutes on each side, or until opaque throughout. Transfer to a platter.

3 To make the sauce, pour the reserved marinade into a small saucepan and add the stock and cream. Bring to a boil over high heat, reduce the heat to a simmer, and cook for about 5 minutes, or until slightly thickened. Taste for seasoning. Pour the sauce over the turkey slices and sprinkle with the cilantro. Serve immediately.

MARINATED ROAST TURKEY

SERVES 10 TO 14

This is my favorite recipe for roast turkey because the marinade infuses into the skin and the breast meat, producing a tender, juicy bird. It is especially enjoyable for Thanksgiving. The soy and balsamic marinade forms the basis for a rich, dark sauce or gravy. Use a fat separator when draining the drippings for the gravy. If you're roasting a larger bird, just increase the marinade ingredients accordingly. You can also stuff this turkey with Corn Bread, Leek, and Red Pepper Stuffing (page 254), but it takes about an hour longer to cook when stuffed. This marinade is also excellent on a turkey breast when you don't feel like cooking the entire bird (see note). Remember to start this recipe a day ahead.

Recommended Wine

Pair this dish with Syrah, Pinot Noir, or Zinfandel.

Note

If you're roasting a turkey breast, use the same amount of marinade and roast at 325°F for 18 to 20 minutes per pound, or to an internal temperature of 170°F.

Advance Preparation

Can be prepared through step 1 up to 1 day ahead, covered, and refrigerated.

MARINADE

2 medium shallots, finely chopped

3 tablespoons balsamic vinegar

2 tablespoons soy sauce

2 tablespoons olive oil

2 tablespoons chopped fresh thyme or 2 teaspoons dried

¼ teaspoon salt

Pinch of freshly ground black pepper

One 14- to 16-pound turkey, rinsed and patted dry

1 large orange, unpeeled, sliced (if not stuffing)

1 onion, sliced (if not stuffing)

2 onions, coarsely chopped

2 carrots, peeled and sliced

2 cups Easy Brown Turkey or Chicken Stock (page 343) or Turkey or Chicken Stock (page 342), or more if needed

Rich Turkey Gravy (page 196) for serving

1   The day before you want to cook the turkey, marinate it. To make the marinade, whisk together the ingredients in a large, nonaluminum mixing bowl. Taste for seasoning. Starting around the main body cavity, carefully slip your hand under the turkey skin, being sure not to break the skin. (You may need to wear gloves if you have long fingernails.) Place the turkey in the bowl. Massage some of the marinade under the skin and pat all over the bird. Refrigerate overnight, covered with plastic wrap. Baste with the marinade a few times.

2 The next day, preheat the oven to 325°F. If you have not stuffed the turkey, place the sliced orange and sliced onion in the cavity and tie the legs together. To stuff the turkey, place the stuffing loosely in the neck and main cavity and close the flaps with skewers. Rub the marinade remaining in the bowl all over the turkey. Place the chopped onions and carrots in the bottom of a large roasting pan. Pour the stock over the vegetables. Set a nonstick roasting rack in the roasting pan and place the turkey on top, breast side up.

3 Place the turkey in the center of the oven and roast, basting about every 45 minutes with the accumulated pan juices, until a thermometer inserted into the thickest part of the thigh registers 170°F and the juices run clear. You may need to add more stock if the pan becomes too dry. A 16-pound turkey should take about 4 hours, or 5 hours if it's stuffed. Be sure to check the temperature at 30-minute intervals as the finish time approaches. A number of variables can affect the cooking time.

4 Remove the turkey from the oven and transfer to a large platter or carving board. Let the turkey rest for at least 20 minutes before carving. Discard the vegetables and set aside the pan drippings for making the gravy, using a fat separator to avoid excess fat. Carve the turkey and serve with the gravy.

TRUSSING POULTRY

The easiest way to truss poultry is to use bamboo skewers. Insert one skewer in the thigh portion of the bird all the way through and out the other side. Do the same thing in the wing portion, making sure to go all the way through the bird and out the other side with each skewer. When you're ready to serve the bird, simply push the skewers all the way out in one swift move. No fuss, no mess, and best of all, the bird still looks great.

RICH TURKEY GRAVY

MAKES ABOUT 3½ CUPS

Advance Preparation

Can be prepared through step 2 up to 2 days ahead, covered, and refrigerated. Reheat gently.

Preparing the gravy at the last minute, after the turkey comes out of the oven, can create a lot of extra pressure when you still have to put everything on the table. Try this method and have the gravy ready and waiting for the defatted pan drippings from the turkey, cutting down the last-minute work to just a few moments.

To make the process even easier, prepare your stock weeks ahead and freeze it. The intense flavor of rich brown turkey stock makes the difference between a good and a great gravy. You can add cooked giblets, mushrooms, diced chestnuts, or roasted garlic for texture and flavor twists.

½ cup unsalted butter

½ cup all-purpose flour

4 cups Easy Brown Turkey Stock (page 343), defatted and warmed

½ cup dry red wine

Salt and freshly ground black pepper

Defatted drippings from roast turkey (page 194)

OPTIONAL ENRICHMENTS (CHOOSE ONE)

½ cup cooked chopped giblets

½ cup sautéed mushrooms

½ cup diced roasted chestnuts

1 tablespoon Roasted Garlic Purée (page 353)

1   In a heavy large saucepan over medium heat, melt the butter, watching care-
    fully so it does not burn. Add the flour slowly and whisk briskly until bubbles
    form. Continue whisking for a few minutes until the mixture thickens and
    turns a golden brown color. The color of this roux is important, because it
    determines the final color of the sauce.

2   Add the stock and wine and whisk until the roux is completely blended into
    the liquid. Continue cooking the gravy over medium heat for 15 to 20 minutes,
    until it is thickened and no taste of flour remains. Add the salt and pepper
    to taste.

3   After you remove the turkey from the oven, strain the pan drippings into a
    gravy separator and pour the defatted drippings into the gravy. Warm the
    gravy over medium heat and season to taste. If desired, add one of the enrich-
    ments to the gravy.

GREAT GADGETS: THE FAT SEPARATOR

If you make a lot of soups, stock, or sauces, this gadget will be very useful. It looks
like an old-fashioned garden watering can. The spout originates at the very bottom,
and the grease rises to the top on its own when left to sit for a minute. The technique
is to pour the stock or drippings off the bottom slowly until the grease line reaches
the top of the spout hole. Then stop pouring and discard the grease.

TURKEY

VEGETABLE

COBBLER

SERVES 6

When you crave a comforting old-fashioned, home-cooked meal, look no further. This sophisticated version of pot pie includes a hefty sprinkling of mixed fresh California herbs and big chunks of turkey. A golden cobbler-style dough enriched with Parmesan crowns the top.

If you're in a hurry, use thawed small white frozen onions to save time. Fresh baby peas are at their peak in early spring; otherwise, use frozen baby peas. Reddish orange chanterelles, with their distinctive fruity, peppery, nutlike flavor, add an elegant touch. Sometimes I add a few extra ounces of dried mushrooms to give the sauce an earthier flavor. Think of this cobbler when Thanksgiving is over and you can't face another plain turkey dinner.

Recommended Wine

A rich, well-oaked Chardonnay works very well with this dish, as does a Pinot Noir or Merlot.

Advance Preparation

The cobbler can be prepared through step 7 up to 1 day ahead, covered well, and refrigerated. Bring to room temperature before baking. It can also be baked 1 day ahead, covered, and refrigerated. Bring to room temperature and reheat gently in a 325°F oven for 20 minutes, or until bubbly hot.

10 ounces fresh or thawed frozen white pearl onions
3 medium carrots, peeled and cut into large dice, or 10 ounces baby carrots
½ cup (8 tablespoons) unsalted butter
1 medium leek, white and light green parts only, cleaned and finely chopped
½ pound white mushrooms, brushed clean and cut into large dice
¼ pound fresh chanterelle, morel, cremini, or shiitake mushrooms, cut into large dice
¼ cup dried shiitake or chanterelle mushrooms, softened in boiling water and drained (optional)
1 cup cooked fresh baby peas or thawed frozen baby peas
1½ pounds cooked turkey breast, cut into large chunks (about 4 cups)
7 tablespoons all-purpose flour
2 cups warm Easy Brown Turkey or Chicken Stock (page 343) or Turkey or Chicken Stock (page 342)
1 cup warm half-and-half
¼ teaspoon salt
¼ teaspoon freshly ground white pepper
2 tablespoons finely chopped fresh flat-leaf parsley
2 tablespoons finely chopped fresh chives
1 teaspoon finely chopped fresh thyme
1 tablespoon finely chopped fresh winter savory (optional)

1¾ cups all-purpose flour

1 tablespoon baking powder

½ teaspoon salt

4 tablespoons freshly grated Parmesan cheese

6 tablespoons frozen unsalted butter, cut into small pieces

½ cup heavy (whipping) cream

1 large egg, beaten

1. If you're using fresh onions, submerge them in a saucepan of boiling water for 30 seconds, then rinse in cold water. Trim off the fuzzy portion of the roots, being sure not to cut the roots off completely. Remove the outside skin and the first layer of the onions with your fingers. Cut a shallow X into the root end of each onion so they will cook evenly and not burst. Bring a medium saucepan of water to a boil and simmer the onions for 10 minutes, or until slightly tender when pierced with a fork. Drain and set aside in a large mixing bowl. If you're using thawed frozen onions, set aside in a large mixing bowl.

2. Add the carrots to a saucepan of boiling water and simmer for about 7 minutes, or until crisp-tender. Drain and add the carrots to the bowl with the onions.

3. In a medium skillet over medium heat, melt 2 tablespoons of the butter. Add the leeks and sauté for about 3 minutes. Add all the mushrooms and sauté for 3 more minutes. Add the leeks and mushrooms along with the cooking juices to the other vegetables in the bowl. Add the peas and turkey chunks to the vegetables and set aside.

4. Melt the remaining 6 tablespoons butter in a large saucepan over medium heat. Sprinkle in the flour and cook, stirring constantly, for 3 minutes. Slowly add the stock, half-and-half, salt, and white pepper and whisk the sauce until thickened and smooth. Add the herbs and pour over the turkey and vegetable mixture and mix well. Taste for seasoning.

5. Preheat the oven to 400°F. Butter a deep 9-by-13-inch baking dish. Pour the turkey mixture into the dish.

continued on next page

6 To make the dough, combine the flour, baking powder, salt, and 3 tablespoons of the Parmesan in a food processor fitted with the metal blade. Add the frozen butter and process until all the flour is incorporated. With the machine running, add the cream and process until the dough forms a ball.

7 Roll out the dough to fit the top of the dish, or drop spoonfuls of dough on top of the turkey mixture, distributing them evenly. Brush the dough with the egg and sprinkle the remaining 1 tablespoon Parmesan evenly over the top. Place the cobbler on a baking sheet.

8 Bake for 30 to 35 minutes, or until the crust is nicely browned, checking during the last few minutes to make sure it does not burn. Serve immediately.

Bruce Aidells, sausage-maker extraordinaire, suggested that I use a combination of fresh and dried apples to give this chicken sausage a concentrated apple flavor. Fresh tarragon is a savory option. This sausage is delicious for breakfast or brunch. It's also an excellent foundation for Thanksgiving stuffing. Apples have residual sugar, so the sausages tend to burn when cooked over high heat. Remember to start this recipe a day ahead.

3 pounds boneless chicken legs and thighs

½ cup cold water

2 cups peeled, cored, and diced pippin apples, cut into ¼-inch pieces (about 2 medium apples)

1 cup chopped dried apples, soaked in ½ cup hot water for 20 minutes, squeezed dry, and finely chopped

2 teaspoons salt

1½ teaspoons freshly ground black pepper

½ teaspoon ground coriander

¼ teaspoon freshly grated nutmeg

1 to 2 teaspoons finely chopped fresh tarragon or ½ teaspoon dried (optional)

1   Remove the chicken skin and finely mince it. Cut the chicken meat into ¾-inch cubes. In a food processor fitted with the metal blade, process the meat and skin in small batches, about 1 pound at a time, by pulsing on and off until a fine texture is achieved. *Do not overprocess.* It should be slightly chunky, not a purée. Place the chicken mixture in a large mixing bowl.

2   Add the remaining ingredients to the chicken and mix together. Knead by hand until well blended.

3   Turn out the chicken mixture onto a 22-inch-long sheet of wax paper. Using 2 rubber spatulas, smooth the mixture into a long sausage shape, about 2 inches in diameter, extending it to within 2 inches of each end of the paper. Fold the paper ends up and roll the paper around the sausage. Place the sausage on a baking sheet, seam side down. Refrigerate overnight.

4   To cook, slice the sausage into ½-inch-thick slices and either sauté in a combination of oil and unsalted butter, or cut into 1½- to 2-inch slices and grill over a medium-heat fire until browned on all sides, 2 to 3 minutes each side. Serve immediately.

Recommended Wine

On their own, these sausages combine well with Chardonnay. When among other dishes, other wines—Pinot Noir, Zinfandel, Merlot, or even Cabernet Sauvignon—might be appropriate.

Advance Preparation

The sausage can be prepared through step 3 up to 3 days ahead and refrigerated, tightly wrapped. It can also be frozen for up to 2 months. If freezing the sausage, divide into 4 portions so you can thaw a small amount for each occasion. Thaw before cooking.

Making Poultry Sausage

Sausages have become a big business in California. They're available not only in supermarkets but also at baseball games, at specialty fast-food restaurants, and from carts on the street. You can find just about any variety imaginable. But sometimes I feel like making my own—they're really not difficult to make. You don't have to put sausages in a casing, just form them into logs or patties.

Bruce Aidells, Berkeley cookbook author and owner of the famous Aidells Sausage Company, suggests making a large quantity of poultry sausage at once, since you can freeze it for future use at a moment's notice. Be sure, however, to freeze these sausages in small batches so they can be thawed for individual servings. Both of the sausage recipes here can be halved, if you prefer.

A meat grinder gives the best texture, but since most home cooks don't have one, a food processor does a good job. These recipes use boneless chicken or turkey legs and thighs as the primary ingredients. The poultry skin is used instead of the customary pork fat to keep the sausage moist. Remove the skin and mince it before it goes into the food processor to avoid having large pieces of skin in the mixture, which the food processor cannot break down. When time is at a premium, you can simply sauté or grill either of these sausages as you would a hamburger.

These sausages are great served like hamburgers on your favorite rolls, sautéed and sprinkled on pizza, or added to pasta sauce. The anchovies and capers lend a Mediterranean taste that works well with the simple but distinctive turkey flavor. Keep these in your freezer wrapped in single layers of aluminum foil, for easy access.

TURKEY SAUSAGES WITH SUN-DRIED TOMATOES

MAKES 3 POUNDS OR ABOUT

FOURTEEN 4-OUNCE PATTIES;

SERVES 6 TO 8

3 pounds boneless turkey thighs

¾ cup drained chopped oil-packed sun-dried tomatoes

1 tablespoon anchovy paste

1 tablespoon capers, well drained and rinsed

2 teaspoons salt

1½ teaspoons freshly ground black pepper

¼ cup finely chopped fresh basil or 2 tablespoons dried

1 tablespoon finely chopped fresh thyme or 1½ teaspoons dried

½ cup Zinfandel or Merlot

1   Remove the turkey skin and finely mince. Cut the turkey meat into ¾-inch cubes. In a food processor fitted with the metal blade, process the meat, the skin, and half of the sun-dried tomatoes in small batches, about 1 pound at a time, by pulsing on and off until a fine texture is achieved. *Do not overprocess.* It should be slightly chunky, not a purée. Place the turkey mixture in a large mixing bowl.

2   Add the remaining ingredients to the turkey mixture and mix together. Knead by hand until well blended. Shape into the desired-size patties. Separate with layers of wax paper and refrigerate.

3   Prepare a grill for medium-heat grilling. Grill the sausage patties about 3 inches from the heat for 4 to 6 minutes on a side, depending on their size. Or, cook the patties in a skillet with a bit of olive oil. Serve immediately.

Recommended Wine
Try a fruity young red such as a Zinfandel or Merlot with this sausage.

Advance Preparation
The sausages can be prepared through step 2 up to 3 days ahead and refrigerated, tightly wrapped. They can also be frozen for up to 2 months.

206 Grilled Skirt Steak with Avocado-Tomato Salsa

209 Grilled Roast Beef with Shallot-Chive Sauce

211 Grilled Flank Steak with Smoky Salsa

212 Grilled Steaks with Olivada and Port Wine Sauce

214 Brisket of Beef with Sun-Dried Tomatoes, Zinfandel, and Thyme

217 Grilled Lamb Chops with Cranberry-Rosemary Marinade

218 Rack of Lamb with Mint Crust

220 Lamb Brochettes with Raita

222 Indonesian Leg of Lamb

224 Lamb Stew with Dates and Zinfandel

226 Panfried Noodles with Vegetables

228 Grilled Veal Chops with Zucchini-Corn Relish

230 Light Meatballs with Double-Tomato Herb Sauce

232 Veal Stew with Orange Sauce

234 Braised Stuffed Shoulder of Veal

237 Sautéed Pork Medallions with Mustard-Herb Sauce

238 Loin of Pork with Dried Fruits and Gewürztraminer

240 Asian Glazed Pork Tenderloin

MEAT

GRILLED SKIRT STEAK WITH AVOCADO-TOMATO SALSA

SERVES 6

Recommended Wine
The lively, spicy flavors of the salsa are surprisingly compatible with a soft, well-rounded Cabernet Sauvignon or Merlot.

Note
When working with chiles, always wear rubber gloves; wash the cutting surface and knife immediately. The tortillas can be warmed right on a grill or on a gas burner for 30 seconds on each side, using tongs to turn them. Keep the tortillas warm by wrapping them in heavy napkins and placing them in a basket.

This Mexican-style dish is perfect for parties or for a last-minute dinner. Skirt steak should be purchased in long strips, rather than rolled up, for this recipe. This particular tasty cut of beef is used frequently in Latin cooking.

If you have the time, make your own tortillas or scout out good fresh ones at a Mexican market or restaurant. Begin with Griddled Quesadillas with Caramelized Onions, Chicken, and Jack Cheese (page 37) and serve Vanilla Caramel Cream (page 318) for dessert.

MARINADE

2 tablespoons olive oil

½ cup fresh lime juice (from about 8 limes)

1 garlic clove, minced

½ small onion, thinly sliced

¼ teaspoon salt

¼ teaspoon freshly ground black pepper

2 pounds skirt steak

SALSA

1 large tomato, peeled, seeded, and finely chopped

1 medium ripe avocado, pitted, peeled, and finely chopped

2 tablespoons finely chopped red onion

2 tablespoons finely chopped fresh cilantro

1 jalapeño chile, seeded and finely chopped (see note) or 1 tablespoon (or to taste) store-bought spicy green salsa

1 tablespoon fresh lemon juice

½ teaspoon salt

¼ teaspoon freshly ground black pepper

12 medium Corn Tortillas (page 281), warmed (see note)

1 To make the marinade, combine all the ingredients in a large, nonaluminum mixing bowl and whisk to combine. Taste for seasoning. Place the skirt steak in the mixing bowl, being sure to flatten it out, and turn to coat all sides evenly with the marinade. Refrigerate, covered, for at least 2 hours and up to 4 hours.

2 Meanwhile, to make the salsa, toss together the ingredients in a medium serving bowl. Taste for seasoning. Set aside.

3 Prepare a grill for medium-heat grilling. Remove the steak and the onion slices from the marinade and grill about 3 inches from the heat for 4 to 6 minutes on each side for medium-rare. Grill the onion slices, making sure that they don't fall through the grill, until they are lightly charred and soft. Arrange the steak and onions on a carving platter and thinly slice the meat on the diagonal. Serve with the salsa and the warmed tortillas.

Advance Preparation
Can be prepared through step 2 up to 4 hours ahead, covered, and refrigerated.

Chile Peppers

Mexico's influence on California cooking is apparent from our extensive use of fresh and dried chiles that add depth and complexity to many dishes and marinades. There are those who like their food hot and spicy, but even people who don't enjoy hot food often appreciate a hint of chile flavoring.

Don't forget to wear rubber gloves when preparing chiles, and be sure to remove all interior ribs and seeds, where much of the heat resides. The volatility of chile oil should not be underestimated—some people are much more sensitive to it than others.

Some Common Chiles

Anaheim

From 6 to 8 inches long and tapering from a narrow base, the Anaheim is the mildest of the chiles (although occasionally it can be surprisingly hot) and turns from pale green to dark green to red as it ripens. Fresh Anaheim chiles are very popular for stuffing. They are also available canned.

Jalapeño (Chipotle When Dried and Smoked)

This bright green, 1½-inch-long pepper is hot to very hot and is one of the most commonly used and most versatile peppers. It is available canned or fresh and is sometimes seen in its bright red state. Some jalapeños are smoked and dried to make chipotle peppers, usually only available canned in the United States. The chipotle's distinctive smoky flavor is well worth seeking out at a specialty market, where you will find it canned with garlic, tomatoes, and vinegar and labeled *chipotles en adobo*. Purée the chipotles in a food processor and store the paste in the refrigerator; it will keep for up to 2 months. A little touch of chipotle purée enlivens many dishes.

Poblano (Ancho When Dried)

From 3 to 5 inches long with a very wide base, the dark green poblano (sometimes called a *pasilla*) is also used for stuffing. Its hotness can range from mild to medium. The dried form, called the *ancho*, is commonly used in Mexican cooking. Ancho chiles should always be toasted briefly over high heat in a skillet and then covered with boiling water to soften them before using.

Serrano

This little pepper packs an awful lot of punch for its size, which is just over 1 inch long and very slender. These bright green chiles turn red as they ripen and are usually very hot. This is the chile for true aficionados; serrano chiles should be used sparingly by those unfamiliar with their power.

Peeling Chiles

The poblano and Anaheim chiles need to be peeled. Select firm-fleshed, thick-skinned chile peppers so they will retain their texture when grilled or broiled. Place the chiles in a broiler pan or on a grill and broil or grill about 4 inches from the heat until the skin is blistered and slightly charred on all sides. Always use long tongs to turn the peppers. Never pierce the peppers, or the juices will escape. Put the peppers in a brown paper bag and close it tightly. Let the peppers rest for 10 minutes. Remove the peppers from the bag and drain the peppers. Peel off the skin with your fingers, being sure to use rubber gloves to protect yourself from the fiery resins. Make a slit in each chile and open it up. Core the chiles and cut off the stems. Scrape the seeds and ribs from the chiles and cut into the desired-size pieces. If you're in a pinch and don't have kitchen gloves, cover your hands in cooking oil to protect them.

For barbecued beef, my favorite cut is the triangle tip roast, sometimes called bottom sirloin or tri-tip. It is in fact triangular and is marbled for flavorful cooking on the grill. This simple shallot-chive sauce is a refreshing accompaniment whether the meat is served hot or at room temperature. Serve with Pasta with Tomatoes, Basil, and Balsamic Vinaigrette (page 128). For dessert, consider Glazed Lemon–Sour Cream Cake (page 304).

GRILLED ROAST BEEF WITH SHALLOT-CHIVE SAUCE

SERVES 4 TO 6

MARINADE

2 garlic cloves, minced

1 medium shallot, finely chopped

1 tablespoon fresh lemon juice

2 tablespoons olive oil

¼ teaspoon freshly ground black pepper

½ teaspoon salt

One 2-pound triangle tip roast

SHALLOT-CHIVE SAUCE

1 medium shallot, finely chopped

1 tablespoon finely chopped fresh chives

2 tablespoons fresh lemon juice

¼ cup olive oil

¼ teaspoon Hot Pepper Oil (page 356), or to taste

½ teaspoon salt

¼ teaspoon freshly ground white pepper

GARNISH

Snipped fresh chives

Recommended Wine

This beefy dish is compatible with virtually every full- to medium-bodied red wine: Cabernet Sauvignon, Merlot, Zinfandel or Syrah.

continued on next page

Note

If you're using a charcoal grill without a lid, cook the meat over a medium fire and turn every 5 to 7 minutes.

Advance Preparation

Can be prepared up to 1 day ahead and refrigerated, if the beef is to be served chilled. Bring the sauce to room temperature 1 hour before serving. If you're serving the meat hot, the sauce can be prepared 1 day ahead and the meat can be marinated up to 1 day ahead and refrigerated.

1 To make the marinade, combine the ingredients in a small mixing bowl and whisk to combine. Place the beef in a shallow, nonaluminum dish and turn to coat evenly. Cover and refrigerate for 4 hours; turn several times to make sure the marinade covers all the meat.

2 Meanwhile, make the sauce: combine all the ingredients in a small mixing bowl and whisk together until well blended. Taste for seasoning. Cover and set aside.

3 Prepare a grill with a lid (see note) for medium-high-heat grilling. Remove the beef from marinade and grill about 3 inches from the heat for about 3 minutes on each side. Move to a medium-heat area of the grill. Cover the grill and grill for about 10 minutes longer on each side, until an instant-read thermometer registers 135°F for rare, 145°F for medium-rare. Let rest for 10 minutes.

4 If the meat is to be served hot, heat the sauce gently over medium heat while you slice the beef on the diagonal about ¼ inch thick. Overlap the slices on a platter, pour a little warmed sauce over the meat, and garnish the platter with the snipped chives. To serve chilled, let the beef cool to room temperature, then refrigerate until well chilled. Slice and serve with the sauce at room temperature on the side.

A smoky tomato salsa and beer make up both the marinade and the sauce for this quick and tasty main course. It's best to marinate flank steak and then cook it quickly to achieve a robust flavor and tender texture. Cut the steak across the grain for best results. Serve these flank steak slices accompanied by warm Corn Tortillas (page 281), sour cream, Smoky Salsa (page 360), and Green Pea Guacamole (page 33).

GRILLED FLANK STEAK WITH SMOKY SALSA

SERVES 4 TO 6

---

1 cup Smoky Salsa (page 360)

1 cup full-bodied beer

1½ pounds flank steak

1 Combine ½ cup of the salsa and ¾ cup of the beer in a medium mixing bowl and mix until well blended. Flatten out the flank steak in a large, shallow, nonaluminum dish. Pour the marinade over it and refrigerate, covered, for at least 2 hours and up to 24 hours; the longer, the more tender.

2 In a small serving bowl, combine the remaining ½ cup salsa and ¼ cup beer for the sauce and mix together. Taste for seasoning.

3 Prepare a grill for medium-heat grilling. Remove the steak from the marinade and grill about 3 inches from the heat for 5 to 7 minutes on each side for medium-rare. Transfer to a carving platter and thinly slice across the grain. Serve immediately with the sauce.

Recommended Wine

The strong flavors in this dish need to be paired with a wine that has power and depth but not much subtlety. It goes well with Zinfandel, Petite Sirah, big and youthful Cabernet Sauvignons, and Rhône varieties.

Advance Preparation

Can be prepared through step 2 up to 1 day ahead and refrigerated.

GRILLED STEAKS WITH OLIVADA AND PORT WINE SAUCE

SERVES 4

Earthy olive paste offers a Mediterranean twist to grilled steaks that are also complemented by a slightly sweet port wine sauce. The first time I tasted this, at Campanile Restaurant in Los Angeles, a large entrecôte section of beef was served in a rustic presentation. At home, New York steaks work best on the grill, served attractively in overlapping slices.

Simple techniques for reducing the sauce and grilling the steak make this a dish that even the beginner cook can accomplish with finesse—a good thing, because this is a wonderful dinner-party dish. You can easily double the recipe.

Olivada, or olive paste, is available at specialty-food stores, or you can make your own: 25 pitted Niçoise olives puréed with 1 tablespoon olive oil in a food processor makes 3 tablespoons of olive paste.

Serve the steaks with White Bean Stew with Spinach and Tomatoes (page 253), Oven-Roasted Potatoes with Parmesan (page 262), or Roasted Winter Vegetables (page 247) for dinner on a cold night. Follow with Essencia Zabaglione with Fresh Fruit Compote (page 299) and biscotti.

Recommended Wine

This is an aggressively flavored dish that goes very nicely with Zinfandel, Syrah, Merlot, or a young Cabernet Sauvignon.

Advance Preparation

The sauce can be prepared up to 4 hours ahead and refrigerated. Reheat gently over low heat.

SAUCE

1 tablespoon unsalted butter

2 medium shallots, finely chopped

½ cup dry red wine

½ cup port wine

1 cup Easy Brown Veal Stock (page 344) or beef stock

2 tablespoons heavy (whipping) cream

¼ teaspoon salt

1 teaspoon freshly cracked black pepper

4 New York steaks, each about ¾ inch thick

Salt and freshly ground black pepper

2 tablespoons black olivada, store-bought or homemade (see recipe introduction)

GARNISH

Fresh watercress or parsley sprigs

1   To make the sauce, melt the butter in a heavy, medium saucepan over medium heat. Add the shallots and sauté until softened, 3 to 5 minutes. Add the red wine and port, raise the heat to high, and cook until reduced by one-half to a syrupy glaze. Add the stock and reduce by a one-fourth or until the sauce barely coats the back of a spoon. Add the cream and reduce for another few minutes, until the sauce coats the spoon. Add the salt and cracked pepper and taste for seasoning. Set aside.

2   Prepare a grill for medium-high-heat grilling or preheat the broiler. Grill or broil the steaks about 3 inches from the heat for about 4 to 5 minutes on each side, or until browned but still rare. Place the steaks on a carving platter, season lightly with salt and pepper, and spread the top of each steak with a thin coat of the olivada. Cut the steaks into ½-inch-thick slices. Spoon some sauce onto a serving plate and place the steak slices, slightly overlapping, on top. Garnish with the herb sprigs and serve immediately.

OLIVADA

Use this luscious olive paste:

- spread on Parmesan Toasts (page 274).
- added to mashed potatoes.
- to flavor your favorite vinaigrette.
- spread on chicken breasts and roast at a high heat to create a crust.
- added to a tomato pasta sauce.
- added to sour cream, red onion, and capers to top corn cakes or pizza.
- added to steamed vegetables.
- added to garlic mayonnaise.

BRISKET OF BEEF WITH SUN-DRIED TOMATOES, ZINFANDEL, AND THYME

SERVES 6 TO 8

Recommended Wine

Although most red wines will go nicely with this dish, I recommend sticking with the wine used in the recipe: full-bodied Zinfandel.

Advance Preparation

Can be prepared up to 1 day ahead. Place in an ovenproof serving dish, cover, and refrigerate. Remove from the refrigerator 1 hour before reheating. Reheat in a 350°F oven for ½ hour before serving.

This dish makes a wonderful alternative to the simple family brisket served during the Jewish holidays. Based on a traditional pot roast recipe, this brisket brings together California ingredients in a sauce that tastes lighter than the usual standby but is still flavorful and hearty. Don't forget to start this a day ahead.

Large plastic cooking bags work extremely well for long braises because they lock in moisture and slowly tenderize the meat. You can also cook the brisket in a roasting pan with a cover. I prefer using the flat, or "first," cut of brisket, which is a bit more expensive but has a much lower fat content. When braised, it becomes very tender. Serve with Crispy Potato Pancakes with Vegetables (page 259) and a simple green vegetable.

One 4- to 5-pound first-cut brisket

MARINADE

3 carrots, peeled and thinly sliced

1 large onion, thinly sliced

2 celery ribs, thinly sliced

3 garlic cloves, minced

1½ ounces dry-packed sun-dried tomatoes, softened in boiling water for 10 minutes and drained

½ teaspoon salt

¼ teaspoon freshly ground black pepper

1 cup full-bodied Zinfandel

2 tablespoons all-purpose flour

2 large tomatoes, peeled, seeded, and diced

2 cups Easy Brown Veal Stock (page 344) or beef stock

1 teaspoon fresh thyme leaves or ½ teaspoon dried

½ cup full-bodied Zinfandel

2 tablespoons olive oil

1 pound mushrooms, brushed clean and sliced

1 teaspoon salt

¼ teaspoon freshly ground black pepper

2 garlic cloves, minced

½ cup full-bodied Zinfandel

1 teaspoon finely chopped fresh thyme leaves or ½ teaspoon dried

¼ cup finely chopped fresh flat-leaf parsley

GARNISH

2 tablespoons finely chopped parsley

1 In a large plastic storage container or a large, nonaluminum pan, place the brisket fat side down. To make the marinade, scatter the carrots, onion, celery, garlic, and sun-dried tomatoes around the meat. Sprinkle the brisket with the salt and pepper and pour the 1 cup Zinfandel over it. Cover the dish and refrigerate overnight. Turn the meat over at least once to distribute the marinade ingredients evenly.

2 Preheat the oven to 325°F. Sprinkle the flour into a large plastic cooking bag. Place the meat, marinade ingredients, fresh tomatoes, stock, thyme, and the ½ cup Zinfandel in the bag and close with the tie. Be sure to make slits in the bag for even cooking. Place the bag in a large, heavy-duty roasting pan. (You can also cook it directly in the roasting pan.) Roast for 3 to 4 hours, checking for tenderness after 3 hours. The meat should be very tender.

3 While the meat is cooking, begin making the sauce: Heat the oil in a medium sauté pan over medium heat. Add the mushrooms and sauté for about 5 minutes, until softened, draining off and reserving the excess juice. When the mushrooms are cooked, add the salt, pepper, garlic, ½ cup Zinfandel, and thyme. Raise the heat to high and boil for 2 to 3 minutes, or until the alcohol burns off. Set aside.

continued on next page

4 When the meat is done, remove it from the oven and let cool. To finish the sauce, transfer the braising liquid and vegetables to a large saucepan or a food processor fitted with the metal blade. Purée the sauce in the pan using an immersion blender or in the food processor, being sure to leave a slight texture. Return to the pan if necessary. Add the mushroom mixture, the reserved mushroom juices, and the parsley and bring to a simmer over medium heat. If the sauce is too thick, add a bit of veal or beef stock. Taste for seasoning.

5 Place the brisket on a carving board. Slice the meat across the grain into ½-inch slices. Arrange the slices overlapping on a serving platter, and pour the sauce over the meat. Garnish with the parsley and serve immediately.

FRESH TOMATOES VS. CANNED TOMATOES

For tomato sauce or recipes in which the tomatoes are cooked, you'll frequently get a better result using canned tomatoes if fresh tomatoes are not in their prime. Look for the organic canned variety that has extra flavor and a deep red color. These tomatoes have been packed at the peak of their ripeness and will give off more flavor than an unripened fresh tomato. If you need fresh uncooked tomatoes, skip the recipe until tomatoes are in season.

The relatively exotic combination of lamb with pomegranate juice was a favorite in California rancho kitchens in the early 1800s. The pomegranate juice may have been intended to mask the strong-flavored lamb produced on the ranches in those days. Pomegranate juice can be difficult to find, so I experimented with cranberry juice and came up with this last-minute marinade fragrant with fresh rosemary and garlic.

This quick entrée has been a life saver when I'm in a hurry and want something a bit out of the ordinary. Begin with La Scala Chopped Salad (page 77) and serve the lamb with Confetti Rice Pilaf (page 269).

MARINADE

1 garlic clove, peeled

1 shallot, peeled

1 tablespoon finely chopped fresh rosemary or 1½ teaspoons dried

½ cup cranberry juice cocktail

¼ cup full-bodied red wine such as Merlot or Cabernet Sauvignon

2 tablespoons olive oil

¼ teaspoon salt

Pinch of freshly ground black pepper

8 thick French rib lamb chops, about ¾ inch thick

GARNISH

Fresh rosemary leaves

Fresh cranberries (optional)

Recommended Wine

Ordinarily, Cabernet Sauvignon is the ideal wine for lamb, but the sweetness of the cranberry juice in the marinade suggests a fruitier wine such as Sangiovese, Pinot Noir, or Syrah.

Advance Preparation

Can be prepared through step 2 up to 4 hours ahead, covered, and refrigerated.

1   To make the marinade, in a food processor fitted with the metal blade, finely chop the garlic and shallot. Add the rosemary, cranberry juice, wine, oil, salt, and pepper. Process until well blended. Taste for seasoning.

2   Arrange the lamb chops in a large, shallow, nonaluminum dish. Pour the marinade over the lamb chops and turn to coat evenly. Refrigerate, covered, for at least 30 minutes and up to 4 hours.

3   Prepare a grill for medium-high-heat grilling. Remove the lamb chops from the marinade and grill 3 inches from the heat for 5 to 7 minutes on each side for medium-rare, depending on their thickness. Place 2 lamb chops on each serving plate. Garnish with the rosemary and the cranberries, if desired. Serve immediately.

RACK OF LAMB WITH MINT CRUST

SERVES 4 TO 6

After I finished training at the Cordon Bleu in London, I had a beginner's repertoire of classic dishes that I could prepare with panache. Rack of lamb *persillade* was a favorite among them. This adaptation adds the complementary flavor of fresh mint to the typical crispy bread topping. A standard brown sauce is enriched with a mint-flavored, nutty, roasted garlic purée.

Rack of lamb is a wonderful company dish. For a pretty presentation, criss-cross the ends of the lamb chops and surround them with some sauce. Begin with Smoked Salmon and Caviar Torta (page 18) and serve the lamb with Grilled Polenta with Confit of Red Onions and Prosciutto (page 140). For dessert, try Mango and Macadamia Nut Brown-Butter Tart (page 312).

Recommended Wine

Here is a great opportunity to roll out your best well-aged Cabernet Sauvignons or Merlots. This lamb dish is an ideal foil for these complex wines, especially if they have some eucalyptus/mint character.

Note

If you use a larger rack of lamb, increase the cooking time. Test the temperature every few minutes.

Advance Preparation

Can be prepared through step 2 up to 6 hours ahead, covered, and refrigerated. Gently reheat the sauce.

SAUCE

1 large head of garlic

1 teaspoon olive oil

5 fresh mint leaves

1 cup Easy Brown Veal Stock (page 344) or beef stock

1 teaspoon Dijon mustard

2 tablespoons dry red wine

1 tablespoon heavy (whipping) cream

1 tablespoon unsalted butter, softened

1 tablespoon finely chopped fresh mint leaves

¼ teaspoon salt

⅛ teaspoon freshly ground black pepper

2 racks of lamb (8 chops or about 3 pounds each), trimmed of excess fat and meat scraped 1½ inches up on each bone (have the butcher do this for you)

1 cup fresh French bread crumbs

2 medium shallots, finely chopped

2 tablespoons finely chopped fresh mint

2 tablespoons finely chopped fresh parsley

¼ teaspoon salt

⅛ teaspoon freshly ground black pepper

3 tablespoons olive oil

2 tablespoons Chicken Stock (page 342)

Fresh mint leaves

1   To make the sauce, preheat the oven to 425°F. Cut a piece of aluminum foil to fit a whole head of garlic. With a sharp knife, cut off the top of the head to expose the cloves, then score it gently, just cutting through a few layers of the papery skin, all around the diameter. Pull off all the loose skin from the top half, trying not to remove every shred. (This will make it easier to squeeze out the cooked cloves later.) Place the garlic head in the center of the foil, drizzle the oil over it, and surround the garlic with the mint leaves. Bake for 1 hour, or until the cloves are very soft. Let cool. Squeeze the garlic pulp with your fingers into a small ramekin.

2   In a medium saucepan over a medium-high heat, combine the garlic pulp, veal stock, mustard, wine, and cream. Bring to a boil and cook until reduced by one-fourth. Swirl in the butter and add the chopped mint, salt, and pepper. Taste for seasoning and set aside.

3   Preheat the oven to 450°F. Place the racks of lamb in a roasting pan, bone side down, and roast for 20 to 25 minutes, depending on their size, for medium-rare, or until an instant-read thermometer inserted into the thickest part of the lamb registers 135°F. Let the lamb rest for 5 minutes. Drain off all the fat in the roasting pan.

4   While the meat is roasting, combine the bread crumbs, shallots, herbs, salt, pepper, olive oil, and chicken stock in a small bowl and mix well.

5   Preheat the broiler. Spread the bread crumb mixture evenly on the meat side of the racks. Place the lamb under the broiler until it is lightly browned, 2 to 3 minutes. Be careful not to let it burn. Meanwhile, gently reheat the sauce.

6   To serve, place the racks on a serving or carving platter and slice by cutting between the bones. Serve 2 or 3 chops per person, garnished with the mint leaves, and pass the sauce on the side.

LAMB BROCHETTES WITH RAITA

SERVES 4 TO 6

Cooling minted yogurt sauce, an Indian staple condiment called raita, functions as both a marinade that tenderizes the meat and a crunchy, refreshing sauce to serve on the side. Serve the brochettes on a bed of Tomato-Mint Bulgur (page 267).

MARINADE AND SAUCE

2 cups plain nonfat yogurt

2 tablespoons finely chopped fresh mint

1 garlic clove, minced

¼ cup fresh orange juice

⅛ teaspoon ground cumin

½ teaspoon salt

Pinch of freshly ground white pepper

2 pounds boneless lamb loin, cut into 2-inch cubes

½ medium English (hothouse) cucumber, finely chopped

1 To make the marinade and sauce, in a bowl, combine the ingredients and mix well. Taste for seasoning. Place the lamb in a medium, nonaluminum bowl and pour ¾ cup of the marinade over it, mixing to coat the meat evenly. Reserve the remaining yogurt mixture for the sauce. Refrigerate, covered, for at least 30 minutes and up to 8 hours.

2 Preheat the broiler or prepare a grill for medium-high-heat grilling. Thread the lamb on metal skewers. Cook the brochettes about 3 inches from the heat, turning a few times and basting with the marinade, until the meat is browned and done as desired, 15 to 20 minutes.

3 Stir the cucumber into the reserved yogurt mixture.

4 Place the brochettes on serving plates and pass the minted yogurt sauce at the table.

Recommended Wine

The creamy, tangy character of the yogurt suggests a young red, such as a Zinfandel, Pinot Noir, or Syrah.

Advance Preparation

Can be prepared through step 1 up to 8 hours ahead, covered, and refrigerated.

Marinades

Marinades are an important technique in California cooking because they add flavor to whatever you're cooking, with minimum effort and without masking the natural flavor of the food.

Most marinades are a combination of an acid, such as citrus juice, vinegar, wine, or even yogurt, and vegetable or olive oil. Spices, herbs, and mustards are often added for distinctive flavor. Add a minimum of salt since it can toughen the meat. I like to use a ratio of 2 parts acid to 1 part oil. Let the marinade rest for a few minutes to allow the flavors to develop. Use glass, porcelain, or enamel for marinating since aluminum will give the food a metallic taste. Be sure all surfaces of the food are covered with the marinade.

Some General Rules

- Meats can be marinated for up to 24 hours without changing their texture.

- Generally, poultry needs a shorter time, up to 6 hours. Fish should never be marinated for more than 2 hours if there is a high acid content to the marinade.

- If you are marinating food in the refrigerator, remove it ½ hour before grilling so that it can come to room temperature before cooking.

- Use the marinade to baste during cooking to give it extra moisture and flavor.

- Don't forget about marinating vegetables, which are particularly good grilled. Marinate vegetables for 30 minutes to 4 hours.

- Pastes or herb coatings are another type of marinade. Plan on spreading the paste on the meat, poultry, or seafood up to 4 hours ahead of cooking. Pastes that contain little acid can marinate for up to 8 hours.

Here are a few pastes that are delicious on meat, chicken, or fish.

- Sun-dried tomato, garlic, basil, capers, and olive oil

- Rosemary, thyme, garlic, shallots, olive oil, and fresh lemon juice

- Dijon mustard, orange zest, balsamic vinegar, and chives

- Hoisin sauce, scallions, dark sesame oil, and ginger

INDONESIAN LEG OF LAMB

SERVES 8 TO 10

I first tasted a version of this leg of lamb at Chef Mark Ellman's restaurant Avalon in Maui. The restaurant is long gone, but the recipe lives on. This scrumptious dish is a good choice for a dinner party. Boned and butterflied leg of lamb works nicely for barbecuing. Ask your butcher to pound the lamb into a uniform thickness so it will cook evenly.

Star anise, the star-shaped spice from China, is included for its slight licorice flavor. If you have the time, marinate the lamb overnight so it can soak up the exotic flavors. While I suggest reducing the marinade with a bit of stock as a sauce, you can also just serve the sliced lamb as is, drizzled with the juices from the carving board.

Begin with Asian Gravlax with Ginger-Mustard Sauce (page 20) and accompany the lamb with Confetti Rice Pilaf (page 269) or Rice Pilaf with Fresh Corn and Peanuts (page 270). Try Tiramisu with Toasted Hazelnuts and Chocolate (page 316) for dessert. Since the leg is a large portion, I usually have some left over. Little cubes of this full-flavored lamb are a great addition to Panfried Noodles with Vegetables (page 226).

Recommended Wine

The forward, spicy flavors of this dish require a full-bodied red wine. I have found it does best with Zinfandel, Petite Sirah, Syrah, or other Rhône varieties.

Note

If you're using a charcoal grill without a lid, cook the meat over a medium fire and turn every 5 to 7 minutes.

Advance Preparation

The marinade can be prepared up to 2 days ahead and refrigerated. The meat can be marinated for up to 24 hours, covered and refrigerated.

MARINADE

¼ cup soy sauce

¼ cup sake

2 tablespoons honey

1 tablespoon crushed star anise

2 tablespoons peeled and minced fresh ginger

2 tablespoons minced garlic

1 tablespoon dark sesame oil

⅓ cup finely chopped fresh mint

¼ cup whole-grain mustard

One 7-pound leg of lamb, about 4½ to 5 pounds, boned and butterflied by the butcher

1 cup Easy Brown Veal Stock (page 344) or beef stock

1 In a large, nonaluminum mixing bowl, combine all the ingredients for the marinade and mix well. Reserve ½ cup of the marinade. At least 12 hours and up to 24 hours ahead, place the lamb in the marinade and turn to coat evenly. Cover with plastic wrap and refrigerate, turning occasionally.

2 Prepare a grill with a lid (see note) for high-heat grilling. Remove the lamb from the marinade, reserving the marinade. Place the lamb on the grill about 3 inches from the heat and sear the meat for 3 minutes on each side. Move to a medium-heat area of the grill. Cover the grill, and grill, basting occasionally with the marinade in the bowl, for 15 to 20 minutes on each side, until an instant-read thermometer registers 140°F for medium-rare, 150°F for medium. You may need to cut a piece off before the rest is finished if the lamb is much thicker in certain places. The meat should be pink on the inside for the best flavor and texture. Transfer the lamb to a carving board or wooden platter and let rest for about 10 minutes. Slice the meat across the grain on the diagonal into ¼-inch slices.

3 While the meat is resting, combine the reserved marinade with the stock in a medium saucepan over medium-high heat. Boil the sauce until it is reduced to about ¾ cup. Taste for seasoning. Serve the lamb with the sauce on the side.

LAMB STEW WITH DATES AND ZINFANDEL

SERVES 6 TO 8

This lamb stew features dried dates, fresh ginger, and Zinfandel to create a slightly sweet sauce reminiscent of a Middle Eastern lamb stew. Dates are grown in Indio, California, close to Palm Springs, where they have their own festival celebrated with date recipes and camel rides. On the drive from Los Angeles to Indio, you'll see stands that feature Date Shakes, well worth the detour. Dates are also good as flavor enhancers in bread puddings or smoothies. Serve this stew on a chilly winter day. Begin with Mixed Greens with Beets and Peppers (page 84) and serve with Spicy Almond Couscous (page 268) without the raisins. For dessert try Banana Split Ice Cream Torte (page 334) or Chocolate Freakout (page 329).

Recommended Wine

Serve the same wine, perhaps a fruity Zinfandel, that you are using in the dish. Zinfandels from the Paso Robles region would be a good choice.

Advance Preparation

Can be prepared up to 2 days ahead. Reheat gently. Taste for seasoning just before serving.

6 tablespoons olive oil

2 medium onions, finely chopped

3 carrots, peeled and chopped

3½ pounds leg of lamb, cut into 1½-inch cubes

½ cup all-purpose flour

Salt and freshly ground black pepper

3 medium garlic cloves, minced

1 teaspoon ground cumin

⅛ teaspoon ground coriander

1 tablespoon peeled and minced fresh ginger

1 cup dry, full-bodied red wine such as Zinfandel

1½ cups beef stock

1 cup crushed tomatoes

1 cup chopped pitted dried dates

Juice and grated zest of 1 orange

GARNISH

2 tablespoons finely chopped fresh flat-leaf parsley

2 tablespoons finely chopped fresh cilantro

1   Preheat the oven to 350°F. Heat 2 tablespoons of the olive oil in a large, ovenproof casserole or Dutch oven over medium heat. Add the onions and sauté until softened, about 5 minutes. Add the carrots and sauté for another 3 minutes, or until slightly softened. Transfer to a bowl and set aside.

2   Pat the meat dry. Place the flour in a large lock-top plastic bag and add salt and pepper to taste. Shake it to mix. Place the lamb in the bag and seal tightly. Shake until the lamb is lightly coated on all sides with the flour.

3   Add 2 tablespoons of the remaining olive oil to the casserole over medium-high heat. Add half of the meat and brown on all sides, 4 to 5 minutes, transferring the browned meat to the bowl with the vegetables as they brown. Add the remaining oil, if necessary, and brown the remaining meat. Return the onion-meat mixture to the casserole.

4   Add the garlic, cumin, coriander, and ginger and stir to coat the meat and vegetables, about 1 minute. Add the wine, stock, and tomatoes and bring to a boil over high heat, scraping up the browned bits on the bottom of the pot. Add the dates and orange juice and zest and return to a boil.

5   Cover the casserole, transfer to the oven, and bake for 1½ to 2 hours, or until the meat is tender.

6   If the sauce is very thin, remove the meat and vegetables with slotted spoon and boil the sauce on top of the stove to thicken it. Return the meat and vegetables to the casserole and stir. Taste for seasoning. Transfer to a serving bowl and garnish with the fresh parsley and cilantro. Serve immediately.

PANFRIED NOODLES WITH VEGETABLES

SERVES 4 TO 6

Recommended Wine

Depending on which meat you use
in this dish, there are lots of choices
here. If using chicken and serving the
dish as part of a luncheon, you might
think about accompanying it with a
ripe, oaky Chardonnay. If using lamb,
a young Zinfandel or Cabernet Sauvignon would be a better choice.

For this one-dish main course, I like to use the Japanese version of Chinese wheat
noodles, *chuka soba* noodles, which are precooked and dried. By crisping the
noodles first, you'll create varied textures. Use any leftover meat or chicken you have,
but this is a last-minute meal that can't be made ahead, so plan accordingly.

½ cup dried shiitake mushrooms

One 8-ounce package chuka soba noodles

SAUCE

2 tablespoons cornstarch

3 tablespoons soy sauce

2 tablespoons dry sherry wine

2 tablespoons dark brown sugar

½ cup Chicken Stock (page 342)

2 teaspoons dark sesame oil

Pinch of hot red pepper flakes

4 tablespoons peanut oil

6 scallions, both white and green parts, finely sliced

1 tablespoon peeled and finely chopped fresh ginger

2 garlic cloves, minced

2 carrots, peeled and sliced

½ pound sugar snap peas, trimmed

6 fresh white mushrooms, brushed clean and sliced

2 cups cooked and cubed chicken, beef, or lamb

1. Pour boiling water over the shiitake mushrooms in a bowl and let them soften for at least 10 minutes.

2. Meanwhile, in a large pot of boiling water, cook the noodles for 3 to 4 minutes, or until al dente. (Do not overcook the noodles, because they are going to be cooked again.) Drain the noodles well and spread them out on a kitchen towel to dry slightly.

3. To make the sauce, in a small mixing bowl, combine the ingredients and whisk to blend, making sure that the cornstarch is dissolved. Drain the shiitake mushrooms, reserving the soaking liquid. Strain the soaking liquid through cheesecloth and add ½ cup to the sauce. Trim the stems of the shiitakes, coarsely chop, and set aside.

4. In a wok or large, nonstick skillet over high heat, heat 2 tablespoons of the peanut oil. Add the noodles and toss using 2 large forks or spoons until crisp and golden brown, 3 to 5 minutes. Transfer the noodles to a bowl.

5. Heat the remaining 2 tablespoons peanut oil in the wok or skillet over medium-high heat. Add the scallions, ginger, and garlic and quickly stir-fry for 1 to 2 minutes. Add the carrots, peas, and fresh mushrooms and continue to stir-fry, stirring and tossing constantly, until the vegetables are crisp-tender, about 2 to 3 minutes longer.

6. Add the shiitakes and the sauce to the vegetables. Raise the heat to high. Add the meat and stir until the meat is heated throughout and the sauce is slightly thickened, about 3 minutes. Taste for seasoning.

7. Just before serving, stir the noodles into the stir-fry just to heat them through. Transfer the mixture to a serving bowl and serve immediately.

GRILLED VEAL CHOPS WITH ZUCCHINI-CORN RELISH

SERVES 6

Veal chops taste best grilled medium-rare. In the colder months, complex mushroom sauces are a wonderful counterpoint to the veal's delicate flavor. In the summer, when fresh corn is plentiful, this relish is a lighter, fresher approach, especially since the vegetables are grilled rather than sautéed.

Serve Oven-Roasted Potatoes with Parmesan (page 262) and a bowl of Roasted Tomato Jam (page 361) alongside for a satisfying meal. For dessert, try Peach Melba Buckle (page 306).

Recommended Wine

Sangiovese, Rhône varieties, and Pinot Noir are the best choices for this dish.

Advance Preparation

Can be prepared through step 2 up to 8 hours ahead, covered, and refrigerated.

RELISH

2 medium zucchini, cut lengthwise into ¼-inch slices

½ small red onion, cut into ¼-inch slices (about 3 slices)

½ medium peeled red pepper (page 27), finely chopped

1 ear of fresh corn, husked

3 tablespoons olive oil

2 tablespoons balsamic vinegar

2 tablespoons fresh lemon juice

2 tablespoons finely chopped fresh basil

2 tablespoons finely chopped fresh flat-leaf parsley

½ teaspoon salt

¼ teaspoon freshly ground black pepper

3 tablespoons olive oil

1 tablespoon balsamic vinegar

6 veal rib chops, 12 ounces each

½ cup Easy Brown Veal Stock (page 344) or beef stock

GARNISH

Large fresh basil leaves

1   To make the relish, prepare a grill for medium-heat grilling. Place the zucchini and red onion slices on the grill about 3 inches from the heat and grill them for about 4 minutes on each side, or until slightly charred. Remove the zucchini and onions from the grill, chop them into ¼-inch pieces, and place them in a medium mixing bowl along with the red pepper.

2   Place the corn on the grill and grill until charred slightly on all sides, about 3 to 4 minutes. Remove the corn from the grill and, when it is cool enough to handle, using a sharp knife, cut the corn kernels off into the bowl with the other vegetables. Add the remaining ingredients and mix well. Taste for seasoning. Set the relish aside.

3   Combine the olive oil and vinegar in a small bowl and brush each side of the veal chops with the mixture. Turn up the grill or rearrange the coals as needed for medium-high-heat. Place the veal chops on the grill about 3 inches from the heat and grill for 5 to 7 minutes on each side for medium-rare; the veal should be very pink inside.

4   Meanwhile, combine the stock with ¼ cup of the relish in a small saucepan and bring to a simmer. In another small saucepan, warm the remaining relish.

5   Transfer the veal chops to serving plates and spoon a generous tablespoon of the sauce on top of each. Arrange a few basil leaves on the plates and spoon a large dollop of the warm relish on top of the basil. Serve immediately.

LIGHT MEATBALLS WITH DOUBLE-TOMATO HERB SAUCE

MAKES ABOUT 30 MEATBALLS;

SERVES 8 TO 10

A mixture of veal and turkey instead of beef lightens these unusual baked meatballs. Airy and fluffy, these meatballs owe much of their flavor and moistness to the shredded carrot and zucchini that replace the usual fat or cream. Shred or grate the carrot and zucchini very finely, and taste the zucchini to make sure it isn't bitter. Serve the meatballs alone, with your favorite pasta, or on a baguette with the tomato sauce spooned over them.

This recipe can also be adapted to a meat loaf. Form the mixture into a large loaf shape, place it in a baking pan, and bake it for 1 hour at 400°F. For extra flavor, spoon over some of the sauce while the meat loaf is cooking.

2 tablespoons olive oil
1 medium onion, finely chopped
2 garlic cloves, minced
2 medium carrots, peeled and finely shredded
1 medium zucchini, finely shredded
1 pound lean ground turkey
1 pound lean ground veal
⅓ cup fine dried bread crumbs
2 large eggs
1 large egg white
¼ cup finely chopped fresh flat-leaf parsley
¼ cup freshly grated Parmesan
2 tablespoons Dijon mustard
1 teaspoon finely chopped fresh rosemary or ½ teaspoon dried
½ teaspoon finely chopped fresh thyme or ¼ teaspoon dried
1 teaspoon salt
¼ teaspoon freshly ground black pepper
3 cups Double-Tomato Herb Sauce (page 347)

Recommended Wine

Here, a ripe, full-bodied Chardonnay does very nicely. If you want to pour a red wine, try Pinot Noir.

Advance Preparation

Can be prepared through step 3 up to 1 day ahead, covered, and refrigerated. Reheat in a 350°F oven for 20 minutes, occasionally basting with tomato sauce. The cooked meatballs can also be frozen, tightly wrapped, for up to 2 months.

1   Preheat the oven to 375°F. In a medium skillet over medium heat, heat the olive oil. Add the onions and sauté for 7 to 10 minutes, or until softened and translucent. Add the garlic and sauté for another minute. Stir in the carrots and zucchini and cook for about 2 minutes, or until slightly softened.

2   Transfer the cooked vegetables to a large mixing bowl and add the remaining ingredients except for the tomato sauce. Using a large spoon or your hands mix all the ingredients together until well blended.

3   Using your hands, gently roll the mixture into meatballs about 1½ inches in diameter. Place them in a large roasting pan lined with aluminum foil. Bake the meatballs for 35 minutes, or until cooked through. Meanwhile, gently reheat the tomato sauce.

4   To serve, arrange the meatballs in a serving dish and spoon the hot sauce over them.

VEAL STEW WITH ORANGE SAUCE

SERVES 4 TO 6

In this splendid flavor combination, cubes of veal are braised in a light orange sauce subtly flavored with bacon. Ask your butcher for veal shoulder meat, which retains its tender texture when stewed slowly. Begin with Mixed Greens with Beets and Peppers (page 84). Simple buttered egg noodles are all that you need to accompany the stew.

3 pounds veal stew, cut into 2-inch cubes, patted dry

2 medium onions, finely chopped

¼ pound bacon, finely chopped

3 tablespoons all-purpose flour

Juice of 1 medium orange (about ½ cup)

1 cup dry white wine

1 tablespoon finely chopped orange zest

2 tablespoons balsamic vinegar

2 garlic cloves, minced

10 ounces baby carrots, peeled, or regular carrots, peeled and sliced into 1-inch pieces

1 tablespoon olive oil

1 pound medium white or cremini mushrooms, quartered

1 cup Chicken Stock (page 342) or Easy Brown Veal Stock (page 344) (optional)

½ teaspoon salt

¼ teaspoon freshly ground white pepper

GARNISH

¼ cup finely chopped fresh flat-leaf parsley

Thin orange slices

1 tablespoon finely chopped orange zest

Recommended Wine

The hearty flavors of this dish require a hearty wine to balance it. Zinfandel would be best, but a big Merlot, Syrah, or even Cabernet Sauvignon does almost as well.

Advance Preparation

Can be prepared up to 3 days ahead, covered, and refrigerated. This stew also freezes well. Thaw in the refrigerator before reheating gently. Adjust the seasonings before serving.

1   Preheat the oven to 450°F. In a large roasting pan, combine the veal, onions, bacon, and flour and toss to coat all the ingredients evenly. Roast for about 30 minutes, using long oven mitts and a long-handled spoon to toss the meat mixture every 10 minutes, until lightly browned on all sides.

2   Remove the pan from the oven and transfer all the ingredients to a large ovenproof, flameproof casserole or Dutch oven. Place the roasting pan over medium heat on top of the stove. Add the orange juice and wine, deglazing the pan by scraping up the browned bits from the pan bottom. Add the deglazed juices to the casserole and place over medium heat. Add the orange zest, vinegar, and garlic and stir to mix. Bring to a simmer. Cover the casserole and simmer over low heat for 1¼ hours, or until the meat is tender, stirring once or twice to evenly cook the meat.

3   While the meat is cooking, add the carrots to a medium saucepan of boiling water over high heat and simmer for 10 minutes, or until the carrots are cooked but slightly firm. Drain and set aside. Heat the olive oil in a large skillet over medium heat, add the mushrooms, and sauté until softened, about 3 to 4 minutes. Remove from the heat and set aside.

4   After the stew has cooked for 1¼ hours, add the mushrooms to the stew and continue cooking over low heat, covered, for 15 minutes. If the sauce is too thick, add the stock to reach the desired consistency. Add the carrots, salt, and pepper and cook for about 5 minutes longer, or until the carrots are heated through. Taste for seasoning.

5   Spoon the stew into a large serving bowl, garnish with the parsley, orange slices, and orange zest, and serve immediately.

BRAISED STUFFED SHOULDER OF VEAL

SERVES 8 TO 10

While a student at the University of California at Berkeley in the late 1960s, I visited many ethnic restaurants in nearby San Francisco. One of my fondest memories finds me sitting at Vanessi's counter watching one of the first California-style open kitchens operate in high gear. Aromatic sizzling pans, the clicking of wire whisks against copper bowls preparing zabaglione, and the smell of just-baked bread—it was easy to imagine I was in Italy.

When I decided to re-create a dish from that kitchen, I chose Vanessi's braised veal, a favorite of mine. I didn't realize how long the recipe would take to prepare. But don't be put off by the long preparation time; just plan a day when you can enjoy leisurely cooking. I usually make this 1 day ahead because the flavors improve with time. You'll need a trussing needle for this recipe.

If your time is at a premium, prepare the veal without the stuffing. It will still be delicious but much less work will be required. The veal will still need to be tied, a task your butcher can perform, and will take about 2 hours to cook without the stuffing.

The veal shoulder clod is country-elegant, filled with Italian-style stuffing, rolled into a tight package, browned, and braised in a fragrant tomato-Madeira sauce until tender. When sliced, the green, mushroom-flecked filling is a perfect contrast to the milky white veal interior. Enjoy this with steamed green beans or sweet spring peas.

Recommended Wine

There is a definite affinity between wines and dishes of similar geographic provenance, so an Italian variety such as Sangiovese, Barbera, or Dolcetto goes nicely with this Italian dish. Zinfandel, which is thought to be an Italian variety, is also an excellent match.

Advance Preparation

Can be prepared up to up to 1 day ahead, covered, and refrigerated. Reheat the veal in the sauce before slicing.

STUFFING

⅓ cup pine nuts

2 medium bunches spinach, leaves only, cleaned and left wet

1 tablespoon olive oil

4 medium shallots, finely chopped

½ pound white mushrooms, brushed clean and coarsely chopped

2 garlic cloves, minced

⅓ cup dry white wine

2 cups fresh French bread crumbs

¼ pound thinly sliced prosciutto, coarsely chopped

¼ pound thinly sliced mortadella, coarsely chopped

2 tablespoons finely chopped fresh flat-leaf parsley

1 tablespoon chopped fresh thyme or 1 teaspoon dried

1 tablespoon chopped fresh rosemary or 1 teaspoon dried

½ teaspoon salt

¼ teaspoon freshly ground black pepper

2 large eggs

5 pounds boned veal shoulder, clod portion, with a pocket cut into the thick part
of the shoulder

3 tablespoons olive oil

1 large onion, finely chopped

2 medium carrots, peeled and finely chopped

2 celery ribs, finely chopped

½ cup dry white wine

½ cup Madeira

2 cups Easy Brown Veal Stock (page 344)

3 large fresh tomatoes, peeled, seeded, and finely chopped, or 1½ cups well-
drained chopped canned tomatoes

2 garlic cloves, minced

1 tablespoon chopped fresh rosemary or 1 teaspoon dried

1 teaspoon salt

¼ teaspoon freshly ground black pepper

1 tablespoon finely chopped fresh parsley

GARNISH

2 tablespoons finely chopped fresh parsley

1 To make the stuffing, preheat the oven to 350°F. Spread the pine nuts in a single
   layer on a baking sheet and toast for 5 minutes, or until lightly browned. Watch
   carefully, as they burn quickly. Transfer immediately to a plate and set aside.

2 Place the moist spinach in a large skillet over medium-high heat, cover partially, and steam for about 2 minutes. Remove the spinach from the heat and
   place it in a strainer. Pour cold water over it to stop the cooking. Drain carefully and place it in a dry kitchen towel. Wring the spinach out until all excess
   liquid is removed. Finely chop the spinach and set aside.

3 In a large skillet over medium heat, heat the olive oil. Add the shallots and
   sauté for about 3 minutes, or until softened. Add the mushrooms and continue
   cooking, stirring often, for about 2 minutes, or until the mushrooms are just
   tender. Add the garlic and sauté for 30 seconds. Pour in the wine, cook for
   another minute, and remove from the heat.

continued on next page

4   In a medium mixing bowl, combine the spinach, mushroom mixture, bread crumbs, prosciutto, mortadella, herbs, salt, and pepper. Taste the stuffing for seasoning. Then add the eggs and pine nuts and mix again.

5   Preheat the oven to 350°F. To stuff the veal, slide the stuffing, a small handful at a time, into the pocket, making sure it is evenly distributed. Pat the veal down to help distribute it.

6   With a trussing needle threaded with string, sew up the end of the veal that has the pocket opening. Make sure to sew it securely so that the stuffing will not escape during cooking.

7   Press the veal into a compact package with your hands. Using kitchen string, wrap the veal in a tight package. Tie it lengthwise and crosswise to hold it together.

8   In an ovenproof, flameproof casserole or Dutch oven large enough to hold the veal comfortably, heat 2 tablespoons of the oil over medium-high heat. Add the veal and brown it evenly on all sides, using 2 spoons to turn it. Transfer to a platter.

9   Reduce the heat to medium. Add the remaining 1 tablespoon oil to the casserole and add the onion, carrots, and celery. Sauté until slightly softened, about 5 minutes. Pour in the white wine and Madeira and boil for 3 minutes, scraping up the browned bits from the bottom of the pan to enrich the sauce. Add the stock, tomatoes, garlic, and rosemary.

10 Return the veal to the casserole, cover, and transfer to the oven. Bake for 2½ hours, or until an instant-read thermometer inserted in the meat but not touching the stuffing registers 160°F. Remove the veal from the oven and remove all the string from around the meat. Place the veal on a carving board and let rest.

11 Return the casserole to the stove top and boil the sauce down for about 5 minutes, until slightly thickened. Skim off the fat from the surface. Add the salt, pepper, and parsley. Taste for seasoning.

12 Cut the veal into 1½-inch slices, being careful to keep the stuffing intact. Overlap the slices on a large serving dish and pour the sauce around the veal. Ladle the sauce down the center of the slices and garnish with the remaining parsley. Serve immediately.

Serve this main dish with Roasted Broccoli with Toasted Bread Crumb Gremolata (page 248) and Roasted Onions and Baby Potatoes (page 263).

(page 248) and Roasted Onions and Baby Potatoes (page 263).

SAUTÉED PORK MEDALLIONS WITH MUSTARD-HERB SAUCE

SERVES 6

2 pork tenderloins (about 1¼ pounds each)

Salt and freshly ground white pepper

2 tablespoons unsalted butter

2 tablespoons olive oil

2 medium leeks, white and light green parts only, cleaned and finely chopped

½ cup dry white wine

1 cup Chicken Stock (page 342)

2 medium cloves garlic, minced

½ cup crème fraîche

3 tablespoons whole-grain mustard

1 tablespoon finely chopped fresh tarragon

2 tablespoons finely chopped fresh chives

GARNISH

2 tablespoons finely chopped fresh parsley

1   Cut each tenderloin into 6 medallions about 2 inches thick and season with salt and pepper.

2   In a very large skillet melt 1 tablespoon of the butter with 1 tablespoon of the oil over medium-high heat. Add the medallions and sauté for about 5 minutes, then turn with tongs. Continue cooking until browned and just cooked through, about 4 minutes longer. Transfer to a platter and cover with aluminum foil.

3   Add the remaining 1 tablespoon butter and 1 tablespoon oil to the skillet and heat until foamy. Add the leeks and sauté, stirring frequently, for about 3 to 5 minutes, or until softened. Add the wine, stock, and garlic and bring to boil, scraping up the browned bits from the bottom of the pan. Boil until slightly reduced, about 4 minutes.

4   Whisk in the crème fraiche and mustard and return to a boil. Cook until slightly thickened again, about 2 minutes. Add the tarragon, chives, and salt and pepper to taste and whisk well. Taste for seasoning.

5   Return the pork and juices to the skillet and cook for 2 minutes longer. Arrange on a serving platter and garnish with the parsley. Serve immediately.

Recommended Wine

This flexible dish works well with Chardonnay, Cabernet, Zinfandel or a Pinot Grigio.

Advance Preparation

This is best made just before serving.

LOIN OF PORK WITH DRIED FRUITS AND GEWÜRZ-TRAMINER

SERVES 6

California wineries have taken an active role in educating food and wine lovers on the successful pairing of wines with California-style foods. Fetzer Winery led the way with its Valley Oaks Garden Center in Mendocino County. This facility includes a 4½-acre organic garden with more varieties of herbs, fruits, and vegetables than you can possibly imagine and a stunning demonstration kitchen and conference center. Throughout the year food events are held there to celebrate contemporary California cooking.

John Ash, former culinary director at Fetzer's Vineyards, is a leader in California wine country cooking. Here I've adapted one of John's recipes that shows off the natural attraction between pork and spicy flavors like ginger, Gewürztraminer, and dried fruit. Serve this pork on a chilly winter evening accompanied by Crispy Potato Pancakes with Vegetables (page 259).

Recommended Wine

It would seem appropriate to stick with the Gewürztraminer used in the recipe. Try to find one that is not too high in residual sugar (more than 3 percent is excessive). If you want to branch out, try a Syrah or a fresh, young Pinot Noir.

Advance Preparation

Can be prepared through step 3 up to 8 hours ahead, covered and refrigerated. Reheat the sauce and the meat gently over low heat.

One 2½- to 3-pound loin of pork, tied

1 tablespoon olive oil

SAUCE

1 tablespoon olive oil

1 medium red onion, finely chopped

2 garlic cloves, minced

2 tablespoons peeled and finely chopped fresh ginger

2 cups fresh orange juice

2 teaspoons finely chopped orange zest

1 serrano chile, seeded and finely chopped (see note)

1 cup Gewürztraminer

1 cup Chicken Stock (page 342)

1 cup coarsely chopped dried apple slices

1 cup coarsely chopped dried apricots

1 teaspoon ground allspice

One 2-inch cinnamon stick

2 teaspoons dark brown sugar

2 tablespoons heavy (whipping) cream

Salt and freshly ground black pepper

GARNISH

2 tablespoons finely chopped fresh parsley

1   In a heavy, flameproof casserole or Dutch oven large enough to hold the pork comfortably, heat 1 tablespoon of the olive oil over medium-high heat. Add the pork and brown evenly on all sides, turning the meat with 2 large spoons or tongs, about 15 minutes. Transfer the pork to a platter.

2   To begin the sauce, reduce the heat to medium and add the oil to the casserole. Add the onion and sauté for 3 minutes, or until softened. Add the garlic and sauté for another minute. Add the ginger, orange juice and zest, chile, wine, stock, dried fruits, allspice, and cinnamon stick and stir to mix. Return the pork to the casserole. Reduce the heat to low, cover, and simmer, turning the meat occasionally for even cooking, for 45 to 60 minutes, or until an instant-read thermometer inserted into the middle of the loin registers 160°F.

3   Transfer the pork loin to a platter and cover loosely with aluminum foil. Discard the cinnamon stick. To finish the sauce, add the brown sugar and cream and cook the sauce until slightly thickened, 3 to 5 minutes. Add the salt and pepper to taste.

4   To serve, remove the strings from around the pork, cut it into ½-inch slices, and overlap the slices on a rimmed platter. Spoon the sauce over the meat, garnish with the parsley, and serve immediately.

Note

When working with chiles, always wear rubber gloves. Wash the cutting surface and knife immediately.

ASIAN GLAZED PORK TENDERLOIN

SERVES 4

These tender pork tenderloins are bathed in a fragrant Asian-Californian mix of ingredients. You can either roast the pork or grill it. Hoisin sauce and sesame oil are available in the Asian section of well-stocked markets.

Begin with Asian Guacamole (page 34) and serve the pork with Rice Pilaf with Fresh Corn and Peanuts (page 270). For dessert, try Nectarine Crisp with Dried Cherries (page 308).

Recommended Wine

To balance the sweetness in the glaze, the best wine choices are Zinfandel, Pinot Noir, or Syrah.

Advance Preparation

Can be prepared through step 2 up to 4 hours ahead, covered, and refrigerated.

MARINADE

1 garlic clove, minced

1 teaspoon peeled finely chopped fresh ginger

1 tablespoon hoisin sauce

2 scallions, white and light green parts only, finely sliced

1 tablespoon sherry vinegar

1 teaspoon finely chopped orange zest

⅓ cup fresh orange juice

½ teaspoon dark sesame oil

1 tablespoon vegetable oil

¼ teaspoon salt

Pinch of freshly ground black pepper

2 pork tenderloins, about ¾ pound each

½ cup Chicken Stock (page 342)

GARNISH

Orange slices

1 To make the marinade, in a medium mixing bowl, combine all the marinade ingredients and whisk until well blended. Taste for seasoning. Reserve ¼ cup of marinade for the sauce.

2 Place the tenderloins in a shallow, nonaluminum dish. Pour the marinade over the tenderloins, rolling them around to evenly coat. Refrigerate, covered, for at least 2 hours and up to 4 hours.

3 Preheat the oven to 400°F. Place the pork tenderloins in a roasting pan and roast for 15 to 20 minutes, or until an instant-read thermometer inserted into the thickest part registers 160°F. Remove the pork from the oven and let rest for 10 minutes. (Alternatively, grill the pork on a medium-high-heat grill about 3 inches from the heat for about 15 to 20 minutes, turning to brown on all sides.)

4 While the pork is roasting, combine the reserved ¼ cup marinade with the stock in a small saucepan, bring it to a boil, and cook until slightly thickened.

5 To serve, cut the tenderloins into ¼-inch slices and arrange the slices overlapping on a platter. Garnish with the orange slices and spoon the sauce over the meat. Serve immediately.

144   Sautéed Green and Yellow Beans with Garlic and Basil

145   Tricolor Vegetable Sauté

146   Cauliflower Purée with Two Cheeses

147   Roasted Winter Vegetables

148   Roasted Broccoli with Toasted Bread Crumb Gremolata

150   Butternut Squash Gratin with Tomato Fondue

151   Home Ranch Butternut Squash

152   Fava Beans with Red Onions and Bacon

153   White Bean Stew with Spinach and Tomatoes

154   Corn Bread, Leek, and Red Pepper Stuffing Terrine

156   Onion, Dried Plum, and Chestnut Compote

158   Roasted Garlic Mashed Potatoes with Leeks

159   Crispy Potato Pancakes with Vegetables

161   Potatoes Vaugirard

162   Oven-Roasted Potatoes with Parmesan

163   Roasted Onions and Baby Potatoes

164   Orange-Glazed Beets

165   Spiced Sweet Potato Pudding

167   Tomato-Mint Bulgur

168   Spicy Almond Couscous

269   Confetti Rice Pilaf

270   Rice Pilaf with Fresh Corn and Peanuts

271   Spinach Rice Timbales

SIDE DISHES

SAUTÉED GREEN AND YELLOW BEANS WITH GARLIC AND BASIL

SERVES 4 TO 6

Sautéing yellow wax beans and green beans over high heat gives them a rich, golden brown color. Mixing the beans with the Italian favorite combination of garlic and fresh basil brings out their inherent sweetness. Be sure to buy tender medium-size beans for best results. When I'm in the mood for just vegetables, a plate of these beans with a baked potato makes a satisfying supper. Or serve these with any simple grilled, roasted, or braised main course.

¾ pound tender yellow wax beans, ends trimmed

¾ pound tender green beans, ends trimmed

2 tablespoons olive oil

1 garlic clove, minced

2 tablespoons finely chopped fresh basil

Salt and freshly ground black pepper

1 In a large saucepan, bring enough water to cover the beans to a boil. Add the beans and cook until tender but slightly resistant, 5 to 7 minutes. Rinse the beans in cold water and drain them well.

2 Heat the oil in a medium skillet over medium heat. When the oil begins to sizzle, add the beans and stir, turning up the heat. Continue stirring the beans until they just begin to brown. Add the garlic and basil and for cook another 30 seconds. Remove from the heat, add the salt and pepper to taste, and toss to combine. Taste for seasoning. Transfer the beans to a serving dish and serve immediately.

Advance Preparation

Can be prepared through step 1 up to 4 hours ahead and kept at room temperature.

This simple, colorful vegetable accompaniment goes with many entrées. Be sure to cut the vegetables the same size for even cooking.

1 tablespoon olive oil
2 medium zucchini, cut into 2-by-½-inch pieces
2 medium Japanese eggplant, cut into julienne or 2-by-½-inch pieces
1 seeded red bell pepper, cut into julienne or 2-inch-by-½-inch pieces
1 garlic clove, minced
2 tablespoons finely chopped scallions, white and light green parts only
¼ cup Chicken Stock (page 342)
Salt and freshly ground black pepper

1   In a medium skillet over medium-high heat, heat the olive oil. Add the vegetables and sauté, turning frequently, until slightly browned, 3 to 5 minutes. Reduce the heat to medium, add the garlic and 1 tablespoon of the scallions, and continue sautéing for another minute.

2   Raise the heat to medium-high, add the stock, and continue cooking until the liquid is just about evaporated, about 1 to 2 minutes. Add the salt and pepper to taste.

3   Transfer to a serving dish and garnish with the remaining scallions. Serve immediately.

TRICOLOR VEGETABLE SAUTÉ

SERVES 4 TO 6

Advance Preparation
This is best made just before serving.

CAULIFLOWER PURÉE WITH TWO CHEESES

SERVES 4

Cauliflower and cheese have a natural affinity. Here a purée of steamed cauliflower is enhanced by piquant yogurt and a combination of Cheddar and Parmesan cheeses. Sometimes I serve this purée instead of mashed potatoes. Sweet baby peas make a nice accompaniment.

1 large head of cauliflower, cut into florets, tough stems removed

3 tablespoons plain nonfat yogurt or sour cream

½ cup shredded sharp Cheddar cheese

¼ cup freshly grated Parmesan cheese

½ teaspoon salt

Pinch of freshly ground white pepper

GARNISH

2 tablespoons finely chopped fresh parsley

Advance Preparation

Can be prepared up to 1 day ahead, covered, and refrigerated. Reheat gently.

1   Place the cauliflower florets in a large saucepan fitted with a steamer basket and fill to the bottom of the basket with water. Cover, bring to a boil, reduce the heat to a simmer, and steam for about 12 to 15 minutes, or until tender. Drain well.

2   Place the cauliflower in a food processor fitted with the metal blade and process to purée. Add the yogurt, cheeses, salt, and pepper and process until well blended. Taste for seasoning. Spoon the cauliflower into a serving bowl and garnish with the parsley.

Sweet potatoes, sweet bell peppers, zucchini, and mushrooms are just a few other vegetables that can be added to this cozy vegetable mélange. It's difficult to make enough of this dish because even people who are not ordinarily vegetable lovers will ask for seconds. If you're feeding a crowd, it's easy to double or even triple this recipe.

Chicken stock adds moisture while reducing the need for excess oil. Adding the corn kernels at the end provides a delightful fresh corn flavor. Serve this colorful vegetable dish with Marinated Roast Turkey (page 194), Chicken with Garlic and Lime (page 184), or Rack of Lamb with Mint Crust (page 218).

ROASTED WINTER VEGETABLES

SERVES 4

3 carrots, peeled and cut into 1-inch chunks

2 medium leeks, white and light green parts only, cleaned and finely chopped

1 quart brussels sprouts, stems trimmed, cut in half if large

3 tablespoons olive oil

1½ cups Chicken Stock (page 342)

1 teaspoon finely chopped fresh thyme or ½ teaspoon dried

¼ teaspoon salt

¼ teaspoon freshly ground black pepper

1 cup fresh corn kernels (from about 2 medium ears) or thawed frozen corn

GARNISH

2 tablespoons finely chopped fresh flat-leaf parsley

Advance Preparation
Can be prepared through step 2 up to 4 hours ahead, covered, and kept at room temperature. Preheat the oven to 425°F before continuing.

1   Preheat the oven to 400°F. In a large metal roasting pan, combine the carrots, leeks, and Brussels sprouts with 2 tablespoons of the olive oil and 1 cup of the stock. Add the thyme, salt, and pepper and mix well, making sure to coat all the vegetables evenly.

2   Roast for 30 minutes, turning the vegetables occasionally. Add the remaining 1 tablespoon olive oil and ½ cup stock to the pan and continue roasting for 30 more minutes. The mixture should be browned and caramelized. (You may need to raise the oven temperature to 425°F to help the vegetables caramelize a few minutes before adding the corn.)

3   During about the last 5 minutes of cooking, stir in the corn and continue roasting until the corn is heated through and browned. Taste for seasoning. Spoon the vegetables into a large serving bowl and garnish with the parsley. Serve immediately.

ROASTED BROCCOLI WITH TOASTED BREAD CRUMB GREMOLATA

SERVES 4 TO 6

I love all sorts of roasted vegetables and am always trying different ones. It turns out that broccoli is a great vegetable for roasting. It tastes quite different than steamed broccoli, and the crisp, Italian-style bread topping adds a definite layer of flavor and texture. Serve with Baked Salmon with Red Onion Sauce (page 154) or Crispy Roast Chicken (page 188).

1½ pounds broccoli, cut into florets, tough stems removed (about 1 pound 2-inch florets)

3 tablespoons olive oil

Salt and freshly ground black pepper

Juice of ½ lemon

GREMOLATA

3 tablespoons coarse fresh bread crumbs

1 tablespoon olive oil

1 shallot, finely chopped

3 tablespoons finely chopped fresh parsley

Zest of 1 lemon

Salt and freshly ground black pepper

Advance Preparation

This is best made just before serving.

1   Preheat the oven to 425°F. In a large shallow roasting pan or baking sheet combine the broccoli, oil, and salt and pepper to taste and mix well, being sure to coat all the vegetables evenly. Spread the broccoli in a single layer.

2   Roast for 20 to 25 minutes, stirring occasionally, or until crisp, lightly browned and tender. When the broccoli is cooked, sprinkle the lemon juice evenly over and stir to combine. Roast for another minute.

3   While the broccoli is roasting, make the gremolata: Put the bread crumbs in a nonstick skillet over medium heat. Toast, swirling the pan often, for about 2 minutes, or until golden brown. Remove from the heat and transfer to a small bowl. Add the olive oil to the hot skillet and then add the shallot. Sauté for about 2 minutes over medium heat, or until the shallot is golden brown. Transfer to the bowl with the bread crumbs. Add the parsley, lemon zest, and salt and pepper to taste and mix to combine. Taste for seasoning. Set aside.

4   Spoon the broccoli into a serving bowl and sprinkle over the gremolata. Serve immediately.

HIGH-HEAT ROASTING

Whether you're roasting meat, poultry, or fish, high-heat (425° to 450°F) roasting produces a crisp outer skin and a moist inner flesh. Certain vegetables with natural sugar, like corn, onions, and carrots, become particularly delicious and slightly caramelized when cooked in this manner with a little olive oil and simple seasoning. Tomatoes come alive when the high heat concentrates and enhances their natural sweetness. Make sure to use a low-sided roasting pan that is large enough to avoid overcrowding the vegetables. It's difficult to give exact cooking times for each of the vegetables because of all the variables—freshness, thickness, and variety. Occasional stirring is necessary to brown the vegetables uniformly and keep them from sticking. This cooking method is an efficient alternative to other traditional techniques. It's also a lighter approach than sautéing because you need less oil. High-heat roasting also makes it possible to make rich chicken, turkey, or veal stock in the oven, using only one pan, with great results.

BUTTERNUT SQUASH GRATIN WITH TOMATO FONDUE

SERVES 6 TO 8

Advance Preparation
Can be prepared through step 3 up to 8 hours ahead, covered, and refrigerated. Bring to room temperature before baking.

I used to make this dish by first sautéing the squash in olive oil. Now I steam the squash to eliminate extra oil, and it actually tastes better. You can use any cheese you like. My favorites here are nutty Swiss, mild Monterey jack, or extra-sharp Cheddar. You can also substitute other winter squash. Serve with a simple grilled entrée or as a vegetarian main dish. Begin with Mixed Greens with Beets and Peppers (page 84).

One 3-pound butternut squash

2 tablespoons olive oil

3 medium leeks, white and light green parts only, cleaned and finely chopped

2 pounds fresh tomatoes, peeled, seeded, and chopped, or about 4 cups well-drained diced canned tomatoes

1 tablespoon finely chopped fresh basil or ½ tablespoon dried

1 teaspoon finely chopped fresh thyme or ½ teaspoon dried

1 teaspoon salt

½ teaspoon freshly ground black pepper

⅓ pound sharp Cheddar, Monterey jack, or Swiss cheese, shredded (about 1½ cups)

1   Preheat the oven to 425°F. Cut the squash in half and scoop out the seeds. Carefully cut the peel from the squash and cut the flesh into 1-inch slices. Bring 2 inches of water in a large saucepan fitted with a steamer basket to a boil. Using tongs, carefully place the squash slices in the steamer, cover, and steam over medium heat for 15 to 20 minutes, or until the squash is tender when pierced with a fork. Transfer the squash to an oiled 9-by-12-inch oval gratin dish.

2   In a medium skillet over medium heat, heat the olive oil. Add the leeks and sauté for about 5 minutes, or until softened. Raise the heat to medium-high, add the tomatoes, and cook, stirring frequently, for 10 minutes. Add the basil and thyme and cook until the sauce has thickened, about 5 minutes. Add the salt and pepper and taste for seasoning.

3   Spoon the tomato mixture over the squash and sprinkle the cheese evenly over the top.

4   Bake for 15 to 20 minutes, or until the cheese is lightly browned and bubbling. Serve immediately.

On a trip to the Home Ranch in Steamboat Springs, Colorado, I tasted a dish of quickly sautéed butternut squash that was remarkable for its simple, clear flavor. Inspired by that memory, I experimented with adding garlic and cumin to bright orange butternut squash, with surprisingly savory and slightly sweet results. This is a wonderful accompaniment to Glazed Halibut with Orange-Chive Sauce (page 160) or any simple grilled chicken, beef, or fish dish.

One 2-pound butternut squash

2 tablespoons olive oil

1 garlic clove, minced

¼ teaspoon ground cumin

¾ cup Chicken Stock (page 342)

½ teaspoon salt

¼ teaspoon freshly ground white pepper

2 tablespoons finely chopped fresh parsley

1   Cut the squash in half and scoop out the seeds. Carefully cut the peel from the squash and cut the flesh into ¼-inch dice.

2   In a large sauté pan over medium heat, heat the olive oil. Add the squash and sauté for 3 to 5 minutes, or until lightly browned. Add garlic and cumin and toss to coat, sautéing for a minute. Add the stock, raise the heat to medium-high, cover, and cook for 5 to 7 minutes longer, or until the squash is tender when pierced with a fork. Remove from the heat, add the salt, white pepper, and parsley, and mix to combine.

3   Taste for seasoning. Heat further if any excess moisture remains. Spoon into a serving bowl and serve immediately.

Advance Preparation

Can be prepared through step 2 up to 4 hours ahead, covered, and kept at room temperature.

FAVA BEANS WITH RED ONIONS AND BACON

SERVES 4 TO 6

Fava beans, sometimes called broad beans or horse beans, have a distinctive creamy, nutty flavor. In the past the best place to find fava beans was the local Italian market. Today, in the spring and summer months, fava beans make their appearance in farmers' markets across the state as well as in many supermarkets.

While it takes a bit of time to shell and peel fresh fava beans, it's fun to enlist a friend or your kids to do the work together, discovering the different textures inside. Look for smaller, younger beans, which have better flavor and are more tender. This dish goes well with a simple grilled fish or chicken entrée. It also makes a good first course, served slightly chilled with a touch of Basic Vinaigrette (page 355).

Ingredients
3 pounds fresh young fava beans
3 strips of bacon
1 tablespoon olive oil
1 medium red onion, finely chopped
2 teaspoons balsamic vinegar
2 tablespoons finely chopped fresh parsley
¼ teaspoon salt
Pinch of freshly ground black pepper

Advance Preparation

The fava beans can be shelled up to 8 hours ahead; the dish can be prepared through step 3 up to 4 hours ahead and kept at room temperature.

1   Shell the fava beans by removing them from their pods. If the beans are very young, they may not need to be skinned after shelling, but if they are older and larger, the outer skin of each bean should be removed, as it makes them tougher. Place the beans in a medium saucepan and set aside.

2   In a medium skillet over medium heat, cook the bacon until crisp. Drain on paper towels and let cool. Crumble into tiny pieces and set aside.

3   Wipe the skillet clean, add the oil, and heat over medium heat. Add the onion and sauté for about 7 minutes, or until softened. Add 1 teaspoon of the vinegar and continue cooking until the onions are lightly browned and just beginning to caramelize, about 2 minutes longer. Set aside in the pan.

4   Cover the beans with water by ½ inch, bring to a simmer over medium heat, and cook for about 3 to 5 minutes, or until tender.

5   Add the beans to the pan with the onions and place over medium heat. Add the bacon, the remaining 1 teaspoon vinegar, the parsley, salt, and pepper and stir to mix. Cook until heated throughout, about 1 minute. Taste for seasoning. Serve immediately.

White beans become creamy as they cook, allowing the juices to thicken slightly. Fresh seasonings of tomato and spinach heighten the simple white bean's taste. Serve this stew as an accompaniment to Grilled Steaks with Olivada and Port Wine Sauce (page 212). I also like to serve it as a main-course dish for a luncheon that begins with Peppery Greens with Gorgonzola and Pine Nuts (page 80). If you're serving the stew as a main or first course, present it in shallow soup bowls and pass the Parmesan separately.

WHITE BEAN STEW WITH SPINACH AND TOMATOES

SERVES 6

2 cups (1 pound) dried large white beans, picked over and rinsed

2 tablespoons olive oil

1 medium onion, finely chopped

2 garlic cloves, minced

2 medium tomatoes, peeled, seeded, and finely chopped

4 cups Chicken Stock (page 342)

1 large bunch of spinach, leaves only, cleaned and torn into bite-size pieces

1 teaspoon salt

¼ teaspoon freshly ground black pepper

1 teaspoon balsamic vinegar

¼ cup freshly grated Parmesan cheese

Advance Preparation
Can be prepared up to 8 hours ahead and kept refrigerated. Bring to room temperature and reheat gently over low heat.

1   Soak the beans overnight in enough cold water to cover generously. (Alternatively, do a quick soak: Bring the beans to a boil in just enough water to cover, boil for 2 minutes, then cover and let stand for 1 hour.) Drain the beans and set aside.

2   In a large, heavy saucepan or Dutch oven over medium heat, heat the oil. Add the onion and sauté for about 3 minutes, or until softened. Add the garlic and sauté for another minute. Add the tomatoes, stock, and beans. Simmer, covered, for 1½ to 2¼ hours, or until the beans are tender.

3   Add the spinach and cook, covered, for 3 minutes, or until the spinach is slightly wilted. Add the salt, pepper, and vinegar and mix to combine. Taste for seasoning.

4   To serve, spoon the beans into a serving bowl or individual bowls and sprinkle with the Parmesan. Serve immediately.

CORN BREAD, LEEK, AND RED PEPPER STUFFING TERRINE

SERVES 8 TO 10

This savory dish is a holiday showstopper. Crusty corn-bread stuffing is molded into a terrine shape, then baked, unmolded, and surrounded by a parsley garnish, or by my favorite, Roasted Winter Vegetables (page 247). Be sure to have both a flat serving spatula and a large spoon on hand for serving. Water chestnuts impart a crunchy contrast to the smooth stuffing texture. You can substitute toasted pecans for the water chestnuts, if you prefer. Serve with turkey, chicken, or duck.

In my home, stuffing is a highly prized part of the holiday dinner, so I make at least two kinds. If you like a more complex stuffing, omit the bell pepper and water chestnuts and add ½ pound cooked Chicken and Apple Sausage (page 201), ½ cup finely chopped dried apricots, ½ cup dried cranberries, and some cooked fresh chestnuts; add up to ½ cup extra melted butter and ½ cup chicken stock. If you like, this recipe makes enough to stuff a 16-pound bird, with enough left over to fill a medium casserole.

Note

You can also bake the stuffing in a medium baking dish and serve it right from the dish.

Advance Preparation

Can be prepared through step 3 up to 1 day ahead, covered, and refrigerated. Remove from the refrigerator 1 hour before baking.

---

7 tablespoons unsalted butter

2 tablespoons olive oil

3 medium leeks, white parts only, cleaned and finely chopped

4 celery ribs, sliced

1 pound white mushrooms, brushed clean and sliced

1 medium red bell pepper, seeded and chopped into ½-inch pieces

2 garlic cloves, minced

6 cups Corn Bread for Stuffing (page 346), crumbled and toasted

One 8-ounce can sliced water chestnuts, rinsed and well drained

½ cup finely chopped fresh parsley

1 teaspoon finely chopped fresh sage or ½ teaspoon dried

1 teaspoon finely chopped fresh thyme or ½ teaspoon dried

¼ teaspoon freshly ground black pepper

½ teaspoon salt

½ cup Turkey or Chicken Stock (page 342)

GARNISH

Fresh watercress or parsley sprigs

1   Preheat the oven to 375°F. In a large skillet over medium heat, melt 2 table-
    spoons of the butter with 1 tablespoon of the olive oil. Add the leeks and sauté
    until softened, about 5 minutes. Transfer the leeks to a large mixing bowl.
    Melt 1 tablespoon of the remaining butter and the remaining 1 tablespoon
    olive oil in the skillet over medium heat. Add the celery and mushrooms and
    sauté until slightly softened, 3 to 5 minutes. Add the bell pepper and garlic and
    sauté for a few more minutes, making sure the red pepper is still firm. Transfer
    to the bowl with the leeks.

2   In a small saucepan over medium heat, melt the remaining 4 tablespoons butter.
    Reserve 2 tablespoons of the toasted corn bread and add the rest, along with
    the water chestnuts, parsley, sage, thyme, salt, and pepper to the bowl with the
    vegetables and mix well. Add the stock and 3 tablespoons of the melted butter.
    Mix carefully, the stuffing should be moist but not too compact (especially if
    you are planning to stuff a turkey). Taste for seasoning.

3   Grease a 9½-by-5½-inch loaf pan and transfer the stuffing into it, packing
    firmly. (The stuffing can be compacted because it will not expand in the pan.)
    Sprinkle the reserved crumbled corn bread on top and drizzle with the remain-
    ing 1 tablespoon melted butter. Cover the stuffing tightly with aluminum foil.

4   Bake the stuffing for 1 hour. Remove the foil for the last 15 minutes of baking
    to create a crunchy topping. To unmold, invert the stuffing onto a plate, and
    then invert again onto a serving platter so that the browned side is facing up.
    Garnish with the herb sprigs and serve immediately. A cake slicer works best
    for serving.

ONION, DRIED PLUM, AND CHESTNUT COMPOTE

SERVES 8 TO 10

My friend Laurie Burrows Grad suggested I prepare a version of this unusual compote for Thanksgiving. The particular combination of tastes and textures—California dried plums, roasted cooked chestnuts, and braised baby onions—turned out to be inspired. Now I include this compote on my holiday table each year, served warm or at room temperature. Buy vacuum-packed cooked chestnuts to save a lot of time shelling them. Although similar to a relish, this compote seems more like a vegetable when served warm.

1 pint pearl onions
3 tablespoons unsalted butter
1½ cups Easy Brown Veal Stock (page 344) or beef stock
1 cup good-quality sweet or semisweet port
2 cups pitted dried plums
2 cups bottled roasted or steamed whole chestnuts
½ teaspoon salt
½ teaspoon freshly ground black pepper
2 teaspoons finely chopped fresh thyme, preferably lemon thyme, or 1 teaspoon dried

GARNISH

Fresh thyme leaves

Advance Preparation

Can be prepared 3 days ahead, covered, and refrigerated. Bring to room temperature before reheating gently over low heat. The mixture may become very thick. To thin, add a small amount of additional stock and/or port and reheat gently until the sauce is slightly thickened. Taste for seasoning.

1   Submerge the onions in a large pan of boiling water for 15 seconds. Rinse them with cold water and drain. Trim off the top and bottom of the onions, being sure to keep the root on. Remove the outside skin and first layer with your fingers. Cut a shallow X into the root end of each onion so that they will cook evenly and not burst.

2   Melt 2 tablespoons of the butter in a medium skillet over medium heat. Add the peeled onions and sauté, rolling them to coat evenly, until nicely browned on all sides, about 7 to 10 minutes. Add 1 cup of the stock and bring to a boil. Reduce the heat to low and simmer, covered, until the onions are translucent and soft, about 20 to 25 more minutes. (If the heat is too high, the onions will burst before they finish cooking.) Remove from the heat and set aside.

3   Combine ¾ cup of the port, the dried plums, and the remaining ½ cup stock in a medium saucepan over medium-high heat. Bring to a boil, then reduce the heat to low and simmer for about 10 minutes, or until the plums are soft but not mushy. Transfer the plums and juices to the skillet with the onions and cook over medium heat until the liquid is reduced to a thin glaze, about 3 more minutes. Set aside and keep warm.

4   Melt the remaining 1 tablespoon butter in another medium skillet over medium heat. Add the chestnuts and cook until heated throughout. Add the remaining ¼ cup port and cook until the liquid has reduced and the chestnuts are lightly glazed, about 3 minutes. Transfer the chestnuts to the skillet with the onion-plum mixture and stir in the salt, pepper, and thyme. Taste for seasoning. Spoon into a serving bowl and garnish with the thyme leaves. Serve warm or at room temperature.

ROASTED GARLIC MASHED POTATOES WITH LEEKS

SERVES 6 TO 8

When you're in the mood to indulge, try these creamy mashed potatoes. Nutty-rich roasted garlic, sweet sautéed leeks, and extra-virgin olive oil add a California-Mediterranean touch to simple mashed potatoes. These are a must on my holiday dinner table. Use as a bed for a simple grilled salmon or as an accompaniment to Marinated Roast Turkey (page 194), or Roasted Cornish Hens with Honey-Tangerine Marinade (page 191).

2 tablespoons unsalted butter
1 medium leek, white and light green parts only, cleaned and finely chopped
3 pounds Yellow Finn, Yukon Gold, or White or Red Rose potatoes, peeled and cut into 3-inch chunks
1 tablespoon Roasted Garlic Pureé (page 353)
2 tablespoons unsalted butter, cut into pieces
1 tablespoon extra-virgin olive oil
1 cup half-and-half, warmed
Salt and freshly ground white pepper

GARNISH

2 tablespoons finely chopped fresh parsley

1   In a medium sauté pan over medium heat, melt the butter. Add the leeks and sauté for 5 to 7 minutes, or until softened. Set aside.

2   Immerse the potatoes in cold water for 5 minutes to remove excess starch. In a large pot of boiling salted water, cook the potatoes for about 15 minutes, or until tender when pierced with a fork. Drain the potatoes and return them to the pot. Over high heat, dry the potatoes, tossing them occasionally, for 1 to 2 minutes, or until all the moisture has evaporated.

3   Put the potato cubes and the garlic pulp through a ricer or mash them with a potato masher in a large mixing bowl. Add the butter and olive oil and slowly pour in the half-and-half, stirring until the potatoes are very creamy but not soupy. Add the leeks and salt and pepper to taste.

4   To serve, transfer the potatoes to a serving bowl and garnish with the parsley. Serve immediately.

Advance Preparation

Can be prepared completely up to 2 hours ahead, covered, and kept at room temperature. Reheat gently in the top of a double boiler over medium heat. Add extra half-and-half as needed. Taste for seasoning.

Fresh potato pancakes, or *latkes,* taste best when they're still warm. But it's a trick to cook large quantities of latkes and have them stay crisp and warm at the same time. From years of experience I have found a number of shortcuts to make the chore more manageable.

If you follow my method for freezing the pancakes, you'll have excellent means for serving up whole, hot, crispy batches easily. Also, this one-step food processor method makes the usually tedious work of making the pancakes a snap. You make the batter without shredding the potatoes and vegetables, yielding near-perfect results.

Remember, you can make as many batches of potato pancakes as you want, pour them into a large mixing bowl, and fry the pancakes as needed. In this version, carrot and zucchini are added for color and texture. If you prefer all potatoes, simples omit the carrot and zucchini and add an additional potato. Serve these with Asian Pear-Quince-Apple Sauce (page 364).

1 medium onion, quartered
2 large eggs
1 medium baking (russet) potato, peeled and cut into 1-inch cubes
1 small zucchini, cut into 1-inch cubes
1 small carrot, cut into 1-inch cubes
½ teaspoon salt
Pinch freshly ground black pepper
2 tablespoons all-purpose flour
Vegetable oil for frying
1 cup Asian Pear-Quince-Apple Sauce (page 364) or your favorite apple sauce

continued on next page

CRISPY POTATO PANCAKES WITH VEGETABLES

MAKES 12 TO 14 PANCAKES;

SERVES 6 TO 8

Advance Preparation

To freeze the pancakes, overlap them in two rows on a double sheet of aluminum foil and enclose the pancakes tightly in the foil. Make sure the pancakes are cool and then place the packets on a flat surface in the freezer. When ready to serve, preheat the oven to 425°F and place the foil packets on a baking sheet. Remove the top sheet of foil so that the pancakes will become crispy. Bake the frozen pancakes for 7 to 10 minutes, or until they are hot throughout and crispy.

1   Purée the onion and eggs together in a food processor fitted with the metal blade until the mixture is smooth and fluffy. Add the potatoes, zucchini, and carrot and pulse until the mixture is finely chopped but retains some texture. Add the salt, pepper, and flour and quickly process to combine. Do not over-process. Pour the batter into a medium mixing bowl.

2   Let the batter sit for 15 minutes, covered with plastic wrap to prevent discoloration.

3   Heat ¾ inch of oil in a large, nonstick skillet over medium-high heat. Pour a tablespoon of batter into the skillet to test the oil. If it is hot enough, the pancake will begin to sizzle and brown. Spoon tablespoons of the batter into the skillet, making sure that there's a little room between each pancake. Flatten them with the back of a spoon and use a spatula to round out the sides, if necessary. Fry the pancakes until they are golden brown on one side, then turn them and brown the other side.

4   Transfer the pancakes to a baking sheet lined with 2 layers of paper towels. Let the excess oil drain. If serving immediately, place the pancakes on a platter and serve with the Asian Pear-Quince-Apple Sauce.

When I lived in Paris, I often made this simple dish using potatoes from the open-air market and cheese from the local *fromagerie*. Named after the Vaugirard market where I shopped each Sunday, these potatoes are easy to make and a real favorite among my family and friends.

I tried many different cheeses and potatoes for those leisurely Sunday lunches, and I thought I had found the best varieties. When I returned to Los Angeles, however, I discovered that creamy Yellow Finn or Yukon gold potatoes work best for this potato dish. They give off their own buttery qualities, making the addition of butter to flavor and moisten the potatoes unnecessary. Don't worry if you can't find these golden gems, however. The recipe works well with plain old russets. I serve this dish frequently with roasted meats, grilled meats, and poultry.

POTATOES VAUGIRARD

SERVES 6

2½ pounds Yellow Finn, Yukon gold, or Idaho (russet) baking potatoes, scrubbed but unpeeled

3 cloves garlic, minced

2 tablespoons finely chopped fresh parsley

1½ cups shredded Swiss Gruyère cheese

¼ teaspoon freshly ground black pepper

1½ cups Chicken Stock (page 342)

Advance Preparation
Can be prepared through step 2 up to 2 hours ahead, covered, and kept at room temperature.

1 Preheat the oven to 375°F. Using the medium slicing disk of a food processor or a sharp knife, cut the potatoes into ¼-inch slices. Combine the garlic, parsley, cheese, and pepper in a small mixing bowl.

2 Grease a 2-quart baking dish such as a soufflé dish. Layer the potatoes in thirds, sprinkling the garlic-cheese mixture over each layer, reserving the last third of the garlic-cheese mixture. Pour the stock over the potatoes and then sprinkle the rest of the garlic-cheese mixture evenly over the top.

3 Bake, uncovered, for 50 to 60 minutes, or until the top is browned and crusty and the potatoes are tender when pierced with a fork. Serve immediately.

OVEN-ROASTED POTATOES WITH PARMESAN

SERVES 6

These crispy potato wedges taste like French fries, though very little oil is used. Serve as an accompaniment to Broiled Orange Roughy with Salsa Glaze (page 164) or Grilled Roast Beef with Shallot-Chive Sauce (page 209).

3 pounds medium Idaho, Yellow Finn, or Yukon gold potatoes, scrubbed but unpeeled
3 tablespoons olive oil
1 teaspoon salt
¼ teaspoon freshly ground black pepper
½ cup freshly grated Parmesan cheese
2 tablespoons finely chopped fresh flat-leaf parsley

1   Preheat the oven to 425°F. Pat the potatoes dry. Cut each potato into 2-inch wedges.

2   Whisk together the olive oil, salt, and pepper in a large mixing bowl. Add the potato wedges and toss until evenly coated.

3   Arrange the potato wedges on an oiled baking sheet and bake for 25 to 30 minutes, turning every 10 minutes since they tend to stick to the pan. The potatoes are done when they're tender and golden brown.

4   Transfer the potatoes to a large serving dish and toss them with the Parmesan cheese and parsley, evenly coating all the wedges. Serve immediately.

Advance Preparation

Can be prepared through step 3 up to 2 hours ahead and kept at room temperature. Reheat in a 350°F oven for 10 to 15 minutes and then toss with the Parmesan and parsley just before serving.

This is one of those versatile potato dishes that goes with almost any main course. The potatoes turn incredibly smooth on the inside and crusty and brown outside, while the onion slices and leeks add a rich caramel crispness. I like to use golfball-size or even smaller creamer potatoes for this dish. If you can't find small ones, just cut larger ones in 1½-inch pieces. This dish is equally appropriate as an accompaniment to a frittata at brunch or with Grilled Veal Chops with Zucchini-Corn Relish (page 228) or Rack of Lamb with Mint Crust (page 218) at dinner.

ROASTED ONIONS AND BABY POTATOES

SERVES 4 TO 6

2 pounds red or purple new potatoes

2 tablespoons olive oil

¾ teaspoon salt

¼ teaspoon freshly ground black pepper

2 medium onions, cut in eighths and sectioned

1 medium leek, white part and light green parts only, thinly sliced

½ cup Chicken Stock (page 342)

1 tablespoon finely chopped fresh chives

1   Preheat the oven to 425°F. Combine the potatoes, olive oil, salt, and pepper in a roasting pan. Stir with a large spoon to coat the potatoes evenly or shake the pan from side to side until all the potatoes are coated.

2   Roast the potatoes for 20 minutes. Add the onion sections, leek, and stock and stir to combine evenly. Continue roasting, shaking the pan every 10 to 15 minutes, until the potatoes are browned and crusty and the onions are lightly caramelized, 45 minutes to 1 hour longer. Taste for seasoning. Spoon into a serving bowl and garnish with the chives. Serve immediately.

Advance Preparation
This is best made just before serving.

ORANGE-GLAZED BEETS

SERVES 4 TO 6

I think of beets as one of nature's culinary wonders because of their unique natural sweetness and rich, deep red color. These simmered beets are finished with a light orange glaze that reinforces the sweet beet flavor. Helpful tips to deal with the red-dye effect beets leave on your skin: Wear rubber gloves and place a sheet of wax paper on your cutting board. Serve with Grilled Lamb Chops with Cranberry-Rosemary Marinade (page 217) or Crispy Roast Chicken (page 188).

Advance Preparation

Can be prepared through step 1 up to 1 day ahead and refrigerated. Bring to room temperature to finish cooking.

6 medium beets, trimmed, peeled, and quartered

1 cup Chicken Stock (page 342)

2 tablespoons balsamic vinegar

¼ cup fresh orange juice

1 teaspoon olive oil

½ tablespoon unsalted butter

1 tablespoon finely chopped fresh flat-leaf parsley

½ teaspoon salt

⅛ teaspoon freshly ground black pepper

1 Combine the beets, stock, vinegar, orange juice, and olive oil in a nonaluminum Dutch oven casserole over medium heat. Bring to a simmer, then reduce the heat to low and braise for 30 to 45 minutes, or until the beets are tender when pierced with a fork.

2 Raise the heat to high and reduce the remaining liquid until it glazes the beets, stirring occasionally to coat the beets evenly. Add the butter, parsley, salt, and pepper and toss to coat. Taste for seasoning and serve immediately.

During the holidays, people seem to gravitate toward the familiar no matter how adventurous they are in their eating habits during the rest of the year. I find myself at odds with my family each year as I try to suggest an alternative to sweet potatoes with marshmallows. This spicy sweet potato pudding has been my only success.

With its a creamy interior and sweet, crunchy topping, this comforting soufflé pudding begs the question—is it a side dish or dessert? However you serve it, it's always a hit. I prefer the deep reddish mahogany-skinned sweet potato (often called a yam) for its sweeter flesh and creamier texture over the lighter-colored sweet potato.

You can usually find amaretti cookies, wrapped two to a package, at Italian delicatessens. If they aren't available, substitute gingersnaps. A 2-quart soufflé dish makes a pretty presentation. Serve with Marinated Roast Turkey (page 194).

TOPPING

½ cup coarsely chopped blanched slivered almonds

10 Amaretti cookies, crumbled

¼ cup dark brown sugar

4 medium sweet potatoes (about 2 pounds)

4 tablespoons unsalted butter

½ cup half-and-half

½ cup fresh orange juice

3 tablespoons dark brown sugar

2 tablespoons orange marmalade

1 teaspoon ground cinnamon

¼ teaspoon ground ginger

¼ teaspoon ground allspice

⅛ teaspoon freshly ground white pepper

⅛ teaspoon freshly grated nutmeg

2 teaspoons finely chopped orange zest

4 large egg yolks

5 large egg whites

¼ teaspoon salt

¼ teaspoon cream of tartar

Advance Preparation
Can be prepared through step 2 up to 1 day ahead, covered, and refrigerated. Bring to room temperature before continuing. The topping can be covered and kept at room temperature.

continued on next page

1   To make the topping, preheat the oven to 350°F. Spread the almonds in a single layer on a baking sheet and toast for 7 to 10 minutes, or until lightly browned. Combine the toasted almonds with the cookie crumbs and brown sugar in a small bowl and mix well. Set aside.

2   Raise the oven temperature to 400°F. Wrap each sweet potato in aluminum foil, place on a baking sheet, and bake for 45 to 60 minutes, or until very soft. Reduce the oven temperature to 350°F and grease a deep 2-quart casserole dish. Let the potatoes cool, then spoon the pulp into a medium mixing bowl; you should have about 4 cups. Melt 2 tablespoons of the butter in a small saucepan. Add the melted butter, half-and-half, orange juice, brown sugar, marmalade, spices, and orange zest to the sweet potato pulp and mix with an electric mixer on low speed. Beat in the egg yolks, incorporating one at a time.

3   In a large mixing bowl, using an electric mixer, beat the egg whites until foamy, and then add the salt and cream of tartar. Continue beating until stiff peaks form. Fold them into the potato mixture carefully, making sure no streaks remain. Spoon the mixture into the prepared dish. Sprinkle the topping over the pudding evenly. Cut the remaining 2 tablespoons butter into small pieces and dot on top.

4   Bake the pudding for 1¼ hours, or until puffed and browned. Serve immediately.

Bulgur is wheat that has been steamed and then dried before being ground or crushed, which is why it cooks so quickly. Don't mistake bulgur for cracked wheat, which takes much longer to cook and has an entirely different texture. This Mediterranean-inspired dish gives the heavy-textured bulgur grain a fresh, light style. Serve with Lamb Brochettes with Raita (page 220).

TOMATO-MINT BULGUR

SERVES 6

2 tablespoons olive oil

1 medium onion, finely chopped

1½ cups coarsely ground bulgur

3 cups Chicken Stock (page 342)

2 tablespoons finely chopped fresh mint

8 red or yellow cherry tomatoes, or a combination, quartered

½ teaspoon salt

¼ teaspoon freshly ground black pepper

GARNISH

Fresh mint sprigs

Advance Preparation
This is best made just before serving.

1   In a large, deep skillet over medium heat, heat the olive oil. Add the onion and sauté for 5 minutes, or until softened. Add the bulgur and toast for 2 to 3 minutes, stirring frequently.

2   Add the stock and bring the mixture to a boil. Reduce the heat to low, cover, and cook for 12 to 15 minutes, or until all the liquid is absorbed. Remove from the heat and add the mint, tomatoes, salt, and pepper, blending carefully so that the tomato pieces stay whole. Taste for seasoning. Garnish with the mint sprigs and serve immediately.

SPICY ALMOND COUSCOUS

SERVES 4

Be sure to buy the 5-minute couscous for this recipe. This is a wonderful last-minute side dish with assertive flavors, so match it up with harmonious-flavored dishes. You can double the recipe if you're serving a large group. Try serving with Grilled Lamb Chops with Cranberry-Rosemary Marinade (page 217) or Glazed Orange-Hoisin Chicken (page 190).

2 tablespoons blanched slivered almonds
1½ cups water
1 small zucchini, cut into ¼-inch dice
1½ cups Chicken Stock (page 342)
1 tablespoon unsalted butter
1 cup quick-cooking couscous
¼ teaspoon ground cumin
1 tablespoon finely chopped fresh cilantro
1 tablespoon finely chopped fresh mint
3 tablespoons golden raisins
½ teaspoon salt
¼ teaspoon freshly ground black pepper

Advance Preparation

Can be prepared up to 2 hours ahead and kept at room temperature. Reheat gently in the top of a double boiler over medium heat for 10 minutes.

1   Preheat the oven to 350°F. Spread the almonds in a single layer on a baking sheet and toast for 5 to 7 minutes, or until lightly browned. (Alternatively, place them in a nonstick skillet over medium heat and toast for 3 to 4 minutes, or until lightly browned.) Set aside.

2   Bring the water to a simmer in a medium saucepan over medium-high heat. Add the zucchini, cover, and cook for 4 minutes. Drain the zucchini in a colander and set aside.

3   Combine the stock and butter in another medium saucepan over medium-high heat and bring to a boil. Add the couscous and stir. Cover, remove from the heat, and let stand for 5 minutes.

4   Add the zucchini and the remaining ingredients and toss to combine. Taste for seasoning. Serve immediately.

When you're looking for a rice side dish that is flavorful but not overpowering, this is it—a dish I fall back on time and time again. Sautéing the rice first results in a more intense flavor. Leeks, carrots, zucchini, and parsley add lots of color. Serve with Asian Glazed Pork Tenderloin (page 240), Glazed Halibut with Orange-Chive Sauce (page 160), or Roasted Cornish Hens with Honey-Tangerine Marinade (page 191).

CONFETTI RICE PILAF

SERVES 4 TO 6

2 tablespoons olive oil

1 small leek, white part only, cleaned and finely chopped

1½ cups long-grain rice

1 small carrot, peeled and shredded

1 small zucchini, shredded

3 cups hot water or Chicken Stock (page 342)

1 teaspoon salt

¼ teaspoon freshly ground black pepper

2 tablespoons finely chopped fresh parsley

2 tablespoons freshly grated Parmesan cheese

Advance Preparation

Can be prepared up to 2 hours ahead and kept at room temperature. Reheat gently in the top of a double boiler over medium heat for 10 minutes.

1   In a medium saucepan over medium heat, heat the oil. Add the leek and sauté for 3 minutes, or until slightly softened. Raise the heat to high and add the rice. Toast the rice for about 3 minutes, stirring constantly. Reduce the heat to medium, add the carrot and zucchini, and continue to cook, stirring, for another minute.

2   Add the hot water to the rice, stir, and bring to a boil. Cover and reduce the heat to medium-low. Simmer for about 20 minutes, or until all the liquid has been absorbed and the rice is tender.

3   Add the salt, pepper, parsley, and Parmesan and blend them in with a large fork. Taste for seasoning and serve immediately.

RICE PILAF WITH FRESH CORN AND PEANUTS

SERVES 4

Advance Preparation

Can be prepared up to 2 hours ahead and kept at room temperature. Reheat gently in the top of a double boiler over medium heat for 10 minutes.

Here's a rice dish that multiplies easily and goes well with Asian entrées like Indonesian Leg of Lamb (page 222) or Glazed Orange-Hoisin Chicken (page 190). Dry roasted peanuts and corn create unusual textural interest.

1 tablespoon olive oil
4 scallions, white and light green parts only, finely chopped
1 cup long-grain rice
2 cups Chicken Stock (page 342)
½ cup fresh corn kernels (from about 1 medium ear)
½ teaspoon salt
¼ teaspoon freshly ground black pepper
¼ cup roasted peanuts, coarsely chopped
2 tablespoons finely chopped fresh parsley

1. In a medium saucepan over medium heat, heat the oil. Add the scallions and sauté for 3 minutes, or until slightly softened. Raise the heat to high and add the rice. Toast the rice for about 3 minutes, stirring constantly.

2. Add the stock, stir, and bring to a boil. Reduce the heat to medium-low, cover, and simmer for 12 to 15 minutes, until almost all the liquid has been absorbed. Add the corn and cook for 3 to 5 minutes longer, until the rice and corn are tender.

3. Add the salt, pepper, peanuts, and parsley and blend them in with a large fork. Taste for seasoning and serve immediately.

These little towers of green rice make a particularly pretty presentation. You can also serve this as a side dish without molding the rice. Just spoon it into a bowl and serve.

SPINACH RICE TIMBALES

SERVES 6 TO 8

2 tablespoons olive oil
2 medium shallots, minced
4 medium white mushrooms, brushed clean and finely chopped
One 10-ounce bunch of spinach, tough stems removed, cleaned and torn into 1-inch pieces
1 quart water or Chicken Stock (page 342)
2 cups long-grain rice
¼ teaspoon salt
Pinch of freshly ground black pepper
1 cup freshly grated Parmesan cheese
2 tablespoons finely chopped fresh basil or parsley

Advance Preparation
Can be prepared through step 1 up to 4 hours ahead and kept at room temperature.

1   In a large skillet over medium heat, heat 1 tablespoon of the oil. Add the shallots and sauté for 3 minutes. Add the mushrooms and continue sautéing until the mushrooms are soft and there is no liquid remaining in the pan, 3 to 4 minutes longer. Add the spinach, raise the heat to medium-high, cover, and cook for 2 to 3 minutes, or until the spinach is wilted, stirring once. Set aside.

2   Combine the water or stock and remaining 1 tablespoon oil in a medium saucepan and bring to a boil over medium-high heat. Stir in the rice, cover, and reduce the heat to medium-low. Cook the rice for 15 to 20 minutes, or until all the liquid is absorbed. Add the spinach mixture, salt, pepper, Parmesan, and herbs and stir to mix with a large fork. Taste for seasoning.

3   Lightly oil six 8-ounce or eight 6-ounce timbale molds or custard cups. Spoon the rice mixture evenly into the molds and pack firmly. To serve, invert the molds onto serving plates by tapping the molds to release them. Serve immediately.

274   Parmesan Toasts

275   Sun-Dried Tomato Toasts

276   Spiced Pumpkin-Hazelnut Bread

278   Ciji's Scones with Currants

279   Fresh Pear Bread

280   Maple Corn Muffins

281   Corn Tortillas

282   Crisp Tortilla Chips

283   Pizza Dough

286   Country Sourdough Bread

288   Sourdough Rye Rolls

290   Walnut Bread

292   Jalapeño Cheese Bread or Rustic Bread Sticks

294   Focaccia

B R E A D S

PARMESAN TOASTS

MAKES 24 TOASTS

In the 1950s Perino's Restaurant in Los Angeles was famous for what we used to call "Continental cuisine" and for its warm pumpernickel toasts. These delectable little toasts of French bread with a melted layer of freshly grated Parmesan are more traditional, though they're also good made with pumpernickel. I like to serve these crispy toasts with a variety of tapenades. You can easily double or triple this recipe for a large party.

24 thin slices French or sourdough baguette

2 tablespoons unsalted butter, melted

2 tablespoons olive oil

⅓ cup freshly grated Parmesan

1 Preheat the oven to 375°F. Arrange the bread slices on a baking sheet and toast for 5 minutes.

2 Meanwhile, in a small bowl, whisk together the melted butter and the oil. Brush each toast with the mixture. Spread the Parmesan on a flat plate and press each toast into the cheese to coat evenly. Return the toasts to the baking sheet and bake for 5 to 7 minutes longer, or until the cheese is melted but not browned. Watch carefully. Let cool.

Advance Preparation

Can be prepared up to 1 week ahead and stored in an airtight container.

You can make your own sun-dried tomato paste by combining softened sun-dried tomatoes with a bit of olive oil in a food processor and puréeing the mixture to a paste. But, of course, store-bought paste works fine as well. These crispy toasts are delicious with cheese and on top of soups or salads for extra flavor.

SUN-DRIED
TOMATO TOASTS

MAKES 24 TOASTS

---

24 thin slices French or sourdough baguette

⅓ cup olive oil

2 to 3 tablespoons sun-dried tomato paste or Pesto (page 349)

---

1 Preheat the oven to 375°F. Arrange the bread slices on a baking sheet and toast for 5 minutes.

2 Meanwhile, in a small mixing bowl, combine the oil and tomato paste and mix until well blended. Brush the tomato mixture evenly on each toast. Return the toasts to the baking sheet and bake for 5 minutes longer, or until baked through. Let cool.

Advance Preparation
Can be prepared up to 1 week ahead and stored in an airtight container.

SPICED PUMPKIN-HAZELNUT BREAD

MAKES TWO 4-BY-8-INCH LOAVES

I love the smell of bread baking in my kitchen, and this recipe has a particularly wonderful fragrance. Toasted hazelnuts add just the right flavor to this orange-scented bread. If you can't find hazelnuts, sliced almonds are a good alternative. You can use 2 teaspoons prepared pumpkin pie spice in place of the spices given here.

Offer small slices of this quick bread accompanied by orange-honey butter (see page 280) and a hot cup of tea on a cool afternoon. If you're wondering why this recipe makes two loaves, look in the desserts chapter. There you'll find Pumpkin Bread Pudding with Eggnog Brandy Sauce (page 320), a sublime ending to any cold-weather meal, which is a great use for the second loaf.

Advance Preparation

This bread tastes best on the day it's baked. It freezes well wrapped in aluminum foil for up to 2 months.

½ cup chopped hazelnuts

4 tablespoons unsalted butter, at room temperature

½ cup plus 2 tablespoons firmly packed dark brown sugar

½ cup granulated sugar

2 large eggs

1 teaspoon finely chopped orange zest

½ cup fresh orange juice

1 cup canned pumpkin purée

2 cups all-purpose flour

¼ teaspoon salt

2 teaspoons baking powder

½ teaspoon baking soda

½ teaspoon ground cinnamon

½ teaspoon freshly grated nutmeg

½ teaspoon ground ginger

½ teaspoon ground allspice

½ cup golden raisins

1   Preheat the oven to 350°F. Grease and flour two 4-by-8-inch loaf pans. Spread the hazelnuts in a single layer on a baking sheet and toast for 5 to 7 minutes, or until lightly browned. Transfer to a plate and set aside.

2   In a large mixing bowl, beat the butter with the sugars using an electric mixer on medium speed until well blended. Add the eggs, orange zest and juice, and pumpkin and blend well on low speed.

3   In a medium mixing bowl, whisk together the flour, salt, baking powder, baking soda, and spices.

4   Add the dry ingredients to the pumpkin mixture and beat on low speed, mixing until blended. *Do not overmix.* Add the raisins and hazelnuts and mix just enough to combine.

5   Divide the batter evenly between the loaf pans and bake for 45 to 50 minutes, or until a toothpick inserted into the center comes out clean. Let cool in the pans for at least 15 minutes, then turn the loaves out onto a wire rack and let cool completely. Serve at room temperature.

CIJI'S SCONES WITH CURRANTS

MAKES 16 TO 18 SCONES

My friend Ciji Ware, the historical novelist, is also a serious scone maker. Teatime, California style, means enjoying a basketful of these warm crumbly treats with your favorite fruit spread instead of the traditional thick clotted cream. Ciji's recipe calls for low-fat milk for glazing the scones instead of the usual cream, yet the scones still become golden brown. This currant-studded quick bread is perfect for a late afternoon break. Serve with small bowls of assorted fruit spreads.

Advance Preparation

This is best made just before serving.

2 cups all-purpose flour
1 tablespoon baking powder
1 teaspoon baking soda
Pinch of salt
¼ cup sugar
6 tablespoons cold unsalted butter
⅓ cup dried currants
1 large egg plus enough low-fat milk to make ¾ cup

1   Preheat the oven to 350°F. Grease a large baking sheet. Sift the flour together with the baking powder, baking soda, and salt into a bowl. Stir in the sugar.

2   Cut the butter into small pieces and blend it into the dry ingredients with a wooden spoon to create a crumbly mixture. Add the currants.

3   In a glass measuring cup, mix the egg and milk and reserve 2 tablespoons to glaze the scones. Add the rest to the flour mixture, mixing just enough to create a dough mixture that can be pressed into a ball.

4   On a lightly floured board, roll or pat out the dough into a circle about 1 inch thick.

5   Dust a round 1½- or 2-inch cookie cutter with flour and cut the dough in rounds. Pat the trimmings into a ball, roll out again, and cut more scones. Place the scones on the prepared baking sheet. Brush with the reserved egg mixture.

6   Place the scones in the middle of the oven and bake for 15 to 18 minutes, or until golden brown and firm to the touch. Serve hot.

Select pears that are slightly underripe, since the cooking process tends to soften them. Fresh winter pears, unlike most other fruits, develop their sweet flavor and superb juiciness when ripened off the tree. Use the juicy, fine-textured Comice or Bosc pear. The pleasing contrast of the sweet fruit and the nutty pecans, nutmeg, and ginger makes this a satisfying fresh quick bread that can be served at breakfast or with eggs for brunch.

FRESH PEAR BREAD

MAKES ONE 9-BY-5-INCH LOAF

⅔ cup coarsely chopped pecans

2 cups all-purpose flour

1 teaspoon baking soda

½ teaspoon salt

¼ teaspoon ground ginger

¼ teaspoon freshly grated nutmeg

½ cup (1 stick) unsalted butter, at room temperature

¾ cup sugar

2 large eggs

¼ cup sour cream

1 teaspoon vanilla extract

1 large Comice or Bosc pear, peeled, cored, and coarsely chopped

Zest of 1 lemon, finely chopped

Advance Preparation
This bread tastes best on the day it's baked, but it can be prepared up to 1 day ahead and kept at room temperature, wrapped in aluminum foil to retain its moisture.

1   Preheat the oven to 350°F. Butter and flour a 9-by-5-inch loaf pan. Spread the pecans in a single layer on a baking sheet and toast for 5 to 7 minutes, or until lightly browned. Transfer to a plate. Sift together the flour, baking soda, salt, ginger, and nutmeg into a bowl.

2   In a large mixing bowl, using an electric mixer, beat the butter and sugar on medium speed until light and fluffy. Beat in the eggs one at a time. Beat in the sour cream and vanilla. Add the sifted flour mixture and blend well on low speed. Add the pear, pecans, and lemon zest and mix well on low speed.

3   Transfer the batter to the prepared pan and bake for about 1 hour, or until a toothpick inserted into the center comes out clean.

4   Let cool in the pan for 10 to 15 minutes, then turn the bread out onto a wire rack. Let cool completely before slicing.

MAPLE CORN MUFFINS

MAKES 12 REGULAR OR

48 MINI MUFFINS

Advance Preparation
The muffins can be prepared up to 8 hours ahead and reheated in a 350°F oven just before serving.

These sweet little corn nuggets are a big hit on my holiday table. I serve them with orange-honey butter. To make orange-honey butter, combine orange zest with softened unsalted butter and orange blossom honey and mix until well blended. Combining flour with cornmeal lightens the batter, and the sweet maple and brown sugar flavors bring out the inherent creamy sweetness of the corn. You can also make these in the mini-muffin size. Serve with tea in a pretty napkin-lined basket with your favorite butter and preserves.

2 cups all-purpose flour

1 cup yellow cornmeal

1 tablespoon baking powder

½ teaspoon salt

¼ cup firmly packed light brown sugar

2 large eggs

6 tablespoons unsalted butter, melted

1 cup milk

⅓ cup maple syrup

½ cup fresh corn kernels (from about 1 medium ear)

Orange-honey butter for serving (optional; see recipe introduction)

1 Preheat the oven to 350°F. Grease a standard 12-cup muffin tin or 48-cup mini muffin tin. Whisk together the flour, cornmeal, baking powder, and salt together in a large mixing bowl.

2 In a medium mixing bowl, whisk the brown sugar into the eggs until well blended. Add the melted butter, milk, and maple syrup and mix well.

3 Pour the wet ingredients over the dry ingredients and fold together with a rubber spatula until the dry ingredients are completely blended. Add the corn kernels and stir just until combined. Spoon the batter into the muffin cups, filling them two-thirds of the way up. Bake for 20 minutes for mini muffins or 25 to 30 minutes for standard muffins, or until the tops are golden brown and a toothpick inserted into the center comes out clean. Let cool in the pan for 15 minutes. Serve immediately, with the orange-honey butter if desired.

There is nothing better than a properly cooked fresh tortilla. The method here is the traditional one, which requires a conventional tortilla press, a clever gadget that really works, available in most Mexican markets or a gourmet cookware store. Just shape the masa into small balls of dough, then place one in the middle of the tortilla maker and press down to flatten and cook the dough at the same time. The process is even easier if you buy good-quality fresh masa dough at a *tortilleria;* 1 pound yields about 12 tortillas. It's very entertaining to make these as your guests watch. Tortillas are particularly good with Sweet Potato–Jalapeño Soup with Tomatillo Cream (page 48), Grilled Chicken, Black Bean, and Corn Salad with Salsa Dressing (page 98), and Grilled Skirt Steak with Avocado-Tomato Salsa (page 206).

CORN TORTILLAS

MAKES 12 TORTILLAS

2 cups masa harina
1½ cups warm water

1   Have ready twenty-four 7-inch squares of wax paper. Combine the masa harina and warm water in a medium bowl. Blend the mixture with a fork until it forms a smooth ball. Divide the dough into 12 pieces. Form the pieces into balls and cover the balls of dough with an inverted bowl.

2   Put a piece of wax paper on the bottom half of a tortilla press and place a dough ball on it, opposite the handle and slightly off center toward the edge of the press. Flatten the ball slightly and cover it with another wax paper square. Lower the top of the press onto the wax paper and press down firmly on the lever until the tortilla measures about 6 to 6½ inches in diameter. Make all the tortillas in the same way with the remaining dough.

3   Heat a griddle over high heat until hot. Carefully peel off the top paper square from a tortilla and invert the tortilla onto the griddle. After 5 seconds, peel off the remaining wax paper. Cook the tortilla for 1 minute; turn it and cook until it looks dry and flecked with golden spots, 30 seconds to 1 minute longer. Transfer the tortilla to a plate or a napkin-lined basket. Cook the remaining tortillas in the same way. If they're not used immediately, wrap them in stacks of 4 in aluminum foil.

Advance Preparation
The tortillas can be made up to 1 day ahead and refrigerated. Reheat wrapped in aluminum foil in a 350°F oven for 10 minutes for best taste, or place on a gas burner for 20 seconds on each side, using tongs to turn them.

CRISP TORTILLA CHIPS

SERVES 6

These tasty, crunchy chips are not deep-fried or greasy. Serve with Shrimp Salsa (page 23), Asian Guacamole (page 34), or Green Pea Guacamole (page 33).

6 Corn Tortillas (page 281), cut into triangles
Salt and freshly ground black pepper

1 Preheat the oven to 400°F. Arrange the tortilla triangles on a baking sheet. Bake for 10 minutes, or until crisp. Transfer to a bowl. Season with salt and pepper to taste and serve immediately.

Advance Preparation

The chips can be made up to 8 hours ahead and stored in an airtight container.

This food-processor method for pizza dough is very easy. Rye and cornmeal are combined with all-purpose flour for a more interesting flavor.

Two ¼-ounce envelopes active dry yeast or two ⅗-ounce cakes fresh yeast

1 teaspoon sugar

1 cup lukewarm water

2½ cups all-purpose flour

½ cup rye flour

2 tablespoons yellow cornmeal

1½ teaspoons salt

2 tablespoons olive oil

1   Sprinkle the dry yeast or crumble the fresh yeast and sugar over ¼ cup of the warm water in a glass measuring cup and let stand for 10 minutes, or until small bubbles form. Stir to dissolve the yeast.

2   In a food processor fitted with the metal blade, process the flours, cornmeal, and salt briefly to mix. Add the remaining ¾ cup warm water and the oil to the dissolved yeast. With the machine running, slowly pour in the yeast mixture. If the dough is too dry to come together, add an extra tablespoon of water and process again. Process for 1 minute to knead the dough.

3   Transfer the dough to a lightly oiled bowl and turn to coat. Cover with a damp cloth and let rise in a warm place for about 1 hour, or until doubled in volume.

4   Punch the dough down and knead it again briefly on a lightly floured work surface until smooth and elastic. Divide the dough into 2 equal balls and press each out with your fingertips into a 9-inch round on an oiled baking sheet. Cover the dough with a damp cloth or plastic wrap and let rise for 30 minutes.

5   Proceed with the recipe or refrigerate until ready to use.

Advance Preparation

Can be prepared through step 4 up to 1 day ahead, wrapped in plastic wrap, and refrigerated. To continue, remove it from the refrigerator, allow at least 1 hour for the dough to come to room temperature, and then let it rise for 20 to 30 minutes. Shape as directed in the recipe. The dough can be frozen indefinitely, but it takes at least 3 hours to thaw (this cannot be hurried in the microwave). Let the dough rise for 20 to 30 minutes and shape as directed in the recipe.

Bread Dough

Here are three basic methods for the preparation of yeast breads. The difference between homemade bread and bread bought in the store is enormous. Ingredient amounts are not specified since they will vary with each recipe.

Active dry or fresh cake yeast

Sweetener

Lukewarm water

All-purpose and/or whole-wheat flour

Salt

To make the dough by hand:

1   Sprinkle dry yeast or crumble fresh yeast into a bowl with the sweetener. Pour a small portion of the warm water over the yeast and let it stand until it becomes foamy (about 10 minutes). Stir to dissolve the yeast.

2   Reserve ½ cup of the flour. Mix the flour(s), salt, and other dry ingredients together in a bowl and make a well in the center. Mix the yeast mixture with the remaining liquid ingredients and stir the mixture into the flour. Mix well until a soft dough forms, adding the reserved flour a little at a time as needed.

3   Knead the dough on a lightly floured work surface until it is smooth and elastic, dusting the surface with flour occasionally if the dough sticks to it.

4   Transfer the dough to an oiled bowl and turn to coat the entire surface. Cover the dough with a damp cloth and let it rise in a warm place for about 1½ hours, or until doubled in volume.

5   Punch the dough down and knead again briefly on a lightly floured work surface until smooth. Shape the dough into the desired form and place it on an oiled pan. Cover the dough lightly with a damp cloth and let rise until doubled in volume again (about 1 hour).

6   Bake as directed in the recipe.

To make the dough in a food processor:

1 Sprinkle dry yeast or crumble fresh yeast into a bowl with the sweetener. Pour a small portion of the warm water over the yeast and let it stand until it becomes foamy (about 10 minutes). Stir to dissolve the yeast.

2 Reserve ½ cup of the flour. In a food processor, combine the flour and other dry ingredients and process briefly to mix them. Mix the yeast mixture with the remaining liquid ingredients and add the mixture to the food processor. Process the dough until it gathers into a ball, adding the reserved flour a little at a time.

3 Process for 1 minute to knead the dough until it is smooth and elastic. Continue with steps 4, 5, and 6 from the by-hand method.

To make the dough in a stand mixer with a dough hook:

1 Sprinkle dry yeast or crumble fresh yeast into a bowl with the sweetener. Pour a small portion of the warm water over the yeast and let it stand until it becomes foamy (about 10 minutes). Stir to dissolve the yeast.

2 Reserve ½ cup of flour. Put the flour and salt into a large bowl of the mixer. With a dough hook turning at low speed, gradually pour in the yeast mixture with the remaining liquid ingredients.

3 Let the machine run until the dough is very smooth and elastic, adding reserved flour as needed. Continue with steps 4, 5, and 6 from the by-hand method.

To freeze dough:

1 After the first rising, punch the dough down and shape it as the recipe directs. Wrap the dough tightly in plastic wrap and then in foil and freeze it for up to 1 month. When you are ready to use it, remove the dough from the freezer and place it in the pan per the recipe, let thaw, and allow it to complete the second rising. Proceed with individual recipe directions.

COUNTRY SOURDOUGH BREAD

MAKES TWO

11-BY-3½-INCH LOAVES

San Francisco is famous the world over for its sourdough bread. The bakers there rightly claim that the special yeasts and moist sea air of the Bay Area give their dough its unique taste. But sourdough, which had its origins in the mining camps of the California gold rush, can be baked anywhere.

What exactly is sourdough? It's simply bread that uses natural, airborne yeast cultures for its leavening rather than commercially cultured yeast. In this recipe, sourdough starter—which takes about 3 days to develop—is used for its flavor and a little yeast is added to ensure that the dough rises properly. Your own sourdough will be different from everyone else's because the wild yeasts vary from place to place. Some starters are handed down from generation to generation, getting more and more sour and delicious as they are repeatedly used and replenished. After you've tried this basic bread, experiment with the Sourdough Rye Rolls (page 288). Sourdough bread is extremely versatile and is excellent with pâtés, spreads, cheeses, and soups.

SOURDOUGH STARTER

One ¼-ounce envelope active dry yeast or one ⅗-ounce cake fresh yeast

1 teaspoon sugar

2 cups lukewarm water

2 cups unbleached all-purpose flour

BREAD

1 cup sourdough starter (above)

1½ cups lukewarm water

5 cups unbleached all-purpose flour

One ¼-ounce envelope active dry yeast or one ⅗-ounce cake fresh yeast

1 tablespoon sugar

2 teaspoons salt

1   To make the starter, sprinkle the dry yeast or crumble the fresh yeast and sugar over ½ cup of the warm water in a large glass bowl and let stand for 10 minutes, or until small bubbles form.

2   Stir 1¼ cups of the remaining water and the flour into the yeast mixture and beat with a wooden spoon until fairly smooth. If a few small lumps remain, they will dissolve during fermentation. Stir in the remaining ¼ cup water and beat briefly. The consistency of the mixture will be like that of thin crepe batter.

Note

Never prepare starter in a metal container. Store unused starter, covered with plastic wrap with a few holes poked in it, in the refrigerator. About once a week, stir in ½ of cup water and ½ cup of flour. Leave the mixture out overnight, then refrigerate.

Advance Preparation

This bread is best on the day it is baked.

3 Cover the starter with a cloth and leave it in a warm place free from drafts for 2 or 3 days, or until the mixture smells sour. If you like a strong sourdough flavor, leave the mixture for up to 5 days. Stir it once every day. If you forget to stir it, a skin may form on top. The skin should be removed.

4 To make the bread, mix 1 cup of the starter with 1 cup of the warm water and 1 cup of the flour. Cover the dough and let stand in a warm place for at least 3 hours or up to overnight.

5 Sprinkle the dry yeast or crumble the fresh yeast and sugar over ¼ cup of the remaining water in a cup or small bowl and let stand for 10 minutes, or until small bubbles form. Stir to dissolve the yeast.

6 Sift the remaining 4 cups flour into a large mixing bowl and make a well in the center. Add the starter mixture, dissolved yeast, remaining ¼ cup water, and salt to the well and mix briefly. Gradually stir the flour into the mixture in the center of the well. When it becomes difficult to stir, knead in the remaining flour. If the dough is dry, knead in an extra tablespoon of water. If the dough is very sticky, knead in 1 or 2 tablespoons flour.

7 Turn the dough out onto a lightly floured work surface and knead until smooth and elastic, dusting the surface occasionally with more flour if the dough sticks to it. Transfer the dough to an oiled bowl and turn to coat the entire surface. Cover with a damp cloth and let rise in a warm place for 1 to 1½ hours, or until doubled in volume.

8 Grease 2 baking sheets. Divide the dough into 2 pieces and, on a lightly floured work surface, roll out each piece into a smooth, oval loaf about 11 by 3½ inches, with the ends slightly tapered. Set a loaf on each prepared baking sheet. Cover and let rise in a warm place for about 1 hour, or until nearly doubled in volume.

9 Preheat the oven to 400°F. Put a pan of water on the bottom of the oven while preheating to provide steam.

10 Brush the loaves lightly with water. Using a very sharp knife, cut a few parallel diagonal slashes across the tops of the loaves (cut carefully and without pressing too hard to avoid deflating the dough).

11 Bake for 40 to 45 minutes, or until the loaves are golden brown. When you tap the bottom of each loaf with your fist, it should sound hollow. Let the bread cool on a wire rack.

SOURDOUGH RYE ROLLS

MAKES 20 ROLLS

These earthy brown rolls feature a balance of three distinct flavors to achieve one original taste. The aromatic sourdough blends well with the heavier rye; both flours are strengthened by the addition of flavor-packed caraway. Serve as an accompaniment to a first course, soup, or salad.

½ cup Sourdough Starter (page 286), stirred before measuring

One ¼-ounce envelope active dry yeast or one ⅗-ounce cake fresh yeast

1 teaspoon sugar

⅔ cup lukewarm water

1 cup rye flour

2 cups all-purpose flour

2 tablespoons vegetable or olive oil

4 teaspoons caraway seeds

2 teaspoons salt

Advance Preparation

The rolls are best on the day they are baked.

1   Prepare the starter at least 3 days before making the rolls.

2   Sprinkle the dry yeast or crumble the fresh yeast and the sugar over ⅓ cup of the warm water in a cup or small bowl. Let stand for 10 minutes, or until small bubbles form. Stir to dissolve the yeast.

3   Sift the flours together into a large mixing bowl, reserving ½ cup, and make a well in the center. Add the starter, remaining ⅓ cup water, dissolved yeast mixture, oil, caraway seeds, and salt to the well and mix briefly.

4   Gradually stir the flour into the mixture in the well. When it becomes difficult to stir, knead in the remaining flour. If the dough is dry, knead in an extra table-spoon of water. If the dough is very sticky, knead in 1 or 2 tablespoons flour.

5   Turn the dough out onto a lightly floured work surface and knead until smooth and elastic, dusting the surface occasionally with more flour if the dough sticks to it. Transfer the dough to an oiled bowl and turn to coat the entire surface. Cover with a damp cloth and let rise in a warm place for 1 to 1½ hours, or until doubled in volume.

6   Grease 2 baking sheets. Knead the dough briefly on a lightly floured work surface. Roll it out to a rope about 18 inches long. Cut the rope into 4 equal lengths, and then cut each length into 5 equal pieces. Roll each piece into a ball between cupped palms. Roll each ball on the work surface into an oval roll about 1¼ by 3 inches. Arrange the rolls on the baking sheets, leaving room between them so they can rise. Cover with a damp cloth and let rise in a warm place for about 1 hour, or until doubled in volume. Preheat the oven to 425°F.

7   Bake the rolls for 10 minutes. Reduce the oven temperature to 400°F. Bake for 10 minutes longer, or until the rolls are firm and browned on the top and bottom. Let cool on a wire rack. Serve warm or at room temperature.

WALNUT BREAD

MAKES ONE 10-INCH-LONG LOAF

Advance Preparation

This bread is best on the day it is baked.

Although the nut itself is originally from Persia, the term *English walnut* is attributable to English merchant marines trading in this delicious commodity around the world. Walnuts were first introduced to California by the Franciscan fathers in the 1700s. The nuts have been grown commercially in California since the mid-nineteenth century. Today California produces 99 percent of our domestic supply, all of them English walnuts.

Walnuts take on different flavors depending upon what they are paired with. Chocolate makes them seem bitter, while cream and Cheddar cheese bring out their underlying sweetness. This bread has a double-walnut flavor because it's made with walnut oil. California walnut oil lacks the depth of flavor unique to its imported counterpart, so I recommend that you invest in a small bottle of French walnut oil; keep it refrigerated after opening.

For an interesting variation, add ½ cup of brandy-soaked currants to the dough after adding the walnuts. This bread is an excellent ending to a light meal when paired with semisoft cheeses such as Monterey jack or goat cheese and fresh fruit. It is also good as a breakfast bread served with butter or cream cheese.

One ¼-ounce envelope active dry yeast or one ⅗-ounce cake fresh yeast

1 teaspoon sugar

1¼ cups lukewarm water

½ cup whole-wheat flour

2½ cups unbleached all-purpose flour

3 tablespoons imported walnut oil

1 teaspoon salt

1 cup chopped walnuts

1   Sprinkle the dry yeast or crumble the fresh yeast and sugar over ¼ cup of the warm water in a cup or small bowl. Let stand for 10 minutes, or until small bubbles form. Stir to dissolve the yeast.

2   Sift the flours together into a large mixing bowl, reserving 1 cup, and make a well in the center. Pour the yeast mixture into the well. Add the remaining 1 cup water, walnut oil, and salt to the well and mix briefly. Stir until the ingredients are thoroughly blended and begin to form a ball.

3   Turn the dough out onto a lightly floured work surface and knead until smooth and elastic, adding some of the reserved flour mixture if the dough sticks. Knead in walnuts by sprinkling about one-fourth of them over the dough and the remainder over the working surface. Roll the dough in the nuts while kneading gently. Transfer the dough to an oiled bowl and turn to coat the entire surface. Cover with a damp kitchen towel and let rise in a warm place for 1½ hours, or until doubled in volume.

4   Grease a baking sheet. Punch the dough down and knead briefly on a lightly floured work surface. Roll it out into a smooth, cylindrical loaf about 10 inches long. Set the loaf on the prepared baking sheet. Cover with a damp cloth and let rise in a warm place for about 1 hour, or until nearly doubled in volume. Preheat the oven to 400°F.

5   Bake the bread for about 15 minutes, or until it begins to brown. Reduce the oven temperature to 375°F and continue baking for about 25 minutes longer. When you tap the bottom of the loaf with your fist, it should sound hollow. Let cool in a wire rack. Serve warm or at room temperature.

JALAPEÑO CHEESE BREAD OR RUSTIC BREAD STICKS

MAKES TWO 9-BY-5-INCH LOAVES

OR 20 TO 24 BREAD STICKS

Whether you bake this in a loaf or make the rustic bread sticks, you'll enjoy this spicy but not overpowering California-style bread. The spiciness of the bread can be altered by increasing or reducing the number of jalapeño chilies. This bread goes nicely with Golden Frittata with Tomatillo Salsa (page 112) or Herbed Scrambled Eggs with Goat Cheese (page 115), especially when toasted. I also recommend this with Chicken Minestrone with Mixed-Herb Pesto (page 64). Try serving the warm bread or bread sticks with softened butter mixed with chopped fresh cilantro, minced garlic, and cumin.

Two ¼-ounce envelopes dry active yeast or two ⅗-ounce cakes fresh yeast

1 tablespoon sugar

2¼ cups lukewarm water

¼ cup oil or melted unsalted butter

1 cup whole-wheat flour

5 cups unbleached all-purpose flour

1 tablespoon salt

4 to 6 jalapeño chiles, to taste, seeded and finely chopped (see note)

2 cups shredded Cheddar cheese (½ pound)

1 egg beaten with 1 tablespoon water until foamy

Cornmeal for sprinkling

1   Sprinkle the dry yeast or crumble the fresh yeast and sugar over ½ cup of the lukewarm water in a cup or small bowl. Let stand for 10 minutes, or until small bubbles form. Stir to dissolve the yeast. Add the remaining 1¾ cups water and the oil.

2   Sift the flours together into a large mixing bowl. Set aside 2 cups of the mixture. Add the salt to the remaining mixture and make a well in center. Pour the yeast mixture into the well, add the jalapeños, and mix briefly.

3   Gradually stir in the reserved flour, ½ cup at a time, until the dough loses its stickiness and can be kneaded easily. Turn the dough out onto a lightly floured work surface and knead until smooth and elastic, dusting the surface occasionally with flour if the dough sticks. Transfer to an oiled bowl and turn to coat the entire surface. Cover with a damp cloth and let rise in a warm place for about 1½ hours, or until doubled in volume. Punch down the dough and let rest for about 5 minutes, covered with the cloth. (This allows the dough to regain elasticity.)

Note

When working with chiles, always wear rubber gloves. Wash the cutting surface and knife immediately. If you are using a food processor to knead the dough, add the chiles and cheese by hand so that the pieces stay intact.

Variations

For a spicy finish, try any of these toppings, which go on after brushing on the egg glaze: hot red pepper flakes, coarse salt, chili powder, or garlic salt.

4 Knead the dough again on a lightly floured work surface. Knead in the cheese by sprinkling it on the bread all at once and kneading until distributed.

For Loaves

If making loaves, proceed here. If making bread sticks, proceed as directed below.

5 Grease two 9-by-5-inch loaf pans. Divide the dough into 2 equal pieces and, on the floured surface, roll out each piece into a smooth, cylindrical loaf about 9 inches long. Put the loaves in the pans seam side down, slash the top lightly 3 times with a serrated knife, cover with a damp cloth, and let rise in a warm place for about 1 hour, or until nearly doubled in volume. Preheat the oven to 375°F.

6 Brush the loaves with the egg mixture. Sprinkle lightly with cornmeal.

7 Bake the loaves for about 15 minutes, or until beginning to brown. Reduce the oven temperature to 350°F and continue baking for another 45 minutes, or until the bread sounds hollow when tapped. Let cool on a wire rack. Serve warm or at room temperature.

For Bread Sticks

5 Divide the dough into 2 equal pieces. On a lightly floured work surface, roll each piece into a rope about 20 inches long. With a sharp knife, cut each rope of dough into 10 to 12 equal pieces. Let rest again, covered with a damp cloth or plastic wrap.

6 Using the palms of your hands, roll each piece of dough into a rope ¾- to 1-inch in diameter and about 9 to 10 inches long (or whatever size will fit on your baking sheet). Twist each piece, if desired, to make twisted bread sticks. Transfer to a lightly oiled baking sheet, making sure each piece is about 2 inches apart. Use 2 baking sheets if necessary.

7 Cover loosely with a damp cloth or plastic wrap and let rise in a warm place until doubled in size. Lightly brush each bread stick with the egg mixture and sprinkle with cornmeal.

8 Preheat the oven to 350°F. For soft bread sticks, bake for 12 to 15 minutes, or until lightly browned. Let cool on a wire rack. If you like crispier bread sticks, bake them in a 300°F oven for about 30 minutes, or until they are very crispy and nicely browned.

Advance Preparation

The bread and breadsticks are best on the day baked.

FOCACCIA

MAKES TWO 9-INCH ROUND

LOAVES OR

ONE 10-BY-15-INCH LOAF

Back in 1946, Genevieve Callahan (*The California Cook Book*) described a bread called *fugaccio* that was available in onion or raisin flavor at her local San Francisco Italian bake shop. Today we call it *focaccia*. However you spell it, this is a satisfying bread that Ms. Callahan properly explained "should look rather rough and bubbly, not smooth and flat."

I like a bready focaccia, so I bake it in a pan with a rim to encourage that quality. A pan with higher sides also helps to keep olive oil from dripping onto the bottom of the oven. Choose either the traditional onion or the spicier olive topping, depending on what you are serving with the focaccia. Serve this bread hot from the oven before dinner, with small bowls of extra-virgin olive oil for dipping. It's a comforting companion to a big bowl of soup or Warm Grilled Vegetable and Shrimp Salad (page 106).

Two ¼-ounce envelopes active dry yeast or two ⅗-ounce cakes fresh yeast

1 teaspoon sugar

1 cup lukewarm water

2¾ cups all-purpose flour

2 tablespoons rye flour

2 tablespoons coarse yellow cornmeal

1½ teaspoons salt

1 teaspoon chopped fresh thyme or ½ teaspoon dried

4 tablespoons olive oil

1 teaspoon coarse salt

OLIVE TOPPING

¼ cup Mediterranean green olives, rinsed, drained, pitted, and coarsely chopped

½ fresh jalapeño chile, seeded and minced (see note)

¼ teaspoon fresh, coarsely ground black pepper

ONION TOPPING

3 tablespoons coarsely chopped red onion

3 tablespoons coarsely chopped fresh rosemary

¼ teaspoon fresh, coarsely ground black pepper

Advance Preparation

Can be prepared through step 3 and the dough wrapped and frozen, in which case it will take at least 3 hours to thaw and begin to rise again. *This cannot be hurried in the microwave.* Alternatively, it can be prepared through step 3, refrigerated overnight, and then brought to room temperature before proceeding.

Note

When working with chiles, always wear rubber gloves. Wash the cutting surface and knife immediately

1   In a 2-cup measuring cup, sprinkle the dry yeast or crumble the fresh yeast and sugar over ½ cup of the warm water. Let stand for 10 minutes, or until small bubbles form. Stir to dissolve the yeast. Add the remaining ½ cup water.

2   In a food processor fitted with the metal blade, combine the flours, cornmeal, salt, thyme, and 2 tablespoons of the olive oil and process briefly to mix. Stir the yeast and water mixture again just to blend and, with the machine running, add to the flour mixture in a slow but steady stream. It should take about 10 seconds to add the liquid, and the dough should form a loose ball within 20 to 30 seconds. If the dough does not form a ball, sprinkle over more water, 1 teaspoon at a time. If the dough is too wet and quickly begins to climb up the center column, sprinkle over more flour, 1 tablespoon at a time. Process the dough for a total time of about 60 seconds, in three pulses.

3   Turn out the dough onto a lightly floured work surface and knead very briefly, just to bring it together into a ball. The dough should be loose and soft, just on the verge of being sticky. Don't be tempted to add too much flour at this stage, because it will inhibit the rising of the dough. Place the dough in an oiled bowl, turn to coat, and cover with a damp cloth. Let rise at warm room temperature for 2 to 3 hours, or until doubled in volume, puffy, and wobbly in appearance.

4   Punch down the dough, divide it into 2 equal pieces, and press each piece firmly into an oiled 9-inch round cake pan, pressing the dough well into the corners. Alternatively, press all the dough into one oiled 10-by-15-inch rectangular pan. Note: if you like your focaccia thin and crispy, proceed directly to step 6. If you like a deep and bready loaf, proceed with step 5.

5   Cover the dough again with a damp cloth and let rise at warm room temperature for about 30 minutes, or until slightly puffed and wobbly.

6   Preheat the oven to 475°F. Poke the dough in 5 or 6 places with your fingertips to give it a dimpled effect. Brush the dough with 1 tablespoon of the remaining oil for each round loaf or 2 tablespoons for the large rectangular loaf and sprinkle the coarse salt over the dough. Sprinkle with the topping of your choice and bake for 20 to 25 minutes, turning the pan around halfway through if it seems to be browning unevenly, until the focaccia is golden and nicely risen. Remove from the oven and let cool in the pan for a softer crust or on a wire rack for a crisp crust. Serve slightly warm or at room temperature. Brush the focaccia with a little more olive oil before serving.

298 Baked Pears in Burgundy and Port Glaze

299 Essencia Zabaglione with Fresh Fruit Compote

300 Mixed Exotic Fruit Gazpacho

301 Fresh Apricots and Strawberries with Sour Cream and Brown Sugar

302 Orange, Almond, and Olive Oil Cake

304 Glazed Lemon–Sour Cream Cake

306 Peach Melba Buckle

308 Nectarine Crisp with Dried Cherries

309 Pear-Raspberry Almond Tart

312 Mango and Macadamia Nut Brown-Butter Tart

314 Blueberry-Lemon Tart

316 Tiramisu with Toasted Hazelnuts and Chocolate

318 Vanilla Caramel Cream

320 Pumpkin Bread Pudding with Eggnog Brandy Sauce

322 Chocolate Chip Coffee Cake

324 Walnut Cake with Roasted Blueberry Compote

326 Banana Cake with Chocolate Fudge Frosting

328 Warm Mocha Pudding Cakes

329 Chocolate Freakout

331 Bittersweet Chocolate Hazelnut Torte with Banana Custard Sauce

334 Banana Split Ice Cream Torte

336 White Chocolate and Pistachio Cookies

338 Spicy Crinkle Cookies

339 Chocolate Truffle Brownies

DESSERTS

BAKED PEARS IN BURGUNDY AND PORT GLAZE

SERVES 8

Advance Preparation

Can be prepared up to 8 hours ahead and kept at room temperature.

I always used to peel pears before cooking them. What a wonderful discovery it was when I decided to cook the pears whole and unpeeled. As the pears bake, the skin becomes wrinkled, with a shiny, caramelized exterior reminiscent of a French country dessert. These make a marvelous simple dessert for a dinner party. They are excellent, served either warm or at room temperature. Accompany with a plate of biscotti or White Chocolate and Pistachio Cookies (page 336).

2 cups burgundy, or other dry red wine

1 cup tawny port wine

1 cup sugar

1 cinnamon stick, about 4 inches long

One 2-inch piece lemon zest

One 2-inch piece orange zest

8 ripe but firm Bosc pears, with stems attached

GARNISH

Fresh mint leaves

Vanilla ice cream for serving (optional)

1 Preheat the oven to 350°F. In a medium, nonaluminum saucepan over medium heat, bring the red wine, port, sugar, cinnamon stick, and lemon and orange zests to a simmer and stir to dissolve the sugar. Remove the cinnamon stick.

2 Core the pears from the bottom and then cut the bottoms flat so that they can stand upright. Place the pears, stem side up, in a large baking dish and pour the wine mixture over them. Bake the pears for about 1 hour, or until tender when pierced with the tip of a knife, basting every few minutes with the wine mixture.

3 Remove the pears from the oven and pour off the remaining wine mixture into a medium saucepan. Bring the wine mixture to a boil and cook until it's reduced to a glaze. Spoon the glaze over the pears on a large serving platter or on individual dessert plates, garnish with the mint leaves, and serve warm, with the vanilla ice cream, if desired.

Zabaglione is a quick last-minute dessert that is always well received. California's Essencia wine is substituted for Marsala in this variation on the classic zabaglione with outstanding results. Andy Quady, the owner of Quady Winery, also makes a low-alcohol (4 percent) orange muscat dessert wine called Electra, which has hints of melons and berries. If you prefer less alcohol, substitute Electra for the Essencia. Pass a plate of Spicy Crinkle Cookies (page 338).

ESSENCIA
ZABAGLIONE
WITH FRESH
FRUIT COMPOTE

SERVES 6 TO 8

ZABAGLIONE

6 medium egg yolks

3 tablespoons sugar

½ cup Essencia wine

3 tablespoons heavy (whipping) cream

4 medium oranges, peeled and sectioned

2 pints strawberries, hulled and thinly sliced

GARNISH

Fresh mint sprigs

Advance Preparation

If you're serving the zabaglione chilled, it can be prepared through step 2 up to 6 hours ahead, covered, and refrigerated.

1   To make the zabaglione, in the top pan of a medium-size double boiler, combine the egg yolks, sugar, and wine and beat until well blended.

2   Place the pan over (but not touching) simmering water over medium heat and whisk the mixture vigorously until it becomes foamy and begins to thicken. Remove from the heat, add the cream, and whisk until incorporated. The mixture should be thick and custardlike and should coat a wooden spoon.

3   Place the oranges and strawberries in a mixing bowl and toss to mix.

4   To serve, spoon the mixed fruit into small individual serving bowls (wine goblets look pretty). Pour on the zabaglione, garnish with the mint sprigs, and serve immediately. You can also serve the zabaglione chilled. Be sure to whisk it right before serving.

MIXED
EXOTIC FRUIT
GAZPACHO

SERVES 6

Advance Preparation

Can be prepared through step 2 up
to 1 day ahead and refrigerated.

Sitting on the terrace of the Ritz-Carlton in Laguna Niguel, I was served a version of
this elegant, refreshing dessert gazpacho. The chef there prepared a fresh basil sorbet
to accompany the chilled soup, but any high-quality fruit sorbet works here. Decorate
the soup with the fruit, the sorbet, and mint leaves. If you prefer a pure red soup,
cook the mint leaves in the sugar syrup and strain them out before continuing.

1½ cups water
¾ cup sugar
2 pints strawberries, hulled
1 pint raspberries
Juice of 1 lemon
2 tablespoons finely chopped fresh mint
1 mango, peeled and cut into small balls with a small melon baller
1 papaya, peeled, seeded, and finely diced
1 kiwi, peeled and julienned

GARNISH

1 pint fruit sorbet (raspberry or strawberry works well)
Fresh mint leaves

1   In a medium saucepan over medium heat, combine the water and sugar and
    simmer until the sugar is completely dissolved. Set the syrup aside.

2   Reserve ½ pint of the smaller strawberries for garnish and combine the rest
    with the raspberries and lemon juice in a blender or food processor fitted
    with the metal blade. Process until puréed. Strain the berry purée through a
    fine-mesh strainer into a large, nonaluminum bowl and add the sugar syrup
    and chopped mint. Mix well, cover, and refrigerate until well chilled, at least
    2 hours.

3   To serve, cut the reserved strawberries into julienne. Divide the berry purée
    among 6 shallow soup bowls, and then arrange the fruits on top in a whimsical
    pattern. Place a small scoop of sorbet in the center of each bowl and garnish
    with the mint leaves. Serve immediately.

Here's a quick dessert idea that lets summer produce shine. Picture big, juicy red strawberries and velvety apricot quarters on a platter surrounded by small pots of brown sugar and sour cream for dipping. A plate of biscotti or White Chocolate and Pistachio Cookies (page 336) are perfect with the fruit. Serve with a cooling glass of late-harvest Riesling.

12 ripe but firm medium apricots

1 pint large strawberries with stems, cleaned but not hulled

1 cup firmly packed dark brown sugar

1 cup sour cream or crème fraîche

GARNISH

Fresh mint sprigs

1   Cut the apricots in quarters and remove the pits. On the outer edge of a serving platter, arrange the apricot quarters alternating with the strawberries. Put the brown sugar and sour cream in small serving bowls and place in the center of the platter. Garnish with the mint sprigs and serve immediately.

Advance Preparation
This is best made just before serving.

ORANGE, ALMOND, AND OLIVE OIL CAKE

SERVES 8

I was once invited to the McEvoy Olive Oil Ranch in Marin County for lunch on a cold rainy day. As I arrived, Chef Gerald Gass was putting the finishing touches on a rustic orange, almond, and olive oil cake studded with sliced almonds that were cooked right into the batter. We sat in a large kitchen/dining room where the chef prepared a perfect cold-weather menu. Outside a brick oven was fired up, baking crusty baguettes to accompany a hearty cassoulet. A simple salad composed of shredded fennel with olive oil and Meyer lemon juice followed. The whole meal was memorable, but it was thoughts of the unique dessert that inspired me to create one similar. I adapted my recipe from *Feast of the Olive* by Maggie Blyth Klein, and I incorporated Chef Gass's touch of baking sliced almonds in the cake. The unexpected ingredient, extra-virgin olive oil, imparts a fruity flavor and a bit heavier texture. Blood oranges, if in season, intensify the citrus taste and make a beautiful garnish. This citrus and almond cake is pure California, brimming with oranges, almonds, and olive oil. If you like, accompany with a big bowl of mixed berries. Try a California orange after-dinner wine like Quady Winery's Essencia or Electra with this and you'll wish dessert would go on forever.

Advance Preparation

Can be prepared up to 1 day ahead and kept at room temperature, tightly covered.

¼ cup plus 2 tablespoons sliced almonds
6 ounces whole blanched almonds or 1¼ cups almond meal
1 cup all-purpose flour
1 tablespoon baking powder
4 large eggs, at room temperature
1½ cups granulated sugar
Zest of 1 medium orange, finely chopped
Juice of 1 medium orange (about ½ cup)
½ cup extra-virgin olive oil

GARNISH

Powdered sugar
Thinly sliced oranges
Fresh mint leaves
Whipped cream or crème fraîche

1   Preheat the oven to 350°F. Oil a 9-inch springform pan with olive oil. Sprinkle the sliced almonds on the bottom and halfway up the sides of the pan evenly, making sure the almonds stick to the pan.

2   In a food processor fitted with the metal blade, process the whole almonds until finely ground, almost like bread crumbs. In a medium mixing bowl, combine the ground almonds, flour, and baking powder and set aside.

3   In a large mixing bowl, using an electric mixer on medium speed, beat the eggs until frothy. Slowly add the granulated sugar and beat the mixture until it is light, thick, and lemon colored. Slowly add the flour mixture and then add the orange zest and juice and the oil, mixing just to combine.

4   Pour the batter into the prepared pan and bake for 50 to 60 minutes, or until a skewer inserted into the center comes out clean. Let cool, then remove the sides of the pan. Carefully invert the pan onto a serving platter, using a sharp knife to separate the cake from the pan.

5   To serve, sprinkle the powdered sugar in a decorative pattern on top. Cut the cake into wedges and transfer to dessert plates. Arrange the orange slices, mint leaves, and a dollop of whipped cream on the side.

QUICK FRUIT DESSERTS

When you find you're in a last-minute pinch for dessert, think of simple fruit desserts. Fruit looks particularly appealing when served in a large balloon wineglass. Here are some suggestions:

- Strawberries with a splash of balsamic vinegar and freshly ground black pepper
- Cut-up nectarines or peaches with a splash of Muscat Canelli
- Blueberries with a vanilla crème anglaise
- Sliced ripe pears with chunks of Roquefort cheese
- Dried cherries marinated in a brandied sugar syrup and served in compote dishes with crumbled blue cheese
- Sliced and peeled apples or pears sautéed in butter and then caramelized with sugar, spooned over French vanilla ice cream
- Fresh figs, quartered and served with honey-ricotta cheese
- Sliced oranges with candied orange zest

GLAZED LEMON–SOUR CREAM CAKE

SERVES 8 TO 10

I have tried at least ten different lemon cake recipes in search of one that would satisfy my personal preference for a clean lemon flavor, fine crumb, moist texture, and ease of preparation. Most of the recipes I found called for lemon juice in the cake, which seems to cause textural problems. I finally experimented with using lemon extract in the batter and fresh lemon juice for the glaze, with an outstanding result bursting with flavor. When I tested this recipe for my family, the cake was a big hit. Many years later, it is still my daughter Laura's favorite.

Lightweight Bundt pans distribute heat more evenly, so invest in one if you do a lot of baking. I like the way this cake freezes and usually keep one on hand for last-minute emergencies. Serve with seasonal berries and a dollop of whipped cream, Essencia Zabaglione with Fresh Fruit Compote (page 299), or a scoop of French vanilla ice cream. You might also try serving this for afternoon tea, or even for breakfast.

Advance Preparation

Can be prepared up to 3 days ahead and kept at room temperature, tightly covered. The cake can also be tightly wrapped and frozen in aluminum foil for up to 2 months.

1¾ cups all-purpose flour

1 teaspoon baking soda

1 teaspoon baking powder

1 cup unsalted butter, at room temperature

1 cup granulated sugar

3 large eggs, at room temperature

1 tablespoon minced lemon zest

2 teaspoons lemon extract

1 cup sour cream

GLAZE

1½ cups powdered sugar

⅓ cup strained fresh lemon juice

2 teaspoons finely minced lemon zest

1   Preheat the oven to 350°F. Butter and flour a 9-inch lightweight Bundt pan.

2   Sift the flour, baking soda, and baking powder together into a medium mixing bowl. Set aside.

3   In a medium mixing bowl, using an electric mixer on medium speed, or in a food processor fitted with the metal blade, beat the butter and granulated sugar together until light and fluffy, about 4 minutes. Beat in the eggs, minced zest, and lemon extract and mix for 2 more minutes.

4   Reduce the speed to low, or pulse with the food processor. Add half of the flour mixture and mix until well combined. Add half of the sour cream, mixing constantly, and then add the rest of the flour and sour cream, ending with the sour cream.

5   Pour the batter into the prepared pan. Bake for about 35 to 40 minutes, or until a skewer inserted into the center comes out clean. Let cool in the pan for 10 minutes, then invert onto a wire rack and remove the pan. Make the glaze while the cake is still warm.

6   To make the glaze, using a fine-mesh strainer, sift the powdered sugar into a small, nonaluminum mixing bowl. Add the lemon juice and minced zest and whisk to break up any lumps.

7   Transfer the cake to a rack placed over a rimmed baking sheet lined with wax paper. Using a long skewer, poke holes in the cake at 1-inch intervals, *almost* going through the bottom. Slowly pour the glaze over the cake, giving it time to absorb as you pour. Let the cake cool to room temperature. Cut into wedges and serve.

PEACH MELBA BUCKLE

SERVES 6 TO 8

A buckle is one of those early American country desserts like a pandowdy, grunt, or cobbler that combines fruit with biscuits or cake. The source for this recipe idea is Florida Chef Clair Epting, who prepared a blood peach–raspberry crisp with a peach-honey sauce for dessert one evening at the Cakebread Winery in Napa Valley. The late summer peaches grown by the Cakebread's neighbors were unbelievably fragrant and juicy, with bright red centers. This buckle takes a similar approach to California's wonderful peaches, combining them with raspberries, a spiced cake, and a toasted almond streusel-like topping.

Advance Preparation

Can be prepared up to 8 hours ahead and kept at room temperature.

TOPPING

½ cup coarsely chopped almonds

½ cup all-purpose flour

½ cup firmly packed dark brown sugar

¼ cup granulated sugar

½ teaspoon ground cinnamon

Pinch of freshly grated nutmeg

Pinch of ground ginger

½ cup unsalted butter, cut into small pieces

CAKE BATTER

½ cup unsalted butter

¾ cup granulated sugar

1 large egg

2 cups all-purpose flour

2 teaspoons baking powder

½ teaspoon ground ginger

½ cup milk

1 pint raspberries, picked over and rinsed

3 medium peaches, peeled, pitted, and cut into ¼-inch pieces

French vanilla ice cream for serving (optional)

1   To make the topping, preheat the oven to 350°F. Spread the almonds in a single layer on a baking sheet and toast for about 7 to 10 minutes, or until lightly browned. Transfer to a plate and cool. Leave the oven on. Butter and flour a 9-by-12-inch baking dish.

2   In a medium mixing bowl, combine the almonds, flour, sugars, and spices. Add the butter and mix together until the mixture is crumbly. Set the topping aside.

3   To make the cake batter, combine the butter and granulated sugar in a large mixing bowl. Using an electric mixer on medium speed, beat them together until the mixture is light and fluffy. Beat in the egg.

4   Sift together the flour, baking powder, and ginger into a bowl. Then add the flour mixture in batches to the butter mixture alternately with the milk, making sure that the ingredients are well blended between additions.

5   Spread the batter evenly in the prepared dish. Sprinkle the raspberries and peach pieces over the batter in an even layer. Sprinkle the topping over the fruit and bake for about 45 to 55 minutes, or until the topping is golden brown and bubbling and a skewer inserted into the center comes out clean. Serve with French vanilla ice cream if desired.

NECTARINE CRISP WITH DRIED CHERRIES

SERVES 6 TO 8

Advance Preparation

Can be prepared up to 8 hours ahead and kept at room temperature.

Quick to assemble and great for parties, this simple dessert is loaded with fresh fruit flavor. Unpeeled nectarines and intensely rich dried cherries are a complementary summer fruit combination. The crust is drizzled with melted butter for a cakey-crunchy baked topping. You can find dried cherries in well-stocked supermarkets or natural- or specialty-foods stores. Serve with French vanilla ice cream or Eggnog Brandy Sauce (page 365), if desired.

TOPPING

¾ cup coarsely chopped pecans

¾ cup all-purpose flour

1⅛ teaspoons baking powder

¾ cup sugar

½ teaspoon ground cinnamon

Pinch of freshly grated nutmeg

Pinch of ground ginger

1 large egg, lightly beaten

10 medium nectarines, pitted and sliced into 1-inch pieces

¾ cup dried cherries, coarsely chopped

6 tablespoons unsalted butter, melted

1   To make the topping, preheat the oven to 350°F. Spread the pecans in a single layer on a baking sheet and toast for 7 to 10 minutes, or until lightly browned. Transfer to a plate and cool. Leave the oven on. Butter and flour a rectangular or oval 9-by-12-inch baking dish.

2   In a medium mixing bowl, combine the pecans, flour, baking powder, sugar, and spices. Add the egg and mix together with your hands or a wooden spoon until the mixture is crumbly. Set the topping aside.

3   Arrange half of the nectarine slices in the prepared dish and then sprinkle on the dried cherries. Cover with the remaining nectarine slices, making an even layer.

4   Sprinkle the topping over the fruit and then drizzle on the butter evenly. Bake for about 35 to 45 minutes, or until the top is golden brown and bubbling. Serve with French vanilla ice cream or Eggnog Brandy Sauce (page 365) if desired.

This elegant showstopper of a dessert features pear halves and raspberries baked with an almond filling inside a flaky crust. Using frozen butter allows you to roll out the pastry immediately. While this dessert takes some time to prepare, it's not difficult, and the result will make you feel like a professional pastry chef. Serve with French vanilla ice cream, if you like.

PEAR-RASPBERRY ALMOND TART

SERVES 8 TO 10

PASTRY

1¼ cups all-purpose or white pastry flour

1 tablespoon powdered sugar

Pinch of salt

½ cup unsalted butter, frozen and cut into small pieces

1 large egg yolk

2 tablespoons ice water

FILLING

1½ cups sliced blanched almonds

¾ cup granulated sugar

4 tablespoons unsalted butter

2 tablespoons all-purpose flour

¼ cup almond liqueur such as amaretto

2 large eggs

TOPPING

4 medium Bosc pears, peeled, cored, halved, and thinly sliced, keeping each half together

½ pint raspberries

2 tablespoons unsalted butter

2 tablespoons granulated sugar

continued on next page

Note

Store any unused glaze in a tightly sealed jar in the refrigerator for up to 2 months.

Advance Preparation

Can be prepared through step 3 up to 8 hours ahead, covered, and refrigerated. The tart shell can be prepared through step 2 up to 1 day ahead, covered, and refrigerated. The finished tart can be kept for up to 8 hours in the refrigerator. Remove the tart from the refrigerator 1 hour before serving. This is best served at room temperature.

GLAZE

1 cup apricot preserves

2 tablespoons fresh lemon juice

GARNISH

2 tablespoons sliced almonds

1   To make the pastry, combine the flour, powdered sugar, and salt in a food
    processor fitted with the metal blade. Process for a few seconds to blend. Add
    the butter and process until the mixture resembles coarse meal, about 5 to 10
    seconds. With the machine running, gradually add the egg yolk and then the
    water and process just until the dough begins to come together and adheres
    when pinched.

2   Transfer the dough to a lightly floured pastry board or work surface. Press
    it into a round shape for easy rolling. Roll the dough out into a circle large
    enough to fit a 10-inch tart pan with a removable bottom. Drape the pastry
    circle over the rolling pin and fit it into the pan. Roll the pin over the rim of
    the pan with moderate pressure to remove excess overhanging dough. Press the
    pastry with your fingers so it adheres to the sides of the pan. If you're using a
    tart pan with straight edges, raise the edges of the pastry ¼ to ½ inch above the
    top of the pan by squeezing the dough from both sides, using your thumb and
    index finger. Place the tart pan on a baking sheet. Preheat the oven to 400°F.

3   To make the filling, grind the almonds in a food processor fitted with the metal
    blade. Add the granulated sugar, butter, flour, and almond liqueur. Turn the
    machine on and off until a meal-like paste is formed. Add the eggs and process
    for 10 seconds to incorporate. Spread the filling evenly in the pastry shell.

4   For the topping, arrange the sliced pear halves flat side down on top of the
    filling, holding them carefully so they retain their shape, in a spokelike pattern,
    with the narrower part of the pear pointing to the middle. The top should
    show 8 pear halves sitting on the filling like the petals of a flower. Arrange
    the raspberries between the pear slices in a consistent pattern. Make a circular
    pattern of raspberries in the middle. Push the raspberries down gently so that
    they are embedded in the almond paste, leaving the tops exposed. Be sure to
    fit the raspberries tightly together.

5   Dot the fruit with the butter and sprinkle evenly with the granulated sugar.
    Bake the tart for 50 to 60 minutes, or until lightly browned on top. If the tart
    becomes too brown, place aluminum foil over it to keep it from burning.
    Remove the tart from the oven and let cool.

6   While the tart is baking, make the glaze: In a small saucepan, combine the
    preserves and lemon juice and bring to a boil over medium-high heat. Strain
    the glaze through a fine-mesh strainer into another small saucepan and set aside.

7   When the tart has cooled, remove the sides of the pan and place on a serving
    platter. Reheat the glaze just to a boil. Brush the glaze on the cooled pears lav-
    ishly to give them a shiny appearance. Garnish with the almond slices and serve.

MANGO AND MACADAMIA NUT BROWN-BUTTER TART

SERVES 6

Advance Preparation

Can be prepared up to 8 hours ahead and refrigerated. Remove the tart from the refrigerator ½ hour before serving. The tart shell can be prepared through step 2 up to 1 day ahead, covered, and refrigerated.

This smooth, nutty, brown-butter filling laced with sweet exotic mango and rich macadamia nut pieces is a good example of Hawaiian regional cooking. A classic concept, here the brown-butter tart is reinterpreted with local Hawaiian ingredients. Fortunately, mangoes and macadamia nuts are available year-round in most supermarkets. Chop the macadamia nuts into small pieces and finely dice the mango for the best texture.

PASTRY

1¼ cups all-purpose or white pastry flour

Pinch of salt

2 tablespoons powdered sugar

½ cup unsalted butter, frozen and cut into small pieces

1 large egg yolk

¼ cup ice water

FILLING

¾ cup unsalted butter

3 large eggs

¾ cup granulated sugar

3 tablespoons all-purpose flour

1¼ cups peeled and finely diced ripe mango (pieces no larger than ¼-inch)

1 cup macadamia nuts, rinsed of all salt and chopped into ¼-inch pieces

GLAZE

½ cup apricot preserves

1 tablespoon fresh lemon juice

GARNISH

2 tablespoons finely chopped macadamia nuts

1   To make the pastry, preheat the oven to 375°F. Combine the flour, salt, and powdered sugar in a food processor fitted with the metal blade. Process for a few seconds to blend. Add the butter and process until the mixture resembles coarse meal, about 5 to 10 seconds. With the machine running, gradually add the egg yolk and then the water and process until the dough just begins to come together and adheres when pinched.

2   Transfer the dough to a lightly floured pastry board or work surface. Press it into a round shape for easy rolling. Roll the dough out into a circle large enough to fit an 11-inch tart pan with a removable bottom. Drape the pastry circle over the rolling pin and fit it into the pan. Roll the pin over the rim of the pan to remove excess overhanging dough. Press the pastry with your fingers so it adheres to the sides of the pan. If you're using a tart pan with straight edges, raise the edges of the pastry ¼ to ½ inch above the top of the pan by squeezing the dough from both sides, using your thumb and index finger.

3   Place the tart pan on a baking sheet. To prevent the pastry from puffing up while baking, line the tart shell with a piece of parchment paper or aluminum foil pressed to fit the sides. Pour pie weights, dried beans, or rice into the paper or foil and distribute evenly. Bake the crust for 15 minutes. Remove the weights and paper or foil and prick the bottom of the pastry shell with a fork. Return the crust to the oven and bake until lightly browned, 5 to 7 minutes longer. Do not overbrown, because the pastry will be baked further. Transfer to a wire rack. Reduce the oven temperature to 350°F.

4   To make the filling, melt the butter in a small saucepan over high heat. Cook, watching carefully, until the butter is dark brown, then immediately remove it from the heat. Strain the butter through a strainer lined with a double thickness of cheesecloth into another small saucepan. There should be no black specks in the butter. Set aside and keep warm.

5   In a medium mixing bowl, using an electric mixer on medium speed, beat the eggs until they are frothy. Beat in the granulated sugar until well incorporated. Sprinkle in the flour and beat until it is well combined and no lumps remain. Add the warm brown butter and mix again. Add the mango and macadamia nuts and mix to combine.

6   Place the baked tart shell on a baking sheet and pour the filling into the crust. Bake for 20 to 25 minutes. The filling should be dark brown and set in the center, and should move just slightly when the pan is moved. Transfer to a wire rack and let cool.

7   While the tart is baking, make the glaze: In a small saucepan, combine the preserves and lemon juice and bring to a boil over medium-high heat. Strain the glaze through a fine-mesh strainer into another small saucepan and set aside.

8   When the tart has cooled, remove the sides of the pan and place on a serving platter. Reheat the glaze just to a boil. Brush the tart with a thin layer of the glaze. Garnish with chopped macadamia nuts. Refrigerate until serving time.

BLUEBERRY-LEMON TART

SERVES 8

Californians love fruit desserts. This two-tiered fruit tart combines a creamy citrus filling with a topping of mild West Coast blueberries. Just a hint of almond flavors the flaky crust. This tart is a delightful finish to Roast Crispy Fish with Warm Lentils (page 156).

Advance Preparation

The tart can be prepared up to 8 hours ahead and kept at room temperature. The tart shell can be prepared through step 2 up to 1 day ahead, covered, and refrigerated.

PASTRY

1 cup plus 2 tablespoons all-purpose or white pastry flour

2 tablespoons finely ground almonds

2 tablespoons powdered sugar

½ cup unsalted butter, frozen and cut into small pieces

1 large egg yolk

¼ cup ice water

FILLING

4 large eggs

1½ cups granulated sugar

2 tablespoons unsalted butter, at room temperature

1 cup fresh lemon juice

2 tablespoons heavy (whipping) cream

1 tablespoon finely chopped lemon zest

1 pint blueberries

GARNISH

Powdered sugar

Fresh mint leaves

Strip of lemon zest

Whipped cream

1   To make the pastry, preheat the oven to 375°F. Combine the flour, almonds, and powdered sugar in a food processor fitted with the metal blade. Process for a few seconds to blend. Add the butter and process until the mixture resembles coarse meal, about 5 to 10 seconds. With the machine running, gradually add the egg yolk and then the water and process just until the dough begins to come together and adheres when pinched.

2   Transfer the dough to a lightly floured pastry board or work surface. Press it into a round shape for easy rolling. Roll the dough out into a circle large enough to fit an 11-inch tart pan with a removable bottom. Drape the pastry circle over the rolling pin and fit it into the pan. Roll the pin over the rim of the pan with moderate pressure to remove excess overhanging dough. Press the pastry with your fingers so it adheres to the sides of the pan. If you're using a tart pan with straight edges, raise the edges of the pastry ¼ to ½ inch above the top of the pan by squeezing the dough from both sides, using your thumb and index finger.

3   Place the tart pan on a baking sheet. To prevent the pastry from puffing up while baking, line the tart shell with a piece of parchment paper or aluminum foil pressed to fit the sides. Pour pie weights, dried beans, or rice into the paper or foil and distribute evenly. Bake the crust for 15 minutes. Remove the weights and paper or foil and prick the bottom of the pastry shell with a fork. (The beans and rice can be reused as pie weights.) Return the crust to the oven and bake until lightly browned, 5 to 7 minutes longer. Do not overbrown, because the pastry will be baked further. Transfer to a wire rack. Leave the oven on.

4   To make the filling, beat the eggs until frothy in a medium mixing bowl with an electric mixer on medium speed or in a food processor fitted with the metal blade. Add the granulated sugar and butter and beat until thick and lemon colored. Add the lemon juice, cream, and zest and mix well.

5   Place the baked tart shell on a baking sheet and pour the filling into the crust. Bake for 10 minutes. Reduce the oven temperature to 350°F and bake for 12 to 15 minutes longer, until the filling is lightly browned and moves just slightly when shaken. Transfer the tart to a wire rack and let cool in the pan.

6   When the tart has cooled, remove the sides of the pan. Place the tart on a serving platter and carefully arrange the blueberries in concentric circles on top, starting on the outside and working towards the center. Dust with the powdered sugar. To serve, garnish each plate with the mint leaves, lemon zest, and a large dollop of whipped cream.

TIRAMISU WITH TOASTED HAZELNUTS AND CHOCOLATE

SERVES 6

Italian everything has swept the restaurant scene in California, and desserts are no exception. Tiramisu, literally "pick-me-up," has become more popular than the hot fudge sundae. This soft, fluffy dessert is easy to prepare. Buy fresh ladyfingers at a bakery and soak them in the espresso quickly, or else they will dissolve.

The filling is made with mascarpone, an incredibly rich, soft Italian cream cheese. Mascarpone has a texture that is a cross between thick crème fraîche and whipped cream cheese, with a mildly sweet and slightly acidic flavor. You can find it in Italian markets or in specialty shops.

This version has hazelnut liqueur in the coffee and is garnished with toasted hazelnuts. Tiramisu is very rich, so it's a fitting finale to a relatively light Italian-style dinner. Begin with Roasted Peppers with Mint Vinaigrette and Goat Cheese Croutons (page 26). For a main course, serve either Indian Summer Pasta (page 120) or Wonton Butternut Squash Ravioli with Spinach Pesto (page 126).

2 tablespoons sliced hazelnuts
1 cup heavy (whipping) cream
½ pound (1 cup) mascarpone cheese
½ cup powdered sugar
3 tablespoons Frangelico or other hazelnut liqueur
1½ cups cooled brewed espresso
2 tablespoons brandy or cognac
30 ladyfingers, pulled in half (two 3-ounce packages)
¼ cup coarsely grated bittersweet chocolate

Variation

Strawberries or raspberries may be added in the middle layer and used as a garnish on top, if desired.

Advance Preparation

Can be prepared up to 8 hours ahead, covered, and refrigerated.

1   Preheat the oven to 350°F. Spread the hazelnuts in a single layer on a baking sheet and toast for 5 to 7 minutes, or until lightly browned. Watch carefully to avoid burning them. Transfer to a plate and cool.

2   In a medium mixing bowl, using an electric mixer on medium speed, beat the cream until soft peaks form. Set aside. In another medium mixing bowl, using the mixer on medium speed, beat the mascarpone for 1 minute. Slowly add the powdered sugar and 2 tablespoons of the Frangelico to the mascarpone and beat until the mixture is well combined. Carefully fold in the whipped cream.

3   In a medium mixing bowl, combine the espresso, brandy, and remaining 1 tablespoon Frangelico. Dip half of the lady fingers quickly into the coffee mixture, one by one, and arrange them, flat side down, in a single layer in an 8-inch square serving dish at least 2 inches deep. Cover the entire bottom of the dish; you will need to cut a few of the ladyfingers in half to fit the ends of the dish.

4   Spread two-thirds of the mascarpone mixture on top of the ladyfingers. Sprinkle 2 tablespoons of the grated chocolate evenly on top. Dip the remaining ladyfingers into the coffee mixture and arrange them, flat side down, in a single layer on top of the mascarpone. Repeat the procedure with the remaining mascarpone mixture, spreading it on the ladyfingers in a thin, even layer.

5   Sprinkle the toasted hazelnuts and then the remaining 2 tablespoons grated chocolate evenly on top for an attractive presentation. Refrigerate for at least 4 hours. Cut into squares to serve.

VANILLA CARAMEL CREAM

SERVES 6

Advance Preparation

Can be prepared up to 3 days ahead, covered, and refrigerated.

This recipe might be the best argument against the false notion that Californians don't like rich desserts. In fact, when Californians dine out, they frequently choose a light first and main course, then dash all pretext of restraint when the dessert menu appears. I don't think it's much different at home.

This soft caramel version of crème brûlée is based on the *crema di vanilla* often served in Italian restaurants. Half-and-half, instead of the usual heavy cream, is the basis for the silky custard that is baked, cooled, and then cloaked with a wickedly rich caramel sauce. Dissolving the sugar in half-and-half creates a finer-textured custard. If you like berries, garnish the top with your favorite variety. Obviously, small servings are recommended.

CUSTARD

2 cups half-and-half

½ cup sugar

1 vanilla bean, split open, or 2 teaspoons vanilla extract

6 large egg yolks

CARAMEL TOPPING

½ cup sugar

¼ cup water

1 teaspoon vanilla extract

½ cup heavy (whipping) cream

1   Preheat the oven to 325°F. To make the custard, in a medium, heavy saucepan over medium-high heat, combine the half-and-half, sugar, and the split vanilla bean, if using. Bring the mixture to a boil, stirring constantly to dissolve the sugar. Remove from the heat and let cool slightly. Remove the vanilla bean. If you're using vanilla extract instead of vanilla bean, add it now.

2   In a medium mixing bowl, using an electric mixer or with a hand whisk, beat the egg yolks for 1 minute. Add the half-and-half mixture in a slow, steady stream while beating on low speed or gently by hand, trying not to create too much foam.

3   Pour the mixture through a fine-mesh strainer into a pitcher or large measuring cup. Arrange six ½-cup ramekins in a shallow baking pan. Pour the custard evenly into the ramekins. Carefully pour hot water into the pan to come halfway up the sides of the ramekins; this helps the custards cook evenly.

4 Bake for about 30 to 35 minutes, or until a skewer inserted into the center of a custard comes out almost clean. Remove the ramekins from the water bath and let cool to room temperature. Place the ramekins in the refrigerator for 2 hours before topping the custard with the caramel.

5 To make the caramel topping, combine the sugar and water in a medium, heavy saucepan. (Do not use a pan with a dark-colored interior, or you will not be able to see the color of the caramel.) Place over low heat and stir to dissolve the sugar. Raise the heat to high and swirl the pan constantly over the heat. The mixture will be bubbly. If sugar crystals form on the sides of the pan, cover it for 1 minute to dissolve them. Boil the mixture just until it turns a dark golden brown. Watch carefully, because caramel can burn easily. (If you make the caramel too dark, it will continue to cook and taste burned.) Remove the caramel from the heat and let cool, making sure it is still liquid. Return to low heat, add the vanilla and cream, and continue cooking. The mixture will look like it has separated, but with patience and constant stirring it will become smooth in a few more minutes. Let the mixture cool. It will thicken slightly.

6 Spoon the cooled caramel over each chilled custard, swirling the ramekin to distribute the caramel evenly. Refrigerate until the caramel is set, at least 2 hours.

PUMPKIN BREAD PUDDING WITH EGGNOG BRANDY SAUCE

SERVES 8

Tired of the prospect of yet another pumpkin pie to end your holiday dinner? This dessert is familiar comfort when you want the flavor of pumpkin pie but not the same old dessert. Actually, once you taste this pudding, it will become a favorite throughout the fall and winter months.

Bread puddings come in all shapes and flavors. This idea is based on my good friend Kathy Blue's gingerbread pudding, which graces her Thanksgiving dessert table every year. Combining pumpkin bread and a pumpkin custard doubles the flavor and brings an unusual taste to bread pudding.

If you like to bake homemade holiday gifts, you can make this dessert in smaller loaf pans and decorate the pans with colored cellophane. The Eggnog Brandy Sauce is optional.

Advance Preparation

Can be prepared through step 3 up to 1 day ahead. Refrigerate the custard and bring to room temperature before assembling. You can also prepare the dish through step 4 up to 1 day ahead and refrigerate until ready to bake. It will be a bit less custardy since the bread will have absorbed the custard.

CUSTARD

½ cup golden raisins

½ cup brandy

4 large eggs

3 large egg yolks

1¼ cups granulated sugar

½ cup canned pumpkin purée

3 cups half-and-half

2 teaspoons vanilla extract

¼ teaspoon ground cinnamon

¼ teaspoon ground allspice

¼ teaspoon ground ginger

¼ teaspoon freshly grated nutmeg

GARNISH

1 loaf of Spiced Pumpkin-Hazelnut Bread (page 276)

Powdered sugar for dusting

Eggnog Brandy Sauce (page 365) or whipped cream for serving (optional)

1   In a small saucepan, combine the raisins and brandy and bring to a boil. Remove from the heat and let stand for 1 hour to plump the raisins.

2   Preheat the oven to 375°F. Butter a 2-quart oval or round baking dish. Place the dish in a larger baking pan that will serve as a water bath.

3   To make the custard, in a large mixing bowl, using an electric mixer on medium speed, beat the whole eggs and egg yolks until frothy. Slowly add the granulated sugar and beat the mixture until thick and lemon colored. Add the pumpkin purée and half-and-half and beat on low speed. Beat in the vanilla and spices, then stir in the plumped raisins and brandy.

4   Slice the pumpkin bread into ⅛-inch-thick slices and arrange the slices, overlapping in the prepared dish. Ladle the custard over the pumpkin bread slices, making sure that the raisins are distributed evenly.

5   Pour enough boiling water into the larger baking pan to reach halfway up the sides of the baking dish. Bake for 40 to 45 minutes.

6   Using heavy oven mitts, open the oven and, with a large spoon, push the bread down. The liquid custard will rise. Spoon the custard evenly over the bread slices. Bake for about 10 minutes longer, or until a skewer inserted into the center comes out clean. Remove the pudding from the water bath and let cool to warm. Dust with the powdered sugar and cut into even pieces. Serve with the Eggnog Brandy Sauce or whipped cream, if desired.

CHOCOLATE CHIP COFFEE CAKE

SERVES 6 TO 8

Advance Preparation

Can be prepared up to 8 hours ahead, but is best eaten warm.

This updated sour cream coffee cake combines a mixture of toasted pecans and almonds with cinnamon and chocolate chips as a filling and a topping. Serve the cake for brunch, tea, or dessert. Don't worry if some of the topping comes off when you invert the cake. A dusting of powdered sugar is all that's needed.

FILLING

1 cup coarsely chopped pecans

1 cup coarsely chopped almonds

2 tablespoons granulated sugar

2 teaspoons ground cinnamon

6 ounces semisweet chocolate chips

CAKE BATTER

1 cup unsalted butter, at room temperature

2 cups granulated sugar

2 large eggs

1 cup sour cream

2 teaspoons vanilla extract

2 cups all-purpose flour

1 teaspoon baking powder

¼ teaspoon salt

GARNISH

Powdered sugar (optional)

1   Preheat the oven to 350°F. Butter and flour a 9-inch lightweight Bundt pan or angel food cake pan.

2   To make the filling, spread the nuts in a single layer on a baking sheet and toast for 5 to 7 minutes, or until lightly browned. Transfer to a plate and let cool. Leave the oven on. Combine the nuts, granulated sugar, cinnamon, and chocolate chips in a small bowl. Set the filling aside.

3   To make the cake batter, in a large mixing bowl, beat the butter and sugar together using an electric mixer on medium speed until the mixture is light and fluffy. Beat in the eggs one at a time. Beat in the sour cream and vanilla.

4   Combine the flour, baking powder, and salt in a medium mixing bowl and mix well. Fold the flour mixture into the butter mixture until well blended. Spread half of the batter in the prepared pan and smooth the top with a spatula. Sprinkle with half of the filling. Spread with the remaining batter and sprinkle the rest of the filling on top in an even layer, pushing the chocolate chips and nuts into the batter.

5   Bake for 60 to 75 minutes, or until a skewer inserted into the center comes out clean. (You may want to put a piece of aluminum foil on top after 45 minutes of baking so the chocolate does not burn.) Let the coffee cake cool in the pan. Invert it onto a wire rack, then transfer to a serving platter. Dust with powdered sugar, if desired. Cut into wedges and serve.

WALNUT CAKE WITH ROASTED BLUEBERRY COMPOTE

SERVES 6

I like using walnuts in desserts for their rich, assertive flavor. Here I have added them as a flavor enhancer to this simple, moist loaf cake. Roasted blueberries become a syrupy sauce and complement the walnut flavor nicely. To gild the lily, a dollop of vanilla cream is placed on top of the berries for a pretty yet casual dessert. You can freeze or refrigerate walnuts in an airtight container for up to 6 months. Make sure to have the walnuts at room temperature before grinding into coarse meal.

Advance Preparation

The cake can be prepared up to 1 day ahead and covered in an airtight container. The vanilla cream can be prepared up to 1 day ahead, covered, and refrigerated.

CAKE

¼ cup chopped walnuts

¾ cup plus 2 tablespoons all-purpose flour

¼ teaspoon salt

½ teaspoon baking soda

6 tablespoons unsalted butter, at room temperature

1 cup granulated sugar

2 large eggs

6 tablespoons sour cream

Zest of ½ lemon

BLUEBERRY COMPOTE

2½ pints fresh blueberries, picked over

2 tablespoons brown sugar

2 tablespoons unsalted butter, cut into small pieces

¼ teaspoon ground cloves

¼ teaspoon ground cinnamon

VANILLA CREAM

¾ cup crème fraîche

1½ tablespoons powdered sugar

1 teaspoon vanilla extract

GARNISH

Fresh mint leaves

1   To make the cake, preheat the oven to 350°F. Butter and flour an 8-inch square baking dish or a 9-by-5-inch loaf pan.

2   In a food processor fitted with the metal blade, chop the walnuts until they resemble coarse meal. Combine the flour, walnut meal, salt, and baking soda in a mixing bowl and stir with a fork to combine. Set aside.

3   In a large mixing bowl, using an electric mixer on medium speed, or in a food processor fitted with the metal blade, combine the butter and granulated sugar and beat or process until light and fluffy. Add the eggs one at a time and mix to combine. Add the sour cream and lemon zest and mix to combine. Slowly add the flour mixture to the batter and mix just until blended.

4   Spread the batter in the prepared pan and smooth the top with a spatula. Bake for 40 minutes, or until a skewer inserted into the center comes out clean. Transfer to a wire rack and let cool. Raise the oven temperature to 375°F.

5   To make the blueberry compote, place the blueberries in a medium baking dish. Sprinkle the brown sugar, butter, and spices over the blueberries and mix to combine.

6   Roast the blueberries until they begin to burst and the juice is syrupy, about 20 minutes. If they overcook, they break down and turn into syrup with little texture, so watch carefully. Let cool for about 10 minutes.

7   Meanwhile, make the Vanilla Cream: In a small mixing bowl, combine the crème fraîche, powdered sugar, and vanilla and stir until well blended.

8   To serve, cut the cake into 8 even pieces and transfer to dessert plates. Spoon a few tablespoons of the blueberry compote around the cake. Top each with a dollop of the vanilla cream. Garnish with the mint leaves. Serve immediately.

BANANA CAKE WITH CHOCOLATE FUDGE FROSTING

SERVES 8 TO 10

Advance Preparation

Can be prepared up to 1 day ahead and refrigerated. Bring to room temperature before serving.

Fluffy banana-scented cake layers are sandwiched between creamy fudge frosting in this old-fashioned homage to the classic chocolate-banana combination.

The frosting is based on a classic ganache, which becomes very thick as it chills, so watch carefully. Be sure to use a good-quality semisweet chocolate. If you like, use 8 ounces of semisweet and 2 ounces of bittersweet for a deeper chocolate flavor. This cake is a perfect ending to a special family dinner or birthday.

CAKE

1¾ cups all-purpose flour

1 teaspoon baking soda

¼ teaspoon salt

1 cup unsalted butter, at room temperature

1 cup sugar

2 large eggs

1 cup mashed banana (about 2 ripe medium bananas)

2 teaspoons vanilla extract

½ cup buttermilk

FROSTING

1¼ cups heavy (whipping) cream

10 ounces semisweet chocolate, cut into small pieces

4 tablespoons unsalted butter, at room temperature

1 tablespoon vanilla extract

1 medium banana, thinly sliced

1   To make the cake, preheat the oven to 350°F. Butter and flour the bottom and sides of two 8-inch round cake pans.

2   Whisk together the flour, baking soda, and salt in a medium mixing bowl.

3   In a large mixing bowl, using an electric mixer on medium speed, beat the butter and sugar together until fluffy and light lemon colored. Beat in the eggs one at a time, then add the mashed banana and vanilla and beat until well blended. Don't worry if the mixture looks curdled.

4   Reduce the speed to low and add the flour mixture and the buttermilk alternately in batches to the banana mixture, beating until they are completely

incorporated before the next addition, ending with the flour. Divide the batter between the prepared cake pans. Bake for 30 to 35 minutes, or until the tops spring back to the touch and are golden brown and a skewer comes out clear. Let the cakes cool in the pans on wire racks for about 15 minutes, then invert them onto the racks and let cool to room temperature.

5   Meanwhile, make the frosting: Bring the cream to a boil in a medium, heavy saucepan over high heat. When boiling, remove the cream from the heat and add the chocolate, butter, and vanilla, stirring until the chocolate and butter are completely melted and the mixture is smooth. Place the pan in the refrigerator. Give it a stir every 15 minutes as it cools. The frosting will begin to set after 50 minutes and will become quite thick. Check every 5 minutes to get the right consistency.

6   To frost the cake, place one layer, smooth side up, on a 12-inch round platter. Spread with one-third of the frosting. Carefully place the banana slices on top of the frosting in an even layer. Place the other cake layer, smooth side up, on the bananas and flatten it with your hand. Frost the top and sides very thickly with the remaining frosting. Make peaks by making quick movements with your hand so the cake looks old-fashioned. Clean the platter with a damp paper towel to remove any excess frosting. Let the frosting set and serve at room temperature.

WARM MOCHA PUDDING CAKES

SERVES 6

These sophisticated pudding cakes require the best quality chocolate you can find. I like bittersweet E. Guittard or Scharffen Berger. You may notice that these chocolate bars have cacao percentages on the label. The higher percentages (usually 65 percent and over) signifies a bittersweet chocolate. You'll find the addition of instant espresso powder rounds out the chocolate flavor in a delightful way. These pudding cakes are a perfect make-ahead dessert for the home cook. You can make these up hours ahead of time and keep them refrigerated until an hour before baking. If you have any baked cakes left over, you'll find that they morph into a delectable cool, rich, almost truffle-like dessert that will also receive raves.

Advance Preparation

Can be prepared through step 3 up to 6 hours ahead, lightly covered with aluminum foil or plastic wrap, and refrigerated. Remove from the refrigerator 1 hour before baking.

6 ounces best-quality bittersweet chocolate, cut into small pieces

½ cup unsalted butter

2 teaspoons instant espresso powder

3 large eggs

3 large egg yolks

⅓ cup granulated sugar

¼ cup all-purpose flour

Powdered sugar or sweetened cocoa powder for dusting

French vanilla ice cream, softened, or crème fraîche for serving

1   Preheat the oven to 375°F. Lightly butter six ¾-cup ramekins.

2   In the top pan of a double boiler set over (but not touching) simmering water over medium heat, melt the chocolate with the butter, stirring until completely melted and blended. Add the espresso powder and mix until dissolved. Remove from the heat and let cool.

3   In a large mixing bowl, using an electric mixer, beat the whole eggs and egg yolks with the granulated sugar until the mixture is a light lemon color, about 5 minutes. Add the flour and beat until completely incorporated. Add the cooled chocolate mixture and mix briefly just to blend. Pour the custard into the prepared ramekins, filling each halfway.

4   Bake for 10 to 12 minutes, or until the cakes are set around the outside edges but the centers jiggle slightly when the ramekins are moved. (Watch carefully; if you overbake the cakes, they will be dry instead of creamy in the center.) Remove from the oven and carefully run a knife around each cake. Invert each cake onto a serving plate.

5   Dust the tops with the powdered sugar or cocoa powder. Serve with small scoops of the softened ice cream or dollops of crème fraîche.

This very intense chocolate dessert falls somewhere between a cake, a torte, and a cheesecake, and it is a chocolate lover's dream. Best of all, you can always store one in your freezer. It tastes almost as good frozen and thawed as it does freshly baked and chilled.

1 pound semisweet or bittersweet chocolate, cut into 1-inch pieces

10 tablespoons unsalted butter

4 large eggs, separated, at room temperature

2 tablespoons all-purpose flour

Pinch of salt

2 tablespoons granulated sugar

GARNISH

Powdered sugar or whipped cream

Advance Preparation
This cake has the best texture when made 1 day ahead, refrigerated, and removed 1 hour before serving. It also freezes well.

1   Preheat the oven to 425°F. Cut a round of wax paper to fit an 8-inch springform pan. Butter the sides and bottom of the pan generously and place the wax paper in the bottom.

2   In the top pan of a double boiler set over (but not touching) simmering water over medium heat, melt the chocolate, making sure no water touches it. Add the butter, stirring until completely melted and blended with the chocolate. (Alternatively, combine the chocolate and butter in a 2-cup microwave-safe glass measuring cup and heat on high power for 1½ minutes or until melted, stirring once.) Remove from the heat and let cool.

3   In a large mixing bowl, using an electric mixer at medium speed, beat the egg yolks until fluffy and light lemon colored, about 5 minutes. Add the flour and continue mixing just until the flour is incorporated. Set aside.

4   In a medium mixing bowl, with the electric mixer at medium speed, beat the egg whites and salt until the whites begin to hold their shape. Increase the speed to high and add the granulated sugar, continuing to whip the egg whites until the peaks are thick and hold their shape but the egg whites are not dry or overly stiff.

continued on next page

5   Add the cooled chocolate mixture to the egg yolk mixture and blend well. With a rubber spatula, slowly fold one-third of the egg whites into the chocolate mixture, mixing from the bottom of the bowl to blend the whites into the chocolate. Add the remaining whites and continue gently folding them in until there are no white streaks left. Pour the batter into the prepared pan.

6   Bake the cake in the center of the oven for exactly 15 minutes. (It will look almost raw but will continue to cook as it cools.) Remove the cake from the oven and let cool to room temperature. To remove the cake from the pan, use a knife to separate the sides from the pan. Place it on a serving platter and dust it with powdered sugar; or decorate with whipped cream all over the cake and then pipe rosettes all around the top in a circular border. Chill until ready to serve.

Remember how delicious frozen chocolate-covered bananas were when you were a kid? This grown-up dessert features intense bittersweet chocolate as the main flavor, enhanced by a burst of tropical banana essence in the custard sauce. While this torte takes some time to prepare, you can make the cake ahead and freeze it with excellent results.

TORTE

6 ounces bittersweet chocolate, cut into small pieces

¾ cup unsalted butter

4 large eggs

¾ cup sugar

3 tablespoons all-purpose flour

3 tablespoons ground hazelnuts

GLAZE

6 ounces bittersweet chocolate, cut into small pieces

½ cup unsalted butter

½ teaspoon safflower oil

1 tablespoon light corn syrup

20 whole hazelnuts

Banana Custard Sauce (recipe follows) for serving

1   To make the torte, preheat the oven to 375°F. Cut a round of wax paper to fit an 8-inch round cake pan. Butter the bottom and sides of the pan and place the paper in the bottom of the pan. Butter the paper generously.

2   In the top pan of a double boiler set over (but not touching) simmering water over medium-low heat, melt the chocolate with the butter, stirring until completely melted and blended. (Alternatively, combine the chocolate and butter in a 2-cup microwave-safe glass measuring cup and heat on high power for 1½ minutes, or until melted, stirring once.) Remove from the heat and let cool.

3   In a large mixing bowl, using an electric mixer on medium speed, beat the eggs until frothy. Slowly add the sugar and beat the mixture until it is pale lemon colored, about 5 minutes. Fold the cooled chocolate mixture into the egg mixture and blend well. Stir in the flour and ground hazelnuts until well combined.

continued on next page

BITTERSWEET CHOCOLATE HAZELNUT TORTE WITH BANANA CUSTARD SAUCE

SERVES 6

Advance Preparation

Can be prepared up to 1 day ahead, covered, and kept at room temperature. The torte can also be refrigerated. Remove it from the refrigerator 1 hour before serving. The torte can be refrigerated until set, wrapped in foil, and frozen for up to 2 months. Remove it from the freezer 8 hours ahead and keep it at room temperature.

4 Pour the batter into the prepared pan. Bake for 25 to 30 minutes, until the outside is firm and the interior is slightly underdone but not runny; a skewer inserted into the center should come out slightly wet. Let the torte cool in the pan, then invert it onto a wire rack and remove the pan. Place the rack on a baking sheet lined with wax paper.

5 To make the glaze, melt the chocolate and butter in the top pan of a double boiler set over (but not touching) simmering water over low heat. Stir the chocolate until it is melted and smooth. (Alternatively, combine the chocolate and butter in a 2-cup microwave-safe glass measuring cup and heat on high power for 1½ minutes, or until melted, stirring once.) Stir in the oil and corn syrup. Remove from the heat and let cool to room temperature. (Make sure the glaze stays at room temperature and that it does not harden. If it hardens, gently soften it in the top of a double boiler or for 20 seconds in the microwave until it is tepid.)

6 Pour the glaze over the cooled torte and tilt the rack so the glaze runs down the sides. Use a long spatula to touch up the sides. When the glaze is set, carefully place the whole hazelnuts in a circular pattern on the outside edge of the top of the torte. Slide a large spatula under the torte and lift it up onto a cake platter lined with a doily. Serve with the Banana Custard Sauce.

Banana Custard Sauce

Makes 1½ cups

1⅓ cups half-and-half
½ vanilla bean, split open (see note)
3 egg yolks
⅓ cup sugar
1 soft banana, cut into small pieces

1 In a small saucepan over medium-high heat, combine the half-and-half and vanilla bean and bring to a simmer. Remove from the heat and cover the pan. Let the vanilla bean steep for 20 minutes. Remove the vanilla bean.

2 Place the egg yolks in the top pan of a double boiler set over (but not touching) simmering water over medium heat. Add the sugar and whisk until thick and lemon colored. Slowly pour in the warm half-and-half, whisking constantly. Continue whisking and cook until the mixture has a custardlike consistency and coats the bottom of a wooden spoon. Do not let the custard boil, or it will curdle.

3 Immediately remove the custard from the heat and add the banana. Using an immersion blender, purée the banana into the custard. (If you don't have an immersion blender, purée the banana in a food processor and then add it to the sauce.) Pour the sauce through a fine-mesh strainer into a bowl for a silky consistency, if desired. Cover the sauce and store in the refrigerator until needed.

Note

If vanilla beans are unavailable, use 1 teaspoon vanilla extract and add it to the sauce when adding the banana.

Advance Preparation

Can be prepared up to 1 day in advance, covered, and refrigerated.

BANANA SPLIT ICE CREAM TORTE

SERVES 6 TO 8

Ice cream pies are a big hit in California for several reasons. They're easy to assemble, pretty to look at, and they work well with our warm climate and informal entertaining style.

You can vary the ice cream, if you like. Just remember that the crust is chocolate and go from there. Other recommended flavors are Oreo, coffee, English toffee, and layers of vanilla and strawberry, like the flavors of an old-fashioned banana split.

This is a great item to keep in your freezer. Remember to remove the torte from the freezer 15 minutes before serving for easy slicing.

Advance Preparation
Can be prepared up to 1 month ahead, covered tightly, and frozen.

CRUST

6 tablespoons sliced blanched almonds

40 chocolate wafers (one 9-ounce box)

5 tablespoons unsalted butter, melted

FILLING

3 bananas, cut into ¼-inch slices

1 quart French vanilla ice cream, softened

6 ounces bittersweet chocolate, finely chopped

GARNISH

2 ounces bittersweet chocolate, grated

1   To make the crust, preheat the oven to 350°F. Spread the almonds in a single layer on a baking sheet and toast for 7 to 10 minutes, or until lightly browned. Transfer to a plate. Set aside 2 tablespoons of the toasted almonds for the garnish.

2   Process the remaining 4 tablespoons of the almonds in a food processor fitted with the metal blade for 10 seconds. Add the cookies and process until they resemble fine crumbs. Transfer the crumb mixture to a medium mixing bowl and add the butter, mixing with your fingers until completely combined. Butter the bottom and sides of a 9½-inch springform pan. Pat the crumb mixture on the bottom and halfway up the sides. (Don't worry if it's not perfectly even.) Refrigerate for at least 4 hours or freeze for 1 hour.

3   To make the filling, purée 2 of the bananas in a food processor fitted with the metal blade. Add the ice cream and process until well blended. With a few pulses, blend in the chopped chocolate and then the remaining sliced banana, making sure not to break it up too much.

4   Pour the filling into the crust in the pan in an even layer, smoothing it down. Cover with wax paper and place on a baking sheet to keep it level. Freeze for 1 hour. When the ice cream is set but not completely frozen, sprinkle the top evenly with the reserved toasted almonds and the grated chocolate. Return to the freezer and freeze the torte uncovered for at least 12 hours, then cover it with plastic wrap. Remove the torte from the freezer 15 minutes before serving and place it on a serving platter. When ready to serve, remove the plastic wrap and release the sides of the pan and remove. Slice with a serrated knife to serve.

WHITE CHOCOLATE AND PISTACHIO COOKIES

MAKES ABOUT 4 DOZEN

The first time I tasted these cookies I couldn't believe how satisfying and sweetly comforting they are. Based loosely on the Toll House recipe, this adaptation combines creamy white chocolate chunks with roasted unsalted green pistachios. Use a good-quality white chocolate such as Lindt.

2¼ cups all-purpose flour
1 teaspoon baking soda
¾ teaspoon salt
1 cup unsalted butter
1 cup firmly packed light brown sugar
½ cup granulated sugar
2 large eggs
1 teaspoon vanilla extract
¾ pound white chocolate, cut into small chunks, or chips
1 cup coarsely chopped unsalted pistachios

Advance Preparation
Can be prepared up to 1 day ahead and kept in an airtight container.

1 Preheat the oven to 350°F. Sift together the flour, baking soda, and salt into a medium mixing bowl and set aside.

2 In a large mixing bowl, using an electric mixer on medium speed, beat the butter, brown sugar, and granulated sugar together until the mixture becomes creamy. Beat in the eggs and vanilla. Add the flour mixture and continue mixing until well blended. Stir in the white chocolate and pistachios.

3. Drop the cookies by rounded teaspoonfuls 2 inches apart onto an ungreased baking sheet. Bake for 10 to 12 minutes, or until lightly browned. They should look slightly underdone when removed from the oven. Let the cookies cool in the pan for a minute before transferring them to wire racks to cool completely.

CALIFORNIA PISTACHIOS

Since the first commercial harvest in 1976, California has become the second-largest producer of pistachio nuts in the world. You can find shelled, unsalted pistachios in most specialty-food markets or natural-foods stores. If you can't find them shelled, you can do this yourself very easily. Do be certain, however, to use the unsalted variety for cooking.

What makes California pistachios so special? They're usually larger in size than their imported cousins, with a vivid green color and a wide split shell that makes them easier to open. The Kerman variety has a smooth, buttery flavor.

In the 1930s, European importers dyed blemished pistachio shells red because of antiquated harvesting and processing methods that bruised the shells. Most California pistachios are sold in their natural tan shell, but some are still dyed red because many consumers have become accustomed to the red color. To keep shelled and unshelled pistachios fresh and flavorful, store them in an airtight container in the refrigerator for up to 1 month.

SPICY CRINKLE COOKIES

MAKES ABOUT 4 DOZEN

These moist, chewy cookies perfumed with sweet spices are perfect with simple fruit desserts or ice cream. I like to serve a plate of these with Mixed Exotic Fruit Gazpacho (page 300) or alongside a platter of Fresh Apricots and Strawberries with Sour Cream and Brown Sugar (page 301).

2¼ cups all-purpose flour

2 teaspoons baking soda

¼ teaspoon salt

½ teaspoon ground cloves

1 teaspoon ground cinnamon

1 teaspoon ground ginger

½ teaspoon freshly grated nutmeg

½ teaspoon ground allspice

¾ cup unsalted butter, at room temperature

1 cup firmly packed dark brown sugar

1 large egg

¼ cup molasses

Granulated sugar for coating

Advance Preparation

Can be prepared up to 1 day ahead and kept in an airtight container at room temperature.

1 In a medium mixing bowl, sift together the flour, baking soda, salt, and spices.

2 In a large mixing bowl, using an electric mixer on medium speed, beat the butter and brown sugar together until creamy. Beat in the egg and molasses. Add the flour mixture and continue mixing until well blended.

3 Refrigerate the dough, covered, for at least 4 hours.

4 Preheat the oven to 350°F. Grease a baking sheet. Lay a large sheet of wax paper on the counter and sprinkle it with the granulated sugar. Roll the dough into balls about the size of a walnut and then roll them in the sugar, creating an even sugar coating. Place the cookies about 2 inches apart on the prepared baking sheet. Bake for about 8 to 10 minutes, or until just set. (They will puff up when cooking, then fall down, forming the crinkle when cooled.) Transfer to wire racks to cool.

The best part about preparing these brownies is that you mix everything right in the top pan of a double boiler. This adaptation on my dear friend Denny Luria's brownie recipe increases the chocolate and reduces the amount of flour, resulting in a crispy-chewy and very moist chocolaty brownie. If you like nuts, add ½ cup of toasted pecans or walnuts. Store the remaining brownies in an airtight container.

1 cup unsalted butter
6 ounces unsweetened chocolate, cut into small pieces
2 cups sugar
4 large eggs
1 teaspoon vanilla extract
½ cup all-purpose flour
½ teaspoon salt
Powdered sugar for dusting

1 Preheat the oven to 325°F. Grease a 9-by-13-inch baking pan.

2 Combine the butter and chocolate in the top pan of a double boiler set over (but not touching) simmering water over medium-low heat and melt slowly, stirring occasionally. (Alternatively, combine the chocolate and butter in a 6-cup microwave-safe glass measuring cup and heat on high power for 1½ minutes, or until melted, stirring once.)

3 When the butter and chocolate are melted, remove from the heat, add the sugar, and whisk vigorously. Add the eggs and vanilla and whisk until completely incorporated. Add the flour and salt and blend in, making sure there are no lumps of flour. The mixture should now be a shiny batter.

4 Pour the batter into the prepared pan and gently smooth the top. Bake in the center of the oven for 40 minutes, or until the top is crisp and dry and a skewer inserted 1 inch from the center comes out barely moist. Let cool to room temperature before cutting into squares or bars. Sprinkle with powdered sugar.

Advance Preparation
Can be prepared up to 1 day ahead and kept in an airtight container at room temperature until serving.

342   Turkey or Chicken Stock

343   Easy Brown Turkey or Chicken Stock

344   Easy Brown Veal Stock

346   Corn Bread for Stuffing

347   Double-Tomato Herb Sauce

348   Mixed-Herb Pesto

349   Pesto

350   Sun-Dried Tomato Pesto

351   Ancho Chile Paste

352   Red Pepper Aioli

353   Roasted Garlic Purée

355   Basic Vinaigrette

356   Hot Pepper Oil

357   Spicy Tomato Salsa

358   Tomatillo Salsa

359   Rustic Salsa

360   Smoky Salsa

361   Roasted Tomato Jam

362   Cranberry-Almond Relish

363   Ginger-Spiced Asian Pear and Cranberry Compote

364   Asian Pear-Quince-Apple Sauce

365   Eggnog Brandy Sauce

B A S I C S

TURKEY OR CHICKEN STOCK

MAKES 3 QUARTS

Soups and sauces always benefit from a rich homemade stock. Make this up and keep it in your freezer in 1- and 2-cup containers.

4 pounds turkey or chicken necks and backs
3 celery ribs
3 medium carrots, peeled
2 medium onions, root ends cut off, cut into halves
2 medium leeks, white and light green parts only, cleaned and sliced
1 bouquet garni (see note)
Salt to taste

1   Combine the poultry parts, vegetables, and bouquet garni in a 6-quart stock-pot and add enough cold water to fill the pot three-fourths full. Bring to a boil slowly over medium heat, uncovered.

2   Reduce the heat to as low as possible and simmer for 3 hours. Add salt to taste.

3   Strain the stock through a colander or strainer lined with cheesecloth. Let cool to room temperature and refrigerate for at least 6 hours or up to overnight. With a large spoon, remove the hardened fat from the surface and discard it.

4   If you're not using it immediately, pour the stock into small containers and refrigerate or freeze.

Note

To make a bouquet garni, wrap a sprig of fresh parsley, a bay leaf, and a sprig of fresh thyme in cheesecloth and tie with kitchen string. Tie the string to the handle of your pan so you can retrieve it easily.

Advance Preparation

If not used within 3 days, the stock should be frozen and then reboiled before use. Freeze in small containers for convenient use.

Sometimes I prefer a dark brown poultry stock instead of the usual white. My friend Kathy Blue makes an incredibly rich brown poultry stock. Her secret lies in reducing the stock for hours on top of the stove. However, this oven technique saves time, requires less cleanup, and doesn't sacrifice any of the delicious results of Kathy's method. I'm not sure I'll ever make brown stock any other way.

6 pounds turkey or chicken necks, backs, and wings, cut up
2 tablespoons all-purpose flour
3 quarts water
2 large carrots, cut into 2-inch pieces
2 large onions, cut into 2-inch pieces
1 bouquet garni (see note)

1   Preheat the oven to 425°F. Place the necks, backs, and wings in a large, heavy roasting pan. Sprinkle the flour on the turkey pieces and toss to coat evenly. Roast, turning occasionally, until browned, about 1½ hours.

2   Using heavy oven mitts, pull the oven rack with the pan on it out halfway, and pour 2 cups of the water, or enough to cover the bones, into the pan. Stir with a wooden spoon, scraping up the browned bits from the bottom of the pan. The water will become a rich brown color. Add the vegetables, the remaining 10 cups water, and the bouquet garni. Continue roasting for another 2 hours. Add more water as it reduces.

3   Remove the pan from the oven, being sure to use the oven mitts, and let the stock cool. Remove the bones and strain the stock through a fine-mesh strainer (a conical strainer is excellent for this purpose) into a large bowl. Let cool to room temperature. Cover and refrigerate for at least 6 hours or up to overnight.

4   With a large spoon, remove the hardened fat from the surface and discard it. The stock should be clear. If you're not using it immediately, pour it into small containers and refrigerate or freeze.

EASY BROWN TURKEY OR CHICKEN STOCK

MAKES 1½ QUARTS

Note
To make a bouquet garni, wrap a sprig of fresh parsley, a bay leaf, and a sprig of fresh thyme in cheesecloth and tie with string. Tie the string to the handle of your pan so you can retrieve it easily.

Advance Preparation
If not used within 3 days, the stock should be frozen and then reboiled before use. Freeze in small containers for convenient use.

EASY BROWN VEAL STOCK

MAKES ABOUT 3 QUARTS

California sauces and reductions often rely on veal stock for its light, meaty richness rather than beef stock, which tends to be heavy and overpowering. Veal stock has another virtue: It assimilates the flavors it's blended with in a most appealing way. Prepare this stock in a large quantity and divide it into small containers to keep in your freezer. Making veal stock from scratch may seem like a big fuss, but this oven method makes it a snap, and the stock is so delicious that you'll want to have it on hand.

1 tablespoon olive oil
4 pounds veal knuckles with some meat on them
1 large carrot, cut into 2-inch pieces
1 large onion, cut into 2-inch pieces
2 celery ribs, cut into 2-inch pieces
2 medium leeks, white and light green parts only, cleaned and finely chopped
1 cup full-bodied, dry red wine such as Merlot or Cabernet Sauvignon
2 tablespoons tomato paste
4½ quarts water
1 bouquet garni (see note)

Note

To make a bouquet garni, wrap a sprig of fresh parsley, a bay leaf, and a sprig of fresh thyme in cheesecloth and tie with string. Tie the string to the handle of your pan so you can retrieve it easily.

Advance Preparation

If not used within 3 days, the stock should be frozen and then reboiled before use. Freeze in small containers for convenient use.

1   Preheat the oven to 425°F. Rub the olive oil on the veal bones and place them in a large, heavy roasting pan. Roast for 1 hour. Add the vegetables and continue roasting for ½ hour, turning occasionally, until well browned, making sure the vegetables are browned but not burned.

2   Using heavy oven mitts, pull the oven rack with the pan on it out halfway, pour the wine into the pan, and stir with a wooden spoon, scraping up the browned bits from the bottom of the pan. Add the tomato paste; the mixture will become a rich brown color. Add 3 quarts of the water and the bouquet garni, making sure the bones are just covered with the water. Return the pan to the oven. Reduce the oven temperature to 325°F and continue roasting for another 1 hour. Add the remaining 1½ quarts water. Reduce the oven temperature to 300°F and roast for 1 hour longer.

3   Remove the pan from the oven, being sure to use the oven mitts, and let the stock cool. Remove the bones and strain the stock through a fine-mesh strainer (a conical strainer is excellent for this purpose) into a large bowl. Let cool to room temperature. Cover and refrigerate for at least 6 hours or up to overnight.

4   With a large spoon, remove the hardened fat from the surface and discard it. The stock should be clear. If you're not using it immediately, pour it into small containers and refrigerate or freeze.

COOKING WITH LESS FAT

There's no question that reducing fat has become a way of life for many of us. But that doesn't mean that you can't have intense, flavorful food. Here are some ways to reduce fat without sacrificing flavor.

- Use olive oil spray instead of coating the ingredient with oil. You still get the same flavor with a far less oily texture. This works particularly well on breads, potatoes, and vegetables.

- Substitute nonfat yogurt when possible for cream or sour cream. The key is to remember that you can't simmer yogurt, but you can add it as a zippy garnish to cold and warm soups, salad dressings, and even mashed potatoes.

- Heavy (whipping) cream is still preferable for finishing certain sauces, but you can reduce the amount and add roasted garlic purée, puréed cooked vegetables, or vegetable or chicken stock to the sauce for extra body with fine results.

- Add a tablespoon or two of boiling water instead of some of the oil to an emulsified vinaigrette to lighten the consistency and fat level, or add a few tablespoons of nonfat yogurt or chicken stock.

- Choose dry-aged cheeses like Parmesan, Pecorino Romano, or dry jack to flavor a dish by garnishing it with thin shards.

- Consider chopped fresh herbs, Dijon mustard, and citrus as low-fat flavor enhancers that really work.

- For fish or poultry, make a crust of mustard and coat with fresh herbs; or make a crust with hoisin sauce and then sprinkle with scallions, peeled and minced fresh ginger, and sesame seeds.

- Use your favorite vegetable salsa as a sauce.

- Try smoking meat, poultry, seafood, or vegetables to add flavor without fat.

CORN BREAD
FOR STUFFING

MAKES 8 CUPS

Don't try to save time by using a packaged corn-bread mix, usually cloyingly sweet and too moist. Making corn bread from scratch is a snap. This basic recipe is studded with corn kernels and is slightly dry, which works well for most stuffing recipes. Because the holidays tend to be such a hectic time, I always make this corn bread right after Halloween and stick it in my freezer in a tightly sealed lock-top plastic bag. Before using, let thaw to room temperature and proceed with your recipe.

Advance Preparation
The corn bread can be prepared up to 2 months ahead, wrapped tightly in a lock-top plastic bag, and frozen. Let thaw before using.

1 cup all-purpose flour

1 cup yellow cornmeal

1 tablespoon baking powder

1 teaspoon sugar

1 teaspoon salt

¼ teaspoon freshly ground black pepper

⅓ cup vegetable oil or melted unsalted butter

1 large egg

1 cup buttermilk

½ cup fresh corn kernels (from about 1 medium ear) or thawed frozen corn

1   Preheat the oven to 425°F. Grease an 8- or 9-inch square baking pan.

2   Combine the flour, cornmeal, baking powder, sugar, salt, and pepper in a large mixing bowl. Add the oil, egg, and buttermilk and whisk until all the ingredients are just blended. Add the corn kernels and mix just to combine.

3   Spoon the mixture into the prepared pan and bake for 20 to 25 minutes or until a toothpick inserted into the center comes out clean. Let the corn bread cool in the pan, then turn it out and cut it into small chunks. Proceed with the recipe or freeze until ready to use.

This California reworking of the classic marinara sauce includes both canned and sun-dried tomatoes for extra-rich flavor. This thick home-style sauce is equally good on pasta, pizza, meatballs, or eggs.

One 3-ounce package dry-packed sun-dried tomatoes

2 tablespoons olive oil

1 medium onion, finely chopped

1 medium carrot, peeled and finely chopped

1 celery rib, finely chopped

One 28-ounce can crushed tomatoes

One 14-ounce can tomatoes, well-drained and diced

2 garlic cloves, minced

1 cup dry, full-bodied red wine such as Chianti or Merlot

2 cups water

¼ cup finely chopped fresh parsley

1 teaspoon finely chopped fresh thyme or ½ teaspoon dried

¼ cup finely chopped fresh basil or 2 tablespoons dried

Salt and freshly ground black pepper

Advance Preparation
Can be prepared up to 5 days ahead, covered, and refrigerated. It also can be frozen in small containers for up to 2 months.

1   Place the sun-dried tomatoes in a small mixing bowl and pour boiling water over them. Let them steep for 5 minutes. Drain the softened tomatoes and set aside.

2   Heat the olive oil in a large, nonaluminum pot over medium heat. Add the onion, carrot, and celery and cook until softened, stirring frequently to prevent burning, about 10 minutes. Add both the canned tomatoes and the softened sun-dried tomatoes, the garlic, wine, water, and herbs. Partially cover and reduce the heat to medium-low. Simmer for 1½ hours, stirring occasionally. Add salt and pepper to taste.

3   Process the mixture in the pot with an immersion blender or in a food processor fitted with the metal blade until the sauce is a fine purée with no large pieces of tomato. You may need to add more water for a saucelike consistency since the sun-dried tomatoes provide extra thickness. Taste for seasoning, add more salt, pepper, or herbs, if desired. Serve hot.

MIXED-HERB
PESTO

MAKES 1¼ CUPS

Basil, parsley, chives, and thyme are combined in this recipe for a spirited pesto. Most herbs are now available year-round, so you can serve this anytime. I prefer to add the cheese right before serving so that I can use the sauce with or without it. Pesto is excellent added to soups, dressings, and sauces and as a glaze for tomatoes.

2 garlic cloves, peeled

2 cups firmly packed fresh basil leaves

¼ cup firmly packed fresh parsley leaves

⅓ cup chopped fresh chives

1 tablespoon fresh thyme leaves

3 tablespoons pine nuts

½ cup olive oil

¼ teaspoon freshly ground black pepper

½ cup freshly grated Parmesan cheese

Advance Preparation
Can be prepared through step 2 up to 1 week ahead and refrigerated. Add the cheese just before serving.

1 Mince the garlic in a food processor fitted with the metal blade. Add the basil, parsley, chives, and thyme and process until finely chopped. Add the pine nuts and finely chop.

2 With the machine running, add the olive oil in a steady stream. Stop and scrape down the sides of the bowl as needed. Add the pepper.

3 Just before serving, add the cheese and process until well blended. Taste for seasoning. Refrigerate the pesto in a tightly covered container until ready to use.

I cook with this uncomplicated pesto when I'm in the mood for the straightforward classic flavors of basil and Parmesan.

PESTO

2 garlic cloves, peeled

2 cups firmly packed fresh basil leaves (about 2 medium bunches)

½ cup firmly packed fresh parsley leaves

2 tablespoons pine nuts

½ cup olive oil

¼ teaspoon freshly ground black pepper

¾ cup freshly grated Parmesan cheese

1   Mince the garlic in a food processor fitted with the metal blade. Add the basil and parsley and process until finely chopped. Add the pine nuts and finely chop.

2   With the machine running, add the oil in a steady stream. Stop and scrape down the sides of the bowl as needed. Add the pepper.

3   Just before serving, add the cheese and process until well blended. Taste for seasoning. Refrigerate the pesto in a tightly covered container until ready to use.

Advance Preparation
Can be prepared through step 2 up to
1 week ahead and refrigerated. Add
the cheese just before serving.

SUN-DRIED TOMATO PESTO

MAKES ABOUT ½ CUP

Whether this recipe originated in Italy or here in California, this luscious pesto is incredibly versatile. It flavors cheese, main courses, dressings, sauces, and pasta. It's also good on lightly toasted bread.

1 garlic clove, peeled
½ cup oil-packed sun-dried tomatoes, drained
2 tablespoons finely chopped fresh basil leaves
2 tablespoon pine nuts
¼ teaspoon salt
⅛ teaspoon freshly ground black pepper

1   Mince the garlic in a food processor fitted with the metal blade. Add the sun-dried tomatoes, basil, pine nuts, salt, and pepper and process to a thick paste. If it is very thick, you may need to add a bit of olive oil. Transfer to a covered container and refrigerate.

VARIATION
For a simpler paste, purée the garlic, tomatoes, salt, and pepper together and add enough oil to form a thick paste.

ADVANCED PERPARATION
Can be prepared up to 1 week ahead and refrigerated.

WHAT TO DO WITH SUN-DRIED TOMATO PESTO OR ANCHO CHILE PASTE

- Add to crème fraîche, sour cream, or mayonnaise for a quick and easy dip for raw vegetables.
- Toss with new potatoes and roast them in aluminum foil or parchment.
- Add to mayonnaise and spread on a sandwich with grilled red peppers, grilled eggplant, and fresh goat cheese.
- Use to season steamed vegetables.
- Use as part of a sauce for sautéed chicken breasts or turkey scaloppini.
- Use as a paste for grilled chicken breasts.
- Use as an addition to basic vinaigrette.

Ancho chiles are a dried version of the poblano chile with a moderately hot flavor. If you can't find ancho chiles, substitute any dried red chile, such as New Mexico or California dried chiles.

In this recipe, garlic and ancho chiles are toasted in a dry skillet, which is a Mexican technique for releasing their flavor. Additions of mild balsamic vinegar and sweet honey bring out the toasted chile flavor. The chiles are then softened, puréed, and strained into a thick paste. This is a wonderful flavoring to have on hand. Try adding it to sour cream, mayonnaise, or butter. It's also a great spicy coating for meat that will be grilled or roasted.

ANCHO CHILE PASTE

MAKES ½ CUP

2 large garlic cloves, unpeeled
6 large ancho chiles (about 3 ounces)
2 tablespoons olive oil
1 tablespoon balsamic vinegar
1 teaspoon honey
½ teaspoon salt

Advance Preparation
Can be prepared up to 1 month ahead and refrigerated.

1   Place the garlic in a small skillet over medium-high heat. Toast the garlic cloves, turning them as they begin to brown. When light brown in color, remove them from the skillet and peel. Set aside.

2   In the same skillet, heat the chiles over medium heat until they begin to expand and the flesh is soft, 1 to 2 minutes. (If you have an overhead fan, turn it on, because the chiles may make you cough.) The chiles should smell rich but should not be charred. Remove from the heat and let cool.

3   Wear rubber gloves when handling chiles. Slit the chiles open and remove the seeds, stems, and any veins. Place the chiles in a small bowl. Pour boiling water over them to cover and let soften for 15 minutes. Drain well and pat dry.

4   In a food processor fitted with the metal blade, process the toasted garlic until minced. Add the chiles, oil, vinegar, honey, and salt and process to a purée, scraping down the sides of the bowl as needed. Push through a fine-mesh strainer to remove all coarse pieces and taste for seasoning. Store the chile paste in an airtight container in the refrigerator.

RED PEPPER AIOLI

MAKES 1¼ CUPS

This simple sauce relies on store-bought mayonnaise to avoid any health risks that might occur from using raw eggs in homemade mayonnaise. Sometimes I add the pulp from a head of roasted garlic for a milder version.

4 garlic cloves
1 roasted, peeled (see page 27), seeded, and finely chopped medium red bell pepper
1 cup mayonnaise
Salt and freshly ground white pepper
Pinch of cayenne pepper

1   Mince the garlic cloves in a food processor fitted with the metal blade. Add the roasted pepper and process until well blended. Add the mayonnaise and process to mix. Add the salt and pepper to taste and the cayenne and taste for seasoning. Refrigerate the aioli in a tightly covered container until ready to use.

Advance Preparation
Can be prepared up to 5 days ahead and refrigerated.

THE NEW CALIFORNIA COOK

Look for peeled garlic cloves, now widely available at well-stocked supermarkets, to cut down on preparation time. You'll find this paste to be a wonderful flavor enhancer for sauces, dressings, and vegetables, among other uses. It is particularly well suited to sweet squashes and adds a depth of flavor.

ROASTED GARLIC PURÉE

MAKES ABOUT ¼ CUP

| 60 peeled garlic cloves |
| 1 tablespoon olive oil |

1. Preheat the oven to 425°F. Place the garlic in a large piece of heavy aluminum foil. Sprinkle with the oil and wrap tightly.

2. Place the package on a baking sheet and bake for 45 minutes to 1 hour, or until the garlic is soft when pierced with the tip of a knife. Remove from the oven and let cool. Mash the softened cloves with a spoon or process in a food processor until smooth.

Advance Preparation
Can be prepared up to 5 days ahead, covered, and refrigerated.

Vinaigrette

These splendid sauces are not just for salads. You can also use them to accompany grilled or steamed vegetables or grilled chicken, fish, or meat, a particularly appealing idea when you want a sauce but don't want to spend hours reducing stock.

A successful vinaigrette depends upon excellent ingredients, the ratio of oil to vinegar, and making sure the two have emulsified. I prefer a ratio of 3 parts oil to 1 part vinegar. If you're watching your fat content, add a little hot water or chicken stock in lieu of some of the oil to lighten the dressing. You can use a food processor or an immersion blender to make vinaigrette because it automatically creates an emulsion that will last at least a few hours. If you don't have a food processor, just put the ingredients in a small jar, cover tightly with the lid, and shake vigorously to emulsify; or whisk the ingredients together in a bowl. Always add the oil last. Vinaigrette will keep in the refrigerator for weeks. Bring it to room temperature before using and stir to emulsify again.

There is an enormous variety of excellent oils and vinegars available that allow you to be really creative. Keep on hand extra-virgin olive oil, safflower oil, aged sherry vinegar, a good-quality red wine vinegar, and balsamic vinegar. Imported hazelnut and walnut oils should be used sparingly because their flavors are very intense. I usually use half nut oil and half olive oil for a nut-flavored vinaigrette.

Almost all vinaigrettes should include a minced shallot and a garlic clove. Dijon mustard is also an excellent flavor enhancer. I like to use just a touch of cream to smooth out the acid in the vinegar for a milder vinaigrette.

Here are some ideas for other combinations.

- Grilled corn and red onion vinaigrette
- Tomato-basil vinaigrette
- Mixed-herb vinaigrette with fresh chervil, dill, chives, and/or burnet
- Chunky tomato–fresh mint vinaigrette
- Black bean, tomato, and fresh cilantro vinaigrette
- Fennel, garlic, and balsamic vinaigrette
- Ginger, orange, and toasted sesame seed vinaigrette
- Chopped Niçoise and green olive, caper, and anchovy vinaigrette
- Roasted mixed red and yellow pepper vinaigrette
- Mixed yellow and red pear tomato vinaigrette
- Roasted garlic and blue cheese vinaigrette

This vinaigrette is my standby salad dressing that will brighten up any variety of salad greens. If you like the full-bodied flavor of balsamic vinegar, you can replace the red wine vinegar with balsamic vinegar, but the dressing will be stronger.

BASIC VINAIGRETTE

MAKES ¾ CUP

1 medium shallot, finely chopped

1 medium garlic clove, minced

1 tablespoon finely chopped fresh parsley

1 tablespoon finely chopped fresh chives

1 teaspoon Dijon mustard

1 tablespoon fresh lemon juice

3 tablespoons red wine vinegar

¾ cup extra-virgin olive oil

Salt and freshly ground black pepper

1 Combine the shallot, garlic, parsley, chives, mustard, lemon juice, and vinegar in medium bowl and whisk until well blended. (Alternatively, combine in a food processor fitted with the metal blade and process until well blended.)

2 Slowly pour the oil into the bowl, whisking continuously (or processing) until blended and emulsified. Add the salt and pepper to taste.

Advance Preparation
Can be prepared up to 1 week ahead, covered, and refrigerated. Bring to room temperature and whisk before using.

HOT PEPPER OIL

MAKES 1 CUP

Use this spicy oil sparingly. It enlivens many dishes, from soup to salad dressings, and will keep in the refrigerator almost indefinitely.

¼ cup hot red pepper flakes

1 cup vegetable oil

1   Combine the red pepper flakes and oil in a small saucepan over medium heat. Bring to a boil and then immediately remove from the heat. Let the mixture cool.

2   Strain the oil through a fine-mesh strainer into a small glass jar and seal tightly. Keep refrigerated.

Variation

Leave the red pepper flakes in the oil. They will fall to the bottom and can be used in seasoning. The oil will become hotter as it stands.

Advance Preparation

Can be prepared up to 3 days ahead, covered, and refrigerated.

All over Mexico you find this traditional salsa in restaurants and in home kitchens. This all-purpose Mexican condiment, sometimes called *pico de gallo* in Texas and *salsa cruda* or *salsa fresca* in Mexico, can be used as a flavoring agent in many dishes, from soups to vegetables.

You can regulate the hotness by the number of chiles included. If you like a more rustic salsa, don't bother to peel and seed the tomatoes. This recipe is typical of California cooking, but you can change the underlying flavors for a salsa with an Italian accent: Simply replace the jalapeños, cilantro, and lime juice with crushed red pepper flakes, chopped fresh basil, and lemon juice.

SPICY TOMATO SALSA

MAKES ABOUT 1 QUART

4 large tomatoes, peeled, seeded, and finely chopped

2 jalapeño chiles, seeded and finely chopped (see note)

2 tablespoons finely chopped fresh cilantro

1 small red onion, finely chopped

1 garlic clove, minced

1 teaspoon fresh lemon or lime juice

1 teaspoon salt

Pinch of freshly ground black pepper

1 Combine all of the ingredients in a medium mixing bowl and mix well. Taste for seasoning.

Note
When working with chiles, always wear rubber gloves. Wash the cutting surface and knife immediately. Canned jalapeños may be used if fresh are unavailable. If you use canned chiles, do not add the lemon juice.

Advanced Preparation
Can be prepared up to 3 days ahead, covered and refrigerated

TOMATILLO SALSA

MAKES 1½ CUPS

Light and spicy, tomatillo sauce is an important basic in California cooking. Here the onion is cooked briefly in stock, which is added to the sauce to lighten it. If fresh tomatillos are unavailable, you can substitute drained canned tomatillos with a pinch of sugar; you won't need to cook them. Use this salsa on grilled meat or fish, or to flavor sauces. It's also great with eggs and fresh corn tortillas.

¾ cup Chicken Stock (page 342)
1 small onion, coarsely chopped
1 pound tomatillos, husked, cored, and quartered
2 jalapeño chiles, seeded and finely chopped (see note)
2 garlic cloves, minced
3 tablespoons finely chopped fresh cilantro
¼ teaspoon ground cumin
½ teaspoon salt
1 tablespoon fresh lemon juice

Note
When working with chiles, always wear rubber gloves. Wash the cutting surface and knife immediately.

Advance Preparation
Can be made up to 5 days ahead and refrigerated in an airtight container.

1 In a large skillet over medium heat, heat the stock. Add the onion and simmer, covered, for about 5 minutes. Add the tomatillos and cook, covered, for another 5 minutes.

2 Pour the contents of the skillet into a food processor fitted with the metal blade and process until coarsely chopped. Add the remaining ingredients and taste for seasoning. Pour the salsa into a storage container and cool. Refrigerate until ready to use.

This chunky, rustic salsa is a combination of red tomatoes and green tomatillos. Unlike other salsas, this one is refined through cooking and chopping coarsely.

RUSTIC SALSA

1 tablespoon olive oil

6 large Roma tomatoes, halved

2 tomatillos, husked, cored, and quartered

1 small red onion, sliced

2 tablespoons finely chopped fresh cilantro

2 garlic cloves, minced

½ teaspoon salt

¼ teaspoon freshly ground black pepper

½ teaspoon mild ground red chile powder

½ cup Chicken Stock (page 342)

Advance Preparation
Can be made up to 5 days ahead and refrigerated in an airtight container.

1   In a large skillet over medium heat, heat the oil. Add the tomatoes and tomatillos and sauté for 6 to 8 minutes. Stir in the onion, cilantro, and garlic and continue cooking for 8 minutes longer, or until the tomatoes and onion are softened. Stir in the salt, pepper, and chile powder. Remove from the heat and let cool.

2   In a food processor fitted with the metal blade, purée the cooled vegetable mixture, being sure to leave some texture. Add the stock and taste for seasoning. Pour the salsa into a storage container and let cool. Refrigerate until ready to use.

SMOKY SALSA

MAKES 2 CUPS

Hugo Molina, former executive chef of the Parkway Grill in Pasadena, created this recipe for the Crocodile Cantina, a fun party of a restaurant serving Central American and Mexican food.

Chipotle chiles canned in adobo sauce, which can be found in the Mexican aisle of supermarkets or in Mexican markets, are used here. Chipotles are smoked jalapeño chiles that are dried, concentrating the charred flavor.

Grilling the ingredients first provides a smoky undertone. Try this on Ricotta Corn Cakes (page 40) or as sauce for Grilled Flank Steak (page 211) or grilled chicken. This salsa is great with a big basket of warm Crisp Tortilla Chips (page 282) or other chips.

Variation
Add a few tablespoons of beer.

Advance Preparation
Can be prepared up to 1 week ahead and refrigerated in an airtight container.

5 large Roma tomatoes, halved
1 small red onion, cut into thick slices
3 scallions, white and light green parts only
⅓ medium bunch of fresh cilantro, tough stems removed
1 garlic clove
1 teaspoon canned chipotle peppers
1 teaspoon apple cider vinegar
1 teaspoon salt
¼ cup Chicken Stock (page 342)

1   Prepare a grill for medium-high-heat grilling. Grill the tomatoes, onion slices, and scallions about 3 inches from the heat until partially charred, turning occasionally. (The onion will take the longest.) Transfer to a plate. Grill the cilantro for about 30 seconds, just to wilt and give it a slightly smoky flavor.

2   Mince the garlic cloves in a food processor fitted with the metal blade. Add the grilled vegetables and cilantro, the chiles, vinegar, salt, and stock and process to a purée. Taste for seasoning. (For a thinner consistency, add more chicken stock.) Pour into a storage container and let cool. Refrigerate until ready to use.

If you've never roasted a tomato, you're in for a treat. The juices of the tomato slowly evaporate, leaving them sweet and slightly caramelized. I usually make this in the summer and early fall months, when tomatoes are as they should be—juicy, vine-ripened, and full of flavor.

Farmers' markets have sprouted up all over California in small and big cities alike. You can find just about any variety of tomato in these markets, from the simple beefsteak to zebra tomatoes, in every imaginable size.

While this rustic condiment requires a long cooking time, it needs little hands-on attention. Serve the jam warm alongside Grilled Veal Chops with Zucchini-Corn Relish (page 228) or any simple flavored chicken breast. Roasted Onions and Baby Potatoes (page 263) make a nice side dish. This is also good on warm pasta.

| 6 pounds tomatoes (about 6 large), peeled, seeded, and coarsely chopped |
| 4 garlic cloves, finely chopped |
| 2 tablespoons olive oil |
| 1 teaspoon finely chopped fresh thyme |
| 1 teaspoon salt |
| ¼ teaspoon freshly ground black pepper |

Advance Preparation
Can be prepared up to 1 week ahead and refrigerated in an airtight container.

1   Preheat the oven to 425°F. In a large, nonaluminum baking pan, combine the tomatoes, garlic, oil, and thyme and mix until well blended. Roast for 2 to 2½ hours, stirring every 30 minutes, until the liquid has evaporated and the mixture has thickened and lightly caramelized. Remove from the oven and let cool. Add the salt and pepper and taste for seasoning. Store in an airtight container.

CRANBERRY-ALMOND RELISH

MAKES 3 TO 4 CUPS

This is a standard dish on my Thanksgiving table. Hot sugar syrup briefly cooks the cranberries so that the fruit is slightly undercooked and crunchy. Raspberries and toasted almonds add a unique touch. This is also good with roast chicken or duck.

½ cup blanched slivered almonds

One 12-ounce bag fresh cranberries, rinsed and picked over

1 cup sugar

1 cup water

1 medium pippin apple, peeled, cored, and quartered

1 medium pear, peeled, cored, and quartered

2 teaspoons minced orange zest

¾ cup fresh or thawed frozen raspberries

¼ cup light rum

Pinch of freshly grated nutmeg

GARNISH

Fresh mint sprigs

Advance Preparation
Can be prepared through step 4 up to 2 days head, covered, and refrigerated. Add the almonds just before serving.

1   Preheat the oven to 350°F. Spread the almonds in a single layer on a baking sheet and toast for 7 to 10 minutes, or until lightly browned. Transfer to a plate and set aside.

2   Add the cranberries to a food processor fitted with the metal blade and pulse a few times to chop coarsely. Transfer to a large mixing bowl.

3   Combine the sugar and water in a medium saucepan over medium heat and bring to a simmer. Cook the syrup until the sugar is dissolved and the liquid is clear. Immediately pour the syrup over the cranberries and mix well.

4   Place the apple and pear in the food processor fitted with the metal blade and coarsely chop. Transfer to the cranberry mixture. Add the orange zest, raspberries, rum, and nutmeg and mix gently to combine. Taste for seasoning.

5   Spoon into a serving bowl and garnish with the mint sprigs. Add the almonds just before serving.

Sometimes I want a simple sauce with clear flavors. This recipe, inspired by Deborah Madison's cranberry quince sauce, is a lively blending of exotic produce (the Asian pear) with the native American cranberry.

According to Elizabeth Schneider in *Uncommon Fruits and Vegetables,* more than 25 varieties of Asian pear were planted by Chinese prospectors as they crossed through the Sierra Nevada mountains during the gold rush days. Asian pears have a mild aroma and a granular texture, making them difficult to overcook. Oddly enough, their flavor intensifies through long cooking, yet they always retain a slight crunch.

Balsamic vinegar provides a sweet-tart finish to the sauce, while fresh ginger is infused during cooking and at the end, creating a layering of flavors. Serve the compote with turkey, poultry, or lamb. I like to serve it at room temperature.

GINGER-SPICED ASIAN PEAR AND CRANBERRY COMPOTE

MAKES ABOUT 6 CUPS

10 cloves
One 2-inch piece fresh ginger, peeled
One 2-inch piece of cinnamon stick
15 allspice berries
1 cup sugar
2 cups water
2 large Asian pears, peeled, cored, and cut into 1-inch chunks
One 12-ounce bag fresh cranberries, rinsed and picked over
2 tablespoons balsamic vinegar
2 teaspoons peeled and finely chopped fresh ginger

Advance Preparation
Can be prepared up to 5 days ahead, covered, and refrigerated. Taste for seasoning before serving; you may need to add a bit more vinegar.

1   Make a bouquet garni by enclosing the cloves, ginger, cinnamon stick, and allspice berries in a piece of cheesecloth tied together with a piece of kitchen string. Tie the string to the handle of a large saucepan.

2   Combine the bouquet garni, sugar, and water in the saucepan and bring the syrup to a boil over high heat. When the sugar has dissolved, reduce the heat to medium and add the pears. Cover and simmer for 40 to 45 minutes, or until the pears are tender but still offer a slight resistance when pierced with the tip of a knife.

3   Stir in the cranberries, raise the heat to medium-high, and cook until the cranberries begin to pop, stirring frequently, 8 to 10 minutes. When the cranberries have cooked, remove from the heat and let cool. Remove the bouquet garni. Add the vinegar and ginger and taste for seasoning. The sauce will firm up as it cools. Transfer to a storage container and refrigerate until ready to use. Taste for seasoning just before serving.

ASIAN PEAR-QUINCE-APPLE SAUCE

MAKES ABOUT 5 CUPS

Sometimes simple additions to a basic recipe can make a grand difference. Quince gives off a tropical fruit perfume, and Asian pears maintain a crisp quality, adding unexpected taste and texture to traditional applesauce. I like to serve this as an accompaniment to Crispy Potato Pancakes with Vegetables (page 259) and Brisket of Beef with Sun-Dried Tomatoes, Zinfandel, and Thyme (page 214). It is delicious served warm, room temperature, or chilled; try it heated gently and spooned over French vanilla ice cream.

1 cup sugar
2 cups water
One 2-inch piece of cinnamon stick
2 quince, peeled, cored, and cut into 2-inch chunks
2 Asian pears, peeled, cored, and cut into 2-inch chunks
2 pippin apples, peeled, cored, and cut into 2-inch chunks

Advance Preparation

Can be prepared up to 1 week ahead, covered, and refrigerated.

1 In a large, heavy saucepan over medium-high heat, combine the sugar, water, and cinnamon stick and cook until the sugar is dissolved. Add the quince, reduce the heat to medium-low, and bring to a gentle simmer. Cover and cook for about 40 minutes, stirring occasionally.

2 Add the pears and apples and continue cooking for about ½ hour longer, stirring occasionally, until the apples have softened. Discard the cinnamon stick. If you prefer a saucelike consistency, purée the sauce in the pot to the desired consistency using an immersion blender. Spoon the sauce into a storage container until ready to use.

A version of this versatile sauce using raw eggs first appeared in my book *The Cuisine of California.* This updated recipe cooks the eggs with superfine sugar to achieve a silky texture and also to avoid any health risks. Brandy and a sprinkling of freshly grated nutmeg enliven this fluffy dessert sauce. This is an exceptional finish to Nectarine Crisp with Dried Cherries (page 308), Pumpkin Bread Pudding (page 320), or any fruit holiday dessert. You can make your own superfine sugar by briefly whirling regular white sugar in a food processor.

EGGNOG
BRANDY SAUCE

3 egg yolks

¾ cups superfine sugar

2 tablespoons unsalted butter, at room temperature

3 egg whites

1 cup heavy (whipping) cream

½ teaspoon vanilla extract

2 to 3 tablespoons brandy, cognac, or applejack brandy

⅛ tablespoon freshly grated nutmeg

1   In the top pan of a double boiler set over (but not touching) simmering water over medium heat, combine the egg yolks, sugar, and butter and whisk until thick and lemon colored (the mixture will be very thick until it begins to cook) and coats a wooden spoon. Be careful not to overcook and curdle the eggs. Let cool.

2   In a medium mixing bowl, beat the egg whites until stiff peaks form.

3   In a small mixing bowl, whip the cream until stiff peaks form.

4   Fold the egg whites and whipped cream alternately into the egg yolk mixture until no streaks remain. Fold in the vanilla, brandy, and nutmeg. Serve immediately.

Advance Preparation
Can be prepared up to 2 hours ahead, covered, and refrigerated. Serve cold. Be careful of the mixture starting to separate. Whisk well if separation occurs.

MENUS

THANKSGIVING OR CHRISTMAS

Pear, Pistachio, and Chicken Liver Mousse (page 16)

Marinated Roast Turkey (page 194)

Rich Turkey Gravy (page 196)

Ginger-Spiced Asian Pear and Cranberry Compote (page 363)

OR

Cranberry-Almond Relish (page 362)

Onion, Dried Plum, and Chestnut Compote (page 256)

Corn Bread, Leek, and Red Pepper Stuffing Terrine (page 254)

Sautéed Green and Yellow Beans with Garlic and Basil (page 244)

Spiced Sweet Potato Pudding (page 265)

Pumpkin Bread Pudding with Eggnog Brandy Sauce (page 320)

SUMMER CELEBRATION FOR WEDDINGS OR GRADUATIONS

This menu works beautifully on a buffet table.

Asian Gravlax with Ginger-Mustard Sauce (page 20)

Asian Guacamole (page 34)

Foccacia (page 294)

Indonesian Leg of Lamb (page 222)

Rice Pilaf with Fresh Corn and Peanuts (page 270)

Tricolor Vegetable Sauté (page 245)

Mango and Macadamia Nut Brown-Butter Tart (page 312)

Bittersweet Chocolate Hazelnut Torte with Banana Custard Sauce (page 331)

WEEKEND BRUNCH

Herbed Scrambled Eggs with Goat Cheese (page 115)

Chicken and Apple Sausage (page 201)

OR

Turkey Sausages with Sun-Dried Tomatoes (page 203)

Roasted Onions and Baby Potatoes (page 263)

Fresh Pear Bread (page 279) with Assorted Preserves

Fresh Melon and Berries

SUNDAY SUPPER

Blood Orange, Mushroom, and Avocado Salad (page 88)

Turkey Vegetable Cobbler (page 198)

Baked Pears in Burgundy and Port Glaze (page 298)

A SUMMER PICNIC

Shrimp Salsa (page 23)

Green Pea Guacamole (page 33)

Crisp Tortilla Chips (page 282)

Grilled Chicken, Black Bean, and Corn Salad with Salsa Dressing (page 98)

Fresh Apricots and Strawberries with Sour Cream and Brown Sugar (page 301)

White Chocolate and Pistachio Cookies (page 336)

INFORMAL HOLIDAY BUFFET

Green Olive Tapenade (page 31)

Sun-Dried Tomato Tapenade (page 32)

Parmesan Toasts (page 274)

Peppery Greens with Gorgonzola and Pine Nuts (page 80)

Grilled Orange-Mustard Chicken (page 180)

Baked Vegetable Rigatoni with Tomatoes and Provolone Cheese (page 122)

Sliced Oranges and Fresh Berries

Orange, Almond, and Olive Oil Cake (page 302)

NO-HASSLE ELEGANT DINNER PARTY

Baked Brie with Sun-Dried Tomato Pesto (page 36)

Broccoli-Leek Soup with Parmesan Cream (page 62)

OR

Farmers' Market Chopped Salad (page 78)

Grilled Lamb Chops with Cranberry-Rosemary Marinade (page 217)

Confetti Rice Pilaf (page 269)

Home Ranch Butternut Squash (page 251)

Chocolate Truffle Brownies (page 339)

A COLD BUFFET

Assorted Grilled Vegetables (page 24)

Grilled Artichoke Halves with Red Pepper Aioli (page 28)

Crispy Roast Chicken (page 188)

Long-Grain and Wild Rice Salad with Corn and Salmon (page 92)

Caesar Salad with Mixed Baby Lettuces and Parmesan Toasts (page 74)

Walnut Bread (page 290) with Assorted Cheeses

Peach Melba Buckle (page 306)

WINTER DINNER

Sweet Potato–Jalapeño Soup with Tomatillo Cream (page 48)

Grilled Steaks with Olivada and Port Wine Sauce (page 212)

White Bean Stew with Spinach and Tomatoes (page 253)

Roasted Winter Vegetables (page 247)

Banana Cake with Chocolate Fudge Frosting (page 326)

FARMERS' MARKET DINNER

Roasted Peppers with Mint Vinaigrette and Goat Cheese Croutons (page 26)

Warm Grilled Vegetable and Shrimp Salad (page 106)

Indian Summer Pasta (page 120)

Fresh Fruit Platter with Assorted Cookies

SPRING LUNCH

Mixed Green Salad with Chilled Asparagus

West Coast Crab Cakes with Grapefruit Sauce (page 165)

Country Sourdough Bread (page 286)

Essencia Zabaglione with Fresh Fruit Compote (page 299)

Spicy Crinkle Cookies (page 338)

LAST-MINUTE DINNER PARTY

Smoked Fish Mousse (page 22) with Toasts

Glazed Orange-Hoisin Chicken (page 190)

Spicy Almond Couscous (page 268)

Tricolor Vegetable Sauté (page 245)

Chocolate Freakout (page 329)

INDEX

A

Aioli, Red Pepper, 352

Almonds
Almond-Caper Relish, 172–73
Banana Split Ice Cream Torte, 334–35
Chocolate Chip Coffee Cake, 322–23
Cranberry-Almond Relish, 362
Orange, Almond, and Olive Oil Cake, 302–3
Peach Melba Buckle, 306–7
Pear-Raspberry Almond Tart, 309–11
Spiced Sweet Potato Pudding, 265–66
Spicy Almond Couscous, 268

Anaheim chiles, 208

Ancho chiles, 208, 351
Ancho Chile Cream, 44–45
Ancho Chile Paste, 350, 351
Pasta with Ancho Chile and Tomato Cream, 118–19

Anchovy, Sun-Dried Tomato, and Tapenade Dipping Sauce, 29

Apples
Asian Pear–Quince-Apple Sauce, 364
Chicken and Apple Sausage, 201
Loin of Pork with Dried Fruits and Gewürztraminer, 238–39
Puffed Apple-Orange Oven Pancake, 113

Apricots
Fresh Apricots and Strawberries with Sour Cream and Brown Sugar, 301
Loin of Pork with Dried Fruits and Gewürztraminer, 238–39

Arroz con Pollo, 186–87

Artichokes, 28
Grilled Artichoke Halves with Red Pepper Aioli, 28
White Bean and Artichoke Soup, 52–53

Arugula and Jerusalem Artichoke Salad with Shaved Pecorino and Orange Vinaigrette, 76

Asian Chicken Noodle Soup with Tofu and Pea Pods, 63

Asian Glazed Pork Tenderloin, 240–41

Asian Gravlax with Ginger-Mustard Sauce, 20–21

Asian Guacamole, 34

Asian pears, 363
Asian Pear–Quince-Apple Sauce, 364
Ginger-Spiced Asian Pear and Cranberry Compote, 363

Asian Salsa, 161–62

Asparagus
Scrambled Eggs with Asparagus and Smoked Salmon, 114
Springtime Salmon Salad, 108–9
Warm Grilled Vegetable and Shrimp Salad, 106–7
Wine Country Chicken Salad, 104–5

Assorted Grilled Vegetables, 24–25

Avocados, 89
Asian Guacamole, 34

Avocado, Cucumber, and Dill Salsa,
153
Avocado-Tomato Salsa, 206–7
Blood Orange, Mushroom, and
Avocado Salad, 88
Cucumber-Avocado Gazpacho, 70
Green Pea Guacamole, 33
Grilled Chicken, Black Bean, and
Corn Salad with Salsa Dressing,
98–99
Shrimp Salsa, 23

B

Bacon
Fava Beans with Red Onions and
Bacon, 252
Grilled Pizza with Leeks, Mozzarella,
Tomatoes, and Pancetta, 146–47
Pasta with Ancho Chile and Tomato
Cream, 118–19
Spinach and Mushroom Salad
with Warm Tomato-Bacon
Vinaigrette, 86–87
Baked Brie with Sun-Dried Tomato
Pesto, 36
Baked Pears in Burgundy and Port
Glaze, 298
Baked Salmon with Red Onion Sauce,
154–55
Baked Vegetable Rigatoni with
Tomatoes and Provolone Cheese,
122–23
Balsamic vinegar, 56
Bananas
Banana Cake with Chocolate Fudge
Frosting, 326–27
Banana Custard Sauce, 333
Banana Split Ice Cream Torte, 334–35

Barley Risotto, Two-Mushroom, 136–37
Basic Vinaigrette, 355
Basil
Mixed-Herb Pesto, 348
Pasta with Tomatoes, Basil, and
Balsamic Vinaigrette, 128
Pesto, 349
Spinach Pesto, 126–27
Beans
Black Bean Soup with Lime Cream,
60–61
Chicken Minestrone with Mixed-
Herb Pesto, 64–65
Fava Beans with Red Onions and
Bacon, 252
Grilled Chicken, Black Bean, and
Corn Salad with Salsa Dressing,
98–99
Grilled Steak and Potato Salad,
96–97
Indian Summer Pasta, 120–21
La Scala Chopped Salad, 77
Pesto Bean Sauce, 178–79
Pinto Bean Soup with Gremolata, 59
Sautéed Green and Yellow Beans with
Garlic and Basil, 244
Spinach, Pasta, and Fagioli Soup,
50–51
Vegetable and White Bean Salsa,
168–69
White Bean and Artichoke Soup,
52–53
White Bean Stew with Spinach and
Tomatoes, 253
Beef
Brisket of Beef with Sun-Dried
Tomatoes, Zinfandel, and
Thyme, 214–16

Grilled Flank Steak with Smoky
  Salsa, 211
Grilled Roast Beef with Shallot-Chive
  Sauce, 209–10
Grilled Skirt Steak with Avocado-
  Tomato Salsa, 206–7
Grilled Steak and Potato Salad, 96–97
Grilled Steaks with Olivada and Port
  Wine Sauce, 212–13
grilling tips for, 171
marinating, 221
Panfried Noodles with Vegetables,
  226–27
Beets
  Mixed Greens with Beets and
    Peppers, 84–85
  Orange-Glazed Beets, 264
Bell peppers
  Baked Vegetable Rigatoni with
    Tomatoes and Provolone Cheese,
    122–23
  California Salad, 82–83
  Corn Bread, Leek, and Red Pepper
    Stuffing Terrine, 254–55
  Mixed Greens with Beets and
    Peppers, 84–85
  Red Pepper Aioli, 352
  Red Pepper–Mint Sauce, 138–39
  Roasted Peppers with Mint
    Vinaigrette and Goat Cheese
    Croutons, 26–27
  roasting and peeling, 27
  Shrimp Salsa, 23
  Tricolor Vegetable Sauté, 245
Bisque, Grilled Seafood, with Red
  Pepper Aioli, 66–67

Bittersweet Chocolate Hazelnut
  Torte with Banana Custard Sauce,
  331–32
Black Bean Soup with Lime Cream,
  60–61
Blood Orange, Mushroom, and Avocado
  Salad, 88
Blueberries
  Blueberry-Lemon Tart, 314–15
  Roasted Blueberry Compote, 324–25
Blue cheese
  California Caponata, 39
  Peppery Greens with Gorgonzola and
    Pine Nuts, 80–81
Braised Stuffed Shoulder of Veal,
  234–36
Bread. See also Pizzas; Tortillas
  Ciji's Scones with Currants, 278
  Corn Bread for Stuffing, 346
  Corn Bread, Leek, and Red Pepper
    Stuffing Terrine, 254–55
  Country Sourdough Bread, 286–87
  dough, freezing, 285
  Focaccia, 294–95
  Fresh Pear Bread, 279
  Goat Cheese Croutons, 26–27
  Jalapeño Cheese Bread, 292–93
  making, 284–85
  Maple Corn Muffins, 280
  Parmesan Toasts, 274
  Pumpkin Bread Pudding with Eggnog
    Brandy Sauce, 320–21
  Rustic Bread Sticks, 292–93
  Sourdough Rye Rolls, 288–89
  Sourdough Starter, 286–87
  Spiced Pumpkin-Hazelnut Bread,
    276–77

Sun-Dried Tomato Toasts, 275
Walnut Bread, 290–91
Brie, Baked, with Sun-Dried Tomato
    Pesto, 36
Brisket of Beef with Sun-Dried
    Tomatoes, Zinfandel, and Thyme,
    214–16
Broccoli
    Broccoli-Leek Soup with Parmesan
        Cream, 62
    Roasted Broccoli with Toasted Bread
        Crumb Gremolata, 248–49
Broiled Orange Roughy with Salsa
    Glaze, 164
Brownies, Chocolate Truffle, 339
Buckle, Peach Melba, 306–7
Bulgur, Tomato-Mint, 267
Butter, Orange-Honey, 280
Butternut squash
    Butternut Squash Gratin with Tomato
        Fondue, 250
    Home Ranch Butternut Squash, 251
    Roasted Garlic and Butternut Squash
        Soup with Ancho Chile Cream,
        44–45
    Wonton Butternut Squash Ravioli
        with Spinach Pesto, 126–27

C
Caesar Salad with Mixed Baby Lettuces
    and Parmesan Toasts, 74–75
Cakes. *See also* Tortes
    Banana Cake with Chocolate Fudge
        Frosting, 326–27
    Chocolate Chip Coffee Cake, 322–23
    Chocolate Freakout, 329–30

Glazed Lemon–Sour Cream
    Cake, 304–5
    Orange, Almond, and Olive Oil Cake,
        302–3
    Walnut Cake with Roasted Blueberry
        Compote, 324–25
    Warm Mocha Pudding Cakes, 328
California Caponata, 39
California Salad, 82–83
Caponata, California, 39
Caramel Cream, Vanilla, 318–19
Carrots
    Confetti Rice Pilaf, 269
    Veal Stew with Orange Sauce, 232–33
Cauliflower Purée with Two Cheeses,
    246
Caviar, 18
    Jewish Breakfast Pizza, 144–45
    Smoked Salmon and Caviar Torta,
        18–19
Cheddar cheese
    Butternut Squash Gratin with Tomato
        Fondue, 250
    Cauliflower Purée with Two Cheeses,
        246
    Golden Frittata with Tomatillo Salsa,
        112
    Jalapeño Cheese Bread, 292–93
    Rustic Bread Sticks, 292–93
    Three-Cheese Macaroni with
        Caramelized Leeks, Prosciutto,
        and Peas, 124–25
Cheese. *See also individual cheeses*
    Butternut Squash Gratin with Tomato
        Fondue, 250
    Cauliflower Purée with Two
        Cheeses, 246

Holiday Lasagne with Roasted
    Vegetables and Pesto, 129–30
La Scala Chopped Salad, 77
Three-Cheese Macaroni with
    Caramelized Leeks, Prosciutto,
    and Peas, 124–25
Cherries, Dried, Nectarine Crisp with,
    308
Chestnut, Onion, and Dried Plum
    Compote, 256–57
Chicken
    Arroz con Pollo, 186–87
    Asian Chicken Noodle Soup with
        Tofu and Pea Pods, 63
    Chicken and Apple Sausage, 201
    Chicken Minestrone with Mixed-
        Herb Pesto, 64–65
    Chicken Salad with Chinese Noodles,
        102–3
    Chicken Stock, 342
    Chicken with Garlic and Lime,
        184–85
    Crispy Roast Chicken, 188–89
    Easy Brown Chicken Stock, 343
    Farmers' Market Chopped Salad,
        78–79
    Glazed Orange-Hoisin Chicken, 190
    Griddled Quesadillas with
        Caramelized Onions, Chicken,
        and Jack Cheese, 37–38
    Grilled Chicken, Black Bean, and
        Corn Salad with Salsa Dressing,
        98–99
    Grilled Chicken Niçoise, 176–77
    Grilled Chicken with Pesto Bean
        Sauce, 178–79
    Grilled Orange-Mustard Chicken, 180
    grilling tips for, 170

Lemon Chicken with Roasted Garlic
    Sauce, 181–82
marinating, 221
Panfried Noodles with Vegetables,
    226–27
Pear, Pistachio, and Chicken Liver
    Mousse, 16–17
Warm Grilled Chicken Salad with
    Pesto, 100–101
Wine Country Chicken Salad, 104–5
Chiles
    Ancho Chile Cream, 44–45
    Ancho Chile Paste, 350, 351
    Avocado-Tomato Salsa, 206–7
    Hot Pepper Oil, 356
    Jalapeño Cheese Bread, 292–93
    Pasta with Ancho Chile and Tomato
        Cream, 118–19
    peeling, 208
    Rustic Bread Sticks, 292–93
    Spicy Tomato Salsa, 357
    Tomatillo Salsa, 358
    varieties of, 208
Chips, Crisp Tortilla, 282
Chocolate
    Banana Cake with Chocolate Fudge
        Frosting, 326–27
    Banana Split Ice Cream Torte,
        334–35
    Bittersweet Chocolate Hazelnut Torte
        with Banana Custard Sauce,
        331–32
    Chocolate Chip Coffee Cake, 322–23
    Chocolate Freakout, 329–30
    Chocolate Truffle Brownies, 339
    Tiramisu with Toasted Hazelnuts and
        Chocolate, 316–17
    Warm Mocha Pudding Cakes, 328

Ciji's Scones with Currants, 278
Cobbler, Turkey Vegetable, 198–200
Coffee Cake, Chocolate Chip, 322–23
Compotes
    Fresh Fruit Compote, 299
    Ginger-Spiced Asian Pear and
        Cranberry Compote, 363
    Onion, Dried Plum, and Chestnut
        Compote, 256–57
    Roasted Blueberry Compote, 324–25
Confetti Rice Pilaf, 269
Confit of Red Onions and Prosciutto,
    143
Cookies
    Spicy Crinkle Cookies, 338
    White Chocolate and Pistachio
        Cookies, 336
Corn
    Corn and Tomato Soup, 68–69
    Corn Bread for Stuffing, 346
    Corn Bread, Leek, and Red Pepper
        Stuffing Terrine, 254–55
    Corn-Tomato Relish, 68–69
    Corn Tortillas, 281
    Farmers' Market Chopped Salad,
        78–79
    Grilled Chicken, Black Bean, and
        Corn Salad with Salsa Dressing,
        98–99
    Indian Summer Pasta, 120–21
    Long-Grain and Wild Rice Salad
        with Corn and Salmon, 92–93
    Maple Corn Muffins, 280
    Rice Pilaf with Fresh Corn and
        Peanuts, 270
    Ricotta Corn Cakes with Smoky Salsa
        Topping, 40
    separating, from the cob, 68

    Shrimp Salsa, 23
    Warm Grilled Vegetable and Shrimp
        Salad, 106–7
    Zucchini-Corn Relish, 228–29
Cornish Hens, Roasted, with Honey-
    Tangerine Marinade, 191–92
Country Sourdough Bread,
    286–87
Couscous, Spicy Almond, 268
Crab Cakes, West Coast, with
    Grapefruit Sauce, 165–67
Cranberries
    Cranberry-Almond Relish, 362
    Cranberry-Rosemary Marinade, 217
    Ginger-Spiced Asian Pear and
        Cranberry Compote, 363
Cream cheese
    Pear, Pistachio, and Chicken Liver
        Mousse, 16–17
    Smoked Salmon and Caviar Torta,
        18–19
Creams
    Ancho Chile Cream, 44–45
    Lime Cream, 60–61
    Parmesan Cream, 62
    Sun-Dried Tomato Cream, 69
    Tomatillo Cream, 48–49
    Vanilla Cream, 324–25
Crisp, Nectarine, with Dried Cherries,
    308
Crisp Tortilla Chips, 282
Crispy Potato Pancakes with Vegetables,
    259–60
Crispy Roast Chicken, 188–89
Croutons, Goat Cheese, 26–27
Cucumbers
    Avocado, Cucumber, and Dill
        Salsa, 153

Cucumber-Avocado Gazpacho, 70
Grilled Swordfish on a Bed of
    Cucumber "Pasta" with Asian
    Salsa, 161–62
Shrimp Salsa, 23
Vegetable and White Bean Salsa,
    168–69
Currants, Ciji's Scones with, 278
Custard
    Banana Custard Sauce, 333
    Pumpkin Bread Pudding with Eggnog
        Brandy Sauce, 320–21
    Vanilla Caramel Cream, 318–19

D

Dates, Lamb Stew with Zinfandel and,
    224–25
Desserts
    Baked Pears in Burgundy and Port
        Glaze, 298
    Banana Cake with Chocolate Fudge
        Frosting, 326–27
    Banana Split Ice Cream Torte,
        334–35
    Bittersweet Chocolate Hazelnut Torte
        with Banana Custard Sauce,
        331–32
    Blueberry Lemon Tart, 314–15
    Chocolate Chip Coffee Cake, 322–23
    Chocolate Freakout, 329–30
    Chocolate Truffle Brownies, 339
    Essencia Zabaglione with Fresh Fruit
        Compote, 299
    Fresh Apricots and Strawberries with
        Sour Cream and Brown Sugar,
        301
    Glazed Lemon–Sour Cream Cake,
        304–5

Mango and Macadamia Nut Brown-
    Butter Tart, 312–13
Mixed Exotic Fruit Gazpacho, 300
Nectarine Crisp with Dried
    Cherries, 308
Orange, Almond, and Olive Oil Cake,
    302–3
Pear-Raspberry Almond Tart, 309–11
Pumpkin Bread Pudding with Eggnog
    Brandy Sauce, 320–21
quick fruit, 303
Spiced Sweet Potato Pudding,
    265–66
Spicy Crinkle Cookies, 338
Tiramisu with Toasted Hazelnuts and
    Chocolate, 316–17
Vanilla Caramel Cream, 318–19
Walnut Cake with Roasted Blueberry
    Compote, 324–25
Warm Mocha Pudding Cakes, 328
White Chocolate and Pistachio
    Cookies, 336
Double-Tomato Herb Sauce, 347

E

Easy Brown Chicken Stock, 343
Easy Brown Turkey Stock, 343
Easy Brown Veal Stock, 344–45
Eggplant
    Baked Vegetable Rigatoni with
        Tomatoes and Provolone Cheese,
        122–23
    California Caponata, 39
    Tricolor Vegetable Sauté, 245
Eggs
    Eggnog Brandy Sauce, 365
    Golden Frittata with Tomatillo Salsa,
        112

Herbed Scrambled Eggs with Goat Cheese, 115
Scrambled Eggs with Asparagus and Smoked Salmon, 114
Espresso
  Tiramisu with Toasted Hazelnuts and Chocolate, 316–17
  Warm Mocha Pudding Cakes, 328
Essencia Zabaglione with Fresh Fruit Compote, 299

F
Farmers' Market Chopped Salad, 78–79
Fat
  reducing, 345
  separator, 197
Fava Beans with Red Onions and Bacon, 252
Fish
  Asian Gravlax with Ginger-Mustard Sauce, 20–21
  Baked Salmon with Red Onion Sauce, 154–55
  Broiled Orange Roughy with Salsa Glaze, 164
  Glazed Halibut with Orange-Chive Sauce, 160
  Grilled Halibut with Red Pepper–Mint Sauce, 158–59
  Grilled Salmon Fillet with Avocado, Cucumber, and Dill Salsa, 153
  Grilled Swordfish on a Bed of Cucumber "Pasta" with Asian Salsa, 161–62
  Grilled Tuna with Vegetable and White Bean Salsa, 168–69
  grilling tips for, 170
  Jewish Breakfast Pizza, 144–45
  Long-Grain and Wild Rice Salad with Corn and Salmon, 92–93
  marinating, 221
  Roast Crispy Fish with Warm Lentils, 156–57
  Roasted Sea Bass with Mustard-Salsa Sauce, 152
  roasting, 249
  Scrambled Eggs with Asparagus and Smoked Salmon, 114
  Smoked Fish Mousse, 22
  Smoked Salmon and Caviar Torta, 18–19
  Springtime Salmon Salad, 108–9
  Tuna Tartare, 41
Focaccia, 294–95
Fresh Apricots and Strawberries with Sour Cream and Brown Sugar, 301
Fresh Fruit Compote, 299
Fresh Pear Bread, 279
Frittata, Golden, with Tomatillo Salsa, 112
Fruits. *See also individual fruits*
  Fresh Fruit Compote, 299
  Loin of Pork with Dried Fruits and Gewürztraminer, 238–39
  Mixed Exotic Fruit Gazpacho, 300
  for quick desserts, 303

G
Garden Risotto, 134–35
Garlic, 183
  California Salad, 82–83
  Chicken with Garlic and Lime, 184–85
  Glazed Onions and Garlic, 184–85
  Roasted Garlic and Butternut Squash Soup with Ancho Chile Cream, 44–45

Roasted Garlic Mashed Potatoes and
Leeks, 258
Roasted Garlic Purée, 353
Gazpacho
Cucumber-Avocado Gazpacho, 70
Mixed Exotic Fruit Gazpacho, 300
Ginger
Ginger-Mustard Sauce, 21
Ginger-Spiced Asian Pear and
Cranberry Compote, 363
Glazed Halibut with Orange-Chive
Sauce, 160
Glazed Lemon–Sour Cream Cake,
304–5
Glazed Onions and Garlic, 184–85
Glazed Orange-Hoisin Chicken, 190
Goat cheese, 26, 115
California Salad, 82–83
Goat Cheese Croutons, 26–27
Herbed Scrambled Eggs with Goat
Cheese, 115
Golden Frittata with Tomatillo Salsa,
112
Gorgonzola, Peppery Greens with Pine
Nuts and, 80–81
Grapefruit Sauce, 165–66
Gravlax, Asian, with Ginger-Mustard
Sauce, 20–21
Gravy, Rich Turkey, 196–97
Green Olive Tapenade, 31
Green Pea Guacamole, 33
Greens, mixed
California Salad, 82–83
Farmers' Market Chopped Salad, 78–79
Mixed Greens with Beets and
Peppers, 84–85
Peppery Greens with Gorgonzola and
Pine Nuts, 80–81

Warm Grilled Vegetable and Shrimp
Salad, 106–7
Gremolata, 59
Griddled Quesadillas with Caramelized
Onions, Chicken, and Jack Cheese,
37–38
Grilled Artichoke Halves with Red
Pepper Aioli, 28
Grilled Chicken, Black Bean, and Corn
Salad with Salsa Dressing,
98–99
Grilled Chicken Niçoise, 176–77
Grilled Chicken with Pesto Bean Sauce,
178–79
Grilled Flank Steak with Smoky Salsa,
211
Grilled Halibut with Red Pepper–Mint
Sauce, 158–59
Grilled Lamb Chops with Cranberry-
Rosemary Marinade, 217
Grilled Orange-Mustard Chicken, 180
Grilled Pizza with Leeks, Mozzarella,
Tomatoes, and Pancetta, 146–47
Grilled Polenta with Confit of Red
Onions and Prosciutto, 140–41
Grilled Polenta with Yellow Cornmeal,
142
Grilled Roast Beef with Shallot-Chive
Sauce, 209–10
Grilled Salmon Fillet with Avocado,
Cucumber, and Dill Salsa, 153
Grilled Scallop Brochettes with
Almond-Caper Relish, 172–73
Grilled Seafood Bisque with Red Pepper
Aioli, 66–67
Grilled Skirt Steak with Avocado-
Tomato Salsa, 206–7
Grilled Steak and Potato Salad, 96–97

Grilled Steaks with Olivada and Port
    Wine Sauce, 212–13
Grilled Swordfish on a Bed of
    Cucumber "Pasta" with Asian
    Salsa, 161–62
Grilled Tuna with Vegetable and White
    Bean Salsa, 168–69
Grilled Turkey Breast in Mustard-
    Bourbon Sauce, 193
Grilled Veal Chops with Zucchini-Corn
    Relish, 228–29
Grilling tips, 170–71
Gruyère cheese
    Golden Frittata with Tomatillo Salsa,
        112
    Potatoes Vaugirard, 261
Guacamole
    Asian Guacamole, 34
    Green Pea Guacamole, 33

H
Halibut
    Glazed Halibut with Orange-Chive
        Sauce, 160
    Grilled Halibut with Red Pepper–
        Mint Sauce, 158–59
    Roast Crispy Fish with Warm Lentils,
        156–57
Ham
    Black Bean Soup with Lime Cream,
        60–61
    Confit of Red Onions and Prosciutto,
        143
    Lentil Soup with Thyme and Balsamic
        Vinegar, 57–58
    Three-Cheese Macaroni with
        Caramelized Leeks, Prosciutto,
        and Peas, 124–25

Hand blenders, 45
Hazelnuts
    Bittersweet Chocolate Hazelnut Torte
        with Banana Custard Sauce,
        331–32
    Spiced Pumpkin-Hazelnut Bread,
        276–77
    Tiramisu with Toasted Hazelnuts and
        Chocolate, 316–17
Herbed Scrambled Eggs with Goat
    Cheese, 115
Holiday Lasagne with Roasted
    Vegetables and Pesto, 129–30
Home Ranch Butternut Squash, 251
Honey-Tangerine Marinade,
    191–92
Hot Pepper Oil, 356

I
Ice Cream Torte, Banana Split, 334–35
Immersion blenders, 45
Indian Summer Pasta, 120–21
Indonesian Leg of Lamb, 222–23

J
Jack cheese
    Butternut Squash Gratin with Tomato
        Fondue, 250
    Griddled Quesadillas with
        Caramelized Onions, Chicken,
        and Jack Cheese, 37–38
    Three-Cheese Macaroni with
        Caramelized Leeks, Prosciutto,
        and Peas, 124–25
Jalapeño chiles, 208
    Jalapeño Cheese Bread, 292–93
    Rustic Bread Sticks, 292–93
Jam, Roasted Tomato, 361

Jerusalem Artichoke and Arugula Salad with Shaved Pecorino and Orange Vinaigrette, 76

Jewish Breakfast Pizza, 144–45

Jicama

    Shrimp Salsa, 23

    Warm Grilled Chicken Salad with Pesto, 100–101

L

Lamb

    Grilled Lamb Chops with Cranberry-Rosemary Marinade, 217

    grilling tips for, 171

    Indonesian Leg of Lamb, 222–23

    Lamb Brochettes with Raita, 220

    Lamb Stew with Dates and Zinfandel, 224–25

    marinating, 221

    Panfried Noodles with Vegetables, 226–27

    Rack of Lamb with Mint Crust, 218–19

Lasagne, Holiday, with Roasted Vegetables and Pesto, 129–30

La Scala Chopped Salad, 77

Leeks

    Broccoli-Leek Soup with Parmesan Cream, 62

    Confetti Rice Pilaf, 269

    Corn Bread, Leek, and Red Pepper Stuffing Terrine, 254–55

    Grilled Pizza with Leeks, Mozzarella, Tomatoes, and Pancetta, 146–47

    Holiday Lasagne with Roasted Vegetables and Pesto, 129–30

    Risotto with Leeks, Tomatoes, and Niçoise Olives, 132–33

    Roasted Garlic Mashed Potatoes and Leeks, 258

    Three-Cheese Macaroni with Caramelized Leeks, Prosciutto, and Peas, 124–25

Lemons

    Blueberry-Lemon Tart, 314–15

    Glazed Lemon–Sour Cream Cake, 304–5

    Lemon Chicken with Roasted Garlic Sauce, 181–82

    Meyer Lemon, Olive, and Dried Cherry Dipping Sauce, 29

Lentils, 157

    Lentil Soup with Thyme and Balsamic Vinegar, 57–58

    Roast Crispy Fish with Warm Lentils, 156–57

Lettuce

    Blood Orange, Mushroom, and Avocado Salad, 88

    Caesar Salad with Mixed Baby Lettuces and Parmesan Toasts, 74–75

    Grilled Chicken, Black Bean, and Corn Salad with Salsa Dressing, 98–99

    La Scala Chopped Salad, 77

    Warm Grilled Chicken Salad with Pesto, 100–101

Light Meatballs with Double-Tomato Herb Sauce, 230–31

Limes

    Chicken with Garlic and Lime, 184–85

    Lime Cream, 60–61

Liver, Chicken, Pear, and Pistachio Mousse, 16–17

Loin of Pork with Dried Fruits and
    Gewürztraminer, 238–39
Long-Grain and Wild Rice Salad with
    Corn and Salmon, 92–93

M

Mangoes
    Mango and Macadamia Nut Brown-
        Butter Tart, 312–13
    Mixed Exotic Fruit Gazpacho, 300
Maple Corn Muffins, 280
Marinades, 221
    Cranberry-Rosemary Marinade, 217
    Honey-Tangerine Marinade, 191–92
Marinated Roast Turkey, 194–95
Mascarpone cheese
    Tiramisu with Toasted Hazelnuts and
        Chocolate, 316–17
Meatballs, Light, with Double-Tomato
    Herb Sauce, 230–31
Menus, 366–69
Meyer Lemon, Olive, and Dried Cherry
    Dipping Sauce, 29
Minestrone, Chicken, with Mixed-Herb
    Pesto, 64–65
Mixed Exotic Fruit Gazpacho, 300
Mixed Greens with Beets and Peppers,
    84–85
Mixed-Herb Pesto, 348
Mousse
    Pear, Pistachio, and Chicken Liver
        Mousse, 16–17
    Smoked Fish Mousse, 22
Mozzarella cheese
    Grilled Pizza with Leeks, Mozzarella,
        Tomatoes, and Pancetta, 146–47
    Pasta Salad with Parmesan Dressing,
        92–93
Muffins, Maple Corn, 280

Mushrooms
    Baked Vegetable Rigatoni with
        Tomatoes and Provolone Cheese,
        122–23
    Blood Orange, Mushroom, and
        Avocado Salad, 88
    Braised Stuffed Shoulder of Veal,
        234–36
    Brisket of Beef with Sun-Dried
        Tomatoes, Zinfandel, and
        Thyme, 214–16
    Corn Bread, Leek, and Red Pepper
        Stuffing Terrine, 254–55
    Garden Risotto, 134–35
    Golden Frittata with Tomatillo Salsa,
        112
    Holiday Lasagne with Roasted
        Vegetables and Pesto, 129–30
    Panfried Noodles with Vegetables,
        226–27
    Spanish Rice Timbales, 271
    Spinach and Mushroom Salad
        with Warm Tomato-Bacon
        Vinaigrette, 86–87
    Turkey Vegetable Cobbler, 198–200
    Two-Mushroom Barley Risotto,
        136–37
    Veal Stew with Orange Sauce, 232–33
    Warm Grilled Chicken Salad with
        Pesto, 100–101
    Yellow Split Pea Soup with
        Mushrooms and Smoked Turkey,
        54–55

N

Nectarine Crisp with Dried Cherries,
    308
Noodles. *See* Pasta and noodles

O

Oil
  Hot Pepper Oil, 356
  olive, 29, 81
  Olive Oil Dipping Sauces, 29
  Orange, Almond, and Olive Oil Cake,
    302–3
Olivada, 212, 213
Olives, 30. *See also* Oil
  Focaccia, 294–95
  Green Olive Tapenade, 31
  Grilled Chicken Niçoise, 176–77
  paste, 212, 213
  Risotto with Leeks, Tomatoes, and
    Niçoise Olives, 132–33
  Vegetable and White Bean Salsa,
    168–69
  Wine Country Chicken Salad,
    104–5
Onions
  Confit of Red Onions and Prosciutto,
    143
  Focaccia, 294–95
  Glazed Onions and Garlic, 184–85
  grilling tips for, 171
  Onion, Dried Plum, and Chestnut
    Compote, 256–57
  Red Onion Sauce, 154–55
  Roasted Onions and Baby Potatoes,
    263
Orange Roughy, Broiled, with Salsa
  Glaze, 164
Oranges
  Blood Orange, Mushroom, and
    Avocado Salad, 88
  Essencia Zabaglione with Fresh Fruit
    Compote, 299
  Glazed Orange-Hoisin Chicken, 190
  Grilled Orange-Mustard Chicken,
    180
  Orange, Almond, and Olive Oil Cake,
    302–3
  Orange-Chive Sauce, 160
  Orange-Glazed Beets, 264
  Orange-Honey Butter, 280
  Orange Vinaigrette, 76
  Veal Stew with Orange Sauce, 232–33
Oven-Roasted Potatoes with
  Parmesan, 262

P

Pancakes
  Crispy Potato Pancakes with
    Vegetables, 259–60
  Puffed Apple-Orange Oven Pancake,
    113
  Ricotta Pancakes with Sautéed Spiced
    Pears, 116–17
Pancetta. *See* Bacon
Panfried Noodles with Vegetables,
  226–27
Parmesan cheese, 131
  Cauliflower Purée with Two Cheeses,
    246
  Holiday Lasagne with Roasted
    Vegetables and Pesto, 129–30
  Oven-Roasted Potatoes with
    Parmesan, 262
  Parmesan Cream, 62
  Parmesan Toasts, 274
  Soft Polenta with Sun-Dried Tomato
    Pesto, 138–39
  Spanish Rice Timbales, 271
  Three-Cheese Macaroni with
    Caramelized Leeks, Prosciutto,
    and Peas, 124–25

Pasta and noodles
  Asian Chicken Noodle Soup with
    Tofu and Pea Pods, 63
  Baked Vegetable Rigatoni with
    Tomatoes and Provolone Cheese,
    122–23
  Chicken Salad with Chinese Noodles,
    102–3
  Holiday Lasagne with Roasted
    Vegetables and Pesto, 129–30
  Indian Summer Pasta, 120–21
  Panfried Noodles with Vegetables,
    226–27
  Pasta Salad with Parmesan Dressing,
    92–93
  Pasta with Ancho Chile and Tomato
    Cream, 118–19
  Pasta with Tomatoes, Basil, and
    Balsamic Vinaigrette, 128
  Spicy Almond Couscous, 268
  Spinach, Pasta, and Fagioli Soup,
    50–51
  Three-Cheese Macaroni with
    Caramelized Leeks, Prosciutto,
    and Peas, 124–25
Peach Melba Buckle, 306–7
Peanuts, Rice Pilaf with Fresh Corn
  and, 270
Pears. See also Asian pears
  Baked Pears in Burgundy and Port
    Glaze, 298
  Fresh Pear Bread, 279
  Pear, Pistachio, and Chicken Liver
    Mousse, 16–17
  Pear-Raspberry Almond Tart, 309–11
  Ricotta Pancakes with Sautéed Spiced
    Pears, 116–17

Peas
  Arroz con Pollo, 186–87
  Asian Chicken Noodle Soup with
    Tofu and Pea Pods, 63
  Green Pea Guacamole, 33
  Indian Summer Pasta, 120–21
  Panfried Noodles with Vegetables,
    226–27
  Pasta with Ancho Chile and Tomato
    Cream, 118–19
  Three-Cheese Macaroni with
    Caramelized Leeks, Prosciutto,
    and Peas, 124–25
  Yellow Split Pea Soup with
    Mushrooms and Smoked Turkey,
    54–55
Pecans
  Chocolate Chip Coffee Cake,
    322–23
  Fresh Pear Bread, 279
  Nectarine Crisp with Dried Cherries,
    308
Peppers. See Bell peppers; Chiles
Peppery Greens with Gorgonzola and
    Pine Nuts, 80–81
Pesto, 349
  Mixed-Herb Pesto, 348
  Pesto Bean Sauce, 178–79
  Spinach Pesto, 126–27
  Sun-Dried Tomato Pesto, 350
Pilaf
  Confetti Rice Pilaf, 269
  Rice Pilaf with Fresh Corn and
    Peanuts, 270
Pinto Bean Soup with Gremolata, 59
Pistachios, 337
  Pear, Pistachio, and Chicken Liver
    Mousse, 16–17

White Chocolate and Pistachio
  Cookies, 336
Pizzas
  Grilled Pizza with Leeks, Mozzarella,
    Tomatoes, and Pancetta, 146–47
  Jewish Breakfast Pizza, 144–45
  Pizza Dough, 283
  toppings for, 147
Plum, Dried, Onion, and Chestnut
  Compote, 256–57
Poblano chiles, 208
Polenta, 139
  Grilled Polenta with Confit of Red
    Onions and Prosciutto, 140–41
  Grilled Polenta with Yellow
    Cornmeal, 142
  Soft Polenta with Sun-Dried Tomato
    Pesto, 138–39
Pork. *See also* Bacon; Ham; Sausage
  Asian Glazed Pork Tenderloin,
    240–41
  grilling tips for, 171
  Loin of Pork with Dried Fruits and
    Gewürztraminer, 238–39
  Sautéed Pork Medallions with
    Mustard-Herb Sauce, 237
Port Wine Sauce, 212–13
Potatoes
  Crispy Potato Pancakes with
    Vegetables, 259–60
  Grilled Steak and Potato Salad, 96–97
  Oven-Roasted Potatoes with
    Parmesan, 262
  Potatoes Vaugirard, 261
  Roasted Garlic Mashed Potatoes and
    Leeks, 258
  Roasted Onions and Baby Potatoes,
    263

Springtime Salmon Salad, 108–9
Squash Vichyssoise, 71
Poultry. *See also individual birds*
  grilling tips for, 170
  marinating, 221
  roasting, 249
  sausage, 202
  trussing, 195
Prosciutto. *See* Ham
Provolone Cheese, Baked Vegetable
  Rigatoni with Tomatoes and,
  122–23
Puddings
  Pumpkin Bread Pudding with Eggnog
    Brandy Sauce, 320–21
  Spiced Sweet Potato Pudding, 265–66
Puffed Apple-Orange Oven Pancake,
  113
Pumpkin
  Pumpkin Bread Pudding with Eggnog
    Brandy Sauce, 320–21
  Spiced Pumpkin-Hazelnut Bread,
    276–77

Q
Quesadillas, Griddled, with Caramelized
  Onions, Chicken, and Jack Cheese,
  37–38
Quince–Asian Pear–Apple Sauce, 364

R
Rack of Lamb with Mint Crust, 218–19
Raita, Lamb Brochettes with, 220
Raspberries
  Cranberry-Almond Relish, 362
  Mixed Exotic Fruit Gazpacho, 300
  Peach Melba Buckle, 306–7
  Pear-Raspberry Almond Tart, 309–11

Ravioli, Wonton Butternut Squash, with
    Spinach Pesto, 126–27
Red Onion Sauce, 154–55
Red Pepper Aioli, 352
Red Pepper–Mint Sauce, 158–59
Relishes
    Almond-Caper Relish, 172–73
    Corn-Tomato Relish, 68–69
    Cranberry-Almond Relish, 362
    Zucchini-Corn Relish, 228–29
Rice
    Arroz con Pollo, 186 –87
    Confetti Rice Pilaf, 269
    Garden Risotto, 134–35
    Long-Grain and Wild Rice Salad
        with Corn and Salmon,
        92–93
    Rice Pilaf with Fresh Corn and
        Peanuts, 270
    Risotto with Leeks, Tomatoes, and
        Niçoise Olives, 132–33
    Spanish Rice Timbales, 271
Rich Turkey Gravy, 196–97
Ricotta cheese
    Holiday Lasagne with Roasted
        Vegetables and Pesto, 129–30
    Ricotta Corn Cakes with Smoky Salsa
        Topping, 40
    Ricotta Pancakes with Sautéed Spiced
        Pears, 116–17
    Smoked Salmon and Caviar Torta,
        18–19
Risotto, 133
    Garden Risotto, 134–35
    Risotto with Leeks, Tomatoes, and
        Niçoise Olives, 132–33
    Two-Mushroom Barley Risotto,
        136–37

Roast Crispy Fish with Warm Lentils,
    156–57
Roasted Blueberry Compote, 324–25
Roasted Broccoli with Toasted Bread
    Crumb Gremolata, 248–49
Roasted Cornish Hens with Honey-
    Tangerine Marinade, 191–92
Roasted Garlic and Butternut Squash
    Soup with Ancho Chile Cream,
    44–45
Roasted Garlic Mashed Potatoes and
    Leeks, 258
Roasted Garlic Purée, 353
Roasted Onions and Baby Potatoes, 263
Roasted Peppers with Mint Vinaigrette
    and Goat Cheese Croutons,
    26–27
Roasted Sea Bass with Mustard-Salsa
    Sauce, 152
Roasted Tomato Jam, 361
Roasted Vegetable Soup, 46–47
Roasted Winter Vegetables, 247
Roasting, high-heat, 249
Rolls, Sourdough Rye, 288–89
Rustic Bread Sticks, 292–93
Rustic Salsa, 359
Rye Rolls, Sourdough, 288–89

S
Salads
    Arugula and Jerusalem Artichoke
        Salad with Shaved Pecorino and
        Orange Vinaigrette, 76
    Blood Orange, Mushroom, and
        Avocado Salad, 88
    Caesar Salad with Mixed Baby
        Lettuces and Parmesan Toasts,
        74–75

California Salad, 82–83

Chicken Salad with Chinese Noodles, 102–3

Farmers' Market Chopped Salad, 78–79

Grilled Chicken, Black Bean, and Corn Salad with Salsa Dressing, 98–99

Grilled Steak and Potato Salad, 96–97

La Scala Chopped Salad, 77

Long-Grain and Wild Rice Salad with Corn and Salmon, 92–93

Mixed Greens with Beets and Peppers, 84–85

Pasta Salad with Parmesan Dressing, 92–93

Peppery Greens with Gorgonzola and Pine Nuts, 80–81

Spinach and Mushroom Salad with Warm Tomato-Bacon Vinaigrette, 86–87

Springtime Salmon Salad, 108–9

Warm Grilled Chicken Salad with Pesto, 100–101

Warm Grilled Vegetable and Shrimp Salad, 106–7

Wheat Berry Vegetable Salad, 90–91

Wine Country Chicken Salad, 104–5

Salami

La Scala Chopped Salad, 77

Salmon

Asian Gravlax with Ginger-Mustard Sauce, 20–21

Baked Salmon with Red Onion Sauce, 154–55

Grilled Salmon Fillet with Avocado, Cucumber, and Dill Salsa, 153

Jewish Breakfast Pizza, 144–45

Long-Grain and Wild Rice Salad with Corn and Salmon, 92–93

Scrambled Eggs with Asparagus and Smoked Salmon, 114

Smoked Salmon and Caviar Torta, 18–19

Springtime Salmon Salad, 108–9

Salsas, 163

Asian Salsa, 161–62

Avocado, Cucumber, and Dill Salsa, 153

Avocado-Tomato Salsa, 206–7

Rustic Salsa, 359

Shrimp Salsa, 23

Smoky Salsa, 360

Spicy Tomato Salsa, 357

Tomatillo Salsa, 358

Vegetable and White Bean Salsa, 168–69

Sauces. *See also* Creams; Pesto; Salsas; Vinaigrettes

Anchovy, Sun-Dried Tomato, and Tapenade Dipping Sauce, 29

Asian Pear–Quince-Apple Sauce, 364

Banana Custard Sauce, 333

Double-Tomato Herb Sauce, 347

Eggnog Brandy Sauce, 365

Ginger-Mustard Sauce, 21

Grapefruit Sauce, 165–66

Meyer Lemon, Olive, and Dried Cherry Dipping Sauce, 29

Orange-Chive Sauce, 160

Pesto Bean Sauce, 178–79

Port Wine Sauce, 212–13

Red Onion Sauce, 154–55

Red Pepper Aioli, 352

Red Pepper–Mint Sauce, 158–59

Shallot-Chive Sauce, 209–10

White Sauce, 129–30

Sausage
Chicken and Apple Sausage, 201
Indian Summer Pasta, 120–21
poultry, 202
Turkey Sausages with Sun-Dried
Tomatoes, 203

Sautéed Green and Yellow Beans with
Garlic and Basil, 244

Sautéed Pork Medallions with Mustard-
Herb Sauce, 237

Scallops
Grilled Scallop Brochettes with
Almond-Caper Relish, 172–73
Grilled Seafood Bisque with Red
Pepper Aioli, 66–67

Scones with Currants, Ciji's, 278

Scrambled Eggs with Asparagus and
Smoked Salmon, 114

Sea bass
Roast Crispy Fish with Warm Lentils,
156–57
Roasted Sea Bass with Mustard-Salsa
Sauce, 152

Serrano chiles, 208

Shallot-Chive Sauce, 209–10

Shrimp
Grilled Seafood Bisque with Red
Pepper Aioli, 66–67
Shrimp Salsa, 23
Tomatillo Grilled Shrimp, 150–51
Warm Grilled Vegetable and Shrimp
Salad, 106–7

Smoked Fish Mousse, 22

Smoked Salmon and Caviar Torta, 18–19

Smoky Salsa, 360

Soft Polenta with Sun-Dried Tomato
Pesto, 138–39

Soups
Asian Chicken Noodle Soup with
Tofu and Pea Pods, 63
Black Bean Soup with Lime Cream,
60–61
Broccoli-Leek Soup with Parmesan
Cream, 62
Chicken Minestrone with Mixed-
Herb Pesto, 64–65
Corn and Tomato Soup, 68–69
Cucumber-Avocado Gazpacho, 70
Grilled Seafood Bisque with Red
Pepper Aioli, 66–67
Lentil Soup with Thyme and Balsamic
Vinegar, 57–58
Mixed Exotic Fruit Gazpacho, 300
Pinto Bean Soup with Gremolata, 59
Roasted Garlic and Butternut Squash
Soup with Ancho Chile Cream,
44–45
Roasted Vegetable Soup, 46–47
Spinach, Pasta, and Fagioli Soup,
50–51
Squash Vichyssoise, 71
Sweet Potato–Jalapeño Soup with
Tomatillo Cream, 48–49
White Bean and Artichoke Soup,
52–53
Yellow Split Pea Soup with
Mushrooms and Smoked Turkey,
54–55

Sourdough Bread, Country, 286–87

Sourdough Rye Rolls, 288–89

Sourdough Starter, 286–87

Spanish Rice Timbales, 271

Spiced Pumpkin-Hazelnut Bread,
276–77

Spiced Sweet Potato Pudding, 265–66

Spicy Almond Couscous, 268
Spicy Crinkle Cookies, 338
Spicy Tomato Salsa, 357
Spinach
    Asian Chicken Noodle Soup with
        Tofu and Pea Pods, 63
    Braised Stuffed Shoulder of Veal,
        234–36
    Spanish Rice Timbales, 271
    Spinach and Mushroom Salad
        with Warm Tomato-Bacon
        Vinaigrette, 86–87
    Spinach, Pasta, and Fagioli Soup,
        50–51
    Spinach Pesto, 126–27
    White Bean Stew with Spinach and
        Tomatoes, 253
Spreads
    California Caponata, 39
    Green Olive Tapenade, 31
    Sun-Dried Tomato Tapenade, 32
Springtime Salmon Salad, 108–9
Squash, summer. *See also* Zucchini
    grilling tips for, 171
    Squash Vichyssoise, 71
Squash, winter
    Butternut Squash Gratin with Tomato
        Fondue, 250
    Home Ranch Butternut Squash, 251
    Roasted Garlic and Butternut Squash
        Soup with Ancho Chile Cream,
        44–45
    Wonton Butternut Squash Ravioli
        with Spinach Pesto, 126–27
Starter, Sourdough, 286–87
Stocks
    Chicken Stock, 342
    Easy Brown Chicken Stock, 343

Easy Brown Turkey Stock, 343
Easy Brown Veal Stock, 344–45
Turkey Stock, 342
Strawberries
    Essencia Zabaglione with Fresh Fruit
        Compote, 299
    Fresh Apricots and Strawberries with
        Sour Cream and Brown Sugar, 301
    Mixed Exotic Fruit Gazpacho, 300
Stuffing
    Corn Bread for Stuffing, 346
    Corn Bread, Leek, and Red Pepper
        Stuffing Terrine, 254–55
Sun-Dried Tomato Cream, 69
Sun-Dried Tomato Pesto, 350
Sun-Dried Tomato Tapenade, 32
Sun-Dried Tomato Toasts, 275
Sweet potatoes, 48
    Spiced Sweet Potato Pudding, 265–66
    Sweet Potato–Jalapeño Soup with
        Tomatillo Cream, 48–49
Swordfish, Grilled, on a Bed of
        Cucumber "Pasta" with Asian
        Salsa, 161–62

T
Tangerine Marinade, Honey-, 191–92
Tapenade
    Green Olive Tapenade, 31
    Sun-Dried Tomato Tapenade, 32
Tarts
    Blueberry-Lemon Tart, 314–15
    Mango and Macadamia Nut Brown-
        Butter Tart, 312–13
    Pear-Raspberry Almond Tart, 309–11
Three-Cheese Macaroni with
        Caramelized Leeks, Prosciutto, and
        Peas, 124–25

Tiramisu with Toasted Hazelnuts and
Chocolate, 316–17
Tofu, Asian Chicken Noodle Soup with
Pea Pods and, 63
Tomatillos
Rustic Salsa, 359
Tomatillo Cream, 48–49
Tomatillo Grilled Shrimp, 150–51
Tomatillo Salsa, 358
Tomatoes, fresh or canned, 216
Asian Salsa, 161–62
Avocado-Tomato Salsa, 206–7
Baked Vegetable Rigatoni with
Tomatoes and Provolone Cheese,
122–23
Braised Stuffed Shoulder of Veal,
234–36
Butternut Squash Gratin with Tomato
Fondue, 250
Chicken Minestrone with Mixed-
Herb Pesto, 64–65
Corn and Tomato Soup, 68–69
Corn-Tomato Relish, 68–69
Double-Tomato Herb Sauce, 347
Grilled Pizza with Leeks, Mozzarella,
Tomatoes, and Pancetta, 146–47
Grilled Seafood Bisque with Red
Pepper Aioli, 66–67
grilling tips for, 171
Indian Summer Pasta, 120–21
Lamb Stew with Dates and Zinfandel,
224–25
Lentil Soup with Thyme and Balsamic
Vinegar, 57–58
Pasta with Tomatoes, Basil, and
Balsamic Vinaigrette, 128
Risotto with Leeks, Tomatoes, and
Niçoise Olives, 132–33

Roasted Tomato Jam, 361
roasting, 249
Rustic Salsa, 359
Shrimp Salsa, 23
Smoky Salsa, 360
Spicy Tomato Salsa, 357
Spinach and Mushroom Salad
with Warm Tomato-Bacon
Vinaigrette, 86–87
Tomato-Mint Bulgur, 267
White Bean Stew with Spinach and
Tomatoes, 253
Wine Country Chicken Salad, 104–5
Tomatoes, sun-dried, 35
Brisket of Beef with Sun-Dried
Tomatoes, Zinfandel, and
Thyme, 214–16
Corn and Tomato Soup, 68–69
Double-Tomato Herb Sauce, 347
Grilled Chicken Niçoise, 176–77
Pasta with Ancho Chile and Tomato
Cream, 118–19
Sun-Dried Tomato Cream, 69
Sun-Dried Tomato Pesto, 350
Sun-Dried Tomato Tapenade, 32
Sun-Dried Tomato Toasts, 275
Turkey Sausages with Sun-Dried
Tomatoes, 203
Torta, Smoked Salmon and Caviar, 18–19
Tortes
Banana Split Ice Cream Torte,
334–35
Bittersweet Chocolate Hazelnut Torte
with Banana Custard Sauce,
331–32
Tortillas
Corn Tortillas, 281
Crisp Tortilla Chips, 282

Griddled Quesadillas with
Caramelized Onions, Chicken,
and Jack Cheese, 37–38
Tricolor Vegetable Sauté, 245
Trussing, 195
Tuna
Grilled Tuna with Vegetable and
White Bean Salsa, 168–69
Tuna Tartare, 41
Turkey
Easy Brown Turkey Stock, 343
Grilled Turkey Breast in Mustard-
Bourbon Sauce, 193
grilling tips for, 170
La Scala Chopped Salad, 77
Light Meatballs with Double-Tomato
Herb Sauce, 230–31
Marinated Roast Turkey, 194–95
Rich Turkey Gravy, 196–97
trussing, 195
Turkey Sausages with Sun-Dried
Tomatoes, 203
Turkey Stock, 342
Turkey Vegetable Cobbler, 198–200
Yellow Split Pea Soup with
Mushrooms and Smoked Turkey,
54–55
Two-Mushroom Barley Risotto, 136–37

V
Vanilla Caramel Cream, 318–19
Vanilla Cream, 324–25
Veal
Braised Stuffed Shoulder of Veal,
234–36
Easy Brown Veal Stock, 344–45
Grilled Veal Chops with Zucchini-
Corn Relish, 228–29

Light Meatballs with Double-Tomato
Herb Sauce, 230–31
Veal Stew with Orange Sauce,
232–33
Vegetables. *See also individual vegetables*
Assorted Grilled Vegetables, 24–25
Baked Vegetable Rigatoni with
Tomatoes and Provolone Cheese,
122–23
Chicken Minestrone with Mixed-
Herb Pesto, 64–65
Crispy Potato Pancakes with
Vegetables, 259–60
Garden Risotto, 134–35
grilling tips for, 171
Holiday Lasagne with Roasted
Vegetables and Pesto, 129
marinating, 221
Panfried Noodles with Vegetables,
226–27
Pasta Salad with Parmesan Dressing,
92–93
Roasted Vegetable Soup, 46–47
Roasted Winter Vegetables, 247
roasting, 249
Tricolor Vegetable Sauté, 245
Turkey Vegetable Cobbler, 198–200
Vegetable and White Bean Salsa,
168–69
Warm Grilled Vegetable and Shrimp
Salad, 106–7
Wheat Berry Vegetable Salad,
90–91
Vichyssoise, Squash, 71
Vinaigrettes, 354
Basic Vinaigrette, 355
Orange Vinaigrette, 76
Vinegar, balsamic, 56

W

Walnuts, 290
  Walnut Bread, 290–91
  Walnut Cake with Roasted Blueberry
    Compote, 324–25
Warm Grilled Chicken Salad with
  Pesto, 100–101
Warm Grilled Vegetable and Shrimp
  Salad, 106–7
Warm Mocha Pudding Cakes, 328
West Coast Crab Cakes with Grapefruit
  Sauce, 165–67
Wheat Berry Vegetable Salad, 90–91
White Bean and Artichoke Soup, White
  Bean Stew with Spinach and
  Tomatoes, 253
White Chocolate and Pistachio
  Cookies, 336
White Sauce, 129–30
Wild Rice and Long-Grain Rice Salad
  with Corn and Salmon, 92–93
Wine Country Chicken Salad, 104–5
Wines, 13
Wonton Butternut Squash Ravioli with
  Spinach Pesto, 126–27

Y

Yams. *See* Sweet potatoes
Yellow Split Pea Soup with Mushrooms
  and Smoked Turkey, 54–55

Z

Zabaglione, Essencia, with Fresh Fruit
  Compote, 299
Zucchini
  Confetti Rice Pilaf, 269
  Crispy Potato Pancakes with
    Vegetables, 259–60

Holiday Lasagne with Roasted
  Vegetables and Pesto, 129–30
Light Meatballs with Double-Tomato
  Herb Sauce, 230–31
Spicy Almond Couscous, 268
Squash Vichyssoise, 71
Tricolor Vegetable Sauté, 245
Warm Grilled Vegetable and Shrimp
  Salad, 106–7
Zucchini-Corn Relish, 228–29

TABLE OF EQUIVALENTS

The exact equivalents in the following tables have been rounded for convenience.

LIQUID/DRY MEASURES

U.S.	METRIC
¼ teaspoon	1.25 milliliters
½ teaspoon	2.5 milliliters
1 teaspoon	5 milliliters
1 tablespoon (3 teaspoons)	15 milliliters
1 fluid ounce (2 tablespoons)	30 milliliters
¼ cup	60 milliliters
⅓ cup	80 milliliters
½ cup	120 milliliters
1 cup	240 milliliters
1 pint (2 cups)	480 milliliters
1 quart (4 cups, 32 ounces)	960 milliliters
1 gallon (4 quarts)	3.84 liters
1 ounce (by weight)	28 grams
1 pound	454 grams
2.2 pounds	1 kilogram

LENGTH

U.S.	METRIC
⅛ inch	3 millimeters
¼ inch	6 millimeters
½ inch	12 millimeters
1 inch	2.5 centimeters

OVEN TEMPERATURE

FAHRENHEIT	CELSIUS	GAS
250	120	½
275	140	1
300	150	2
325	160	3
350	180	4
375	190	5
400	200	6
425	220	7
450	230	8
475	240	9
500	260	10